Reading
through the
Bible
in one year
made easy

Mark Water

HENDRICKSON
PUBLISHERS

*Reading Through the Bible
in One Year Made Easy*
Hendrickson Publishers, Inc.
P.O. Box 3473
ISBN 978-1-56563-792-4

© 2003 by John Hunt Pub-
lishing, Alresford, Hants, UK.
Reprinted with permission.

Text © 2003 by Mark Water

Designed and produced
by Tony Cantale Graphics

Photography supplied by
Artville, Tony Cantale, Digital
Stock, Digital Vision, Foxx
Photos, fstock, Goodshoot,
Illustrated London News,
Nägele stock, Photodisc, and
Salvation Army.

Illustrations by Tony Cantale
Graphics.

First printing — 2003
Second printing — September 2009

Printed in China by South China Printing Co. Ltd.

Contents

Special pull–out chart

Seven steps in reading the Bible, by C.H. Spurgeon

Week 1
Beginnings

"In the beginning God created the heavens and the earth."
Genesis 1:1

DATE	MORNING	MORNING	EVENING
January 1	Genesis 1	Matthew 1	Ezra 1
January 2	Genesis 2	Matthew 2	Ezra 2
January 3	Genesis 3	Matthew 3	Ezra 3
January 4	Genesis 4	Matthew 4	Ezra 4
January 5	Genesis 5	Matthew 5	Ezra 5
January 6	Genesis 6	Matthew 6	Ezra 6
January 7	Genesis 7	Matthew 7	Ezra 7

What to look out for in Genesis

Genesis is the book of beginnings. The book of *Genesis* presents the beginning of everything except God. The beginning of:
• the universe, *1:1*
• humankind, *1:27*
• the Sabbath, *2:2,3*
• marriage, *2:22-24*
• sin, *3:1-7*
• sacrifice and salvation, *3:15,21*
• the family, *4:1-15*
• civilization, *4:16-21*
• government, *9:1-6*
• nations, *11*
• Israel, *12:1-3*

Living without God's Word

"The deceit, the lie of the devil consists of this, that he wishes to make people believe that they can live without God's Word." *Dietrich Bonhoeffer*

Week 2
Opposition

THIS WEEK'S IMPORTANT BIBLE VERSE

"When I heard these things [about Jerusalem's walls being broken down], I sat down and wept. For some days I mourned and fasted and prayed before the God of heaven." *Nehemiah 1:4*

DATE	MORNING	MORNING	EVENING
January 8	Genesis 8	Matthew 8	Ezra 8
January 9	Genesis 9; 10	Matthew 9	Ezra 9
January 10	Genesis 11	Matthew 10	Ezra 10
January 11	Genesis 12	Matthew 11	Nehemiah 1
January 12	Genesis 13	Matthew 12	Nehemiah 2
January 13	Genesis 14	Matthew 13	Nehemiah 3
January 14	Genesis 15	Matthew 14	Nehemiah 4

5

What to look out for in Nehemiah

Note the different forms of opposition that were used against Nehemiah.

- Ridicule, *2:19; 4:1*
- False accusation, *2:19*
- Plots and stirring up people to oppose Nehemiah, *4:8*
- Persistent pretense to have helpful meetings, *6:1,2,10*
- Intimidation, *6:19*

Discovering treasure

"The depth of the Christian Scriptures is boundless. Even if I were attempting to study them and nothing else, from boyhood to decrepit old age, with the utmost leisure, the most unwearied zeal, and with talents greater than I possess, I would still be making progress in discovering their treasures."
Augustine of Hippo

Week 3
Salvation

THIS WEEK'S IMPORTANT BIBLE VERSE

"She will give birth to a son, and you are to give him the name Jesus, because he will save his people from their sins." *Matthew 1:21*

DATE	MORNING	MORNING	EVENING
January 15	Genesis 16	Matthew 15	Nehemiah 5
January 16	Genesis 17	Matthew 16	Nehemiah 6
January 17	Genesis 18	Matthew 17	Nehemiah 7
January 18	Genesis 19	Matthew 18	Nehemiah 8
January 19	Genesis 20	Matthew 19	Nehemiah 9
January 20	Genesis 21	Matthew 20	Nehemiah 10
January 21	Genesis 22	Matthew 21	Nehemiah 11

What to look out for in Matthew

Observe how Matthew presents the kingship of Jesus in his Gospel.

- The presentation of the King, *1:1–4:11*
- The proclamation of the King, *4:12–7:29*
- The power of the King, *8:1–11:1*
- The rejection of the King, *11:2–16:12*
- The preparation of the King's disciples, *16:13–20:28*
- The crucifixion of the King, *20:29–27:66*
- The proof of the King, *28*

Managing without the Word of God

"The soul can do nothing without the word of God, and the soul can manage without anything except the word of God." *Martin Luther*

Week 4
Reflecting Jesus

"And who knows but that you have come to royal position for such a time as this?" *Esther 4:14*

DATE	MORNING	MORNING	EVENING
January 22	Genesis 23	Matthew 22	Nehemiah 12
January 23	Genesis 24	Matthew 23	Nehemiah 13
January 24	Genesis 25	Matthew 24	Esther 1
January 25	Genesis 26	Matthew 25	Esther 2
January 26	Genesis 27	Matthew 26	Esther 3
January 27	Genesis 28	Matthew 27	Esther 4
January 28	Genesis 29	Matthew 28	Esther 5

What to look out for in Esther

Esther's character
- Esther was meek and attractive, *2:1-18*
- Esther depended on God, *4:15-17*
- Esther was brave: *4:16*
- Esther was diplomatic, *5:1-8; 7:1-6*

Mordecai's character
- Mordecai was a caring foster father, *2:7*
- Mordecai was shrewd, *2:19-23*
- Mordecai cared for God's people, *4:1-17*

Haman's character
- Haman was consumed by greed and ambition, *5:10-12*
- Haman was open to flattery, *3:1,2*

Cross references

"Compare Scripture with Scripture. False doctrines, like false witnesses, agree not among themselves."
William Gurnall

Week 5
Faithfulness

THIS WEEK'S IMPORTANT BIBLE VERSE

"Naked came I out of my mother's womb, and naked shall I return thither; the LORD gave, and the LORD hath taken away; blessed be the name of the LORD."
Job 1:21 (KJV)

DATE	MORNING	MORNING	EVENING
January 29	Genesis 30	Mark 1	Esther 6
January 30	Genesis 31	Mark 2	Esther 7
January 31	Genesis 32	Mark 3	Esther 8
February 1	Genesis 33	Mark 4	Esther 9; 10
February 2	Genesis 34	Mark 5	Job 1
February 3	Genesis 35; 36	Mark 6	Job 2
February 4	Genesis 37	Mark 7	Job 3

What to look out for in Job

As you read through the book of *Job* keep the big picture of the breakdown of the book in your mind:

- Satan's attack on Job, *1–2*
- Job's three debates, with his friends and so-called "comforters," Eliphaz, Bildad, and Zophar, *3–14; 15–21; 22–31*
- The solution proposed by Elihu, Job's fourth friend, *32–37*
- God's two challenges to Job, *38:1–42:6*
- Job's deliverance, *42:7-17*

The book of Job

"The greatest poem of ancient and modern times."
Alfred Tennyson, commenting on the book of Job

Light and joy

Lord, thy word abideth,
And our footsteps guideth,
Who its truth believeth
Light and joy receiveth.

O that we discerning
Its most holy learning,
Lord, may love and fear thee,
Evermore be near thee.
H.W. Baker

Week 6
Servant

"For even the Son of Man did not come to be served, but to serve, and to give his life as a ransom for many." *Mark 10:45*

DATE	MORNING	MORNING	EVENING
February 5	Genesis 38	Mark 8	Job 4
February 6	Genesis 39	Mark 9	Job 5
February 7	Genesis 40	Mark 10	Job 6
February 8	Genesis 41	Mark 11	Job 7
February 9	Genesis 42	Mark 12	Job 8
February 10	Genesis 43	Mark 13	Job 9
February 11	Genesis 44	Mark 14	Job 10

What to look out for in Mark

Note how Mark portrays Jesus as a Servant.

- The presentation of the Servant, *1:1–2:12*
- The opposition to the Servant, *2:13–8:26*
- The instructions of the Servant, *8:27–10:52*
- The rejection of the Servant, *11:1–15:47*
- The resurrection of the Servant, *16:1–20*

The Gospels' portrayal of Jesus

"I would very earnestly ask you to check your conception of Christ, the image of him which as a Christian you hold in your mind, with the actual revealed Person who can be seen and studied in action in the pages of the Gospels."
J.B. Phillips

Week 7
Son of Man

"... she [Mary] gave birth to her firstborn, a son. She wrapped him in cloths and placed him in a manger, because there was no room for them in the inn."
Luke 2:7

DATE	MORNING	MORNING	EVENING
February 12	Genesis 45	Mark 15	Job 11
February 13	Genesis 46	Mark 16	Job 12
February 14	Genesis 47	Luke 1:1-38	Job 13
February 15	Genesis 48	Luke 1:39-80	Job 14
February 16	Genesis 49	Luke 2	Job 15
February 17	Genesis 50	Luke 3	Job 16; 17
February 18	Exodus 1	Luke 4	Job 18

What to look out for in Luke 1–11

Observe how Luke writes about Jesus as the Son of Man.

- Luke states the purpose of his Gospel, *1:1-4*
- The events before Jesus' birth, *1:5-56*
- The events surrounding Jesus' birth, *1:57–2:38*
- The events during Jesus' childhood, *2:39-52*
- The events before Jesus' public ministry, *3:1–4:13*
- The Son of Man and his ministry. See *4:14–9:50*
- Increasing opposition to the Son of Man. See *9:51–11:54*

The Bible and source criticism

"**We must not fall into the error of thinking that when we have come to a conclusion about the sources of a literary work we have learned all that needs to be known about it. Source Criticism is merely a preliminary piece of spadework. Whatever their sources were, the Gospels are there before our eyes, each an individual literary work with its own characteristic viewpoint, which has in large measure controlled the choice and presentation of the subject matter. In attempting to discover how they were composed, we must beware of regarding them as scissors–and–paste compilations.**"
F.F. Bruce

Week 8
Exodus

"Therefore, say to the Israelites: 'I am the Lord, and I will bring you out from under the yoke of the Egyptians. I will free you from being slaves to them, and I will redeem you with an outstretched arm and with mighty acts of judgment.'" *Exodus 6:6*

DATE	MORNING	MORNING	EVENING
February 19	Exodus 2	Luke 5	Job 19
February 20	Exodus 3	Luke 6	Job 20
February 21	Exodus 4	Luke 7	Job 21
February 22	Exodus 5	Luke 8	Job 22
February 23	Exodus 6	Luke 9	Job 23
February 24	Exodus 7	Luke 10	Job 24
February 25	Exodus 8	Luke 11	Job 25; 26

Bible reading and meditation

"Begin with reading or hearing. Go on with meditation; end in prayer.

"Reading without meditation is unfruitful; meditation without reading is hurtful; to meditate and to read without prayer upon both, is without blessing." *William Bridge*

What to look out for in Exodus

For an overview of the book of Exodus read Stephen's defense in *Acts 7:17-44*.

Link up the events recorded in Exodus with explanations about them given in the New Testament.

- The Passover. See *John 1:29,36*; *1 Corinthians 5:7*
- The Exodus. See *Romans 6:2,3*; *1 Corinthians 10:1,2*
- The manna and water. See *John 6:31-35,48-63*; *1 Corinthians 10:3,4*
- The high priest. See *Hebrews 4:14-16*; *9:11,12,24-28*

Week 9
Forgiveness

"But while he was still a long way off, his father saw him and was filled with compassion for him; he ran to his son, threw his arms around him and kissed him."
Luke 15:20

DATE	MORNING	MORNING	EVENING
February 26	Exodus 9	Luke 12	Job 27
February 27	Exodus 10	Luke 13	Job 28
February 28	Exodus 11:1–12:21	Luke 14	Job 29
March 1	Exodus 12:22-51	Luke 15	Job 30
March 2	Exodus 13	Luke 16	Job 31
March 3	Exodus 14	Luke 17	Job 32
March 4	Exodus 15	Luke 18	Job 33

13

What to look out for in Luke 12–18

In the light of Jesus' rejection, note the instructions Jesus gives in these chapters.

- **Chapter 12**: Jesus teaching a great crowd
- **Chapter 13**: the kingdom of God
- **Chapter 14**: eating with a Pharisee and the cost of discipleship
- **Chapter 15**: the three stories of the lost
- **Chapter 16**: teaching about money
- **Chapter 17**: teaching about service, the healing of ten lepers, and God's coming kingdom
- **Chapter 18**: teaching about justice and humility, Jesus meets a rich young ruler, and the healing of a beggar

When to read the Bible

"Do not have your concert first and tune your instruments afterwards. Begin the day with God." *James Hudson Taylor*

Week 10
Final days

THIS WEEK'S IMPORTANT BIBLE VERSE

"The Word became flesh and made his dwelling among us. We have seen his glory, the glory of the One and Only, who came from the Father, full of grace and truth." *John 1:14*

DATE	MORNING	MORNING	EVENING
March 5	Exodus 16	Luke 19	Job 34
March 6	Exodus 17	Luke 20	Job 35
March 7	Exodus 18	Luke 21	Job 36
March 8	Exodus 19	Luke 22	Job 37
March 9	Exodus 20	Luke 23	Job 38
March 10	Exodus 21	Luke 24	Job 39
March 11	Exodus 22	John 1	Job 40

What to look out for in Luke 19–24

In these chapters Luke portrays Jesus as the Savior of the world through his death and resurrection in Jerusalem. There are eight scenes to follow:

- Jesus teaching in the temple, *19:45-21:4*
- Jesus speaking about the future, *21:5-38*
- The Last Supper, *22:1-38*
- The scene in the Garden of Gethsemane, *22:39-53*
- Peter's denial, *22:54-62*
- Jesus on trial, *22:63-23:25*
- Jesus' crucifixion and burial, *23:26-56*
- Jesus' resurrection, *24:1-49*
- Jesus' ascension, *24:50-53*

Let the Bible "inflame" you

"Don't stop reading the Bible until you find your heart warmed, see Psalm 119:93. Let it not only inform you but also inflame you, see Jeremiah 23:29; Luke 24:32."
Thomas Watson

Week 11
Witness

THIS WEEK'S IMPORTANT BIBLE VERSE

"This, the first of his miraculous signs, Jesus performed in Cana of Galilee. He thus revealed his glory and his disciples put their faith in him." *John 2:11*

DATE	MORNING	MORNING	EVENING
March 12	Exodus 23	John 2	Job 41
March 13	Exodus 24	John 3	Job 42
March 14	Exodus 25	John 4	Proverbs 1
March 15	Exodus 26	John 5	Proverbs 2
March 16	Exodus 27	John 6	Proverbs 3
March 17	Exodus 28	John 7	Proverbs 4
March 18	Exodus 29	John 8	Proverbs 5

What to look out for in John

Imagine that you are in a courtroom as you read John. Here are four witnesses brought forward who testify that Jesus is the Christ and the Son of God.

1. The witness of the Old Testament, *1:45; 5:39, 46-47; 8:56*
2. The witness of John the Baptist, *1:6-8,15,19-36; 3:25-30; 5:33-36*
3. The witness of people in general, *4:29,39; 9:13-33,38; 11:27*
4. The witness of the apostles, *1:41-46,49; 15:27; 17:20; 20:24-25,28*

Trials

"The great folly of man in trials is leaning to or on his own understanding and counsels. What is the result of this? Whenever in our trials we consult our own understanding, listen to our own reason, even though they appear to be good, the principle of living by faith is stifled, and we will in this way be let down by our own counsels." *Dr John Owen, commenting on Proverbs 3:5*

Week 12
Witness

THIS WEEK'S IMPORTANT BIBLE VERSE

"I have come that they may have life, and have it to the full." *John 10:10*

DATE	MORNING	MORNING	EVENING
March 19	Exodus 30	John 9	Proverbs 6
March 20	Exodus 31	John 10	Proverbs 7
March 21	Exodus 32	John 11	Proverbs 8
March 22	Exodus 33	John 12	Proverbs 9
March 23	Exodus 34	John 13	Proverbs 10
March 24	Exodus 35	John 14	Proverbs 11
March 25	Exodus 36	John 15	Proverbs 12

What to look out for in John

Here are four more witnesses John brings forward to convince his readers that Jesus is the Christ and the Son of God.

1. The witness of the Father, *5:31,32,37; 8:18,38,54; 12:27,28*
2. The witness of the Holy Spirit, *14:26; 15:26; 16:12-15*
3. Jesus' deeds, *2:11,23; 5:36; 9:3,31-33*
4. Jesus himself, and his words and claims, *3:11,32; 8:13,14,38; 6:35,48,51; 8:12; 9:5; 10:7,11,14; 11:25; 14:6; 15:1*

A new attitude

"Read the Bible as though it were something entirely unfamiliar, as though it had not been set before you ready–made. Face the book with a new attitude as something new." *Martin Buber*

16

Most gracious God, our
heavenly Father, in whom
alone dwells all the fullness of
light and wisdom, enlighten
our minds by your Holy Spirit
to truly understand your
Word. Give us grace to receive
it reverently and humbly. May
it lead us to put our whole
trust in you alone, and so to
serve and honor you that we
may glory your holy name and
encourage others by setting a
good example.
John Calvin

Week 13
Principles

THIS WEEK'S **IMPORTANT BIBLE VERSE**

"A gentle answer turns away wrath, but a harsh word stirs up anger." *Proverbs 15:1*

DATE	MORNING	MORNING	EVENING
March 26	Exodus 37	John 16	Proverbs 13
March 27	Exodus 38	John 17	Proverbs 14
March 28	Exodus 39	John 18	Proverbs 15
March 29	Exodus 40	John 19	Proverbs 16
March 30	Leviticus 1	John 20	Proverbs 17
March 31	Leviticus 2; 3	John 21	Proverbs 18
April 1	Leviticus 4	Psalms 1; 2	Proverbs 19

18

Universal purity

"The principles of the Proverbs of Solomon are piety, charity, justice, benevolence, and true prudence. Their universal purity proves that they are the Word of God." *John Calvin*

What to look out for in Proverbs

Look out for the reoccurring themes that are covered in *Proverbs*.

- **Work**, *6:6-11; 22:13; 26:13,14; 21:25,26*
- **Speaking**, *6:16,18,19; 10:11,13,18-21,31,32; 29:11; 31:26*
- **Friends**, *3:29; 14:20; 17:9; 18; 25:17*
- **Poverty and wealth**, *10:15; 18:16; 19; 23:4,5; 30:8, 9*

Week 14
Holiness

"Moses and Aaron then went into the Tent of Meeting. When they came out, they blessed the people; and the glory of the Lord appeared to all the people."
Leviticus 9:23

DATE	MORNING	MORNING	EVENING
April 2	Leviticus 5	Psalms 3; 4	Proverbs 20
April 3	Leviticus 6	Psalms 5; 6	Proverbs 21
April 4	Leviticus 7	Psalms 7; 8	Proverbs 22
April 5	Leviticus 8	Psalm 9	Proverbs 23
April 6	Leviticus 9	Psalm 10	Proverbs 24
April 7	Leviticus 10	Psalms 11; 12	Proverbs 25
April 8	Leviticus 11; 12	Psalms 13; 14	Proverbs 26

What to look out for in Leviticus

The theme of the book of *Leviticus* is holiness. In it God teaches the Israelites how they can approach their holy God, and live holy lives.

Link up your reading of the book of *Leviticus* with the New Testament letter of *Hebrews*. For example, *Leviticus 16:15* links to *Hebrews 7:27* and *Leviticus 16:16* links to *Hebrews 9:25*. Use a Bible that gives you such cross-references to the letter to the *Hebrews*, which is a commentary on the book of *Leviticus*.

Built up

"The Bible applied to the heart by the Holy Spirit, is the chief means by which men are built up and established in the faith, after their conversion."
J.C. Ryle

Week 15
Chasing after the wind

"My God, my God, why have you forsaken me?"
Psalm 22:1

DATE	MORNING	MORNING	EVENING
April 9	Leviticus 13	Psalms 15; 16	Proverbs 27
April 10	Leviticus 14	Psalm 17	Proverbs 28
April 11	Leviticus 15	Psalm 18	Proverbs 29
April 12	Leviticus 16	Psalm 19	Proverbs 30
April 13	Leviticus 17	Psalms 20; 21	Proverbs 31
April 14	Leviticus 18	Psalm 22	Ecclesiastes 1
April 15	Leviticus 19	Psalms 23; 24	Ecclesiastes 2

What to look out for in Ecclesiastes
Note the following three themes:
1. Without God life is meaningless, *1:1-11; 3:15; 6:10,11*
2. All men and women need a divine dimension.
   - God is sovereign, *3:14*
   - God is judge, *3:15-17; 8:12,13*
   - God is our maker, *11:5; 12:1*
3. We should accept what God gives, *2:24-26; 3:1-8,12,13,22; 11:7-10*

Judged by the Bible

"We need to repent of the haughty way in which we sometimes stand in judgment upon Scripture and must learn to sit humbly under its judgment instead."
John Stott

Week 16
Times of trouble

"To you, O Lord, I lift up my soul; in you I trust, O my God."
Psalm 25:1

DATE	MORNING	MORNING	EVENING
April 16	Leviticus 20	Psalm 25	Ecclesiastes 3
April 17	Leviticus 21	Psalms 26; 27	Ecclesiastes 4
April 18	Leviticus 22	Psalms 28; 29	Ecclesiastes 5
April 19	Leviticus 23	Psalm 30	Ecclesiastes 6
April 20	Leviticus 24	Psalm 31	Ecclesiastes 7
April 21	Leviticus 25	Psalm 32	Ecclesiastes 8
April 22	Leviticus 26	Psalm 33	Ecclesiastes 9

What to look out for in Psalms 1–33

Note how specific psalms deal with specific times of trouble:
- *Psalm 3*: "God is all I need."
- *Psalm 4*: "Put our trust in God."
- *Psalm 5*: "Lead me, Lord."
- *Psalm 6*: "I am so tired."
- *Psalm 7*: "God is just."
- *Psalm 10*: "Why do the wicked prosper?"
- *Psalm 11*: "God knows what goes on."
- *Psalm 12*: "God has promised to help."
- *Psalm 13*: "I have trusted in your love."
- *Psalm 25*: "The Lord is good and upright."
- *Psalm 28*: "God has heard my prayer."
- *Psalm 31*: "My times are in your hands."

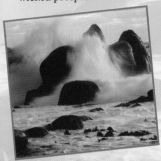

Understanding and revelation

"Christ teaches by the Spirit of wisdom in the heart, opening the understanding to the Spirit of revelation in the word."
Matthew Henry

Week 17
Love songs

"Fear God and keep his commandments, for this is the whole duty of man."
Ecclesiastes 12:13

DATE	MORNING	MORNING	EVENING
April 23	Leviticus 27	Psalm 34	Ecclesiastes 10
April 24	Numbers 1	Psalm 35	Ecclesiastes 11
April 25	Numbers 2	Psalm 36	Ecclesiastes 12
April 26	Numbers 3	Psalm 37	Song of Solomon 1
April 27	Numbers 4	Psalm 38	Song of Solomon 2
April 28	Numbers 5	Psalm 39	Song of Solomon 3
April 29	Numbers 6	Psalms 40; 41	Song of Solomon 4

What to look out for in Song of Solomon

There are two distinct ways of reading the *Song of Solomon*. You can read it at face value and see it as a collection of love songs or love poems, expressing human love, which Christians teach are God's gift for the married. Or you can read the *Song of Solomon* as an extended allegory about God's love for humankind, and Jesus' love for his Church.

Me and the Bible

"When you read God's Word, you must constantly be saying to yourself, 'It is talking to me, and about me.'"
Søren Kierkegaard

Prayer for reading the Bible
Hearing and obeying

O Lord Jesus, let not your word become a judgment on us, lest we hear it and do not do it, or believe it and do not obey it.

Thomas à Kempis

Week 18
Disobedience

"But because my servant Caleb has a different spirit
and follows me wholeheartedly, I will bring him into
the land he went to, and his descendants will inherit it."
Leviticus 14:24

DATE	MORNING	MORNING	EVENING
April 30	Numbers 7	Psalms 42; 43	Song of Solomon 5
May 1	Numbers 8	Psalm 44	Song of Solomon 6
May 2	Numbers 9	Psalm 45	Song of Solomon 7
May 3	Numbers 10	Psalms 46; 47	Song of Solomon 8
May 4	Numbers 11	Psalm 48	Isaiah 1
May 5	Numbers 12; 13	Psalm 49	Isaiah 2
May 6	Numbers 14	Psalm 50	Isaiah 3; 4

Inward illumination

"We acknowledge the inward
illumination of the Spirit of God
to be necessary for the saving
understanding of such things as
are revealed in the Word."
*The Confession of Faith of the
Westminster Assembly of Divines,
1646*

What to look out for in Numbers

Note how the book of *Numbers*
continues the record of God's
people. The Israelites have to
wander in the desert for 40
years because of their
disobedience.

- They had good intentions,
  1:1–10:10
- Their downfall was due to
  grumbling and rebellion,
  10:11–20:29
- Their failures, as well as their
  triumphs, are recorded,
  21:1–36:13

Week 19
Prophecy

"'Woe to me!' I cried. 'I am ruined! For I am a man of unclean lips, and I live among a people of unclean lips, and my eyes have seen the King, the Lord Almighty.'"
Isaiah 6:5

DATE	MORNING	MORNING	EVENING
May 7	Numbers 15	Psalm 51	Isaiah 5
May 8	Numbers 16	Psalms 52–54	Isaiah 6
May 9	Numbers 17; 18	Psalm 55	Isaiah 7
May 10	Numbers 19	Psalms 56; 57	Isaiah 8:1–9:7
May 11	Numbers 20	Psalms 58; 59	Isaiah 9:8–10:4
May 12	Numbers 21	Psalms 60; 61	Isaiah 10:5-34
May 13	Numbers 22	Psalms 62; 63	Isaiah 11; 12

What to look out for in Isaiah

Link up prophecies about Jesus you find in the book of *Isaiah* with their fulfillment recorded in the New Testament. For example:
- *Isaiah 7:14* links with *Matthew 1:22,23*
- *Isaiah 9:1,2* links with *Matthew 4:12-16*
- *Isaiah 9:6* links with *Luke 2:11*; *Ephesians 2:14-18*
- *Isaiah 11:1* links with *Luke 3:23,32*; *Acts 13:22,23*
- *Isaiah 11:2* links with *Luke 3:22*

Classic statement on repentance

"It is generally agreed that this fifty–first psalm is perhaps the classic statement in the Old Testament on the question of repentance [and] is perhaps the classic statement on this whole matter of repentance in the entire Bible."
Martyn Lloyd-Jones, commenting on Psalm 51

Week 20
Times of trouble

THIS WEEK'S **IMPORTANT BIBLE VERSE**

"May God be gracious to us and bless us and make his face shine upon us."
Psalm 67:1

DATE	MORNING	MORNING	EVENING
May 14	Numbers 23	Psalms 64; 65	Isaiah 13
May 15	Numbers 24	Psalms 66; 67	Isaiah 14
May 16	Numbers 25	Psalm 68	Isaiah 15
May 17	Numbers 26	Psalm 69	Isaiah 16
May 18	Numbers 27	Psalms 70; 71	Isaiah 17; 18
May 19	Numbers 28	Psalm 72	Isaiah 19; 20
May 20	Numbers 29	Psalm 73	Isaiah 21

What to look out for in Psalms 34–73

Note how specific psalms deal with specific times of trouble in *Psalms 34–73*.

- *Psalm 38*: "Lord I am sick and sinful."
- *Psalm 42*: "Why am I so depressed?"
- *Psalm 43*: "I will praise God again."
- *Psalm 51*: "Have mercy on me."
- *Psalm 54*: "God is my helper."
- *Psalm 57*: "In the shadow of his wings."
- *Psalm 73*: "Why do the innocent suffer?"

Asking questions

"When you read a verse in the Bible ask yourself, 'What does this verse mean?' Then ask: 'What does it mean for me?' When that is answered ask yourself again: 'Is that all it means?' and do not leave it until you are quite sure that is all it means for the present."
R.A. Torrey

Week 21
Times of trouble

THIS WEEK'S IMPORTANT BIBLE VERSE

"O my people, hear my teaching,
    listen to the words of my mouth."
Psalm 78:1

DATE	MORNING	MORNING	EVENING
May 21	Numbers 30	Psalm 74	Isaiah 22
May 22	Numbers 31	Psalms 75; 76	Isaiah 23
May 23	Numbers 32	Psalm 77	Isaiah 24
May 24	Numbers 33	Psalm 78:1-37	Isaiah 25
May 25	Numbers 34	Psalm 78:38-72	Isaiah 26
May 26	Numbers 35	Psalm 79	Isaiah 27
May 27	Numbers 36	Psalm 80	Isaiah 28

What to look out for in Psalm 74–79

1. Note how specific psalms deal with specific times of trouble in *Psalms 74–79*.
   - *Psalm 74*: "Why have you deserted us?"
   - *Psalm 77*: "Has God forgotten?"
   - *Psalm 79*: "The groaning of the prisoners."
2. As you read *Psalms 74–79* give God praise and thanksgiving in the appropriate psalms.
   - *Psalm 75*: God is in control
   - *Psalm 76*: God is to be given reverence

Delighting in God

"The most valuable thing the Psalms do for me is to express that same delight in God which made David dance."
C.S. Lewis

Week 22
The covenant

28

THIS WEEK'S IMPORTANT BIBLE VERSE

"Lord, you have been our dwelling-place throughout all generations."
Psalm 90:1

DATE	MORNING	MORNING	EVENING
May 28	Deuteronomy 1	Psalms 81; 82	Isaiah 29
May 29	Deuteronomy 2	Psalms 83; 84	Isaiah 30
May 30	Deuteronomy 3	Psalm 85	Isaiah 31
May 31	Deuteronomy 4	Psalms 86; 87	Isaiah 32
June 1	Deuteronomy 5	Psalm 88	Isaiah 33
June 2	Deuteronomy 6	Psalm 89	Isaiah 34
June 3	Deuteronomy 7	Psalm 90	Isaiah 35

What to look out for in Deuteronomy

Be alert to all references about the covenant in *Deuteronomy*. The central message of this book is God. It is only because God is who he is that the covenant can exist at all.

- The God of the covenant, *4:35; 16:18; 32:4; 10:17; 28:1-14*
- The obligations of the covenant, *8:1,11; 11:1; 6:5,13; 13:1-18*
- The benefits from keeping the covenant, *7:22; 28:1,7,13; 28:4,11; 5:16; 7:15*
- The disasters that come from breaking the covenant, *28:20,25; 4:26; 28:22-24,38-40*

A meaningful life

"A knowledge of the Bible is essential to a rich and meaningful life."
Billy Graham

Week 23
Praise and thanksgiving

"He tends his flock like a shepherd:
He gathers the lambs in his arms and
carries them close to his heart;
He gently leads those that have young."
Isaiah 40:11

DATE	MORNING	MORNING	EVENING
June 4	Deuteronomy 8	Psalm 91	Isaiah 36
June 5	Deuteronomy 9	Psalms 92; 93	Isaiah 37
June 6	Deuteronomy 10	Psalm 94	Isaiah 38
June 7	Deuteronomy 11	Psalms 95; 96	Isaiah 39
June 8	Deuteronomy 12	Psalms 97; 98	Isaiah 40
June 9	Deuteronomy 13; 14	Psalms 99–101	Isaiah 41
June 10	Deuteronomy 15	Psalm 102	Isaiah 42

How not to read the Bible

"One of the many divine
qualities of the Bible is this:
it does not yield its secrets to
the irreverent and censorious."
J.I. Packer

What to look out for in Psalms 80–102

As you read *Psalms 80–102*
give God praise and
thanksgiving in the appropriate
psalms.

- *Psalm 81*: Learn from what God has done.
- *Psalm 87*: Zion, city of our God.
- *Psalm 93*: The Lord on high is mighty.
- *Psalm 95*: Let us worship and bow down.
- *Psalm 96*: The judge is coming.
- *Psalm 97*: God loves his own.
- *Psalm 98*: Shout for joy to the Lord.
- *Psalm 99*: The Lord reigns.
- *Psalm 100*: The Lord is good.

Week 24
Praise and thanksgiving

THIS WEEK'S IMPORTANT BIBLE VERSE

"Listen to me, you stubborn-hearted,
    you who are far from righteousness.
I am bringing my righteousness near,
    it is not far away;
    and my salvation will not be delayed." *Isaiah 46:12,13*

DATE	MORNING	MORNING	EVENING
June 11	Deuteronomy 16	Psalm 103	Isaiah 43
June 12	Deuteronomy 17	Psalm 104	Isaiah 44
June 13	Deuteronomy 18	Psalm 105	Isaiah 45
June 14	Deuteronomy 19	Psalm 106	Isaiah 46
June 15	Deuteronomy 20	Psalm 107	Isaiah 47
June 16	Deuteronomy 21	Psalms 108; 109	Isaiah 48
June 17	Deuteronomy 22	Psalms 110; 111	Isaiah 49

What to look out for in Psalms 103–113

As you read *Psalms 103–113* give God praise and thanksgiving in the appropriate psalms.

- *Psalm 104*: The God who made everything.
- *Psalm 105*: The God who led his people out of slavery.
- *Psalm 108*: The One who gives victory.
- *Psalm 111*: God's deeds are very wonderful.
- *Psalm 113*: Who is like the Lord our God?

From Genesis to Revelation

"I know not a better rule of reading the Scripture, than to read it through from beginning to end and, when we have finished it once, to begin it again. We shall meet with many passages which we can make little improvement of, but not so many in the second reading as in the first, and fewer in the third than in the second: provided we pray to him who has the keys to open our understandings, and to anoint our eyes with his spiritual ointment." *John Newton*

**Prayer
for reading
the Bible**

A light
to shine on
my path

O Lord, you have given us your
Word as a light to shine on our path;
grant that we may so meditate on
that Word, and follow its teaching,
that we may find in it the light that
shines more and more until the
perfect day; through Jesus
Christ our Lord.

Jerome

31

THIS WEEK'S
IMPORTANT
BIBLE
VERSE

"We all, like sheep, have gone astray,
    each of us has turned to his own way;
and the Lord has laid on him
    the iniquity of us all." *Isaiah 53:6*

DATE	MORNING	MORNING	EVENING
June 18	Deuteronomy 23	Psalms 112; 113	Isaiah 50
June 19	Deuteronomy 24	Psalms 114; 115	Isaiah 51
June 20	Deuteronomy 25	Psalm 116	Isaiah 52
June 21	Deuteronomy 26	Psalms 117; 118	Isaiah 53
June 22	Deuteronomy 27:1–28:19	Psalm 119:1-24	Isaiah 54
June 23	Deuteronomy 28:20-68	Psalm 119:25-48	Isaiah 55
June 24	Deuteronomy 29	Psalm 119:49-72	Isaiah 56

What to look out for in Psalms 114–119

Before you read *Psalm 119*, the longest chapter in the whole Bible, flick through the pages of your Bible that contain its 176 verses and observe:
- Each section is divided in eight verses.
- There are 22 sections or stanzas. Some Bibles, such as *The New International Version*, give verses 1-8 the heading "Aleph" and give verses 9-18 the heading "Beth." These words are the letters of the Hebrew Bible, as each stanza of *Psalm 119* has eight two-part lines beginning with the same Hebrew letter.

- Note that nearly every verse of this psalm mentions God's law (or commands, statutes, precepts, word, promise, or ways), and see what is taught about the Law in each verse.

The Bible and the cross

"There is not a word in the Bible which is *extra cruem*, which can be understood without reference to the cross." *Martin Luther*

Week 26
Teach us

 THIS WEEK'S IMPORTANT BIBLE VERSE

"Your word is a lamp to my feet and a light for my path."
Psalm 119:105

DATE	MORNING	MORNING	EVENING
June 25	Deuteronomy 30	Psalm 119:73-96	Isaiah 57
June 26	Deuteronomy 31	Psalm 119:97-120	Isaiah 58
June 27	Deuteronomy 32	Psalm 119:121-144	Isaiah 59
June 28	Deuteronomy 33; 34	Psalm 119:145-176	Isaiah 60
June 29	Joshua 1	Psalms 120–122	Isaiah 61
June 30	Joshua 2	Psalms 123–125	Isaiah 62
July 1	Joshua 3	Psalms 126–128	Isaiah 63

What to look out for in Joshua

As you read through this book you should note:

1. What the book of *Joshua* teaches about God:
   - God's promises, *23:14*
   - God's will, *13:1; 18:3*
   - God's goodness, *1:2; 6:16; 10:8*
   - God's power, *3:7-17; 10:12*
2. What the book of *Joshua* teaches about God's people:
   - Their obedience, *1:7,8*
   - Their faith, *3:15; 6:16,20*
   - Their perseverance, *17:14-18*

The Holy Spirit and the Bible

"The Spirit will teach us to love the Word, to meditate on it and to keep it."
Andrew Murray

Week 27
God knows you

THIS WEEK'S IMPORTANT BIBLE VERSE

"Before I formed you in the womb I knew you,
before you were born I set you apart;
I appointed you as a prophet to the nations."
Jeremiah 1:5

DATE	MORNING	MORNING	EVENING
July 2	Joshua 4	Psalms 129–131	Isaiah 64
July 3	Joshua 5:1–6:5	Psalms 132–134	Isaiah 65
July 4	Joshua 6:6-27	Psalms 135; 136	Isaiah 66
July 5	Joshua 7	Psalms 137; 138	Jeremiah 1
July 6	Joshua 8	Psalm 139	Jeremiah 2
July 7	Joshua 9	Psalms 140; 141	Jeremiah 3
July 8	Joshua 10	Psalms 142; 143	Jeremiah 4

34

What to look out for in Jeremiah

Here is an outline of the book of *Jeremiah* so that you can keep your bearings in this prophecy, which is not always in chronological order:

Chapter	Theme
1	Jeremiah's call
2–25	Judah is condemned
26–29	Conflicts Jeremiah endured
30–33	The future restoration of Jerusalem
34–45	The imminent fall of Jerusalem
46–51	Prophecies directed to the Gentiles
52	The fall of Jerusalem

Bible and truth

"The Holy Scriptures, given by inspiration of God, are of themselves sufficient to the discovery of the truth."
Athanasius

Health check, Bolivia.

Week 28
Witnesses

"Let everything that has breath praise the Lord. Praise the Lord."
Psalm 150:6

DATE	MORNING	MORNING	EVENING
July 9	Joshua 11	Psalm 144	Jeremiah 5
July 10	Joshua 12; 13	Psalm 145	Jeremiah 6
July 11	Joshua 14; 15	Psalms 146; 147	Jeremiah 7
July 12	Joshua 16; 17	Psalm 148	Jeremiah 8
July 13	Joshua 18; 19	Psalms 149; 150	Jeremiah 9
July 14	Joshua 20; 21	Acts 1	Jeremiah 10
July 15	Joshua 22	Acts 2	Jeremiah 11

35

Bible and the Fathers

"I ask for Scriptures and Eck offers me the Fathers. I ask for the sun and he shows me his lanterns. I ask: 'Where is your Scripture proof?' and he adduces Ambrose and Cyril. With all due respect to the Fathers I prefer the authority of the Scripture."
Martin Luther

What to look out for in Acts 1–9

The book of *Acts* is the history of God's actions through the lives of the first Christians. Note how *Acts 1:8* is fulfilled in this book: "... you will be my witnesses in Jerusalem, and in all Judea and Samaria, and to the ends of the earth."

Chapters	Theme
1–2	The power of the church
3–8	The progress of the church
9	The witness of Philip

THIS WEEK'S IMPORTANT BIBLE VERSE

"As he [Saul] neared Damascus on his journey, suddenly a light from heaven flashed around him. He fell to the ground and heard a voice say to him, 'Saul, Saul, why do you persecute me?'" *Acts 9:1,2*

DATE	MORNING	MORNING	EVENING
July 16	Joshua 23	Acts 3	Jeremiah 12
July 17	Joshua 24	Acts 4	Jeremiah 13
July 18	Judges 1	Acts 5	Jeremiah 14
July 19	Judges 2	Acts 6	Jeremiah 15
July 20	Judges 3	Acts 7	Jeremiah 16
July 21	Judges 4	Acts 8	Jeremiah 17
July 22	Judges 5	Acts 9	Jeremiah 18

36

What to look out for in Judges

Apart from its introduction, *Judges 1:1–2:5*, and its appendix, *Judges 17:1–21:25*, the book of *Judges* records the events in the lives of twelve judges of Israel.

As you read the book you will see how the following "sin-cycle" repeats itself:

- God's people enjoy a time of peace, but turn to worship idols.
- God abandons his people and they are defeated by foreign powers.
- God's people turn back to him in repentance.
- God sends a deliverer and saves them through a judge.
- God's people enjoy a time of peace, and the sin-cycle starts all over again.

God rebuilds

"Like the New Testament parables, not every part must be pressed for its symbolism for neither nations nor men are lifeless lumps of clay...It is God who molds, breaking down, rebuilds. This power is not exercised arbitrarily and the possibility of renewal by God is conditional on a change of heart."

D.J. Wiseman, commenting on Jeremiah 18

Take away, O Lord,
  the veil of my heart
while I read the scriptures.
Lancelot Andrewes

37

Week 30
Widening circles

"We are witnesses of everything he [Jesus] did in the country of the Jews and in Jerusalem. They killed him by hanging him on a tree, but God raised him from the dead on the third day and caused him to be seen."
Acts 10:39,40

DATE	MORNING	MORNING	EVENING
July 23	Judges 6	Acts 10	Jeremiah 19
July 24	Judges 7	Acts 11	Jeremiah 20
July 25	Judges 8	Acts 12	Jeremiah 21
July 26	Judges 9	Acts 13	Jeremiah 22
July 27	Judges 10:1–11:11	Acts 14	Jeremiah 23
July 28	Judges 11:12-40	Acts 15	Jeremiah 24
July 29	Judges 12	Acts 16	Jeremiah 25

38

What to look out for in Acts 10–16

The Christian church spreads in ever widening circles in *Acts 10–16.*

- The conversion of Saul, *9:1-31*
- The witness of Peter, *9:32–11:18*
- The witness of the early church, *11:19–12:25*
- Paul's first missionary journey, *13–14*
- The council meeting at Jerusalem, *15*
- The start of Paul's second missionary journey, *16*

The Bible and success

"The secret of my success? It is simple. It is found in the Bible, 'In all thy ways acknowledge Him and He shall direct thy paths.'"
George Washington Carver

Week 31
Influence

"In those days Israel had no king; everyone did as he saw fit." *Judges 17:6*

DATE	MORNING	MORNING	EVENING
July 30	Judges 13	Acts 17	Jeremiah 26
July 31	Judges 14	Acts 18	Jeremiah 27
August 1	Judges 15	Acts 19	Jeremiah 28
August 2	Judges 16	Acts 20	Jeremiah 29
August 3	Judges 17	Acts 21	Jeremiah 30; 31
August 4	Judges 18	Acts 22	Jeremiah 32
August 5	Judges 19	Acts 23	Jeremiah 33

What to look out for in Acts 17–28

The book of *Acts* starts with a handful of confused disciples in Jerusalem and ends with the Christian gospel being freely spread in the world's most influential town, Rome.

- The completion of Paul's second missionary journey, *17:1–18:22*
- Paul's third missionary journey, *18:23–21:16*
- Paul arrives in Rome, *21:17–28:31*

Faith in God's Word

"Never did there exist a full faith in the divine word which did not expand the intellect while it purified the heart; which did not multiply the aims and objects of the understanding, while it fixed and simplified those of the desires and passions."
Samuel Taylor Coleridge

Week 32
Serving the Lord

THIS WEEK'S IMPORTANT BIBLE VERSE

"Where you [Naomi] go I [Ruth] will go, and where you stay I will stay. Your people will be my people and your God my God." *Ruth 1:16*

DATE	MORNING	MORNING	EVENING
August 6	Judges 20	Acts 24	Jeremiah 34
August 7	Judges 21	Acts 25	Jeremiah 35
August 8	Ruth 1	Acts 26	Jeremiah 36
August 9	Ruth 2	Acts 27	Jeremiah 37
August 10	Ruth 3; 4	Acts 28	Jeremiah 38
August 11	1 Samuel 1	Romans 1	Jeremiah 39
August 12	1 Samuel 2	Romans 2	Jeremiah 40

What to look out for in 1 Samuel

As you read through *1 Samuel* note:
• how Samuel served the Lord, *1–7*
• how king Saul went wrong, *8–15*
• how David was the Lord's choice, *16–31*

The Bible and human reason

"Scripture is above our natural reason, understanding, and comprehension." *Justin Martyr*

Week 33
Justification by faith

THIS WEEK'S IMPORTANT BIBLE VERSE

"Samuel explained to the people the regulations of the kingship. He wrote them down on a scroll and deposited it before the Lord. Then Samuel dismissed the people, each to his own home." *1 Samuel 10:25*

DATE	MORNING	MORNING	EVENING
August 13	1 Samuel 3	Romans 3	Jeremiah 41
August 14	1 Samuel 4	Romans 4	Jeremiah 42
August 15	1 Samuel 5; 6	Romans 5	Jeremiah 43
August 16	1 Samuel 7; 8	Romans 6	Jeremiah 44; 45
August 17	1 Samuel 9	Romans 7	Jeremiah 46
August 18	1 Samuel 10	Romans 8	Jeremiah 47
August 19	1 Samuel 11	Romans 9	Jeremiah 48

What to look out for in Romans

As you read through *Romans* note how justification by faith without deeds of the law is its reoccurring theme.

A poet's estimate of Romans

"It is the profoundest piece of writing in existence."
Samuel Taylor Coleridge

Chapter	Theme
1:1–3:23	God's faithfulness
3:24–5:21	Faith and justification
6–8	Life in Christ
9–11	Israel
12–15	Humility
16	Greetings

Week 34
Compassion

THIS WEEK'S IMPORTANT BIBLE VERSE

"Because of the Lord's great love we are not consumed, for his compassions never fail."
Lamentations 3:23

DATE	MORNING	MORNING	EVENING
August 20	1 Samuel 12	Romans 10	Jeremiah 49
August 21	1 Samuel 13	Romans 11	Jeremiah 50
August 22	1 Samuel 14	Romans 12	Jeremiah 51
August 23	1 Samuel 15	Romans 13	Jeremiah 52
August 24	1 Samuel 16	Romans 14	Lamentations 1
August 25	1 Samuel 17	Romans 15	Lamentations 2
August 26	1 Samuel 18	Romans 16	Lamentations 3

What to look out for in Lamentations

Picture a city in mourning.

Chapter	Theme
1	The cry of the mourner
2	God seems to be against his people
3	A prayer and cry from the heart to God
4	Jerusalem: past and present
5	A united prayer for God's help

1 Corinthians 1

"Forbid it, Lord, that I should boast,
  Save in the death of Christ my God.
All the vain things that charm me most
  I sacrifice them to his blood."
Isaac Watts

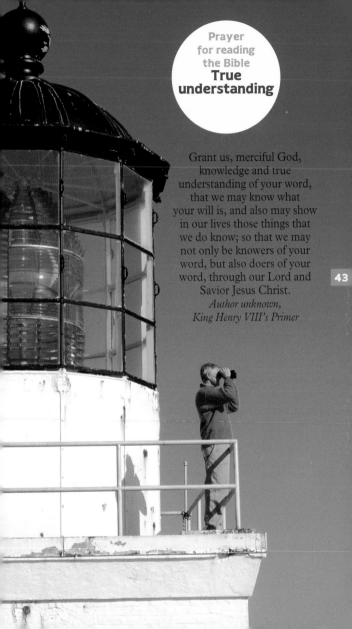

Grant us, merciful God,
knowledge and true
understanding of your word,
that we may know what
your will is, and also may show
in our lives those things that
we do know; so that we may
not only be knowers of your
word, but also doers of your
word, through our Lord and
Savior Jesus Christ.
*Author unknown,
King Henry VIII's Primer*

43

THIS WEEK'S IMPORTANT BIBLE VERSE

"It is because of him [God] that you are in Christ Jesus, who has become for us wisdom from God — that is, our righteousness, holiness and redemption."
1 Corinthians 1:30

What to look out for in 1 Corinthians

As you read Paul's first letter to the Christians at Corinth, remember that it is part of a correspondence.

Standing in judgment over the Bible

"We ought not to criticize, explain, or judge the Scriptures by our mere reason, but diligently, with prayer, meditate thereon, and seek their meaning."
Martin Luther

Chapter	Theme
1:1-9	Introduction
1:10–4:21	Divisions in the church at Corinth
5–11	Disorders in the church at Corinth
12–14	Use and abuse of spiritual gifts
15	Jesus' resurrection
16	Conclusion

Week 36
Visions

THIS WEEK'S IMPORTANT BIBLE VERSE

"And now these three remain: faith, hope and love. But the greatest of these is love."
1 Corinthians 13:13

DATE	MORNING	MORNING	EVENING
September 3	1 Samuel 27	1 Corinthians 8	Ezekiel 6
September 4	1 Samuel 28	1 Corinthians 9	Ezekiel 7
September 5	1 Samuel 29; 30	1 Corinthians 10	Ezekiel 8
September 6	1 Samuel 31	1 Corinthians 11	Ezekiel 9
September 7	2 Samuel 1	1 Corinthians 12	Ezekiel 10
September 8	2 Samuel 2	1 Corinthians 13	Ezekiel 11
September 9	2 Samuel 3	1 Corinthians 14	Ezekiel 12

What to look out for in Ezekiel

Ezekiel is speaking to the Jewish exiles in Babylon during the last days of Judah's decline and downfall. It is a book full of visions.

The Bible and sin

"Either the Bible will keep you away from sin, or sin will keep you away from the Bible!"
C.S. Lewis

Chapters	Theme
1–3	Ezekiel is commissioned to be God's prophet.
4–24	God's judgment will fall on Judah.
25–32	God's judgment will fall on the non-Jews.
33–39	Israel will return to her land.
40–48	Israel will be restored, with a new temple, new worship, and new land.

Week 37
Stand firm

THIS WEEK'S
IMPORTANT
BIBLE
VERSE

"Therefore, my dear brothers, stand firm. Let nothing move you. Always give yourselves fully to the work of the Lord, because you know that your labor in the Lord is not in vain." *1 Corinthians 15:58*

DATE	MORNING	MORNING	EVENING
September 10	2 Samuel 4; 5	1 Corinthians 15	Ezekiel 13
September 11	2 Samuel 6	1 Corinthians 16	Ezekiel 14
September 12	2 Samuel 7	2 Corinthians 1	Ezekiel 15
September 13	2 Samuel 8; 9	2 Corinthians 2	Ezekiel 16
September 14	2 Samuel 10	2 Corinthians 3	Ezekiel 17
September 15	2 Samuel 11	2 Corinthians 4	Ezekiel 18
September 16	2 Samuel 12	2 Corinthians 5	Ezekiel 19

What to look out for in 2 Samuel

2 Samuel records King David's 40-year reign. Note David's failures as well as his faithfulness to God.

The Bible and Jesus

"Remove Christ from the Scriptures and there is nothing left."
Martin Luther

Chapters	Theme
1–5	David's political triumphs
6–7	David's spiritual triumphs
8–10	David's military triumphs
11	David's sins of adultery and murders
12–13	Trouble in David's family
14–24	Troubles in David's kingdom

Week 38
Perfecting holiness

THIS WEEK'S IMPORTANT BIBLE VERSE

"Since we have these promises, dear friends, let us purify ourselves from everything that contaminates body and spirit, perfecting holiness out of reverence for God." *2 Corinthians 7:1*

DATE	MORNING	MORNING	EVENING
September 17	2 Samuel 13	2 Corinthians 6	Ezekiel 20
September 18	2 Samuel 14	2 Corinthians 7	Ezekiel 21
September 19	2 Samuel 15	2 Corinthians 8	Ezekiel 22
September 20	2 Samuel 16	2 Corinthians 9	Ezekiel 23
September 21	2 Samuel 17	2 Corinthians 10	Ezekiel 24
September 22	2 Samuel 18	2 Corinthians 11	Ezekiel 25
September 23	2 Samuel 19	2 Corinthians 12	Ezekiel 26

47

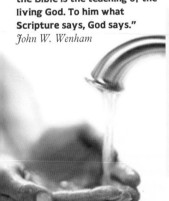

Jesus' view of the Bible

"To Christ the Bible is true, authoritative, inspired, to him the God of the Bible is the living God, and the teaching of the Bible is the teaching of the living God. To him what Scripture says, God says."
John W. Wenham

What to look out for in 2 Corinthians

See what you can learn from the spiritually alive, first-century church at Corinth, as you read this letter.

Chapter	Theme
1:1-11	Introduction
1:12–7:16	The characteristics of Paul's ministry
8–9	Taking the collection of money to the poor at Jerusalem
10:1–13:10	Paul's defense of his apostolic ministry
13:11-14	Conclusion

Week 39
Confusion

THIS WEEK'S IMPORTANT BIBLE VERSE "Evidently some people are throwing you into confusion and are trying to pervert the gospel of Christ."
Galatians 1:7

DATE	MORNING	MORNING	EVENING
September 24	2 Samuel 20	2 Corinthians 13	Ezekiel 27
September 25	2 Samuel 21	Galatians 1	Ezekiel 28
September 26	2 Samuel 22	Galatians 2	Ezekiel 29
September 27	2 Samuel 23	Galatians 3	Ezekiel 30
September 28	2 Samuel 24	Galatians 4	Ezekiel 31
September 29	1 Kings 1	Galatians 5	Ezekiel 32
September 30	1 Kings 2	Galatians 6	Ezekiel 33

48

What to look out for in Galatians

Paul writes this white-hot letter to counter false teachers.

Chapters	Theme
1–2	Paul defends the gospel of grace.
3–4	Justification is by faith, not by deeds, or by the Law.
5–6	The gospel of grace gives the gift of Christian freedom.

Faith alone

"Paul taught that the Gentiles were justified by faith alone, without works of the law."
Martin Luther, commenting on Galatians 2

Week 40
"In Christ Jesus"

THIS WEEK'S IMPORTANT BIBLE VERSE

"For we are God's workmanship, created in Christ Jesus to do good works, which God prepared in advance for us to do."
Ephesians 2:10

DATE	MORNING	MORNING	EVENING
October 1	1 Kings 3	Ephesians 1	Ezekiel 34
October 2	1 Kings 4; 5	Ephesians 2	Ezekiel 35
October 3	1 Kings 6	Ephesians 3	Ezekiel 36
October 4	1 Kings 7	Ephesians 4	Ezekiel 37
October 5	1 Kings 8	Ephesians 5	Ezekiel 38
October 6	1 Kings 9	Ephesians 6	Ezekiel 39
October 7	1 Kings 10	Philippians 1	Ezekiel 40

What to look out for in Ephesians

In this letter the phrase "in Christ," or its equivalent comes 35 times – more than in any other New Testament book. As you come across the phrase see what important truth Paul is emphasizing.

For example, in *Ephesians 1:1* the saints, that is Christians, at Ephesus are said to be "in Christ Jesus." And in *Ephesians 1:4* Paul says that we were chosen "in him."

The Bible's unity

"In the Old Testament the New is concealed.
In the New Testament the Old is revealed."
Augustine of Hippo

Week 41
Rejoice

"So then, just as you received Christ Jesus as Lord, continue to live in him, rooted and built up in him, strengthened in the faith as you were taught, and overflowing with thankfulness." *Colossians 2:6,7*

DATE	MORNING	MORNING	EVENING
October 8	1 Kings 11	Philippians 2	Ezekiel 41
October 9	1 Kings 12	Philippians 3	Ezekiel 42
October 10	1 Kings 13	Philippians 4	Ezekiel 43
October 11	1 Kings 14	Colossians 1	Ezekiel 44
October 12	1 Kings 15	Colossians 2	Ezekiel 45
October 13	1 Kings 16	Colossians 3	Ezekiel 46
October 14	1 Kings 17	Colossians 4	Ezekiel 47

50

What to look out for in Philippians

The word "joy," or "rejoice" comes 16 times in the four chapters of this letter. Note what we should be joyful about, and when we should be joyful.

Understanding the Bible

"In expounding the Bible if one were always to confine oneself to the unadorned grammatical meaning, one might fall into error. Not only contradictions and propositions far from true might thus be made to appear in the Bible, but even grave heresies and follies. Thus it would be necessary to assign to God feet, hands and eyes."
Galileo

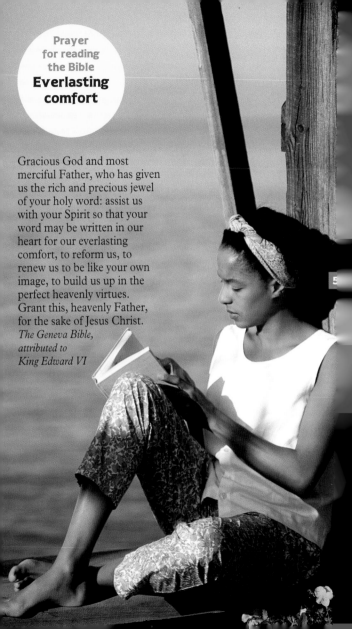

Gracious God and most
merciful Father, who has given
us the rich and precious jewel
of your holy word: assist us
with your Spirit so that your
word may be written in our
heart for our everlasting
comfort, to reform us, to
renew us to be like your own
image, to build us up in the
perfect heavenly virtues.
Grant this, heavenly Father,
for the sake of Jesus Christ.
The Geneva Bible,
attributed to
King Edward VI

Week 42
Our hope

"Now when Daniel learned that the decree had been published [which stated that only King Darius should be prayed to], he went home to his upstairs room where the windows opened towards Jerusalem. Three times a day he got down on his knees and prayed, giving thanks to his God, just as he had done before." *Daniel 6:10*

DATE	MORNING	MORNING	EVENING
October 15	1 Kings 18	1 Thessalonians 1	Ezekiel 48
October 16	1 Kings 19	1 Thessalonians 2	Daniel 1
October 17	1 Kings 20	1 Thessalonians 3	Daniel 2
October 18	1 Kings 21	1 Thessalonians 4	Daniel 3
October 19	1 Kings 22	1 Thessalonians 5	Daniel 4
October 20	2 Kings 1	2 Thessalonians 1	Daniel 5
October 21	2 Kings 2	2 Thessalonians 2	Daniel 6

What to look out for in 1 Thessalonians
Note the helpful and illuminating teaching Paul gives in each chapter about the return of the Redeemer. See *1 Thessalonians 1:10; 2:19; 3:13; 4:13-18; 5:1-11,23.*

Infallible

"The church has always believed her Scriptures to be the book of God, of which God was in such a sense the author that every one of its affirmations of whatever kind is to be esteemed as the utterance of God, of infallible truth and authority."
B.B. Warfield

Week 43
Dependence

"But godliness with contentment is great gain."
1 Timothy 6:6

DATE	MORNING	MORNING	EVENING
October 22	2 Kings 3	2 Thessalonians 3	Daniel 7
October 23	2 Kings 4	1 Timothy 1	Daniel 8
October 24	2 Kings 5	1 Timothy 2	Daniel 9
October 25	2 Kings 6	1 Timothy 3	Daniel 10
October 26	2 Kings 7	1 Timothy 4	Daniel 11
October 27	2 Kings 8	1 Timothy 5	Daniel 12
October 28	2 Kings 9	1 Timothy 6	Hosea 1

What to look out for in 1 and 2 Kings

The first half of *1 Kings* traces the life of one king, King Solomon, *1 Kings 1–11*, while the second half of *1 Kings*, *1 Kings 12–22*, traces the histories of two sets of kings who ruled over the divided kingdom. Note how the underlying theme is: "Men and women cannot rule themselves without conscious dependence on God's help."

Textual attestation

"There is no body of ancient literature in the world which enjoys such a wealth of good textual attestation as the New Testament." *F.F. Bruce*

THIS WEEK'S
**IMPORTANT
BIBLE
VERSE**

"All Scripture is God–breathed and is useful for teaching, rebuking, correcting and training in righteousness, so that the man of God may be thoroughly equipped for every good work."
2 Timothy 3:16

DATE	MORNING	MORNING	EVENING
October 29	2 Kings 10; 11	2 Timothy 1	Hosea 2
October 30	2 Kings 12	2 Timothy 2	Hosea 3; 4
October 31	2 Kings 13	2 Timothy 3	Hosea 5; 6
November 1	2 Kings 14	2 Timothy 4	Hosea 7
November 2	2 Kings 15	Titus 1	Hosea 8
November 3	2 Kings 16	Titus 2	Hosea 9
November 4	2 Kings 17	Titus 3	Hosea 10

What to look out for in Titus

Paul had left Titus in charge of the Christians on the island of Crete. Now he writes to Titus and in this letter there are three summaries of Christian theology. Note how each of them point to the grace of God. See *Titus 1:1-4; 2:11-14; 3:4-7.*

As originally given

"No one, as far as I know, holds that the English translation of the Bible is absolutely infallible and inerrant. The doctrine held by many is that the Scriptures as originally given were absolutely infallible and inerrant, and that our English translation (KJV) is a substantially accurate rendering of the Scriptures as originally given."
R.A. Torrey

Week 45
The Day of the Lord

**"Rend your heart
and not your garments.
Return to the Lord your God,
for he is gracious and compassionate,
slow to anger and abounding in love,
and he relents from sending calamity."** *Joel 2:12*

DATE	MORNING	MORNING	EVENING
November 5	2 Kings 18	Philemon 1	Hosea 11
November 6	2 Kings 19	Hebrews 1	Hosea 12
November 7	2 Kings 20	Hebrews 2	Hosea 13
November 8	2 Kings 21	Hebrews 3	Hosea 14
November 9	2 Kings 22	Hebrews 4	Joel 1
November 10	2 Kings 23	Hebrews 5	Joel 2
November 11	2 Kings 24	Hebrews 6	Joel 3

What to look out for in Joel

The key theme in the book of Joel is "the Day of the Lord," which appears five times, see *1:15; 2:1,11,31; 3:14* (see also *3:18*). It is possible to see five characteristics of the Day of the Lord. See also *Isaiah 2:12-22; Ezekiel 13:1-7; Zephaniah 1:14-23; Zechariah 14:1-21*.

Bible translation

"If God spare my life, ere many years I will cause a boy that driveth the plow to know more of the Scriptures than thou dost." *William Tyndale*

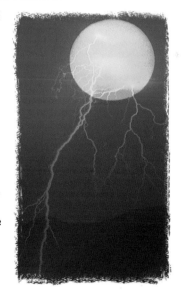

See that justice is done

THIS WEEK'S IMPORTANT BIBLE VERSE

"Let us fix our eyes on Jesus, the author and perfecter of our faith, who for the joy set before him endured the cross, scorning its shame, and sat down at the right hand of the throne of God." *Hebrews 12:2*

DATE	MORNING	MORNING	EVENING
November 12	2 Kings 25	Hebrews 7	Amos 1
November 13	1 Chronicles 1; 2	Hebrews 8	Amos 2
November 14	1 Chronicles 3; 4	Hebrews 9	Amos 3
November 15	1 Chronicles 5; 6	Hebrews 10	Amos 4
November 16	1 Chronicles 7; 8	Hebrews 11	Amos 5
November 17	1 Chronicles 9; 10	Hebrews 12	Amos 6
November 18	1 Chronicles 11; 12	Hebrews 13	Amos 7

What to look out for in Amos

As you read the book of *Amos* you will come across the following four divisions:

1. Eight prophecies, *1:1–2:16*
2. Three sermons, *3:1–6:14*
3. Five visions, *7:1–9:10*
4. Five promises, *9:11-15*

Concern for others

"Concern for the rights and welfare of all [God's] people flows, like a mighty river, from his own heart. Whoever would truly serve him must go with that flow."
D.A. Hubbard, commenting on Amos 5:24

Week 47
Echoes

THIS WEEK'S IMPORTANT BIBLE VERSE

"But Jonah ran away from the Lord and headed for Tarshish."
Jonah 1:3

DATE	MORNING	MORNING	EVENING
November 19	1 Chronicles 13; 14	James 1	Amos 8
November 20	1 Chronicles 15	James 2	Amos 9
November 21	1 Chronicles 16	James 3	Obadiah
November 22	1 Chronicles 17	James 4	Jonah 1
November 23	1 Chronicles 18	James 5	Jonah 2
November 24	1 Chronicles 19; 20	1 Peter 1	Jonah 3
November 25	1 Chronicles 21	1 Peter 2	Jonah 4

What to look out for in James

Note how *James* has a number of echoes from the Sermon on the Mount.

James compared with Matthew

James	Theme	Matthew
1:2	Perseverance	5:10-12
1:4	Sanctification	5:48
2:13	Mercy	6:14-15
4:11	Judgment	7:1-2
5:2	Wealth	6:19

Giving

"He is no fool who gives what he cannot keep to gain what he cannot lose."
Jim Elliot, the young American missionary who was killed by Auca Natives in Ecuador in 1956, commenting on Luke 9:23-25.

Week 48
Persecution

"He has shown you, O man, what is good.
 And what does the Lord require of you?
To act justly and to love mercy
 and to walk humbly with your God." *Micah 6:8*

DATE	MORNING	MORNING	EVENING
November 26	1 Chronicles 22	1 Peter 3	Micah 1
November 27	1 Chronicles 23	1 Peter 4	Micah 2
November 28	1 Chronicles 24; 25	1 Peter 5	Micah 3
November 29	1 Chronicles 26; 27	2 Peter 1	Micah 4
November 30	1 Chronicles 28	2 Peter 2	Micah 5
December 1	1 Chronicles 29	2 Peter 3	Micah 6
December 2	2 Chronicles 1	1 John 1	Micah 7

What to look out for in 1 Peter

Peter wrote his first letter to outline the proper response Christians should have towards suffering. This was especially relevant to his readers, as they were being persecuted. See *1 Peter 2:21; 3:18; 4:1,12-14; 5:9.*

God's fatherly favor

"Thus we learn that we only make due progress in the knowledge of the Word of the Lord when we become really humbled and groan under the burden of our sins and learn to flee to God's mercy and find rest in nothing except his fatherly favor."
John Calvin on 1 John 1:10

Prayer for reading the Bible

Read, mark, learn

Blessed Lord, who hast caused all holy Scriptures to be written for our learning: grant that we may in such wise hear them, read, mark, learn, and inwardly digest them, that by patience and comfort of thy holy Word, we may embrace and ever hold fast the blessed hope of everlasting life, which thou hast given us in our Savior Jesus Christ.

Book of Common Prayer, 1549, Collect, Second Sunday in Advent

59

Week 49
Opposites

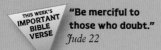

THIS WEEK'S **IMPORTANT** BIBLE VERSE

"**Be merciful to those who doubt.**"
Jude 22

DATE	MORNING	MORNING	EVENING
December 3	2 Chronicles 2	1 John 2	Nahum 1
December 4	2 Chronicles 3; 4	1 John 3	Nahum 2
December 5	2 Chronicles 5:1–6:11	1 John 4	Nahum 3
December 6	2 Chronicles 6:12-42	1 John 5	Habakkuk 1
December 7	2 Chronicles 7	2 John	Habakkuk 2
December 8	2 Chronicles 8	3 John	Habakkuk 3
December 9	2 Chronicles 9	Jude	Zephaniah 1

What to look out for in 1 John

Note John's many antithetical parallelisms in *1 John*.
- Light versus darkness
- Truth versus falsehood
- Love versus hatred
- Love of the world versus love of the Father
- Christ versus antichrists
- Children of God versus children of the devil
- Righteousness versus sin
- Life versus death

The Bible's scope

"**The whole counsel of God concerning all things necessary for His own glory, man's salvation, faith, and life, is either expressly set down in Scripture, or by good and necessary consequence may be deduced from Scripture: unto which nothing at any time is to be added, whether by new revelations of the Spirit, or traditions of men.**"
The Confession of Faith of the Westminster Assembly of Divines, 1646

Perspectives

THIS WEEK'S
IMPORTANT
BIBLE
VERSE

"Here I am! I stand at the door and knock.
If anyone hears my voice and opens the
door, I will come in and eat with him, and
he with me." *Revelation 3:20*

DATE	MORNING	MORNING	EVENING
December 10	2 Chronicles 10	Revelation 1	Zephaniah 2
December 11	2 Chronicles 11; 12	Revelation 2	Zephaniah 3
December 12	2 Chronicles 13	Revelation 3	Haggai 1
December 13	2 Chronicles 14; 15	Revelation 4	Haggai 2
December 14	2 Chronicles 16	Revelation 5	Zechariah 1
December 15	2 Chronicles 17	Revelation 6	Zechariah 2
December 16	2 Chronicles 18	Revelation 7	Zechariah 3

What to look out for in 1 and 2 Chronicles

1 and *2 Chronicles* cover the same period of Jewish history described in *2 Samuel* through *2 Kings*. However, the perspective of *1 and 2 Chronicles* is different. While *2 Samuel* and *1 and 2 Kings* give political history of Israel and Judah, *1 and 2 Chronicles* gives a religious history of the Davidic dynasty. The former were written from a prophetic and moral viewpoint, but the latter from a priestly and spiritual perspective.

Reliability of the Bible

"The Christian can take the whole Bible in his hand and say without fear or hesitation that he holds in it the true Word of God, handed down without essential loss from generation to generation throughout the centuries."
Sir Frederic G. Kenyon, former Director of the British Museum

Future plans

THIS WEEK'S IMPORTANT BIBLE VERSE

"Rejoice greatly, O Daughter of Zion!
Shout, Daughter of Jerusalem!
See, your king comes to you,
righteous and having salvation,
gentle and riding on a donkey,
on a colt, the foal of a donkey." *Zechariah 9:9*

DATE	MORNING	MORNING	EVENING
December 17	2 Chronicles 19; 20	Revelation 8	Zechariah 4
December 18	2 Chronicles 21	Revelation 9	Zechariah 5
December 19	2 Chronicles 22; 23	Revelation 10	Zechariah 6
December 20	2 Chronicles 24	Revelation 11	Zechariah 7
December 21	2 Chronicles 25	Revelation 12	Zechariah 8
December 22	2 Chronicles 26	Revelation 13	Zechariah 9
December 23	2 Chronicles 27; 28	Revelation 14	Zechariah 10

What to look out for in Zechariah

Zechariah writes about God's future plans for his covenant people. You will find this theme running through *Zechariah's* three sections.

- **Eight visions**, *1–6*
  Each vision needs to be interpreted. For example, the sixth vision, *5:1-4*, a flying scroll, symbolizes judgment on those who disobey God's law.
  In the seventh vision, *5:5-11*, a woman in a basket, wickedness which must be removed from Judah, is personified.
- **Four messages**, *7–8*
  These messages state that the fast recalling Jerusalem's

downfall will be replaced by celebrations when God blesses his people.
- **Two burdens**, *9–14*
  The first burden is depicted in chapters *9–11*.
  The second burden, *12–14*, shows how Israel will be victorious and will have a victorious king.

The Bible's purpose

"The Bible was given to bear witness to one God, Creator and Sustainer of the universe, through Christ, Redeemer of sinful man. It presents one continuous story – that of human redemption."
M.F. Unger

Father of mercies, in thy word
What endless glory shines!
For ever be thy name adored
For these celestial lines.

O may these heavenly pages be
My ever dear delight,
And still new beauties may I
    see,
And still increasing light.

Divine Instructor, gracious
    Lord,
Be thou for ever near;
Teach me to love thy sacred
    word,
And view my Savior here.
Anne Steele

Week 52
Revelation

DATE	MORNING	MORNING	EVENING
December 24	2 Chronicles 29	Revelation 15	Zechariah 11
December 25	2 Chronicles 30	Revelation 16	Zechariah 12:1–13:1
December 26	2 Chronicles 31	Revelation 17	Zechariah 13:2-9
December 27	2 Chronicles 32	Revelation 18	Zechariah 14
December 28	2 Chronicles 33	Revelation 19	Malachi 1
December 29	2 Chronicles 34	Revelation 20	Malachi 2
December 30	2 Chronicles 35	Revelation 21	Malachi 3
December 31	2 Chronicles 36	Revelation 22	Malachi 4

What to look out for in Revelation

This book opens with the words, "The revelation of Jesus Christ," which provides an apt title for the whole book. Look for the many presentations of the resurrected Jesus in this book. See *1:1,5,17,18; 2:18; 3:7,14; 5:5,6; 19:11,13,16; 22:13,16,21.*

The Bible's origin

"The chief reason why the Christian believes in the divine origin of the Bible is that Jesus Christ himself taught it."
John Stott

"STRIKES THE READER LIKE AN UNEXPECTED CLAP OF THUNDER . . . BRILLIANT."
—*The Fort Pierce Tribune*

"This thriller offers plenty of passion, sick characters, deadly foes, and old-fashioned blood and guts. But however complicated the plot, Singerman keeps a tight hand on the reins."
—*The Orlando Sentinel*

"A contemporary thriller full of colorful characters and keen suspense . . . The plot is absorbing, the characters are compelling, and the action is exciting—sometimes even kinky. PRANCING TIGER is a first-rate novel of intrigue and adventure. It features original settings and many tense, violent confrontations that will entertain its readers steadily."
—*New Smyrna Beach Observer*

"[Singerman] is lavish in his explorations of a vast array of human experience. . . . You'll stay with the story because it's a heck of a good mystery, and you'll care about the solution."
—*St. Petersburg Times*

"In *Prancing Tiger* Philip Singerman has succeeded in the difficult task of writing a thriller that spans decades and generations. He deftly weaves the threads of Troy's investigation and the story of his life without losing his readers somewhere in the mud of Laos or the dust of Texas."
—*BookPage*

Also by Philip Singerman:

AN AMERICAN HERO: The Red Adair Story

PRANCING TIGER

Philip Singerman

IVY BOOKS • NEW YORK

Ivy Books
Published by Ballantine Books
Copyright © 1994 by Philip Singerman

Library of Congress Catalog Card Number: 94-2635

ISBN 0-8041-1428-5

This edition published by arrangement with William Morrow and Company, Inc.

Manufactured in the United States of America

First Ballantine Books Edition: December 1995

10 9 8 7 6 5 4 3 2 1

For Marcia

mi amor, mi vida

I would like to thank Larry Hughes, editor at large at William Morrow, for his enthusiastic support and invaluable assistance. I would like to thank Rose Marie Morse, my editor at Morrow, as well. Her devotion and skill did much to shape this book. I am also deeply grateful to my agent, Bob Diforio, extraordinary partner and friend, whose efforts on my behalf are equaled only by his willingness to listen, day or night, and to always offer wise counsel.

Prologue

$\blacklozenge$

Billy Roseman saw a light on in the office of his barn. It was one in the morning, Sunday, and he had no idea who might be in there. Returning to Florida from a brief but disastrous adventure on the banks of the Rio Grande, Roseman had come directly from the airport to the track to check on his horses. Billy was injured and in a state of complete exhaustion, but neglect of animals was unthinkable to him, a crime for which there was no excuse.

Roseman trained and raced harness horses—standardbreds, as they are called. Recently, his stable had fallen into financial disarray, and Billy was in debt to nearly everyone he knew. Maybe his guest was a bill collector. They had come looking for him at stranger hours than this. Intense pain knifed through his left shoulder, he was sure his ribs were bruised, and his head was on fire from a deep gash in his forehead, hastily bandaged by a woman who had probably saved his life. The last thing he needed was a conversation with someone to whom he owed money. Then he thought about the Mexicans who had nearly killed him—who very well may have tracked him east, or called ahead to friends—and decided a bill collector wouldn't be such bad company after all.

Before walking unsteadily to the small window of the office to see who was, in fact, inside, he made sure to lock the brown envelope stuffed with hundreds inside the trunk of the Lincoln Town Car he'd rented. In the glow of the Lincoln's trunk light he saw that the envelope was flecked with dried blood. Roseman had no idea whether the blood had come from his head or from his friend Myron McBride, who had lured him to the Mexican border with the promise of a quick fix for Billy's monetary woes.

1

"Horses for money," McBride had said. "A simple and time-honored exchange." McBride had left the guns and the drugs out of the equation, but Billy should have known. There would be no quick fix for Billy Roseman. Not now. Not for McBride, either. Certainly not for him.

Roseman approached the window and breathed a sigh of relief. Nikki Waters's black Porsche was parked in the dark passway that ran through the center of the barn. Billy peered in the window and saw Nikki stretched out on the old leather couch, reading a book. The revolver he kept locked in his desk was lying on the coffee table in front of her.

"Hey, don't get excited," he said through the window. "It's only me. I'm coming in through the door. Leave that gun where it is."

As he eased into the room she put the book down and stared at him, her eyebrows arching. "Hey, yourself, sugar," she said. "You better sit down. I ain't gonna ask what kind of day you had. You look like you been stomped by a mule."

"Well, you look good enough for both of us," he said. He had always considered her an attractive woman, but he had never seen her in a dress before, made up with a professional model's sense of allure. Jeans, an old work shirt, and running shoes were all she ever wore around the stable where, for a couple of days a week during the past two training seasons, she had hot-walked, bathed and fed his horses, and helped him with his books. For free. For some reason he had not divined. "I like horses and I like you," she had said when he asked her. Roseman, in need of any help he could get, had probed no further.

She had one leg bent at a forty-five-degree angle, the heel and sole of her shoe resting on a cushion. He could see the top of her stocking and the garter that held it in place. After what he'd been through in the past couple of days, he thought perhaps he was hallucinating.

"Where you goin'?" he said. "Where you been? What the hell you doin' with my gun?"

"I can answer those in order," she told him. "I ain't goin' anywhere, least not for a while. I been stood up. And I got your gun out 'cause I think I'm bein' followed."

"That forty-five's a helluva piece for a lady to protect herself with," he said. "Watch out you don't blow off your foot."

The gun was a Colt Wyatt Earp Buntline Special single-action army revolver, a commemorative produced in 1964 on the thirty-fifth anniversary of Earp's death. It had a twelve-inch barrel and was gold-plated, with black rosewood grips. Only 150 had been made. Roseman had fired the gun once, straight up into the air, the day after he bought it in 1980 for nine hundred dollars, when he signed the papers incorporating his business, Quickdraw Stable.

"Shit, my uncle Jewel taught me how to use his Ruger Blackhawk when I was sixteen. And that was a forty-four," she said. "We hunted hogs with it. I know I told you that story at least twice."

"I forgot about your uncle Jewel," he said. "And huntin' hogs."

"Maybe we should take a ride to the emergency room," she said. "Get your head looked at."

"No," he said. "I'll be all right."

"Cool Babba laid some smoke on me," she said. "Jamaica's finest. He claims it's *ganja of de utmost kind*. I rolled a couple before you got here. What say you and me give it a try and find out. Maybe that'll be the ticket. For you *and* me."

"Nikki, I don't know," Roseman said. "There's places I been just recently I'd as soon not revisit in my head, not tonight."

"Well you ain't in those places now, sugar," she said. "You're here with me, who's all dressed up with no place to go. A confluence of kindred spirits. Roll with it." She lit a joint and took a couple of deep hits.

Billy leaned against the file cabinet, watching Nikki's face, watching her eyes narrow against the smoke. She smiled slightly. Should he tell her about Mexico? Maybe she already knew. He'd seen her talking to McBride a couple of times recently. All Billy had said to Fulton Tasmeeda, his groom, was that he had to go away for a couple of days and to make sure everything got done around the barn. But that sorry asshole McBride, his friend, his late friend, always wanted to impress the ladies, always

wanted to be the hot shot. Did he talk up his big-time deal?
Did McBride tell Nikki Waters about his grand scheme that
left him lying in the dirt by the Rio Grande with his face
blown off, unless by now they'd stuffed him in a hole?

She thought someone was following her, she said. What
about him, Billy wondered. Who was after his ass? There
could be a whole lot more confluence out there than either
one of them had bargained for. One minute he'd been hiding in his cave, watching again and again the video of his
greatest race, his singular triumph, as his life slid slowly
downhill. The next minute he had stepped into the open,
into the middle of an avalanche. Really, he thought, there
was no difference. One way was simply quicker than the
other.

He took the joint from her and smoked, still watching
her face, watching her dress move ever so slightly further
up her leg, rolling with it, rolling with the notion of making
love to her in spite of his pain. In fact, the idea had occurred to him more than once when he watched her supple
body bend and twist as she worked around the barn. Something had always kept him from making a pass at her, some
elusive quality about her, some unspoken barrier that was
no longer there.

They were halfway into the second joint when she called
to him. It sounded like she was at the end of a long, narrow
hallway. She held out her arms, beckoning; he could feel
her hot breath across the room. Flashes of light jumped
from her fingertips, reflected off her silvery eyelids and off
the faint beads of perspiration on her upper lip. He concentrated on the light and his pain diminished.

It was warm in the office from the electric heater. He had
unbuttoned his shirt and pulled it out of his jeans so that
when he knelt above her on the couch it hung around her
like a pink tent. She drew his head down to her, his lips to
hers, drawing on him, working her tongue deep into his
mouth as her fingers tore at the buttons of his fly, freeing
him with both her hands.

"No," she said, when he was ready for her. "Not yet.
Wait." She took his hands and placed them on the collar of
her dress, above the row of buttons that ran down to the

waist. "Rip it open," she said. "Rip it so I can show you
my tits. Do it. Do that for me. That's what I need."

He was in the tunnel with her now, the dope obliterating
everything but her body arched under him, opening to him,
and her voice, coiled like velvet rope around his head. "I
want to come with you," she whispered. "Do what I need
to make me come. Rip it." She raked his forearms with her
nails as he tore the buttons open. Then she had the gun,
somehow she had picked up the gun, holding it by the cyl-
inder, pressing the smooth black wood of the grip into his
hand, and the barrel, the end of the long, gold-plated barrel
was against her lips.

"Do this to me," she said, running the barrel in and out
of her mouth, running her tongue along its length, biting on
it, baring her teeth. He was lost inside her then, caught up
in the lasciviousness of her shredded clothing and disheveled hair and the gold barrel circled by her reddened lips,
coming with her as her fingers drummed against his belly
and then pulled wildly at her own breasts.

He needed air, and so he left her sleeping on the couch
and stumbled into the night. He limped toward the rented
Lincoln, looking for something to lean on, and lay on his
back across the hood. At some point, shivering and cold but
too weary and in too much pain to trudge even the thirty
yards to his office, he opened the car door and collapsed on
the back seat. The car seemed to be flying to a height
where he was weightless. He looked down and saw a river.
The river was filled with horses, swimming upstream
against the current, swimming for their lives from a tall
man in a long coat with a rifle who was firing at them from
the bank. He could hear the rifle booming and see the water
churning from the horses' frantic hooves.

They had not been alone in the office. There was someone hidden above them. This person had climbed from a
stall to the narrow loft that ran the length of the barn, crept
silently along a joist to a position of observation—a slit in
the rough-hewn boards of the ceiling—and remained motionless throughout the couple's passion. Clad in a dark
blue hooded sweatshirt, black jeans, skin-tight black gloves,
and black socks pulled over sneakers so the soles would not

leave prints, the figure waited while the woman slept and
the man went out for air. Finally, after more than half an
hour, when the man did not return, the figure crept back
down the joist, down into the stall, and over to the office
door, noting on the way that the man had passed out in the
car.

The figure moved quickly; there had been plenty of time
in the loft to think things through. Originally, the plan was
to cut the woman's throat with an ebony-handled, double-
edged knife, but the appearance of Billy Roseman changed
that. Now, the double-edged knife remained sheathed on the
figure's hip. Instead the gun, the Wyatt Earp Buntline Special, was gripped by the long, gold barrel and the hammer
was pulled back. The end of the barrel, meeting no resistance, was reinserted between the sleeping woman's lips
and a gloved finger was pressed firmly against the trigger.
The woman's body bucked once from the impact of the
bullet and was motionless. A black-gloved hand put the gun
down on the table. The hooded figure turned back to the
woman, paused for just a second, removed the ebony-
handled knife from its sheath, cut swiftly at the dead woman's flesh, and was gone before the echo of the revolver's
roar had left the room.

I

✦

Just after dawn, Roland Troy, wrapped in an old plaid blanket, emerged onto his front porch with a steaming mug of coffee. He sat down in a rocking chair mounted high like a throne on concrete blocks, put his feet up on the porch railing, and sipped from the mug, watching the first shafts of sunlight sift between the tall pine trees on the far side of his pond. Soon, various shades of ocher, from deep orange to a yellow that was almost white, made paths across the flat water.

Once, the house itself had been bright yellow. Here and there, in places always shaded from the sun, the wood was colored like the horns of an old ram, but mostly it was bare. Two front windows, one on each side of the sagging porch, reached almost to the ground, their sills obscured by weeds. The porch was gone directly by the door, and across the gaping hole was tacked a blue four-by-eight–foot sheet-metal sign with white letters that read BRAKE AND FRONT END SPECIALISTS—WHEEL ALIGNMENT. Footsteps on this sign boomed and crackled like a rain of baseballs on a tin-roofed shed. It was impossible to come into the house, at least through that door, without being heard.

The night before, Roland Troy had stayed up late, putting the finishing touches on a model of a bank. Before it met Troy's satisfaction, the dimensions had to be just right. The cross streets, the parking lot, the trees and shrubs, the stores next door, the gas station across the road, all were in precisely scaled proportion to the place itself, where a robbery had occurred, two hostages taken, and a bank guard shot dead. That afternoon Troy would deliver the model to the county courthouse where the state attorney would then use it in a trial.

Formerly, Roland Troy had been a homicide detective, the best in Florida, the best in all of the southeastern United States, according to those who'd worked with him and to those he'd run to ground. Now, building models such as these was what he did for a living, though in a sense that wasn't true since he didn't need the money. The models he built were renowned for their quality. They had helped the state attorney countless times in his presentation of a case to the jury. Troy built them out of friendship and for pride. They were a way he could contribute, a way he could help out, though he never would admit it. He said he built them all for art.

Dozens of them filled a room inside his house. (Part of his deal with the state attorney, a man closer to Troy than his own brother, was that he'd get them back once they were no longer needed.) If the rate of serious crime in central Florida kept rising at its present rate, Troy reckoned, this room would house most all of it in miniature within ten years. Troy's favorite featured a giant teacup, a replica of one from the Mad Hatter ride at the Magic Kingdom. One Thursday evening, several years before, a man had shot his wife and both her lovers who were sitting all together in the cup. Troy had built two nearby rides as well to give a sense of relative distance to the scene. The job had taken him two weeks, working straight, twelve hours a day. When the trial was over a woman from Montreal who had been a witness to the crime offered to buy the model for ten thousand dollars. Troy politely declined the offer, not wanting to profit from human misery.

His coffee finished, Troy went back inside the house, but soon came out again, dressed in tan Levi's corduroy jeans and a dark green flannel shirt. He walked to the edge of the pond, climbed into his canoe, untied it from the dock and began paddling to the northeast. The morning was chilly and he had considered a jacket, but there was no wind and he would soon be warm enough from his exertion. At the corner of the pond furthest from his house, Troy eased between a tangled outcropping of mangrove roots. Here the pond let out into a narrow passage, no more than five feet wide, that someone unfamiliar with the shoreline would never have found.

The passage ran for fifty yards beneath a canopy of vines, then widened into a vast lagoon filled with cypress trees whose knees protruded from the surface like the gnarled supports of some primeval bridge. These knees, which are extensions of the tree's root system and may be up to ten feet tall, function in a way not altogether known to man. It may be that they help provide the roots with oxygen or that they help support the tree itself. To Roland Troy, they were signposts on a road map of a dark watery forest he knew like no one else. From the time he was a child he had explored this water, learned where deer and bear and panther came to drink, where eagles nested and alligators lurked. On the high ground that bordered it he had hunted and camped, searched for Indian relics and buried treasure that legend said was there. A hundred and eighty acres of this tenebrous cypress swamp was part of an eight-hundred-acre tract that Roland Troy owned. The land had been in Troy's family for five generations, ever since his great, great-grandfather bought it, back in 1883, from the federal government for eleven dollars an acre.

On early maps of the region, the dark, winding river that ran through the land appears with several different names, but Troy's grandfather, Wiley, renamed it the Coacoochee—the Indian word meaning wildcat—to commemorate his sighting of a panther on its banks.

Wiley Troy spent his life running a fishing camp on the Coacoochee and guiding hunters through his woods. Unlike other members of the Troy family who moved out, regarding Florida as nothing more than an uncultured breeding ground for snakes and insects, Wiley was seduced by the lush splendor of the land and explored every square foot of it. He grew accustomed to the extreme heat and even in the middle of summer would tramp through the woods, examining plants and searching out animal lairs. The tropical storms that tore through the region, terrifying others, excited him and filled him with vitality. It was from his grandfather that Roland Troy received his wilderness education, from him that he learned to hunt, fish and track, and to respect the land.

Roland's father was shot down on a bombing mission over Germany in 1945, when Troy was two years old. His

mother, Gretta, returned to her home in New York City
with Roland and his older brother, Lansford. With her two
sons she moved into her parents' enormous apartment on
Central Park South, just up the street from the Plaza Hotel.
When they were old enough, she enrolled the boys in an
exclusive private school and exposed them constantly to
museums and concerts of classical music. Her parents were
the owners of a well-known art gallery (Gretta's mother, so
the story went, once shared an apartment in Paris with
Modigliani and Jacques Lipshitz) and entertained a constant
stream of painters and sculptors in their home. Lansford
Troy absorbed with fervor this culture that his mother and
her parents so loved, but Roland hated New York. Twice
he tried to run away, and finally, at the age of ten, was
shipped back to Florida to live with his paternal grandparents.

Wiley Troy and his wife Eunice both died in 1963, and
the land was split between Roland and his older brother, a
musical prodigy, now a cellist with the New York Philharmonic Orchestra. Lansford sold his thousand acres to a
Canadian land speculator in 1970 for 250 dollars an acre.
Roland Troy sold two hundred acres to developers twelve
years later for two and a half million but kept the rest, despite the developers' persistent entreaties and escalating offers. When he died, Roland's will decreed, the land would
belong to his daughter, Katherine. She would be allowed to
sell off another two hundred acres, but the rest would be
preserved forever wild.

There were people living on Roland Troy's land. Some
were squatters who came and went by boat, leaving no
more behind them than a few charred pieces of wood from
a campfire on the banks of the river. Others, well known to
Troy, were his permanent guests. It was to the home of one
of them, an Indian named Sheridan Halpatter, that Roland
Troy now made his way by canoe, through the cypress av-
enues of the swamp.

Halpatter, or *halpatah*, is the Seminole word for alligator,
and hunting alligators is what Sheridan Halpatter did, pur-
suing the occupation he believed had been bestowed on
him at birth. It was a classic example of a man following
his name to his destiny. Halpatter, like his father and grand-

father before him, hunted in the traditional Timucuan manner: he killed alligators by ramming sharpened poles down their throats, just as his ancestors had done long before white men showed up in Florida with guns. He hunted other game with feathered arrows tipped with razor-sharp flint or fish bone, propelled from a handmade yew-wood bow of such tensile strength it took two normal men to bend it. Halpatter was deadly with this bow up to a hundred yards, and on more than one occasion, Troy had seen him kill prey at over a hundred and fifty.

Halpatter was sitting on his dock, tying hooks on a trot-line, when Troy rounded a sandy point of land and came into view. He stood up, waved with both arms, and smiled broadly, revealing two rows of very large white teeth.

Sheridan Halpatter was one of the most remarkable-looking human beings Roland Troy knew. He had dark, smoldering eyes, smooth, copper-colored skin that was luminous, and waist-length black hair streaked with silver he wore almost always in a braid. Although several inches shorter than Troy, who was six-one, he outweighed him by at least forty pounds, most of it muscle. All of Halpatter's parts—his head, his shoulders, his chest, his arms and legs—were enormous, giving the Indian the aspect of a six-foot ten-inch giant who had been stuck in a press and shortened by twelve or fourteen inches. In general, Halpatter moved with a slow, rolling gait, as though he were walking on the deck of a ship in a stormy sea, but he was deceptively agile and very quick. Troy once saw him win a thousand-dollar bet by shinnying up a thirty-foot flagpole in less than ten seconds.

The most unusual of Sheridan Halpatter's parts, however, were his feet. Halpatter had been alive for fifty-six years, and for the last forty-five of them had not once put on a pair of shoes. Summer and winter he wore faded blue bib overalls from the legs of which these feet protruded like two prehensile beings independent of the man who lived above them. The long, powerful toes were splayed and topped by horny plates that looked much more like claws than nails. The feet themselves, nearly twice as wide as most men's, were fissured and blackened from four and a half decades of exposure to the elements, and were covered

top and bottom with calluses so thick they had repelled the
fangs of water moccasins and rattlesnakes. There was no
way they would any longer fit into a pair of shoes, which
is what Halpatter told his wife when he went barefoot to his
son's college graduation and his daughter's wedding.

"Hey, hey, hey," he said, throwing Troy a line. "I been
looking for you. You must'a finally got my message from
Tom Waxe. I been trying to get you on the phone for three
days. Don't read the paper, don't watch the TV, disconnect
your telephone. You're an isolated man, Roland. This and
that could happen and you'd never know."

"You should talk," Troy said. "Living out here with a
seven-foot water moccasin for a next-door neighbor. Wife's
gotta take a boat to get to the grocery store."

"I'm constantly in touch," Halpatter said. "I have a satellite dish. I read *Time* magazine and *Scientific American*.
And I don't unplug my phone."

In fact, although Roland Troy did not subscribe to the local Orlando newspaper, he read *The New York Times* and
The Wall Street Journal daily, as well as a wide selection of
magazines that ran from *Guns & Ammo* and *Popular
Hotrodding* to *The New Republic* and *Mother Earth News*.
Moreover, every evening he sat out on his porch, smoked
a cigar, and listened to the BBC's world news roundup on
his shortwave radio. He saw no need, however, to mention
this to Halpatter. Nor did he mention his second phone line
that was never unplugged. That number was known only to
Troy's daughter and an old friend and former employer
who lived on a farm in Virginia, not far from Washington.

"I'm sorry it took you so long to reach me, Sheridan,"
Troy said. "I was working on a model."

"No matter," Halpatter said. "I could have paddled over
to your place. Come on inside and we'll talk."

Halpatter turned, and Troy followed him down the dock
to his house, built Indian-style on cypress poles rising six
feet above the water. When they reached the kitchen,
Halpatter took a jug of homemade wine from the counter
and poured himself a large glass.

"There's apple juice in the fridge if you're thirsty," he
said. "And Pepsi. I know you don't want any of this." He
finished the wine in two long gulps and poured some more.

"What's wrong, Sheridan?" Troy asked. Rarely had he seen the Indian agitated enough to be drinking wine this early in the day.

"People on the island, three of them, two men and a woman. I asked them very politely to leave. They told me to get fucked. I thought you should go back there with me. You have a cooler head. I can't reason with people like that. I don't want to hurt anybody if I don't have to."

"How long they been there, on the island?"

"A week. Maybe a day or two more."

"You only been calling me three days."

"I waited. I wanted to think about it a little. Indians on that island been buried a thousand years, maybe more. I figured, what's a few days?"

Sheridan Halpatter's family lived on the land now owned by Roland Troy when his great, great-grandfather Phineas bought it from the government. Sheridan's great, great-grandfather, Osia Halpatter, had been a good friend to Phineas, and Phineas saw to it that Osia and his family were not removed to Oklahoma, as almost all the other Seminoles had been. Halpatters had lived safely and securely on the Troys' property since, watching over it, protecting it, not in a proprietary sense, for that was not the Indian way, but out of respect for the land and for the bones of those buried underneath it.

In the middle of the land, in the middle of a pond connected to the river by a stream, was a small island, about two acres in size. In the center of the island was an ancient Indian burial mound, fifty feet square and almost four feet high. The island was a holy place, not only to Sheridan Halpatter, but to Roland Troy as well.

When Troy was ten and first living with his grandparents, his grandfather brought him there by canoe. He showed him the burial mound and then made him sit perfectly still for half an hour, his back against a tree. Water lapped gently at the mangrove roots on the shore and the wind blew through the oak trees and the cabbage palm. Otherwise the island was still.

"What do you notice about this place that's different?" his grandfather asked him.

"It's quiet," Troy replied.

"That's because there are no animals here," his grandfather said. "There are no birds nesting in the trees. No snakes under the bushes. I've never seen another place like it in all my life. An engineer I used to know said it was a quirk of nature, something to do with the electromagnetic field that made the animals uncomfortable and kept them away. He said there were other places on earth he'd heard about where the same thing happened. I wasn't convinced. I told a zoologist from the University of Florida about it. He didn't believe me, so I brought him here. He went away shaking his head. He didn't have an answer. I'm not sure I have one either, but the Indians do. They say it is a holy place that should not be disturbed. They say there is an aura around the mound and that this aura keeps the animals and the birds away."

"Do you believe the Indians?" Troy asked his grandfather.

"What I believe is that there are things on this earth we don't understand," Wiley Troy said. "I believe this is one of them. The reason I'm showing this place to you and telling you these things is not to scare you, but so you'll know what I'm talking about when I tell you this island should be left alone. I don't know why, but I believe it. You can come and sit here, come and think. It's good for that. But never disturb it. I know it sounds strange, but I think that would be a mistake. In any case, it's sacred to the Indians and as far as I'm concerned that's reason enough to let it be."

At first, Troy considered approaching the encampment directly in his canoe so that he and Halpatter could be plainly seen, but then rejected the idea. It was better, he decided, to demonstrate to whoever was there that they were vulnerable. He and Halpatter checked the smoke from the campfire on the island and landed unobserved on the other side.

No one, not even Halpatter, could move as skillfully through the woods as Roland Troy, so the Indian let Troy lead them toward the camp. When they were ten yards from the campfire they could see the two long-haired men who were cooking fish and bacon in a large frying pan. Cooking utensils, packages of food, and dirty pots and dishes were strewn around them. There was a small outboard runabout tied up to a mangrove root with a large cooler and fishing gear inside.

The men sat facing the water, their backs to the woods. One of them was tall and fat, with a walrus mustache. The other was short, skinny, and ferret-faced. The woman was not visible. Probably she was in the tent that was pitched close to the pond. Troy signaled to Halpatter to watch the tent and silently crept up on the men.

Both of them were covered with tattoos and wore ragged jeans, Harley-Davidson T-shirts, and boots. The big one had a Buck knife on his hip; the little one had a holstered, short-barreled pistol—probably a snub-nosed .38. Most likely they were bikers, but they weren't local. Local bike club members didn't camp on Troy's land. His instincts told him they weren't hiding from anybody; they seemed completely unconcerned about the broad column of smoke from their cook fire. Bike week was still more than a month away, but maybe they were on a long vacation from the snow and ice, hanging out in the woods before getting down with their buddies in Daytona. Troy looked over at Halpatter, gave him a one-handed thumbs-up, and strolled calmly over to the campfire.

"How y'all doin'?" he said, squatting across the fire from the men.

"Who the fuck are you?" said the small one. "You're gonna get your ass shot off walkin' up on people like that." His hand moved to the butt of the .38.

"Don't do that," said Troy. "That would be a mistake, 'cause my friend, Mr. Halpatter, standing over there next to your tent with the forty-five, would be moved to shoot you." The small man paused, his hand frozen in the air above his pistol, and swiveled his head. Halpatter had Troy's Colt .45 pointed directly at his back.

"Yeah, he'd do it," said Troy. "He already told me he didn't think you guys could be reasoned with. I said, 'No, I believe they can be talked to. I believe they'll listen to reason.'" The fat man shifted his position slightly. He looked from Troy to the frying pan.

"Go ahead," said Troy. "I don't want your breakfast to burn. But move it real, real slowly. Mr. Halpatter *will* shoot you if you fuck up. This the first time you been down here. From where? Ohio?"

"Michigan," said the big one. "Grand Rapids."

A young woman with permed blond hair and puffy eyes came out of the tent. "What's goin' on?" she said. "What's happening?" She turned and saw Halpatter. "Oh," she said, "Oh shit. I just woke up. I didn't do nothin'. Can I sit down? I have to sit down. I feel sick. Don't shoot me." Halpatter motioned with his head to the ground. The woman sat and rested her forehead on her hands.

"How I know you ain't been down before is 'cause you're packing," said Troy. "Bikers don't pack when they come down here for bike week, didn't anybody tell you that? You have any idea what the highway patrol or the local sheriff's departments or the Daytona cops do when they catch a biker with a gun? Bike week'll come and go a couple more times before you get to see Grand Rapids again, I can tell you that.

"Now then, you gentlemen are on my land. Mr. Halpatter asked you to leave a week or so ago and you insulted him. No, don't say anything. Just listen. You and I are going to make a deal. I ain't gonna run you off. I'm gonna let you stay here the rest of this week. That means next Sunday morning you and all your stuff are gone. What you're gonna do, your end of the deal, is number one apologize to Mr. Halpatter, and number two clean every last little bit of trash off this island before you leave. That's every empty beer can, every cigarette butt, every fish bone. You don't . . . you leave this place a mess . . . you better drive straight on back to Grand Rapids, 'cause the Daytona cop I'm gonna send after your ass will make you wish you'd drowned in this here pond. And lose that piece. It's only gonna get you into trouble."

They had started into the woods on their way back across the island when the fat biker, named Pete, came crashing after them. "Wait, man. Wait a second," he said. He came up on them, breathing heavily. "Look, man, we didn't mean no harm. We really didn't. We were just, you know, tryin' to get away from things, in the woods, and . . . I appreciate your not runnin' us off. So does Kirby and Lisanne. So . . .

I really am sorry about what we said to Mr. Halpatter, you know, not just 'cause you had the drop on us and all."

"Good," said Troy. "Enjoy the rest of your stay."

"One other thing. You own all the land up and down the river?"

"I don't know what you mean by all," Troy said. "I own a good chunk in both directions from where we're at here, but sooner or later you ain't gonna be on my property anymore. Why?"

"Me an' Kirby were exploring in the boat a couple of nights ago. We found this place, you go up the river a ways and turn by where this big tree hangs all the way across, go down a ways through these trees. Spookier 'n shit at night, man, I'm tellin' ya'. Like Mars. We hadn't a had the four-cell flashlight, we'd 'a never got out. As it is we bumped into about twenty of 'em, like to bust every tooth in my mouth. After a while, you come to this piece of land, it's like somebody stuck a big dinner plate in the middle of the swamp? And there's this cabin on it? Nobody livin' there. I was just thinkin' if you owned it you maybe wouldn't mind if we stayed there a few days."

"I know the place you're talkin' about," said Troy. "It ain't mine. You're smart you'll stay out of it. Guy owns it ain't as nice as me."

"He own a Porsche?"

"I don't know, he might. He owns a lot of things. Why?"

"I heard one. We saw lights comin' when we were leavin' so we rowed instead of startin' the outboard. At first I couldn't see it, but I knew it was a Porsche. I've fixed enough of 'em. That's what I do back home. I'm a foreign car mechanic. This Porsche here'd been worked on. Had a hot exhaust. Made me curious so I rowed us back in, real slow and quiet. There it was, poppin' and cracklin' no more 'n thirty feet from the dock. Cam wasn't stock, that's for damn sure. There was a woman in it, sittin' there with the door open. Then all of a sudden she slammed the door and took off. We thought maybe she'd spotted us, so we beat it too."

Troy shrugged. "Do yourself a favor. You leave this is-land, you bring that outboard back to wherever you rented it, get on your bikes, and go north a ways up the back roads. You'll be smack in the middle of the Ocala Forest. You don't bother nobody, nobody'll bother you. You'll love it."

"The Ocala Forest. Yeah, man. Good idea. Nice name."

"That was a good plan, Roland," Halpatter said when they were back in Troy's canoe. "But I must tell you, I'm not surprised. You have a good way with situations. Me, I probably would have speared one of 'em in the ass with my alligator pole, which would have been most unfortunate. It would be a terrible thing to spill blood on that island."

II
✦

On a cold, gray, December afternoon a month before Nikki Waters's death, a Cessna Citation, flying northwest from Savannah, Georgia, broke through the clouds and began its approach to a private airstrip in western North Carolina. The plane banked steeply between two thickly wooded mountain peaks, swept low over a jagged ridge, and descended across a long, narrow valley on which lay a remote runway barely long enough to accommodate a jet. The pilot of the Cessna was unperturbed. He had once spent a year ferrying all manner of military aircraft to and from the secret mountain airbase at Long Tieng, in Laos, an installation considerably more perilous to reach than this. He landed smoothly and taxied up to a large barn, in front of which sat a Jeep Cherokee, its motor running.

Three men got out of the plane, leaving the pilot on board. Two of the three were tall, muscular Caucasians with very short hair. They wore jeans and running shoes. Lightweight parkas concealed their sidearms. One of these men remained next to the plane. The other walked just ahead of the third man, the short, powerfully built Oriental named Chotoku Nakama, known also by the nickname "Bassai," the Japanese word meaning "to breach fortifications."

Nakama had a large, round head that appeared to sit directly on his sloping shoulders without the benefit of a neck. His hair, also cut very short, was pure white. He was dressed in a very expensive dark blue suit, black wing-tipped shoes, a starched white shirt, and a silk regimental stripe tie in navy, crimson, and green. He was sixty-seven years old but moved like a man of forty, striding with a quick, straight-backed gait to the Jeep and hopping nimbly

into the front passenger seat while his bodyguard climbed
in behind the driver.

The Jeep drove along a path that ran beside the barn and
soon disappeared into thick woods. It crossed a wooden
bridge suspended above a rushing stream and pulled up in
front of a beautifully crafted four-thousand-square-foot two-
story lodge made of rough-hewn timbers and stone. The
lodge was built into the side of a steep slope that rose in
steps from the stream. Next to it was another building that
housed a generator and served as a workshop. On the roof
of the workshop was a satellite dish and a shortwave-radio
antenna.

Two men, dressed in chinos and flannel shirts, were
standing on the front porch of the lodge. From where they
stood they could easily have cast a fishing line into the
stream twenty feet below. Both men were about six feet
tall. They were slightly overweight and appeared to be in
their forties. One had a prominent jaw and blond hair that
fell boyishly across his forehead. His name was Drew
Parabrise, and he was a United States Senator from Florida.
The other man, with dark, slicked-back hair and slightly
protruding eyes, was John Varney, the financier. He owned
the lodge, the valley with its airstrip, and two hundred additional acres of extremely precipitous terrain. Surrounded
by national forest, Varney's property was accessible only by
air or by a single dirt road that snaked through the mountains. Neither the road nor the airstrip appeared on any
map.

Parabrise and Varney waved hello as Nakama emerged
from the Jeep. Nakama did not seem to acknowledge them
at all, but instead looked around him and took several deep
breaths of the cold mountain air. Varney, who did not know
him well, thought perhaps Nakama was concerned about
his safety. There were, after all, any number of people who
would have paid to see the Oriental dead. Parabrise, who
had known Chotoku Nakama for more than twenty-five
years, thought the old man was simply tired, maybe a little
dizzy, and was getting his bearings before climbing the
stairs to the porch.

In fact, neither of them was right, for Nakama was in-
dulging in a rare moment of nostalgia brought on by the

rushing stream and the wind, whistling through the trees like the cry of the Chinese wolf, who hunts alone. He was thinking of his own mountain retreat in Burma that he probably would never see again.

Once on the deck Nakama bowed slightly to the two men, or perhaps he only nodded, it was difficult to say, but at that moment the two of them moved apart as though blown by a strong current of air. Nakama walked between them and proceeded into the lodge as though it were his own. Parabrise and Varney followed. Nakama's bodyguard and the driver of the Jeep remained outside.

"So, Drew-san, it has been some time since we've seen one another," Nakama said. "And now you are not only a senator but an important one too. A committee chairman. Commerce, Science and Transportation. Quite a mouthful. And at such a young age. Estimable, *ne?*"

It had been twelve years since Drew Parabrise was last in Nakama's company. During that time, when he had rapidly ascended to a position of considerable power, he had grown accustomed to deferential treatment. Nakama's tone, and his reference to Parabrise's age—he was forty-eight—rankled him, and in spite of himself he pursed his lips and expelled air through his nose in a snort of irritation. To the senator's relief, Nakama appeared not to notice his displeasure; incurring the Oriental's wrath was the last thing Parabrise wanted.

The three men were seated in armchairs that formed a semicircle before a blaze that crackled and sparked in the huge stone fireplace of the lodge's living room. Parabrise and Varney were on either side of Nakama who sat in the middle, facing the fire. At his feet was a leather attaché case just given to him by John Varney.

"And so the business with the horse has finally been concluded," Varney said to Nakama.

"Finally," Nakama said. "A year for the insurance company to pay off. Almost another year for the rest of your financial maneuvers. A considerable length of time for a deal like that. Assuming that in fact it is, as you say, concluded."

"I don't think I ought to be listening to this," Parabrise said. He held up both hands, palms outward, as though he were fending off a blow, and rose from his chair. He assumed there was a great deal of money in the attaché case but had refrained from discussing it with Varney before Nakama's arrival. He wanted no knowledge of any transactions between the two of them, even though he was the one who first arranged their meeting several years before.

"And what is it you should be listening to?" Nakama asked, pivoting in his seat. In that instant Parabrise knew Nakama had been aware of his annoyance. The senator sat down and stared, not at the Oriental's face, which was impassive, but at his hands, resting on the arms of his chair like poised weapons.

Save for dire circumstances, Nakama had long since given up the practice of violence personally, preferring to let people he employed put their lives at risk, but he still trained in an ancient Okinawan martial art for at least an hour every morning at dawn, as he had since he was twelve years old. The first knuckles of the index and middle fingers on both Nakama's hands were the size of acorns and covered with fissured callus; the thick outside edges of both palms were hard as horn. Parabrise had never seen Nakama strike another human being, but he had heard the stories, and many years before had on two occasions been forced to witness demonstrations of the barbarity Nakama was capable of inflicting. The senator bit a piece of dead skin off his lower lip and was silent.

"I had not planned to bring it up," Nakama went on, "but maybe you should listen to the story of Lumen Spofford, your esteemed colleague, the former chairman of your committee, who now has AIDS. Just how do you imagine that came to be?"

"Everyone in the country knows how Lou Spofford got AIDS," Parabrise answered. "He got it from a blood transfusion."

Six months earlier, when Spofford announced he would not seek reelection to the Senate, he had told the nation, on a CNN interview show, that in 1983, during an emergency appendectomy, he had received the AIDS virus from a transfusion of untested blood. After thirty-six years, he said tearfully, he was leaving the Senate to devote what time he had remaining on earth to helping other AIDS victims.

Nakama nodded to John Varney. "There wasn't a thing in the world wrong with the blood they gave Senator Lumen Spofford," Varney said. "What got him AIDS was the tube-steak transfusion he gave Angela Bernardino, a twenty-two-year-old topless dancer from Fort Lauderdale. And it wasn't in 1983. It was in the winter of eighty-seven, at the little ole condo Spofford keeps on the beach in Boca Raton."

"So he picked up some bimbo . . ." Parabrise began.

"Uh, uh, partner," said Varney. "She picked *him* up. At the racetrack in Pompano. It was all arranged. Not that she had to work real hard with the old son of a bitch. Her time was running out. She had a four-year-old son and no life insurance. Given her mode of employment, she wouldn't. The boy's seven now, up in Indiana with his granny and fifty thousand dollars in the bank. And you're the committee chairman. My good buddy the rising star. The man on the road to the big house." Varney whistled a couple of bars of "Hail to the Chief."

In spite of the heat from the fire Drew Parabrise suddenly shivered involuntarily. He felt waylaid, conspired against, yanked from the cozy cocoon of admirers and flatterers in which he now spent his time. Two days before he had traveled from his house in Virginia to Orlando, his hometown, where he had been invited to address the Florida Citrus Council. He had just finished a round of golf with two citrus growers who contributed heavily to his re-election in 1988 when Varney called and told him Nakama wanted to see the two of them. This was highly unusual; ordinarily, Nakama communicated with Parabrise through obscure, untraceable channels, not through someone who had run one of his campaigns.

Nakama was an elusive, shadowy figure virtually unknown to most of the Western world. From the end of World War Two, during the entire period of American involvement in Southeast Asia, and on through the post-Vietnam era, his name never surfaced in the press. Only in a single arcane book on legendary martial artists was there a reference to a particularly ruthless practitioner known as Bassai, who may or may not have been Nakama. The Bassai in this book was considered without peer in his use of the long wooden fighting staff, or *bo*. Bassai, the book said, fashioned his own *bo* from Mongolian oak, and, within an area of three hundred square feet, was more lethal with it than the average man was with a gun.

Still, obscure though he was, it was far too risky for a United States Senator to be seen with Nakama. Though he now had legitimate business interests in various parts of the world, he was believed to have formerly made his living smuggling precious gems, running guns, and moving opium. Rumor had it that he first became rich commanding a fleet of pirate vessels in the South China Sea. No one really knew for sure, nor did anyone seem to know the size of his fortune, nor, for that matter, where he actually lived. This was the result of an all but impenetrable cloud of secrecy that enveloped Nakama, who traced his roots back to a clandestine fourteenth-century band of warriors and smugglers based in Swatow on the southeast China coast. This band called itself "Prancing Tiger," and prized, above all else, loyalty and silence.

It was presumed, however, that the CIA had a file on Nakama. No doubt several other intelligence agencies did as well. In addition to that, Nakama himself believed that at least two Asian underworld organizations with operatives in the United States had put a price on his head, the result of a nasty territorial war along the Laotian–Chinese border.

Drew Parabrise first met Nakama more than a quarter of a century earlier, in Southeast Asia, when he unwittingly tried to rob him. Parabrise was allowed to go free, but thereafter he was indebted to the Oriental whose markers lasted a lifetime. He was uneasy in the wake of Varney's call, but after assuring his guests he would return to Orlando in plenty of time for the Citrus Council meeting, flew up to North Carolina that morning with Varney and his wife in their Baron. They enjoyed a lovely lunch of fresh trout together, then Varney's wife drove into town for supplies while the two men awaited Nakama's arrival.

While they waited they walked along the stream, looking for wildlife and talking about a possible fishing trip to Alaska the following summer. The atmosphere had been extremely cordial. It was Parabrise, after all, who had seen how profitable it would be for Varney and Nakama to connect. He had kept his distance, but he had been the catalyst.

Now it seemed that Varney had taken a cue from Nakama and was toying with him, rubbing his nose in shit as though he were a dog that needed to be housebroken. He wondered whether Nakama had told Varney how they had met.

"Well, gentlemen," Nakama said, "much as I would enjoy staying here to breathe more of this fresh mountain air, I must go. To Kansas City, and Phoenix and San Antonio. Then maybe I will fly somewhere to rest."

He rose, gripping the attaché case, and walked to the door, then turned back to face Parabrise and Varney. "I know what you are thinking, Drew-san," he said. "You are thinking I brought you here to implicate you in something. You are thinking, 'Who does that old bastard think he is, coming here to the woods in his blue suit, talking to me, a senator of the United States, in this way?' "

He held up his free hand. "Don't protest. It's of no importance. From time to time we all forget who we really are. Anyway, you are wrong. Why would I bother to further implicate you in something you are already sitting in up to your neck? The reason I asked you to come was to show you how our mutual success depends on careful planning and cooperation. On restraint. Which brings me to the subject of your girlfriend, who seems to have run amuck."

Parabrise, who was under the impression that there were no problems concerning the woman in Orlando, felt as though he had been kicked in the stomach by a mule. That Nakama would even mention her was terrifying to him. He fought to maintain his composure.

"My suggestion to you is that you fly back to Orlando and give your speech to the citrus people," Nakama said. "Then go back to your wife and children in Virginia . . . oh, I forgot, your children are away at school. To just your wife, then. When the children come home for vacation, enjoy the holidays with your family and stay away from the girl. You know, she has been talking about horses with Raimundo Villegas, trying to concoct something. I must consider what to do about that." He sighed. "Ah, Drew-san. I wish I could get my *chimpo* as hard as some people's heads."

When his plane was airborne, Nakama moved from the passenger compartment to sit up front next to Brownie, the old Air America pilot who'd flown for him since 1975. He'd known Brownie for thirty years, and had never seen the man show any sign of greed. For this reason Nakama had come to trust him, unlike the two men he'd just left on the ground. Nakama swiveled in his seat and glanced back at the attaché case Varney had given him. His brief visit to North Carolina had nothing to do with the money inside. Far greater sums were transferred to his accounts daily from various interests around the world. The reason for his stopover was to look both of them—the politician and the wheeler-dealer—in the eye, to remind them who they were, to remind Parabrise in particular who was in charge. Many years ago his instincts told him this Parabrise, with his blond hair and his big square face and his booming voice that made gibberish sound so important, was just what the American public desired in a leader, but maybe he had been wrong. And the other one, the one who was so good at making money out of air. That one would turn on you in an instant. You could maneuver him, but only so far.

Nakama closed his eyes and pictured the two of them as hens, rushing around in a pen, scattering feed with their beaks as fast as they could lest the other get more. They would have fun now, thinking about the girl in Orlando. Varney's wife, a former Miss Hawaiian Tropic runner-up, would be hard pressed keeping the conversation lively at dinner.

"So, Bassai," Brownie said. "We go to Kansas City."

"No, my friend, I think instead we go to Costa Rica," said Nakama. "I think probably it's a good idea to stay out of this country for a while."

III

✦

From the porch of his house, from her seat in his rocking chair up on blocks, Clara Roseman could see Roland Troy coming across the pond. He was kneeling in his canoe, his arms sweeping the paddle through the shimmering water in powerful, rhythmic strokes, propelling the craft silently toward her. She was sure he saw her, though he gave no sign, but that was his way. He would show nothing until he had time to reflect on why she might be there. He wouldn't ask her, either. He would hide behind small talk. They hadn't seen each other in over ten years, but she knew he would let her sit there all day, all week . . . hell, he'd let her move into his house and wait for a year until she was ready to tell him why she'd come. That was Roland Troy, the man she had once loved.

He tied up at the dock, and with the paddle in one hand and his pistol case in the other, walked slowly up the path to the house. *After all this time he still has that little bit of a limp,* she thought, *but he still stands as straight as a smokestack. He won't be one of those men who curve into themselves when they get old. His head won't look as though it's about to tumble off his neck and roll away. In his case it's conviction as much as genetics and lack of fat. He has never not believed he was doing the right thing.*

She noticed that his long, curly hair, sprouting from under a baseball cap, was still thick, but it was now streaked with gray, and around his chin and below his ears his beard was turning white. As he came up onto the porch she saw the long, jagged scar, a raised, mottled rivulet, beneath the beard on the left side of his face. That hadn't changed, nor had his eyes, which were the color of weathered slate.

27

"Busy morning," he said, setting down the paddle and the gun. "You been here long?"

She had known him since they were both seventeen and even then it sounded to her like the roll of distant thunder when he spoke. It occurred to her that he was probably the only person she had ever known who never raised his voice.

"Almost an hour," she said. "You didn't shoot anything. Calm as the wind is, I'd have heard that gun go off."

"There were a couple of guys and a girl camping on the burial mound island. They gave Halpatter some shit, but it was no big deal."

She had come to him for help. Billy, her son, had been arrested for murder. She started to tell him this, to simply blurt it out, but suddenly she felt a knot form in her chest and she couldn't speak. She cleared her throat.

"You all right?" he asked.

"Yeah," she said. "I'm okay. I could use a drink, though. Some water or juice, if you've got any." She was feeling light-headed and gripped the arms of the rocker with both hands.

"Sit tight," he said. "I'll be right out."

He went inside and the metal sign crackled. In a minute he returned with two tall glasses of cranberry juice. A cigar was sticking out of his shirt pocket and the half-empty bottle of juice was wedged under his arm. He handed one glass to her and set the bottle and the other glass down on the porch railing. While she drank, refilled her glass, and drank some more, he pulled another rocker over from the far side of the porch, lifted it onto the concrete block platform, and sat down beside her.

"You feel better?" he asked.

She nodded. He put his feet up on the porch railing, tugged the baseball cap lower over his eyes, and lit the cigar.

He's never stopped wearing those strange desert boots, she thought. *Those rough-out things with the sticky soles made over in Africa somewhere. Or the corduroy Levi's. Someday they'll bury him in corduroy Levi's and desert boots.* She drank some more, set her glass down, and breathed deeply. She had been racing around frantically since arriving in Orlando the previous afternoon. She decided not to tell him for a moment—to sit there and collect herself.

They stared out over the pond. A pair of great blue herons stood motionless in the shallows near the far shore, watching the water for something to eat. They could stand this way, like statues, for long periods of time, waiting for a frog or snake or fish to take back to their nest. A breeze ruffled the long black plumes on top of their heads and the white feathers along the front of their blue-gray chests. Something startled them and they flew off into the swamp.

"Look at that old gator," Troy said, puffing on his cigar. "There, you can just make out the top of her head. That pair of herons been coming here every winter for years now, and every winter that same mamma gator tries to catch 'em right there in that very spot. It's like a game they play over and over again. I used to think sooner or later the gator would win, but not anymore. The herons are smarter."

"How's Katherine?" she asked.

"Oh, fine. She's doin' fine. She went to Denmark for six months after she graduated from Miami. Stayed with her mother. Traveled around Europe. Now she's up in Massachusetts, at Woods Hole, workin' in a marine biology research lab. Got herself a boyfriend who's a treasure hunter. She's havin' fun. How's Louis doin'?"

"Louis died two and a half years ago."

"I didn't know. Nobody told me. Hell, this goddamn town changes so fast ninety-five percent of the people here now probably never even knew who he was. I'm sorry to hear that. What was it, his heart?"

"He had a triple bypass back in eighty-five. Afterwards he checked out great. The doctor said he could resume a normal life, joggin', tennis, you name it. One day he came in the house from playin' nine holes of golf, sat down in his recliner in the den, and took off his shoes. I went to get him a glass of iced tea. When I came back he was dead. I know you never thought much of him, but he was good to me, Roland."

"Him and his partners tore the living shit out of half this county, Clara. I know it ain't proper to speak ill of the dead, but that's what he did. Raped the land and cleared out. I hope at least he left you in good shape."

"His kids got most of it. I have the place in Hilton Head. Enough money so I don't have to work."

"Well, at least he did that. That's somethin'. His buddy the senator come to the funeral?"

"He sent a card. He was off studying the ocean in California."

"I would have thought . . ."

"I know what you would have thought, Roland. I know what you've always thought. You told me once, and I know. But Jesus Christ, I thought *you* were dead. Everybody thought you were dead, and that was twenty-three years ago. Are you going to hold Drew Parabrise against me for the rest of your life? You trusted him too, you know, once, just like I did. I don't know why you did. I don't know the circumstances. You never told me that part. Twenty-three years is a long time not to forgive somebody. It's a long fucking time not to forgive yourself."

He turned his gaze from the pond and looked at her. She was a beautiful woman, tall and thin, with the grace of a dancer even while she sat, but she was forty-seven years old, forty-eight in three more months. There were creases around her eyes and mouth, a loss of tautness in her skin, a blurring of lines and angles that makeup couldn't hide. Roland Troy noticed none of that, or if he did, it made no difference. What he saw was the young woman, still almost a girl, with long dark hair blowing about her face, and flashing eyes, dark, defiant eyes that grabbed onto anyone she looked at and held fast. She was standing outside the small café at the harness track wearing a man's blue oxford shirt that hung down almost to her knees and huge gold hoops in her ears that made her look like a gypsy. Troy had never seen her before. She had a proprietary look on her face that told him she wasn't visiting, a way she stood, as though, arriving at that spot from some distant place, she had immediately made it her own. She had a baby in her arms, but she wasn't wearing a ring. When Troy looked at her and smiled from inside his pickup truck she turned away.

That was in March of 1960. Roland Troy was a junior in

high school and had just turned seventeen. He was a good student, a sprinter on his school's track team and a receiver and defensive back in football. He liked defense best and was considered a candidate at that position for all-state honors in his senior year.

He was on his spring vacation, doing chores around the house, and his grandmother had sent him to the Ben White Raceway for some manure. Local residents were welcome to come there and take what they wanted for their gardens. Troy filled the bed of his pickup, drove back around to the café, parked, and went inside. There was no sign of the girl he'd seen earlier. He sat down at the counter and ordered a Coke, hoping maybe she'd appear.

Two men eating at one of the tables called him over. They knew Troy not only from his exploits on the football field, but because they hunted now and then on his grandfather's land and used Wiley Troy as their guide. One of them was Bucky Frennel, who owned a local lumber yard. The other was a lawyer named Johnny Wallace. Wallace weighed 375 pounds and wheezed every time he opened his mouth to speak.

"You boys up there in Seminole County gonna have yourselves a team next season," Wallace said.

"I hope so, sir," said Troy.

"It's kickin' ass that gets it, not hopin', ain't that right?" Wallace said to his friend. "I've seen this here boy out on the field. He knows what I mean. You give any thought to where you want to go after you graduate?"

"No, sir, I haven't. Tell you the truth, I'd be grateful just to have the chance to play," Troy said. Actually, he wanted to go to Alabama, but he knew better than to reveal that to these men. He had heard the new coach there, Bear Bryant, liked small, fast players who were willing to work. Although he was slightly over six feet tall, Troy only weighed 165 pounds.

"Well, son, I think you'd make a helluva Gator," said Wallace. "I ain't gonna say no more about it, but I bet your grandpa agrees with me, don't he?"

"I expect he does, sir," said Troy. The sight of the strange dark-haired girl had put him in a state of considerable agitation and he was having difficulty drawing a deep breath. He wanted desperately to escape from these men. "Well, I guess I better be going," he said. "I have to get a load of horse manure back to my grandma."

"You say hello to both of them for us," Frennel said. "And think about what Johnny said."

"Yes, sir, I will." Troy hurried out of the café and got into his truck. He was driving along the bumpy dirt road leading out of the track when he saw the girl again. She was standing outside the barn where Pat Wittinger's horses were stabled, talking to Drew Parabrise, Wittinger's nephew. "Shit," Troy muttered. "Figures one of those Chicasaw sons of bitches would find her before anyone else." He spit through the truck's open window into the dirt and drove away.

Roland Troy was a born tracker who instinctively understood the woods. His grandfather knew it the first time he took Troy back into the swamp with him to find a rogue alligator that had attacked and seriously wounded a fisherman. This was when Roland Troy was ten years old. By the time he was twelve, Wiley Troy was sending him out alone to scout possible hunting sites and report anything unusual on the land.

"I've never seen anyone like him," Wiley told his wife one night when the two of them were lying in bed. "That boy's eyes catch fire out there. His body . . . it's like it goes through a transformation of some kind, like something that's been bound up is set loose."

"His father was like that," Eunice Troy said.

"No, Bobby was different," Wiley said. "Bobby became good at it because that's what he thought I wanted from him. He *was* good, don't misunderstand me. But it was always work. Always, 'Was that right, Daddy? Did I do a good job? Are you proud of me?' With Roland . . . he *feels* it, Eunice. I hardly ever need to tell him anything. It's like he's tapped into the rhythm of the wilderness, like his heart beats in tune with it. He'd rather be alone out there than with someone else. He's a wild animal himself."

When he began playing football, Roland Troy searched for the same rhythm that made him at home in the woods. He was lightning-fast, with superb reflexes, and he was fearless, but relying on his physical talents alone didn't satisfy him. He was convinced every game had a pulse of its own, an ebb and flow created by the two teams on the field. He believed he could tap into this pulse if he concentrated hard enough. Once he did, once he made the game's rhythm his own, he was able to anticipate—more often than anyone imagined—the direction of a play before it developed.

By the end of his second season of varsity football, Troy was one of the best receivers in his conference, but that was not where he was happy. On offense his success was to a large degree determined by the agility and accuracy of the quarterback. It was on defense, in the backfield, that he felt at home. There, he felt dependent on no one but himself. In his mind, he saw his role as that of a lone jungle cat prowling behind the line of scrimmage, lying in wait, watching the action unfold in front of him, daring an opposing receiver to venture into his territory.

In his junior year, Troy averaged almost two interceptions a game. Opposing teams tried to throw away from him, to the other side of the field, but it seemed he could read their minds and streak across to where the ball was going. That season he was burned for a touchdown only once, when he slipped on a muddy field and fell down.

By the time Roland Troy was seventeen, he knew Drew Parabrise very well. Parabrise was the quarterback at General Jesup High School in Orlando, the arch rival of Micanopy High, Troy's school, north of the city. Though Troy had only spoken a few words to him, he had studied Parabrise very carefully, much the way he studied the habits of animals in the woods.

Parabrise's father was an insurance salesman, successful enough to afford a nice home on a lake in the best part of town, successful enough to buy a new Buick every other year and have a membership at the exclusive Chickasaw Country Club, but not anywhere near as rich as the fathers of Drew Parabrise's friends.

Even as a young boy, Drew Parabrise had an instinct for making the right moves, getting laughs, drawing approbation from his peers. His preppy clothes, casual but never sloppy, hung right on his tall frame. His blond hair, not too long but never with a freshly barbered edge, looked right.

His easy walk and the insouciant modulation of his voice
were right. Other kids wanted to be around him, wanted to
be his friend. In grade school he was the captain of the
safety patrol. In junior high and high school he was president of the student council, the acknowledged leader of his
class.

Though he was careful to display appropriate self-
effacement, Drew Parabrise was well aware of his magne-
tism and as a teenager began using it to make the right
connections. He was the kind of boy adults said would go
far. No one told him this, but he was smart enough to
know the journey would be much easier with the right as-
sociates. His close friends were all selected from rich, influential families, all members of the Chickasaw Country
Club.

A week before the game with General Jesup, Roland
Troy traveled to Orlando to watch Drew Parabrise and his
teammates play. Halfway through the third quarter he saw
the pattern in Drew Parabrise's game. It was almost imper-
ceptible and undoubtedly had never been noticed by his
coaches, but whenever he was going to pass there was a
slight alteration in the way Parabrise held his body as he
bent above the center. It was a change in balance more than
position, and if he were asked, Roland Troy could not have
put it into words. Troy saw something else, too. Whenever
Parabrise was going to pass long, he ran the thumb of his
passing hand twice across the insides of that hand's fingers.
His coaches should have noticed that. Troy could almost
feel the increase in Parabrise's tension before he took the
snap for a passing play. *He doesn't really like to put it up,*
Troy thought. *I wonder why that guy's a quarterback.
Somewhere inside him there's a part that doesn't like to
throw the ball.*

IV

✦

"Today, your body is here without your head," said Shima. "That's okay. You're a human being, not a machine."

"I'm sorry," said Troy. "It's this girl I met. Well, not met. Saw. I saw her and I *want* to meet her."

"Oh, don't worry. If you want to, you will," Shima said.

"I don't know," said Troy. "I got this feeling it might not be that easy."

"There's nothing hard about meeting," said Shima. "Whether there are difficulties afterwards is another story. But simply meeting someone is easy. Look how easy it was for you to meet me."

Troy was sixteen when he met Shima. Actually, Roland's grandfather met him first. "Got this guy moved into the cabin by the spring," he said one night at dinner. "Little Oriental fella works for Benny Butler. Helluva carpenter, Benny says. Only been with him two weeks, but Benny says he's the best he's ever had. I was over there at the place he's buildin' on Semoran and Benny says, 'See that guy up there workin' on the roof? The guy with the dress shirt on? He's lookin' for a place to stay. Been livin' out of his car. He's a good man, you hear of anythin' . . .' I said lemme talk to him. I don't know where the hell he learned his English but he speaks it real well. He's from Okinawa originally, but he's traveled around, I think. I told him, look, I'll make you a deal. I got this little cabin you can stay in for nothin' if you fix it up. It's got water and electricity but it's a goddamn mess, near to fallin' over. He says, 'Sounds good to me.' I figure what the hell, Eunice, what's the worse can happen? He burns it down, which is

35

what one them drunks that holes up in it is gonna do sooner
or later anyway."

This was in the summer before Roland Troy's junior year
in high school, when he was helping his grandfather run his
fishing camp. Very early one hot humid Sunday morning,
two weeks after Wiley Troy made his announcement about
the cabin, Roland was paddling his canoe through wispy
fog on the river. He had arisen at dawn and run three miles
on a path that snaked through the woods and was now
completing that day's training regimen with an upperbody
workout against the river's current. He came around a bend
and saw a strange figure standing on the bank with a fishing pole in his hand. The fisherman was a small Oriental
man with a large head, wearing a starched white dress shirt
and creased slacks. His line had become tangled in some
branches under the water on the far side of the river and it
appeared that he was unsure about what to do. Troy thought
maybe he was going to jump into the river without bothering to take off his clothes.

"Stay right there," Troy shouted. "I think I can get that
line free for you." He paddled over to the branches and saw
the silvery lure at the end of the line glittering just below
the surface. It was hooked into a piece of bark. By lying
flat on his stomach in the canoe, Troy was able to reach
deep enough into the water to free the hook without having
to jump into the river.

"You look like you've done that before," said the man.
"If I'm correct then I do not feel quite as foolish, since oth-
ers have no doubt tangled themselves up in a similar way.
My name is Ansai Shima and I am very grateful to you."

"I'm Roland Troy, and you're very welcome," Troy said.
He climbed up onto the bank and shook the man's hand. "I
been fishing this river for six years and I still foul my line.
It's no big thing." This had to be the man who was living
in the old cabin. Troy had been meaning to take a ride
down and see what he was doing to the place, but he'd
been too busy. "Have you done much fishing before?" he
asked.

"You are wondering what kind of person would get
dressed like this to go into the woods, am I right?" Shima
said. "Looks like maybe I ran away from church?"

"Well . . ." Troy blushed.

"To answer your question, actually, no. I've never been fishing before this morning. I was going to drive over to Cocoa Beach to buy some fish from the fishermen there. Get them fresh right off the boat. But then I said, 'I'm right near a perfectly good river. Let me see if I can catch a couple myself.' So I bought this pole and here I am."

"I gotta work for my grandpa all day or I'd go out with you," Troy said. "He runs a fishing camp. Maybe another day. I could show you the best places. There's some good fish in this river. Some even better ones in the ponds back in the woods."

"You're Mr. Wiley Troy's grandson?"

"Yes, sir, I am."

"He's a wonderful man. A very generous man. I'm living in his cabin by the spring. You have to come over and visit some time. You won't recognize it."

"Mr. Shima, if you don't mind me asking, what happened to your hands?"

Shima looked down at his palms, then turned his hands over and studied the tops. "My hands?" he said.

"Your knuckles."

"Ah, my knuckles." Shima clenched and unclenched his fists several times rapidly and laughed. "You want to know why they're so big. That's funny. I've lived with them for so many years that now I no longer notice anything unusual. My knuckles are this way from *makiwara*."

"I don't understand," said Troy.

"*Makiwara*. It's a special piece of wood you strike to build up strength in your punch. Makes your wrist very strong. Makes your knuckles hard as the stones on a riverbank. Makes the *shuto* edge of your hand—the outside part of the palm—like the bottom of an elephant's foot. Just tonight I'm putting the finishing touches on a new *makiwara* that will be outside the cabin. Come visit me and I'll show you. I'll teach you about *makiwara*, you teach me fishing. How's that?"

Shima was bent over a workbench resting on two sawhorses beside the cabin when Troy pulled his truck into the yard. The small Oriental turned his head and smiled. "Look, it's almost finished," he said.

An eight-foot oak four-by-four post lay on the bench. It had been gradually tapered at one end so that the top two feet, though still four inches wide, were only three quarters of an inch thick. Shima lifted the post, carried it around to the back of the cabin, and dropped it into a four-foot-deep hole he had dug. Troy helped him mix up a small batch of concrete that Shima poured into the hole, then held a level to the post while Shima filled the top of the hole with dirt and tamped it down. "Ah, that looks excellent," said Shima when they were done. "Now we will let the concrete cure for a week. Then I will wrap the very top with special rice rope to punch against and it will be ready. You see, the top of this *makiwara* is a perfect height for a small guy like me. You will have to squat down further than I do when you punch it, but that is good. The squatting will help build up your legs and hips."

"Me?" asked Troy.

"You," said Shima. "You are going to be my student, unless you've changed your mind. Remember? You will teach me fishing. I will teach you *ka-ra-te*. *Makiwara* is only a tiny part of *ka-ra-te*. If you're going to learn it you should learn it all."

"What is *ka-ra-te*?"

Shima paused for a moment and stared at the *makiwara*. "You wait here," he said. "I will be right back."

He went inside the cabin, which already looked like a very different place than the rickety shack Troy and his friends used as a fort when they were twelve and thirteen. Part of the roof had been replaced, as well as most of the windows, and the front porch, formerly tilted at a thirty-degree angle, was now as level as a pool table. A sturdy front door hung where previously there was none; no doubt Shima had put up a back door as well. The walls were filled with gaping holes where the old rotten boards had been pried off, and a large pile of used brick lay nearby, obviously for a fireplace and chimney Shima intended to construct.

"It's still very rough, but at least now it won't fall down," Shima said. "I thought the best idea was to do the outside first. Get it weatherproof. Then I'll turn my attention to the inside."

He was standing on the porch dressed in baggy white cotton pants and a white cotton jacket with baggy sleeves and no buttons. The jacket was secured by a black belt wound twice around his waist and tied in what looked to Troy like a square knot. "This is a *gi*," Shima said. "It's the uniform you wear when you practice *ka-ra-te*. I'll get one for you, but yours will have a white belt. I began studying when I was nine years old. My teacher did not give me this black belt until I was fifteen. Now, you sit up there on the worktable and watch."

Shima leaped from the porch to the front yard. For an instant he stood still, his heels together, his toes pointed out. His shoulders were relaxed and his arms hung loose. His hands lay one over the other, palms toward his body, resting against his *gi* below the black knot at his waist. He breathed deeply twice, then he moved, twisting his hips, lashing out with his fists and feet, blocking the attack of an imaginary opponent, his cheerful face now a mask of fury. Shima's arms and legs were a blur, and each of his kicks and punches brought a loud snap from the material of his *gi*, as though it were a flag in a strong wind. Troy had never seen anyone move with such speed, nor with such control; from where Troy sat on the worktable, the tiny man did not look so small to him anymore. Even when Shima paused between moves an extraordinary energy seemed to emanate from him, as though he had somehow tapped the source of absolute power. At one point he let out a piercing shriek, a *ki-ai*, and Troy's stomach muscles contracted in fear. Then, as suddenly as he had begun, Shima returned to his relaxed position, his face once again peaceful and benign, and it was over.

"*Ka-ra-te* means 'empty hand,' " he said. "It is a very ancient art used for self-defense, but as you will see it is much more than that. It is a way of life. When it was brought to Okinawa from China, it was called '*ch'uan fa*.' My ancestors in Okinawa began practicing it more than a thousand years ago. Of course it has changed over the centuries just as everything does, but one thing has remained the same. *Karate ni santinash*—there is no first move in *ka-ra-te*.

"What I just did was a *kata*. A *kata* in a way is like a dance, a set of moves with a beginning a middle and an end that a man must do over and over a thousand times before it belongs to him. There are many *katas*, some very difficult, but each begins with a block. *Karate ni santinash*. It means never do you attack first. Since you are going to be my student, you must understand that above all else." Shima was sweating profusely from his exertion and stopped to take a drink of water from the thermos resting on his worktable.

"Roland, it is a great responsibility to teach this art to another person. A *sensei*, a teacher, can produce men who only want to fight, who become animals capable of inflicting great harm to other human beings. Believe me, this is true. I have seen it happen. But a *sensei* can teach so that his students do everything possible to avoid violence. That is my way, though I did not invent it. Itosu, a master who lived more than a hundred years ago, believed *karate* was not a path to violence or glory, but a way to develop true character. Other *senseis* before him believed the same. I myself have had only two other students, in Hawaii, where I lived for many years. Now I have you, unless you decide you don't want to study. If you do study, I will tell you what I told them. A true student of *karate* learns dignity which he extends to all men. I feel you understand this. I felt that when I met you at the river. That's why I told you about *makiwara* and showed you this *kata*, which is called *ku-san-ku*. So now it is up to you. You teach me fishing, I teach you *karate*."

"I heard of it from a guy who was over there right after the war," Wiley Troy said, "but I never saw it. You want to study with him, you go ahead. Long as you get your work done around here. Once school starts, well, then we'll see. One thing, though. You're smart, you'll keep it to yourself."

"That's what Mr. Shima told me," Roland said.

They trained in the morning as soon as it was light, when the air near the spring was still cool and fragrant from the

pine trees and jasmine. At first, while Shima was getting
the cabin in order, they worked outside on a small section
of level ground where the small Oriental drilled his tall
teenage pupil endlessly in correct posture and balance, in
proper punching, kicking and blocking techniques, and later
in the moves of the *katas*. Together they alternately struck
the *makiwara* until Troy's knuckles, like Shima's, were en-
larged and calloused. When Troy's friends asked him about
it he told them, in partial truth, it was from doing push-ups
on his knuckles to strengthen his wrists. They shook their
heads and laughed. Most of them already thought he was
partly crazy from all the time he spent in the woods.

In the fall, because of school and football, Troy reduced
his karate workouts down to four a week, on Saturdays and
Sundays in the very early morning and twice during the
week at night. He helped Shima build a sub-floor out of
two-by-fours and cover it with plywood in the small garage
out behind the cabin. They cut windows in the garage's
walls, put in screens, then ran an electric line from the
cabin and installed a fan and an overhead light. "Remember, no job is of less importance than another, not here in
this garage or anywhere else in life," Shima said before
they began to construct the *dojo*. "Treat each one with pre-
cision and attention to detail, as though it were a *kata*."

On the wall, Shima mounted a samurai sword sheathed
in a scabbard that had been given to him by his *sensei* and
was over two hundred years old. Below it, he painted the
ideographs for karate and those of a poem by the great
seventeenth-century fencing master, Musashi Miyamoto:
"Under the sword lifted high there is hell making you tremble; But go ahead and you have the land of bliss."

"Now we have a real *dojo*, a place built for a single purpose," he said. "That is most important. We've been taking
it easy, you and I. Now you will see how hard we can
train." Secretly, Shima was amazed at the dedication and
diligence of his young pupil, as well as his power of concentration. In twenty-one years of karate training he had
only known two others who had studied with Troy's intensity: himself, and his cousin, Chotoku Nakama, master of
the *bo* staff, to whom he had given the nickname Bassai.

He was thirty-two, a *shichi-dan*, or sixth-degree black

belt, but other than saying he had lived for years in Hawaii he never spoke about his past. Instead, he told Troy about the legendary karate masters of the past—Yara, who, barehanded, killed three samurai swordsmen when they attacked a helpless girl; Agena, whose hands were so strong and fingers so toughened by years of training he could tear the bark from an oak tree. He would talk to Troy about the philosophy of karate as it had been handed down to him, about respect for one's elders, about kindness and modesty, and about the quest through years of disciplined training for *mushin*, the egoless state of mind that knows no fear of failure or of death, the state of mind in which the *kata* would perform itself.

He never missed a day of work for Benny Butler, never was in a foul mood, but he kept to himself, reading at night in the cabin that he turned into a snug, pristine dwelling of brick and wood, lit inside with Japanese lanterns and filled with paperback books. Occasionally, on the weekend, he would tell Troy to train by himself, then drive off in his black 1951 Ford. "I'm going sightseeing," he would say, but he never offered to take Troy with him. Come Monday morning he was always back on the job, hammering, sawing, bounding around on the unfinished structures with twice the energy of the other men on the crew.

Once, Troy asked him how he wound up living near Orlando. "Oh, it wasn't my actual destination," Shima said. "I was heading for Miami, but as I drove along this country road one evening a powerful thunderstorm struck, so I pulled over. The rain was so strong I couldn't see the front of my car, but I could smell the orange blossoms. After the storm passed, I could see the sun, low in the sky, shining through some trees. It was so peaceful. As I sat there I thought of a haiku I once read by a poet named Shiki. 'The thunderstorm goes by; on one tree evening sunlight—a cicada cry.' I decided the reason I remembered the haiku was that this must be the place for me."

They had gone fishing that day, on a lake filled with bass north of the Troys' land. Shima landed three good-sized fish and was cleaning them in his sink. "*Sensei*, do you have any family?" Troy asked.

"Everyone has family somewhere," Shima said, and continued to scrape the bass with his knife. Troy didn't press him; he became lost instead in thoughts of his own family. His mother and brother had come to Florida for Thanksgiving and had watched him play in a football game. Afterwards they tried to appear excited about Roland's success and his team's victory, but the two of them lived in a world as distant and foreign to him as the medieval Okinawan villages recreated by Shima in his stories. Troy had not been back to New York City for almost seven years and only saw his mother and brother on their winter trips to Florida to escape the cold.

"You are an unusual boy, Roland," Shima said. "You left your mother's house and followed your own heart at a very early age. It is not common for someone so young to even know what they want, much less act on it. I did something similar, so I know that it isn't the easiest thing in the world to do. Luckily you had your grandparents to take you in, but I think probably you would have left before too much longer even if they weren't here. One fish is all I need. Take these other two to them. And don't worry. Being alone and being lonely are very different things. I am not lonely. Neither will you be, even when you are older and are alone."

V

He never saw her come up to his truck. It was late on a Saturday afternoon in mid-October. That morning he had trained with Shima and done his chores. After lunch he did his homework, then told his grandmother he was going to New Smyrna Beach to join some friends, which truly was his plan. When he reached the main highway, though, he turned south, feeling like a fool and cursing himself but driving to the racetrack just the same. He stopped in front of the café, where he'd parked two dozen times before in the last seven months, and sat there for several minutes, unsure if this time he would actually get out and go inside for a Coke and a hamburger and another glimpse of the girl behind the counter, who wouldn't even smile at him much less say hello.

Troy had tried to find out more about the dark-haired girl, but to everyone he knew she remained a mystery. As his grandfather had told him the previous spring, she lived with her uncle and aunt, Marvin and Sarah Lodish, and worked in their café. She didn't go to school. On the rare occasions she was seen around town, she was either alone or with her baby, driving a four- or five-year-old Cadillac convertible with Texas tags. The car inspired rumors of a liaison with an oil tycoon or a big-time gangster, though evidence of neither had surfaced. The Lodishes were Jews, which provoked an occasional anti-Semitic remark, but to Troy, who was without prejudice, the girl's religion only added to her exotic appeal and intensified his infatuation.

When she leaned her head in the open window on the passenger side of the truck he was so startled he jammed his hand down on the horn, causing a horse that was being

44

shod thirty yards away to whinny and yank frantically against its tether.

"Hi," she said. "My name's Clara." She squatted down and rested her chin between her hands on the windowsill. Her long black hair, hanging partly inside the cab, sparkled in the sunlight. It smelled as though she had just washed it and Troy was seized with an overpowering desire to grab two handfuls and press them against his face. Instead he gripped the steering wheel and stared at her as though she were some wild apparition in a dream.

"Well, are you going to say something or what?" she asked.

"Would you like to go for a canoe ride?" he asked her. His voice sounded unnaturally loud to him, like the hoarse croaking of someone who hadn't spoken to another person for several years. The words themselves seemed ridiculous the instant they were out of his mouth. In fact, showing her the river and its mysterious cypress-filled tributaries and side streams was something he had thought about a hundred times during the past seven months, an adventure that would show her who he was. Now that he had actually set the possibility in motion, he felt as though he had revealed an ill-disguised proposal designed to take advantage of her out in the woods where she would be vulnerable. What an idiot he was. He should have suggested a Coke in the café, or even a ride into town. Now, of course, she would think the worst of him. Her dark eyes riveted him to his seat or surely he would have bolted from the truck. He was confused and terrified and he began to sweat. It occurred to him that in his excitement he had forgotten to introduce himself.

"Yeah, that would be great," she said.

"It would?"

"Yeah, it really would. When do you want to go?"

"We could go right now," he said. "I mean we could go right now from here and get my canoe and pack something to eat and then go. Whatever you want to do is fine with me."

"Let me go in and call my aunt and see if it's all right with her," she said. "She's watching my son."

"Oh, by the way," he said. "My name's Roland."

"I know," she said, smiling as she turned from his truck.

They put in at a bend in the Coacoochee where a sandy shoal stuck out into the water beneath a canopy of vines. Troy did almost all the talking while they paddled, his reticence evaporating in the woods. He told her about the vegetation and wildlife around them and about the Indians who used to roam through the region and whose bones now lay buried all around them. She stared straight ahead; he spoke to her back and to her hair, cascading over the gunwales.

"It's beautiful out here," she said once while they paddled. "This is really nice." Otherwise she was silent. It wasn't until they tied up on the shore of a pond fed by the river and were sitting side by side that she began to speak. When she did, it was as though a floodgate had opened, inundating him without warning.

"Tell me about Texas," he had said. She had stared at him for a moment, saying nothing. "Your car," he said. "It's got Texas tags, so I figured—" She stopped him with a hand on his forearm.

"I'll tell you," she said. "I'll tell you all about Texas. My daddy went there right after the war. He was from Vermont originally, but he met this man named Baker Ledoux in the Marine Corps when he was over in the South Pacific. The two of them made a bunch of money together playin' poker and they decided they were gonna pool all of it and go drillin' for oil. Baker came from some little ole place in Louisiana nobody'd ever heard of and he was a wild man, even crazier than my daddy, which is sayin' somethin'.

"They were wildcat drillers. You know what that is? Wildcatters go in and drill wells where nobody's sure if there's oil or not. They're gamblers. Either they're rich or they're broke. Sometimes it's chicken and sometimes it's feathers, my daddy would say. That was him and Baker Ledoux. Double L Drilling. My daddy's name was Herman Lodish, so Lodish and Ledoux is where they got the double L from. They hit a couple of big ones down around Edna and El Campo and for a while we had lots of money but then they spent a ton drilling nothing but dry holes in Alligator Bayou. This real famous oil man named Michael

Halbouty went there when they were done and he brought one in that's still producing like crazy this very minute, while you and I are sittin' here on the shore of this pond.

"They drilled everywhere, from Louisiana to the Permian Basin way out in west Texas by Kermit and Wink and Monahans and down in the Coyanosa Draws. I liked it out there the best. There was nothin' but empty country for miles and miles and miles. You could see a thunderstorm coming an hour and a half before it reached you. I used to climb way up in the derrick, you know, the great big ole tower where all the drill pipe's hung, and watch the sun set behind the mountains. God, it was so beautiful out there. The sky went on forever.

"See, I traveled all over with my daddy because my mama died when I was five. She had a brain tumor. She was from Providence, Rhode Island. They got married just before he went into the marines and then she had me while he was off fighting in the war. Daddy never remarried. We lived in Houston and I went to a real good private school there because my daddy believed strongly in education, but vacations I was always with him on a location somewhere. I loved it. I love the people who work in the oil patch. They're hard-ass but they're fun. They used to tease me all the time. They'd call me Clara-bell. They'd say 'Clara-bell, cute as hell, hair got black down the oil well.' They were so different from the people I hung around with when I was in school. They seemed more alive.

"My daddy had a plane, a Luscombe. You ever heard of Luscombes? They're high-wing two-seaters, tough as hell to land. Daddy used to fly to where his wells were. He taught me how to fly it when I was thirteen. I can ride a horse and fly a plane. I can drive a bulldozer, too. I learned that from the guys in the oil patch.

"When I was fifteen I met this guy at a seder in San Antonio. You know what a seder is?"

"A seder," Troy said. "Yeah, I know what a seder is. I went to one once, in New York."

Troy welcomed the chance to appear worldly. He knew plenty of girls who rode horses, and one or two who could probably drive a bulldozer, but Clara was the first he'd met who could fly a plane. He wondered whether he'd sounded foolish to her, carrying on about all the trees and the animals living in the woods.

"Well, I wasn't sure," she said, "because, you know, lots of people who aren't Jewish don't know what one is. The guy I met ... His name was Burt Roseman, and he was eighteen. He was a freshman at the University of Texas and he was a rodeo bull rider. I think he was probably the only Jewish bull rider in all of Texas. Maybe the only one in the whole world. He wanted to be a doctor, but first he wanted to be a world champion bull rider. He had a brand-new fifty-seven Chevy Corvette he bought all with his own money he made from bull riding. It was the souped-up one with fuel injection and a four-speed transmission and he used to drive that car just like it was a one of those bulls. It was his parents whose seder we were at. His daddy leased oil-well equipment and he was a good friend of my daddy. Burt was just the most unbelievable person I'd ever met 'cause he was as smart as any of the kids I went to school with and he was funny and sweet and he had these big gorgeous eyes, but he was a cowboy, a wild man like Baker Ledoux and my daddy. I mean he rode those bulls. We fell in love."

She stopped talking and took a drink from the canteen Troy had brought. For a second he thought she was through—that she'd decided she'd said enough.

"Can I trust you?" she asked suddenly. " 'Cause I've never talked about what happened after that with anybody."

"Yes," he said. "You can trust me." He assumed what was coming had to do with the baby. Her hand was still on his arm and she was looking directly into his eyes. "I give you my word," he said.

She shifted her gaze out across the pond. "I promised Daddy I would go to college," she said. "I did real well in school too, and I was accepted at Pembroke but I got pregnant and when I found out and told Burt we decided we'd get married and I'd go to school in Austin instead. So one night he came and got me and we drove down to Richmond and got married by a judge. I never got to tell Daddy. He was havin' all sorts of trouble with these union organizers from up north who were shootin' up wells and beating up people so they'd join and generally terrorizing the whole

damn oil patch and I just didn't want to worry Daddy any
and then one day they blew up one of Daddy's wells and
he got hurt real bad and was in the hospital and Burt and
I went out to this other well Daddy owned to watch it for
him because I was afraid they'd try to blow it up too and
it was the last one Daddy had. It was down by Matagorda,
right near the gulf, and it was gonna be a winner, Daddy
could tell. We were out there and we built a fire to keep
warm and were just sittin' in our sleeping bags talking and
I said as soon as Daddy got out of the hospital I was going
to tell him about us and the baby. That's when they came
up in their car. There were two of them and when they got
out we could see they had shotguns and Burt stood up and
it was dark and one of them said, 'I thought you already
got that bastard' 'cause they thought Burt was Daddy and
they shot him. They killed him right in front of me and I
started screaming and they came after me and I ran up onto
the floor of the derrick to the doghouse where I knew there
was a rifle. They were chasing me and I was so damn
scared. I knew they wanted to kill me too. They fired at me
but they missed 'cause it was so dark. I got hold of the rifle
and the one who had killed Burt was climbing the stairs. I
knew it was him. I knew it because he had a ski hat on and
I shot him. Then the other one drove away. I stayed up on
the rig because I didn't want to see Burt. I stayed up there
crying all night by myself and in the morning when it got
light I could see him lying on the ground where the campfire had been, and then the sheriff came and took me in his
car and told me my daddy had died too. Oh, God, I miss
my daddy so badly. You don't have any idea."

She began to cry. "I know I was mean to you all these
months—ignoring you like I did," she said, "but the thing
is you reminded me of Burt, something about you did, and
every time I saw you I didn't know what to do."

He held her until finally she was still. He had his back
against a cypress tree with her head resting on his chest, her
hair spread like a fan across his lap.

"Always expect the unexpected," Shima had once said to
him. That was fine in theory, and when Troy was older it
would be one of the guiding principles of his life, but then
he was seventeen and in love and Clara's outpouring

stunned him. This tall, thin girl with the beautiful hair and eyes, the girl he had dreamed of holding in his arms like this for months, had had her father and husband murdered and had herself shot one of the killers. He was so shocked by her story that when she finished his head was spinning and his limbs felt like rubber. But at the same time he was exhilarated. She had shared with him the most painful details of her past. She had trusted him. He concentrated on the rise and fall of her chest against his, matching his breathing to hers, hoping, as he'd been told the Indians believed, that in this way their souls would merge.

It was dark and he thought maybe she had fallen asleep, but then she spoke again. "You've got to promise me you'll never tell anyone," she said. "You have to promise. I mean it was in all the Texas papers. It's not as though what happened was a secret. I just . . . just promise me you won't talk about it. About me."

"I swear I won't," Troy said.

"They had a picture of me sittin' on the floor of the drilling rig," she said. "This Texas Ranger had his arm around me. He was the first one there the next morning. You know what he said to me after I told him what happened? He said, 'Honey, that was some good shootin'. Damn shame you didn't get the other one too.' "

Troy said nothing. Instead he put his hand behind her head, lifted her face to his, and kissed her. In the dark, her eyes were only shadows and he was tentative, unsure of how she would react, afraid she might think him totally insensitive and push him away, but her mouth opened to his and she arched her body against him. He moved his other hand down to her waist and reached under her flannel shirt. Her skin was smooth and warm. She kissed him harder and he slid his fingers upward.

"Not yet," she said. "I want to. I want to so much, but not yet. Do you understand?"

"I understand," he said, kissing her eyes, burying his face in her hair, holding her again against his chest.

"I'm glad you brought me here," she said. "I know this sounds corny as hell but . . . I feel . . . you know how with a tree, after a bad storm and it's been damaged, if there's some dead branches you cut 'em off, and maybe you cut off some of the live ones too, but still the tree's okay. It doesn't die. It keeps on growing. That's the way I feel out here. That's the way you make me feel. I have to get back, though. I told my aunt I wouldn't be out too late. Can you get us back in the dark?"

"I'll get us back," he said.

"Having a child changes everything," she said. "You should know that right from the beginning. I mean that is if you want to be with me."

"That's what I want," Troy said. "That's absolutely what I want."

Roland Troy would look back on that night as the beginning of a period in his life that ran for three years in which time was compressed and events tumbled one over another. He pulled a hamstring muscle and missed several football games but still made the all-state team and was offered a scholarship to Alabama.

Clara came to all his games but sat alone, not wanting to mingle with the cheering students from Micanopy High. She had become a familiar figure in Orlando, the subject of all sorts of gossip and speculation and an object of considerable desire among the young men of the area. To all but Roland Troy she remained elusive, working for her uncle in the café and appearing here and there around town with her young son, Billy, in her '56 Cadillac Eldorado convertible, gold with a white top, which she'd driven to Florida from Texas. At first Troy was questioned about her past, but he said nothing, and his friends knew enough not to persist.

On Thanksgiving night he made love to Clara for the first time, on a pile of blankets, on the floor of an abandoned shack on his grandfather's land. They undressed quickly in the dark and embraced standing up, thrusting against each other. He would have entered her right then but she pushed him away. "Wait," she said, and lit the candle they had brought. "I want you to see my face when you're inside me. I want you to see how much I love you."

For the rest of his senior year he was with her as much as possible. Clara was a devoted mother and only rarely would leave Billy during the day. This didn't bother Troy at all. In his mind he had already decided that he and Clara would someday marry and he would help raise Billy as though he were his son. On Sunday afternoons, he and Clara would bundle Billy into Troy's old truck and take off for the beach, or wrap the baby in a life jacket and head out in Troy's canoe for a picnic somewhere along the Coacoochee.

Only once, early in their relationship, did he ask her about Drew Parabrise. "I thought when I saw you talking to him at the track that maybe you were his girl," he said.

"He wanted me to go out with him," she said, "but I told him no. He wasn't used to that. I'd be willing to bet you no girl ever refused him before. He pretty well told me as much. He said he always gets what he's after, sooner or later. I think he's got a thing about you too, from when you played against each other. After he heard about us going out he started calling at the café, saying he wants me to fly up for a football weekend at Virginia. I quit answering the phone and eventually he stopped, but for a couple of weeks he was relentless."

Troy told Clara he would go to the University of Florida instead of Alabama to be closer to her.

"No," she told him. "You go to Alabama where you've always wanted to go, because if you don't then someday you're gonna hold that against me and hate me for it. You listen to me. I know what I'm talkin' about. A few hundred miles is not gonna change the way we feel about each other, or if it does, better we find out before we have three kids and a mortgage."

Shima agreed with her. "Once karate is in your blood you take it with you wherever you are, Alabama, Oklahoma, Australia, the place doesn't matter," he said. "Don't worry about it. If you have time, do some *katas* in the morning when you wake up. You and I will train in summer, on your vacations."

Two years passed and Troy did well. He started the last three games of his sophomore season at Alabama and academically had just over a B average, majoring in history. His plan, after graduating, was to go to law school and then join the FBI Clara became manager of the café, allowing her uncle to pursue his other interests. As often as possible, she and Troy would split the 550-mile drive from Tuscaloosa to Orlando, meeting at the apartment of one of Troy's old high school teammates who was going to school in Tallahassee. Whenever they were together they talked of marrying when he finished school.

Shima worked on with Benny Butler and trained with Troy in the summer. Drew Parabrise quit playing sports at Virginia to concentrate on campus politics. He also joined a naval R.O.T.C. unit and would begin a three-year enlistment when he graduated in 1964. "If the navy was good enough for Kennedy, it'll sure as hell be good enough for me," he told his friends. He was intent on a career modeled after the dashing young president and had taken to wearing his blond hair in the same semi-windblown style. Little did he suspect that he would soon be commanding a patrol boat in a war far different from the one fought by the hero of PT-109.

In May of 1963, a week before Troy was due home for summer vacation, his grandfather was killed in a freak accident. A drunken boater rammed the power pole at the end of the dock at the fishing camp, snapping a high-voltage electrical line. The line landed in the aluminum boat where Wiley Troy sat barefoot and he died instantly. A week later, his wife Eunice passed away peacefully in her sleep. Both were buried in a pine grove on a gentle slope above the river, chosen as the family burial plot by Phineas Troy eighty years earlier.

Roland was inconsolable, his disciplined lifestyle unraveling into wild, unpredictable behavior. He began sleeping during the day and roaming the woods at night, and neither Shima nor Clara seemed able to reach him. If anything, he trained even harder with the Okinawan, but he also began to drink. He bought moonshine a gallon at a time from one of Wiley's old hunting buddies and gulped the clear, potent liquor right out of the jug while careening over the rutted backwoods roads in his truck. He took to racing through the woods with Wiley's .357 next to him on the seat, shooting wildly at anything that moved, or at trees if no animals were about. One night he ran the truck into the swamp at fifty miles an hour, submerging it to the windows. He crawled out and walked barefoot four miles to Shima's cabin, where he passed out on the front porch. He never retrieved the truck but instead bought a 1960 Chevy El Camino with a 348 racing motor and a four-speed.

Clara's aunt and uncle thought Troy had completely lost his mind and suggested she stay away from him before he killed himself and her along with him.

"Clara, you have Billy to think about," her aunt said. "I don't mean to be cruel, but your uncle and I aren't going to be alive forever. Maybe you should start thinking about dating other guys."

"In the oil patch, when a drilling bit meets so much resistance in the hole that it snaps, they say it twisted off," Clara told them. "When a person gets himself all wound up inside tighter and tighter until he finally busts loose of any kind of restraint, they say the same thing. He's twisting off, they say. Usually it's like a two- or three-day drunk and then it's over. My daddy ... your brother did it, when things got more than he could cope with. With Roland ... Roland's just an extreme kind of guy, so he's twisting off like about six normal people rolled into one. It isn't only on account of his grandparents. Them dying was like the last hunk of rock down at the bottom of the well, the piece that snaps the bit, but there was all that stuff he's been drilling through for years. He's twisting off from his whole life. That doesn't mean I don't still love him."

Finally, in early July, Troy jumped into the El Camino, drove straight through to Tuscaloosa, and walked into the building housing Bear Bryant's office. Troy found Bryant sitting behind his desk smoking a cigarette and reading the newspaper. "Well, don't just stand there, Troy, come on in," Bryant growled. It was the first time since he'd recruited Troy that the coach had spoken directly to him. "Jesus Christ, you look like you been swimmin' in buzzard piss," he said. "Whatcha been doin' down there in Florida, rasslin' alligators?"

"Coach, I'm turnin' in my scholarship," Troy said. "I'm takin' a year off from school. My mind just ain't into it right now."

Bryant put the newspaper down and stubbed his cigarette out in a paper cup sitting on his desk. "Troy, you're a helluva football player and a good student too, but you ain't got shit for sense if you drop out of school. It's a damn

shame about your grandparents. But their dyin' ain't reason
for you to quit. You go on home and calm down and think
about it. Practice starts in three weeks. You're smart, you'll
be there."

When football practice started, Roland Troy wasn't there.
"I don't know what I'm gonna do," he told Shima. "I need
some time to think. Maybe I'll come work for Benny Butler with you."

"Roland, everything changes and there is nothing you
can do but make the best of it," Shima said. They were sitting on the porch of the Okinawan's cabin, waiting out a
summer thunderstorm so that they could work out on the
makiwara. "Your girl friend Clara understands that better
than you. Tonight we will not train. Tonight we will do
something I have been thinking about for a long time. You
and I have someplace to go."

They drove north and east in Shima's old Ford, through
orange groves thick with unripe green fruit and forests
where they could feel the summer heat diminish, until the
trees dwindled to scrub oak and low-growing saw palmetto
and they could smell the ocean. "Where are we going,
Sensei?" Troy asked.

"If you want it, I am going to give you a present you
will carry with you for the rest of your life," said Shima.
"You may, however, decide you do not want to accept it,
which is all right, no problem."

"I'd never—"

"No, no wait. Let me finish. Let me tell you the story
first about this present's history. You listen. It's an interesting story.

"Sometime late in the seventh century, during the Tang
dynasty, my ancestors came to Okinawa from China. They
brought with them *ch'uan fa*, the weaponless fighting techniques that became, after many, many years, karate. For
hundreds of years they trained in this art, but they did so
secretly, allowing only a very few students, most of them
family members, to study. In the late fourteenth century,
much larger numbers of Chinese settlers arrived in
Okinawa. They have been called 'the thirty-six families,'
but in fact there were far more people than that. 'Thirty-six

families' is some sort of symbolic number, but its meaning has been lost over time.

"These people were traders who bought luxury items in Southeast Asia and brought them back to Okinawa, where they were reshipped to China, Korea, and Japan. Traveling over thousands of miles of unguarded water, they became the target of pirates who roamed at will from the South China Sea to the Sea of Japan. The traders needed some sort of protection, and for that they turned to those who were trained to defend themselves, who devoted their lives to *ch'uan fa*, to karate.

"For a while, these men were no more than bodyguards paid to travel aboard the merchant ships, but then some of them decided they could do much better if they became traders themselves with their own ships. They formed a society called Prancing Tiger. I'm not sure why they picked this name. Perhaps it comes from a very old *ch'uan fa kata* known as 'the poised tiger,' in which a man appears to be vulnerable to attack but is actually in a most lethal state of readiness. Or it may have been taken because the ancient Chinese considered the white tiger of the West as the king of beasts. In any case, to belong to Prancing Tiger a man had to be at least *go-dan*, at least fifth-degree black belt. Those who belonged were highly respected and greatly feared.

"For the next three hundred years the men of Prancing Tiger were the most successful traders sailing out of Okinawa. Their ships all flew a flag with a picture of a tiger on his hind legs. Painted on the flag below the tiger was a Chinese ideograph. This ideograph is most interesting because it means both 'danger' and 'opportunity.' Pirates who saw these ships left them alone. The pirates knew that if they harmed one Prancing Tiger they would sooner or later have to deal with the rest. They found, through several bloody encounters, that this was not at all in their best interest. From the beginning, it was decided there would never be more than thirty-six members of Prancing Tiger, in honor of the thirty-six families. Prancing Tiger exists to this day, and to this day that remains true. Some members are still traders of many different kinds of goods. Some are not.

"So, Roland. You are sitting there wondering why is he

telling this story to me? There must be a reason. He never tells me stories without a reason. He is like Aesop and his fables that way. The fox and the crow. The Okinawan sailor and the pirate. Right? Well, I'm telling all of this to you because I am a member of Prancing Tiger. And to be a member is the present I am offering you. But you are not *go-dan*. Someday I have no doubt you will be, but now you are only *sho-dan*, first-degree. Remember though, I said to you everything changes. During the past six hundred years there have been exceptions, and in your case I believe an exception should be made as well. The reason for making the exception now is that I am leaving Florida very soon. Don't ask me where I'm going because I can't tell you. Someday maybe, but not now.

"You have been the kind of student a *sensei* looks for all his life ... no, no, don't say anything. Don't protest. It's true. You should feel good about that. I have no doubt you will continue down the same path, but at the moment you are restless. You are confused and angry."

"I know I've been acting like a loony," Troy said.

"Like a loony. That's a good word. A loony. Well, so you have—but then, who hasn't at one time or another. The point is, what to do about it before you run into a tree with your El Camino, or shoot your foot off, or shoot off your *chimpo*, which would be even worse. I think it would be good if you got out of here for a little while. I think a good idea would be for you to go to Okinawa to study in the *dojo* of my friend *Sensei* Miyazato, a *ku-dan*, a ninth-degree. I have already written to him about you. If you decide to go, rest assured you will be very welcome. You can learn much from him. He and his students can learn from you, too. In fact, *Sensei* Miyazato already looks forward to learning about tracking in the woods from you. Unlike me, he knows how to fish, so you don't have to worry about that. I think training there for six months or a year will help restore peace to your soul. But it's up to you. Anyway, let all this sink in. See how you feel about it when we get where we are going."

South of Daytona they crossed the intercoastal waterway over a steel drawbridge and worked their way through a maze of narrow streets filled with tiny houses, some wooden, others built of concrete block. After about ten minutes of twisting and turning through these streets, Shima finally stopped in front of a wooden bungalow painted a garish shade of blue. "Here we are," he said. "Come on, let's go inside."

The man who opened the door for them appeared to be in his early thirties, although it was hard to tell exactly because he was totally bald. He wore a pair of cutoff jeans, was shirtless, and from waist to neck was covered with tattoos. There was also a tattoo of what looked like a tarantula on the top of his hairless head. "Hey," the tattooed man said, "Mr. Shima. C'mon in, man, make yourself at home."

"Name's LaFountain," he said, shaking Troy's hand. "My lady friend there calls me LaFountain of Youth. Ha, ha, ha. Ain't that right, baby? Course she's barely eighteen so, you know, to her I'm like Father Time. Somebody once told her guys over thirty can't get it up more than once a week. Ha, ha, ha."

A very tan young woman in a bikini, sitting cross-legged on the floor with a Martin classical guitar across her lap, looked up and smiled, but said nothing. A piece of sheet music was propped up against a stack of books in front of her. After a moment she went back to her playing. "Diabelli," said LaFountain. "Goddamn difficult piece. She's extremely good. Far better than I am. But then, I'm a better artist, so we're even. C'mon. My workroom's in the back."

"If Roland agrees, I want you to copy this exactly," Shima said, removing his shirt. From years of football and track competition, Troy was accustomed to seeing male bodies in good condition, and like most athletes who've spent countless hours in locker rooms, he rarely paid any attention to them. However, he had never seen Shima without his shirt on before and was instantly mesmerized by his teacher's physique. What was remarkable about the Okinawan's build was not the size of his muscles—he was only five-five and weighed about 135 pounds—but their visibility and motion. Even the slightest bend or turn of Shima's body produced kaleidoscopic ripples and undulations beneath the drum-tight skin laced with veins that bulged like swollen blue rivers.

Then Troy saw the tattoo, about three inches high and exquisitely rendered in shades of blue, green, and red, on Shima's right arm, just below the shoulder. It was of a tiger standing on its hind legs, its mouth open, its front paws poised to strike. Below it was the single Chinese ideograph with the double meaning—opportunity and danger.

"You like that, huh?" LaFountain said. "I touched it up for Mr. Shima a year ago and he said it looked better than when it was brand-new. I'm not cheap but I do good work. You ready?"

"He wants to think it over," Shima said. "It involves more than just a tattoo."

"There's nothing to think over, *Sensei*," Troy said, unbuttoning his shirt. "I'm honored by your gift."

"I'm letting Tom Waxe stay in Shima's house," Troy said to Clara. "His mother was a good friend to my grandmother. If you need anything, any help or anything, you can always go to Tom. Or you could ask Sheridan Halpatter. He's even better, but he's harder to find."

The Indians had such strange names, she thought. Waxe. Waxe the taxi. He drove a broken-down old truck that didn't even have a seat in it—he drove sitting in an old canvas deck chair bolted to the floor—but she always imagined him behind the wheel of a yellow cab. And Halpatter. Every time she heard his name she pictured little children running down a long hallway with a wooden floor. Patter, patter, patter, their feet went. "Who's staying in your house?" she asked.

"You are, if you want. You and Billy. I thought he'd like it out here by the pond. If it's too isolated, you can just use it as a place to get away. Whatever you want to do. It's for you to use. Another thing. I wrote up a will and gave it to Grady Bannister, my grandfather's lawyer. If something happens to me—you know, if the plane I'm on crashes into the ocean or something . . . It won't, but . . . if it does, the house and my land belongs to you. Just promise me you'll never run the Indians off. I mean, I know you never would, but . . ." He sighed. "Clara, don't cry. I'm not gonna crash into the ocean. I'm only going for six months or so. Then I'll come back, finish school, we'll get married, I'll join the

FBI and catch bad guys, we'll have a couple of kids. Billy'll be their big brother. C'mon, cheer up. Did I tell you, the lady at Alabama who does student flights got me on this really cheap charter out of Chicago. I can get a flight to Chicago out of Tampa. I was thinkin' we could go over there a day or two early and stay at the beach. Oh, and I paid up the insurance on the El Camino through the end of the year and I'm leavin' you the keys so you can have it to drive."

"I like my Cadillac," she said. Unable to even look at her dead husband's Corvette, she had sold it before leaving Texas, but vowed never to part with her father's El Dorado.

They made love then, wordlessly and fast. Afterwards, she cried silently in the dark, in his house with the sagging porch, while a barred owl hooted from across the pond. *Why am I so sad?* she thought. *If it's only for six months, why am I so terribly sad?* She had no way of knowing that when she left him at the airport in Tampa, she would not see Roland Troy again for more than five years.

VI

✦

He watched her, his hat low over his eyes, the cigar clenched between his teeth, his large hands with their misshapen knuckles hanging loosely over the arms of his chair. A single tear rolled down her cheek, leaving a sooty trail of mascara. She wiped the tear away with the edge of her index finger, saw the dark smudge on the finger, and sighed softly.

"Aw, shit," she said. "I told myself I was not going to cry. I'm just going to go there and talk to him, I said, as an old friend. As an old friend . . . I'll see if—now I look a mess, don't I?"

"Hell, Clara, you look beautiful. Now don't cry. I'm sorry. I'm truly sorry. I mean, Jesus, I haven't seen you in so long and you come and pay me a visit and what do I do but get you all upset by bringing Parabrise up again. Forget I said anything. Forget it. Parabrise ain't worth it."

"Drew Parabrise isn't why I'm crying, Roland. I'm crying . . . don't you know? Haven't you heard? Well, I expect you wouldn't have since you don't read the local paper and you probably never did get a TV set, did you? You never even listened to the radio 'cause they didn't play any decent jazz. See, I remember things too. I remember your shoes and your corduroy jeans. I remember your El Camino. I see you still have one of those. The cigar's new, though. Even you've changed a little bit."

"Hey, wait a minute," he said. "First Halpatter, now you. What all haven't I heard? I *do* listen to the radio. They got this woman on now plays real fine music, reads poetry, shit I sit back in the kitchen with a mug of herbal tea I think I'm in Greenwich Village."

"The woman on the radio is why I'm here, Roland. She's

dead. They're saying Billy killed her. They're saying he raped her and killed her. Oh Jesus, Roland, you gotta help me. Billy's all I have left. He'd never . . . he's a fuck-up, I know that. He went and got himself tied in with that Varney character . . . oh, Lord, he's such a fuck-up. It's partly my fault. But he'd never kill anybody. I told myself, I'm not going to cry and I'm not going to beg, and I know, Roland, I know you don't investigate crimes anymore. I heard about what happened on that case and I know about the models you build now. They had your teacup on the eleven o'clock news in Savannah. Did you know that? Help me, Roland. I *am* begging you."

He put his hand on her arm. "Of course I'll help you," he said. "I'll do whatever I can, and you don't have to beg me. Not you."

She took a drink of juice. Her hand was shaking, but she was in control of herself. "I have to use the bathroom," she said. "I won't be but a minute. You know, this goddamn porch is a lethal weapon to a woman in high-heel shoes."

"Billy's in jail?" he asked when she returned.

"They're holding him without bail," she said.

"Where'd this happen, this killing?"

"They found her in Billy's office at the track. She was shot with his gun. He was sleeping in a car parked next to the office." She leaned her head against one of the posts supporting the porch and closed her eyes. "There's more," she said. Her voice was ragged, as though she had recently awakened from a deep sleep. "Billy was down in Mexico with a man named Myron McBride—another trainer— doing some sort of horse trading. McBride wound up dead and Billy wound up back here at the track with a whole lot of money, a little bit of cocaine, and the body of the woman on the radio. Nikki Waters is her name. Or was. It's— there's no doubt the two of them were in that office to- gether, but . . ." She held her palms up and shrugged. "Billy says he didn't do it. I say he couldn't have done it. Some helluva defense, huh? 'Mom says son couldn't have done it, he's not that kind of guy.' I talked to Stanton Feinberg about defending Billy and he told me he should plead guilty. He told me the evidence is overwhelming and if

Billy pleads guilty maybe he can get life instead of the electric chair."

"Where you stayin', at Billy's?"

"No. I was afraid of disturbing something. In case there's something there that could help him . . . some evidence . . . I don't know. I thought you might . . . we might check it over. Later. I hate that house anyhow. The way his wife furnished it. Everything is so cold. I took a room at the Park Suite. Connie Alderman tried to get me to stay with her, but I didn't want her hovering over me. I'd rather be by myself."

"I was gonna deliver a model of a crime scene to the state attorney's office. I'll go down to the jail and pay Billy a visit first. Meanwhile, you go get your stuff from the hotel and bring it on back here. Then we'll see what all we're gonna do."

"I can't stay here, Roland. You threw me out of here. Do you know how hard it is for me just to sit on this porch? Do you have any idea?"

"Yeah, I know," he said. "All I'm saying is . . . shit, it's been twenty-three years, Clara. Weren't you the one who just told me that? I was fucked up. When I came back I was so fucked up. When you told me about you and Parabrise, I went nuts. I wasn't very far from nuts to begin with, where I was over there, what happened there. There hasn't been a day since that I didn't regret what I said to you. It's true. It's true. I just . . . I couldn't. I felt betrayed. You and Parabrise. And Shima. I was very confused, Clara. You know Shima was a killer? That's right. All that decency and dignity of man stuff he told me. A hired killer on the run. I found that out over there. The man who saved my life was his cousin. His boss."

"Shima didn't do you any harm, whatever he was," she said. "He thought of you as his son. He told me that once. I didn't do you any harm either. I loved you. I told you about me and Drew Parabrise because I didn't want there to be anything we didn't know about each other. I was afraid if you found out later from somebody else you'd hate me. I never thought . . ." She swallowed twice and took a sip of juice. "I wasn't prepared for this, Roland. I came here because of Billy. I can't even think straight."

"Stay here, Clara," he said. "You don't want to be stayin' by yourself at a time like this. There's four bedrooms in this house and three of 'em are empty. You can take your pick. Make things a whole lot easier anyway if we're in the same place. I'll cook you dinner. You know I'm a vegetarian now. I make this great lentil stew."

He relit his cigar and grinned at her. "You came to the right person, Clara," he said. "You didn't make a mistake."

"I saw your horse run," Roland Troy said. "I saw you drive him. The two of you put on quite a show."

"You did, really?" Billy Roseman said. He was sitting on the bunk in his cell, hunched over, his forearms resting on his thighs. He had lost five pounds since his trip to Mexico and the blue jailhouse coverall hung on him like the clothes on a scarecrow. The bandage on his cut forehead failed to cover the bottom three stitches, his eyes were sunken deep into their sockets, and his face, beneath three days' growth of beard, was the color of old newsprint. Troy had seen dead bodies that looked better.

"I was up in New York," he said. "My mother had a stroke and had to be put into a home. I saw in the paper you were racing up at Yonkers, so I went. I bet on you but by then I think you'd won seven or eight in a row with him, so I didn't make much."

"Man, it feels like that was about a hundred years ago. You should'a come down and said hello. Come and seen Steakhouse up close. You'd 'a loved him. He was all heart."

"Yeah, I probably should have, but I was in a hurry," Troy said. "I had to get over to LaGuardia and catch a plane."

A man in a nearby cell who'd been talking in a low voice since Troy arrived began to holler. "Hey, Jewboy," he shouted. "Tit-man. That your new lawyer? Don't matter you got you ten lawyers, Jewboy. They gonna roast your ass just like the Germans." Roseman raised his eyes but otherwise didn't move.

"I'll be right back," Troy said. He had the guard let him out and crossed the corridor to the loud man's cell. "Peanut Butter, as I live and breathe," he said.

"Sheeit. That you?" Peanut Butter said. "I didn't recognize you, man. I didn't know it was you at all."

"What you in for, Peanut Butter?"

"Sold a man half a key. It was entrapment."

"Yeah," said Troy. "I bet it was. But half a key. That's a lot of toot for fella such as yourself. You're moving up in the world."

Peanut Butter was a very light-skinned black man with mean, hooded eyes. He smiled, showing a front tooth with a gold inset in the shape of a lightning bolt. "I deal with an exclusive clientele these days, my man," he said.

"That right?" said Troy. "They gonna come around and stop the judge from sending you for a long ride, this exclusive clientele? I don't think so, P.B. Whereas I, on the other hand, might be able to put in a word or two in your behalf."

"What I gotta do so you'll put in words in my behalf?" said Peanut Butter.

"Well, for openers you gotta get off my friend's case. And then you gotta get on the drum about what a righteous dude he is, because he may be in here for a while, and if anything should happen to him ... well, P.B., there's a move afoot 'round these parts to throw the book at dope dealers, and I promise you I'll see to it they throw the whole fuckin' library at you. You can bet your black ass on it. You understand what I'm sayin'?"

"That's it? Take care of your boy? That's all I gotta do?"

"That's it. But you take *good* care of him, you hear me? You don't, you won't have to wait for the judge. I'll come back here and cook your shit myself."

"What'd you say to him?" Billy Roseman asked.

"I explained how it would be in his best interests to be your friend," said Troy. "He won't bother you anymore."

Roseman looked up at him then, his eyes feverish, haunted. He licked his lips and swallowed; Troy could hear that his mouth was dry. He started to speak but had to clear his throat. He began again. "Do you think I did it?" he asked. "Killed Nikki? Raped her?"

"If I did, I wouldn't be here," Troy said. "I'd feel terrible for your mother and I'd help her get you a good lawyer but

I wouldn't be around, Billy. I *know* you didn't do it. What I gotta do now ... what we gotta do now is prove it."

"What do you want me to do?" Roseman asked.

"I want you to tell me what happened."

"Where should I start?"

"Start with Mexico," Troy said. "Tell me about this guy McBride."

VII

$\blacklozenge$

"It was anybody else, I'd just take the car, there wouldn't be no conversation, you realize that," Myron McBride said.

Billy Roseman looked away from the giant television screen that occupied almost an entire wall of his den. The screen was filled with standardbreds—harness horses pulling drivers seated on sulkies—careening around the far turn, heading straight at the camera. The track announcer's voice boomed out of two towering speakers set on either side of the screen. Roseman pushed the pause button on the VCR remote and the room was silent, the horses frozen in midstride, veiled by a suspended shower of dirt. He set a bone down on the edge of the paper plate of chicken wings resting in his lap, wiped some sauce from the corner of his mouth with the index finger of his right hand, licked the finger clean, and sighed.

"We've known each other since we were what? Nine, six, one of those early numbers," he said, "and now you come into my house, you don't even knock, and tell me you're gonna pop my car?" Roseman shook his head and smiled up at Myron McBride, like he wasn't really angry, just tired. Like he'd been expecting Myron to come for the car all along.

"You hear that noise, drip, drip, drip?" he said. "That's my roof leaking into a plastic tub I got sitting on the leather couch in the living room. The same couch my soon-to-be ex-wife bought with my ex–credit card two days before she took off with one of John Chadwick's grooms. I was a disappointment, she said. So she hit the road with a guy making two hundred a week hot-walking horses. In my Corvette. Dark-blue convertible with some very subtle gold pinstriping, saddle interior, six-speed transmission, but you probably got all that on your sheet there. You want to pop my car, you gotta find them first. I was you I'd hurry up; the trail's gettin' cold."

Myron McBride sat down in an easy chair across from Billy Roseman and placed his clipboard on the coffee table between them. Though he lived a tumultuous life, McBride prized neatness and organization. His condo was immaculate. He allowed no eating in his car. The disarray of Roseman's house and the pervasive odor of mildew appalled him. Outside, he had noticed, the stucco was cracked and chunks of it lay in the shrubbery. The garage door was askew. Empty fast-food containers, rumpled articles of clothing, and stacks of magazines and newspapers littered the place. Garbage overflowed two large containers in the kitchen. The rug was stained, and through the sliding glass door McBride could see some sort of greenish scum floating on top of the water in the swimming pool.

The last time McBride was in the house, at a party two years before, the pool water was crystal-clear, filled with shimmering pastel beams from the underwater lights. Elegantly dressed people moved around the pool deck, through the living room, all chrome and white leather, with a skylight in the cathedral ceiling, through this very den done in oatmeal tones to match the pine-paneled walls.

The house was on a small lake in Winter Park, just north of Orlando, in a neighborhood of wildly appreciating real estate. Why Roseman didn't just sell the place, take a profit, and straighten out the rest of his finances before he went bankrupt was a mystery to McBride. Instead, he sat there, in his torn jeans and cowboy boots, his long legs hanging over the end of the recliner, his large, callused, horseman's hands hanging out of the frayed cuffs of his pink shirt, watching videotapes of old races while things deteriorated around him.

Grudgingly, McBride had to admit that Roseman himself didn't look all that bad. True, his tanned face had become lined and there were bags under his eyes, but in spite of the crap he ate he still appeared lean and hard, and he hadn't lost a bit of the dark straight hair that hung down to his shoulders. McBride's hair was thinning and he had lately begun to put on some weight. These days, he thought, he wouldn't look so hot in a pink shirt.

For as long as McBride could remember, pink was the only color shirt in Roseman's wardrobe, although he would never say why. He kept a few pink dress shirts for special occasions, but back around 1980 he found out about an outfitter somewhere in Nevada who sold Western-style pink chambray work shirts, all-cotton, with pearlized snap buttons. Roseman ordered three dozen of them and from then on, summer or winter, they were mostly all he wore. He had one of them on now, bleached almost white from a hundred washings and years in the sun, with both elbows worn through.

Roseman was the same way with cars, too. The day he turned sixteen and got his license he went out and bought an old Corvette. He had owned one ever since, even when he was so broke he had to crawl around peeking underneath his furniture looking for enough change to buy gas. Of course, some of them were pretty ratty—oil-burners with headlights that wouldn't close flush with the fenders, and holes in the body panels with strands of fiberglass sticking out, flapping in the breeze—but they were Corvettes.

Roseman bought his house, along with his first brand-new Corvette, and a Ferrari to boot, as well as a condo in Breckenridge, after pocketing $400,000, his share of the race he was now watching on the huge video screen. Roseman's wife told McBride he watched the race, known as the Breeders' Crown, every night while he ate dinner. It was what finally drove her out of the house, she said.

"Look," Billy Roseman said, "this is where Audette makes his move and I hold him off. Look." He hit the play button on the remote but left the sound off. The horses swirled into silent action.

"See, Audette's talkin' to me, tellin' me to take a hole. 'Fuck you,' I said. 'I ain't takin' no hole, I'm goin' right to the front end.' It was all or nothing, Myron. I sold my goddamn dining-room furniture to make the stakes payment and get my ass into that race. I was gonna either win the bastard or finish at the back of the pack. I wasn't takin' no hole, settle for second or third. Uh, uh, motherfucker. Not that night."

Roseman won the Breeders' Crown in October of 1988
at a track in upstate New York. He was driving Steakhouse
Papa, the horse Roland Troy had watched him race, the
horse he'd spent twelve years looking for, the horse most
trainers spend a lifetime looking for and never find. The
first time he'd raced Steakhouse Papa, earlier that spring,
he had started out easy, content to stay near the back end
and let the horse get a feel for the track. After the first
quarter he was in tenth place, dead last, and composed.
Then he felt something pulling at him, through the long
shafts that attach the sulky to the horse and up his legs to
his groin, through the reins and up his arms to his shoulders
and down his spine to the small of his back. It was a surge
of power surprising in a horse who wasn't all that big.

What the hell, he figured, let me swing outside with him
and see how he runs, and when he did, Steakhouse accel-
erated with such thrust he was lifted right out of his seat
and had to hang on to the reins with all his might to keep
from flipping out of the sulky onto the track. In the next
quarter-mile they passed every one of the other nine horses
and won going away, by six lengths. Right then he knew
this horse was the one you found once, if you were lucky.
The next day he sold his dining-room set for fifteen hundred dollars and sent the money in so Steakhouse Papa
could run in the Breeders' Crown.

Coming into the big race, Steakhouse had won ten out of
eleven, taking one second on a muddy track. But Billy
Roseman had little money and could afford to race his
horses mostly on minor-league tracks in Pennsylvania and
Ohio, with only the occasional appearance, in low-level
stakes races, at the Meadowlands in New Jersey or Yonkers
Raceway in Westchester. Steakhouse Papa, therefore, had
never run against Blue Monday, the pride of Orange Blossom Stables, who swept through a season of top-dollar
stakes races at the big-time tracks undefeated. None of the
harness racing cognoscenti thought Roseman had a chance.

John Varney, the banking wonder, was a stockholder
in Orange Blossom Stables. Varney, whose base of opera-
tions was Orlando, was routinely referred to by the local
paper there as "John Varney, the financial wizard." At his
insistence—he claimed security wasn't tight enough at the

racetrack—the rules were bent and Blue Monday was allowed to be stabled away from the track, at a private farm apart from all the other horses. Blue Monday had his own private vet, a trainer and two assistant trainers, and was watched around the clock by guards armed with assault rifles. His driver was Lambert D'Artigue, "the Intimidator," who had earned $800,000 already that year, and often raced at several tracks in an evening, flying from one to another in his own helicopter.

Bart Hendricks, one of the few active harness drivers with earnings in the same ballpark as D'Artigue, approached Billy Roseman as he was changing into his racing colors in the dank locker room in the bowels of the grandstand. Like D'Artigue, Hendricks was a contract driver, a hired gun, affiliated with no particular stable. It was the age of the specialist, and Roseman, who trained and drove his own horses, was considered a dinosaur. "Let me handle this one for you, Billy," Hendricks said. "It's your only shot."

"Not on your life," said Roseman. "Ain't nobody but me drivin' Steakhouse."

Hendricks snorted. "Then you can't blame nobody but you when you get your ass handed to you," he said.

"Here comes Blue Monday," Roseman said. "Here he comes after us with that shitbird D'Artigue beating on him like he was a rug full of dust. See that. See?—I got my whip in the air but I never once touch Steakhouse. I never had to, man. It was never fuckin' necessary."

Roseman leaped out of his chair and the plate of chicken wings in his lap went flying across the room. A bit of sauce landed on Myron McBride's pants and he groaned. Roseman, oblivious to the mess, was almost on top of the video screen now, pointing wildly at it. "This is it," he shouted. "We're past the quarter pole and D'Artigue's so close to me I can smell his cologne, but see, my whip's still behind my ear. Why I don't have to hit my horse is 'cause he *knows*, man. He knows it's now or never, and that little sucker reaches down and turns it on and we're gone. Blue Monday never has a chance."

A month after the race, Billy Roseman made a deal with John Varney. The night of the party, Varney stood beside Roseman's swimming pool, a glass of champagne in his hand, his face smooth and deeply tanned, his dark, slicked-back hair glistening. All the guests gathered around while he announced the syndication arrangement that would make Billy Roseman so rich the $400,000 he'd won in the Breeders' Crown would seem like lunch money.

Clara, in town from Hilton Head for the party, had taken Billy into the garage on the pretext of sitting in her son's new Ferrari. "You know, Billy, all the drivin' around I've done, I don't believe I've ever been in a real honest-to-God Ferrari," she said, pushing her long dark hair away from her face. "Though I did once get a ride in a turbo Porsche from Johnny Wallace. Lordy, that big fat man could hardly fit through the door of that car, and once he got plunked down in the seat he could barely breathe. I thought for sure we'd get ourselves killed."

Though in her mid-forties, she was still lithe as a cat. In spite of the tight dress she was wearing, she slid nimbly into the driver's seat and gripped the wheel. Only then, with Roseman inches away from her on the passenger side, did she stop smiling. She was careful never to publicly embarrass her son.

"Billy, that man John Varney is more slippery than eel shit," she said. "Don't get your ass involved with him. I know men like that. There's dozens of them in this town now, like there must have been in California during the gold rush. They wriggle in and suck the money the way leeches suck blood. They dance on other people's graves."

But it was too late. The deal was done. Shares in Steakhouse Papa were already being sold for $300,000 each. There were fifty shares in all, a fifteen-million-dollar syndication. Fifty-five shares, actually, if you counted the five John Varney gave to Billy in exchange for signing over his half of Steakhouse Papa. A share was good for three breedings a year, each worth $20,000, paid by the owner of the mare. That meant Billy Roseman could look forward to $300,000 per year for the life of the horse. Furthermore, he was free to breed Steakhouse to any five of his own mares each year and either keep the foal or sell it. With a future like that, Roseman borrowed heavily. In addition to the house, the condo, and the cars, he bought fifteen yearlings. Added to the horses he trained for other owners, and ones he owned a piece of, his stable, in the spring of 1989, numbered thirty-seven. It wasn't as big a stable as Chadwick's or the Wadhams brothers', but it was a major-league operation at last.

On the night John Varney's shiny new trailer took Steak-house Papa from Billy Roseman's stable, Billy slept fitfully, awakened several times by what he imagined was the plain-tive whinnying of a horse. The following morning he wan-dered listlessly around his barn feeling depressed and ashamed, believing he had somehow betrayed Steakhouse Papa by bartering him for John Varney's pot of gold, but later, as he drove home in the shiny red Ferrari that drew stares at every stoplight, he felt better, imbued once again with the conviction that Varney, after all, was right. He was in business, and in business there was no room for senti-mentality. Not if you wanted to make it to the big time.

It was in that state of mind that Billy watched pridefully, several weeks later, while Steakhouse Papa raced for the first time with another driver behind him. Billy was sitting in a well-upholstered leather chair in the enclosed air-conditioned section of the grandstand reserved for celebri-ties, wealthy corporate executives, and an exclusive circle of standardbred owners. He was observing the race on closed-circuit television, sipping a glass of John Varney's expensive red wine, when his pride turned to horror as Steakhouse Papa, the horse who still held the world record for a mile at 1:47 flat, the horse who never seemed to get tired, nor ever was injured or sick a day in his life, the horse who was about to make him fabulously rich, dropped dead of a heart attack in the far turn.

"There ain't no trail," Myron McBride said. "With all due respect, your wife, your soon-to-be ex-wife, has the imagination of a turnip. She and the groom are holed up in a trailer on Lee Brown's place in Apopka. Your 'Vette's right there, in the middle of a field, under a very large cam-phor tree, covered with dust and cow shit. I saw it there myself this afternoon. But see, you weren't listening. I didn't say I was gonna pop your car. What I said was, it was anybody but you I would.

"See, on the sheet here I've already written the car isn't on the premises, before you even told me Beverly took off

with it, and the signatory of the loan—that's you—the dude
who ain't paid a fucking dime on his ride for three months,
ain't here either. Which gives you a couple, three more
days to come up with the money. And I'm here to show
you how that can be done."

Roseman had slumped back down in his chair, and for
the first time looked straight at McBride. "The truth of it is,
Myron, that other horse was probably faster," he said. "The
reason we won was because Steakhouse Papa had more
heart. You can't train that in a horse any more than you can
in a human being."

"How many times you watched this thing?" McBride
asked.

"You think I've lost it? That's what my wife thinks. My
soon-to-be ex-wife. She thinks my motor's runnin' but my
wheels don't turn. That what you think?"

"What I think is that you and me are gonna take a ride
out to Apopka and snatch your Corvette. We're gonna park
it in your garage out there, pull the battery, and take off the
distributor. Then you're gonna help me haul some horses
out to Texas, across the Rio Grande into Mexico, and help
yourself to a shit-pile of money so's you can make a bunch
of payments on that dude and fix your roof both. Maybe
get these rugs cleaned in the bargain."

"What are you, makin' a movie, you want me to help
you move horses across the Rio Grande? What the hell
kind of horses are they? Where'd you steal 'em?"

"Jumpers. Six jumpers. We bring 'em to a guy's gonna
sell 'em to the Mexican Olympic team. He just don't want
to pay, you know, taxes, import shit, whatever. They aren't
stolen, Billy. They're bought and paid for. You ride one,
lead two. I do the same thing. You get ten grand. Nice,
huh?"

"Six jumpers? Six good jumpers gotta go three-fifty, four
hundred at least. Six *real* fuckin' jumpers cost you a half
million. What is this, man, some sort of test you see how
nuts I really am? Go to Mexico with jumpers. Sure, why
not? Then after that we take a load of saddle broncs to Yu-
goslavia. What do these horses of yours jump, up and down
when it's time to eat?"

"It ain't no joke, Billy. I got backers. This is a real,

honest-to-God deal. A big deal. It's all set. I got a rig all ready to roll. Got a trailer and a nearly new Freightliner, super stereo, CD player, bed in back. One of us drives, the other sleeps like a baby, here to the Mexican border nonstop."

"So this is the big score, Myron," Roseman said. "Not like all the others. This one has backers, it's all bought and paid for. Ten for me, a ton for you. Is that how it's goin' down? And with a Freightliner, no less."

"And you're the only person I know who can drive one. That also can ride one horse and lead two more across a river," McBride said. He was certain Roseman would go along with him, even if there wasn't any money in it, just for the adventure. Billy always did.

"What if we get caught?" Roseman said. "You consider that possibility? It could happen, you know. Get boogered in some Mexican jail."

"It ain't gonna happen, not where we're crossing. The guy in Mexico knows about these things. Anyway, it ain't like we're rustlers or wetbacks or something. We're respectable American citizens out for a weekend horseback ride."

Billy Roseman sighed, rubbed his eyes with the thumb and index finger of his left hand, and shook his head. "I can't leave my stable," he said. "It's a lot of money, but I can't go."

"Billy, it's Wednesday night. We leave tomorrow, we deliver Friday night. We turn around and haul ass, we're back here Sunday night. That's only four days, and the horses don't even jog Sundays. You got Fulton still workin' for you. Let him take care of business. Hell, what've you got? Three horses, for Chrissake?"

"Five. I got five horses to train. Four of 'em ain't worth all that much, to tell you the truth, but this one filly I'm training for these two Canadians might do something."

"Well, you got a yearling or a lottery ticket, at least you won't be as likely to commit suicide," McBride said. "C'mon, call Fulton, or don't he have a phone?"

"You know, I had it all," Billy Roseman said. "And now . . . and now. I didn't get one fuckin' dime of the insurance money for Steakhouse Papa. There was a clause in the policy somewhere. Only those who actually paid out money, or

put up money, or something. Only they collected. John
Varney collected. His friends collected, whoever they are.
But I didn't put up any money. All I did was sign over the
horse that I found, and raised, and trained, and drove. I
signed him over for future considerations. So I didn't collect.

"You want to know why I watch that tape every night,
I'll tell you. It's because I'm still not sure I won the race.
I keep thinking, this time I'm gonna watch it and
D'Artigue's gonna beat me. Blue Monday's gonna pull it
out. But then, every night Steakhouse Papa blows that
sucker off. Every night I do win. If I didn't, then I'd have
nothing."

Billy Roseman woke to the melancholy voice of George
Jones on the stereo. McBride had insisted on playing nothing but country music once they crossed the Louisiana line,
which was fine with Roseman, who found it easy to sleep
to and no problem when he was driving. Through the tiny
porthole next to the tractor's bunk he could see jagged
peaks and canyons colored brown and purple in the fading
light. In the distance, a dust devil whipped across an empty,
magenta plateau. There were no houses, no signs of any animals, though Roseman knew the territory teemed with
wildlife. Roseman's people were from Texas and he had
made a pilgrimage there when he was eighteen, traveling
all over the state, alone, on the back of an old Norton motorcycle.

He had turned over the wheel to McBride and gone to
sleep in Ft. Stockton, where they left the interstate and
headed southwest toward Presidio on the Mexican border.
While the rig bounced and swayed through the desolate
mountains of southwest Texas, Roseman dreamed that he
was sitting around a campfire with his father. His father
kept trying to yodel, but instead brought up great gobs of
bloody phlegm that sizzled like tallow when he spit them
into the fire. Roseman had never met his father; he knew
him only through two or three old photographs and from
what little his mother told him. His father had been a rodeo
bull rider, but Roseman had no idea if he ever yodeled.

He climbed slowly from the bunk to the passenger seat

beside McBride, who gave him a friendly wave. "According to my map we're almost there," McBride said. "Two, maybe three miles we should reach the place where we unload. Then it's just down a little path to the river. Thirty-seven hours on the money. Not bad, considering two stops to feed and water. Going back empty we should do even better."

They had dropped down out of the mountains, but the road they were on was still lined on both sides by jagged outcroppings of rock. Roseman was about to say something about there being no place to pull off the highway and park the rig when they rounded a curve and the narrow canyon they'd been in opened onto a broad mesa sparsely covered with sagebrush, cactus, and small trees. The lights of two or three buildings twinkled in the distance.

"It's just a garage, couple of cabins, couple of trailers and some sort of café that may or may not be open," McBride said. "Don't ask me what they're doing out here. All I know is we park the truck out back of the garage. There's a trail about a hundred yards behind the café that drops down to the river, just waiting for you and me."

The road ended in a broad clearing of hard-packed dirt where the weatherbeaten, ramshackle buildings and ancient Airstream trailers sat in a haphazard cluster. Only the garage and one of the trailers were lit. A skinny kid, nineteen or twenty years old, in greasy jeans, was working on the engine of an old Chevy Nova with wide tires and a lift kit parked in front of the garage. He had a crew cut and an earring that hung almost to his shoulder, and wore a Guns 'n' Roses T-shirt and a tattered down vest that flapped in the cold wind blowing down off the mountains. He looked up for just a second when they pulled the rig around back, as though it was no big deal, as though the place was a regular truck stop.

"Any hot coffee in that café?" McBride asked him. He and Roseman had unloaded the horses, roped them together, and led them around to the front of the building. The animals moved around nervously, unsteady after so long in the trailer. They pawed the grassless earth and snorted, their breath visible in the night air.

"Uh uh, no," said the kid. He had mean eyes and a jailhouse tattoo on the back of his right hand, between the thumb and index finger. "They all gone to Presidio, to a dance. Shut the kitchen down. There's a hose over there on the side of the building, and a trough, you want to water them horses. You gotta flip the switch to the well pump first. Path to the river's down that way, in that clump of trees. You can't miss it."

The kid went back to his motor, paying no attention while they filled the trough and let the horses drink. When the animals were through, Roseman and McBride mounted up, bareback, and started toward the river. The path, though visible through the underbrush, led down a steep slope and required total concentration to traverse safely, so they rode in silence. At the bottom of the slope they paused momentarily before entering the water. Where they were crossing, the Rio Grande appeared to be only about fifty yards wide, far narrower than Roseman had imagined it. On the other side, they could see a campfire and several shadowy figures moving around it.

"On time, in the right place," McBride said. "Let's get these ponies across, get paid, and go home."

"It's a regular pony express station back there, by the sound of that kid," Roseman said when they were in the water.

"He's just a kid trying to be helpful," said McBride.

"He's a nasty little bastard with a telephone in his Nova. Right next to the Remington."

"You saw that?"

Roseman didn't answer. Instead he held up one hand and reined his horse to a halt with the other. They were almost halfway across the Rio Grande, in dark, muddy water about four feet deep that moved against their horses' bellies at about ten miles an hour. The two horses on either side of him—the ones he was leading—shifted anxiously in the river. Five yards to his left, McBride saw Roseman's upraised hand and stopped moving as well. "What is it? What do you see?" he asked.

Billy Roseman's vision was legendary, even at night. Especially at night. On a harness racing track, he was able to see the slightest shift in position of the sulkies in front of him, enabling him to anticipate an opening—a hole—and move through it before another driver would know it was there. That was how he won races on lesser horses, the only kind he could afford.

Now what he saw, in the pale light of a gibbous moon, were the men walking about in the brush near the campfire across the river. He saw one of them reach under his jacket, remove a long-barreled pistol, examine it, and put it back, undoubtedly in a shoulder holster. So these guys were armed, these hombres who were buying jumpers for their Olympic team. All he and McBride had with them were the clothes on their backs and their boots, slung around their necks by bandannas tied to the pull straps so they wouldn't get wet. They didn't even have a piece back in the Freightliner. It was going to be an interesting night, he was sure of that. He wondered how much McBride had been promised, to send ten grand his way.

"These fellas have guns, Myron," Roseman said.

"Of course they have guns," said McBride. "Hell, everybody in Orlando's got a gun. My fuckin' accountant has a gun, a Magnum he keeps under the seat of his Honda Accord. Why shouldn't they have guns down here? It don't mean they're gonna shoot us."

McBride moved his horses forward with a couple of low clucking sounds and Roseman followed, feeling the warm river water splash against his bare feet, watching the men move about on the far shore.

"*Oye!* You guys," one of them shouted from the bank. "Right up here the footing is not so bad."

The horses came out of the river and sprang up the embankment on the Mexican shore, glad to be on dry land. Roseman and McBride dismounted and tethered the animals to a couple of tree limbs. Steam, rising from the horses' wet flanks, mingled with smoke from the campfire. Roseman and McBride sat on the ground and pulled on their socks and boots while the Mexicans watched, saying nothing.

There were three of them. One was old, maybe seventy, a tiny, corvine figure with a scraggly white beard and only a few teeth. He sat hunched on the tailgate of a battered old Toyota pickup truck wrapped in an oversized Houston Oilers jacket, smoking a thin cigar. The truck was about thirty

yards from the river, in the middle of the small clearing
where the men had built the campfire. At the far side of the
clearing was a dirt road bordered by thick mesquite, leading
away from the river.

The man who called to them, and the third, the one with
the long-barreled pistol, carefully checked each of the
horses. Roseman could see immediately that they knew
what they were doing, feeling the bones, probing for any
inflammation. They were both tall, nearly as tall as
Roseman, who was six-three. The one with the gun had a
substantial gut hanging over a silver belt buckle inlaid with
diamonds that glittered in the firelight. Up close, Roseman
could clearly see the shoulder holster and the butt of a revolver with custom grips under the man's plaid lumber
jacket. The other man was thin, and wore an expensive-
looking leather duster and snakeskin boots. Both of them
had on cattleman-rolled Stetsons. Roseman was sure he had
seen the thin one somewhere before, but it was hard to tell
because of the hat.

"Well, amigos, I see no problem here. No problem at
all," the thin one said. He nodded to his companion. *"Me
parece bien."*

The heavyset Mexican, who had yet to speak, put a hand
into the inner breast pocket of his jacket—on the opposite
side, Roseman was relieved to see, from where he kept his
gun. He came out with a thick brown envelope he handed
to McBride. Then, almost as an afterthought, he dug inside
the outer bellows pocket from which he produced another
brown envelope, somewhat thicker than the first. McBride
pulled up the leg of his jeans and stuffed the first envelope
in his boot. He put the thicker one into the front, zippered
compartment of his ski parka, and winked at Roseman.

He believes it's over, Roseman thought. *He imagines already that he's home, talking about it, flashing the gold
Rolex he's going to buy. Or climbing out of the sharp ride.
A 300ZX. There ought to be enough in those envelopes for
a Z and a Rolex both. He's so excited he can hardly keep
from hugging himself. Which one of us is the bigger fool?
Him for thinking we're going home with that money, or me
for following him here?*

Though he wasn't really cold, Roseman did up the snaps

of his down vest and stuck his hands in his pockets. *I feel like a kid,* he thought. *Like a kid trying to hide in plain sight.* "I gotta piss," he said, and walked over to the bushes in front of the truck. When he had finished and zipped up his pants, he remained leaning against the truck's front fender instead of rejoining the others. The old guy kept his back turned to Roseman, who could see a thin plume of smoke from the man's cigar rising over his shoulder. The man with the gun eyed him suspiciously for an instant, but Roseman pretended not to notice, digging a boot heel into the dirt and scratching his ass, scared shitless, but nonchalant. Clearly, the guy didn't want to start shooting while he was standing next to six strange horses. The whole bunch of them might spook and trample him. Better to wait until he was mounted.

"Diego will take you back across now, in the truck," the thin one said. He motioned into the distance with his free hand, toward the east, along the river, as though he were broadcasting seed. There was no road where he pointed, only a rock-strewn ridge running parallel to the riverbank. "Down that way is the bridge," he said. "Another fifteen minutes from there and you will be back at the garage where you parked. Ernesto and I go in the opposite direction with the horses. Our trailer is a few hundred meters down that road. There is no way to turn it around in this place here. By tomorrow they will be on a rancho near Chihuahua, these fine animals, at their new home. And so, *señores,* our business is concluded and all of us are satisfied."

His smile, filled with great white teeth, was a rictus of ill intent. He climbed aboard the horse Roseman had ridden and steadied the other two, as Ernesto, the heavy one, took the reins from McBride and followed suit. Then they were gone, the dust of the horses mingling with the smoke from the dying campfire. McBride came over to the truck and punched Roseman on the shoulder. "I told you this was a real one. You standing here shitting rivets and me with your ten in my boot. Now all that's left is for us to get on home."

Roseman rode in the truck's bed, declining to sit up front with the old man and McBride, choosing instead to stretch

out on his back, on an old horse blanket, and stare up at the
stars. They were doing about thirty miles an hour, a good
clip considering the rocky terrain, when he heard the shots,
not from any pistol, but from an automatic rifle. He heard
glass shattering and a long, high-pitched scream, and felt a
tremendous thump. The pickup bucked wildly and then he
was flying through the cold dark air, branches tearing at
him, whipping across his face. He bounced two or three
times and was skidding downhill on his stomach, his face
grinding in the dirt, until something struck him hard across
the right shoulder and he stopped. He rolled onto his side,
spitting pebbles and grit, tasting blood that had run down
his face into his mouth from a cut on his forehead. Though
his shoulder was throbbing, he found he could sit up.

He was at the bottom of a ravine. Above him he could
see the ridge line, outlined against the sky. Beyond a tangle
of undergrowth he could hear the gurgle of the Rio Grande,
and in the darkness, ten feet from where he sat, he could
make out the twisted remains of the pickup, resting upside
down. No sounds came from it. He began crawling toward
the truck and was almost there when he found McBride lying on his back, facing downhill. Half of his face was gone
and his legs were splayed almost at right angles to his
torso, but the boot, with the brown envelope sticking out of
it, was still on his right foot.

"Myron, Myron, what the fuck have we done," Roseman
whispered.

There was noise in the brush high above him, and he
could see the beams of two flashlights working their way
down the ravine. *God help me, but it ain't no good to him
anymore,* he thought. He grabbed the envelope from
McBride's boot and scurried toward the river. He had covered only a few yards when he nearly tripped over the body
of the old man. Diego the thin one had called him. A bullet
had taken off the back of his head. *Jesus Christ,* he thought,
they shot their own man.

He was in the river, halfway across, crouched low with
only his head above the water, when he heard one of them
speak. It had to be the one with the belly; he would have
recognized the thin one's voice. *"Oye, Raimundo,"* the man

said. *"Está la cocaína, pero no el dinero. Y no veo al alto con el pelo largo."*

So that was it. That was why the money for six first-rate jumpers could fit in a brown envelope. Myron said the rest—the money owed to his backers—was being held in an Orlando bank. Maybe it was and maybe it wasn't, but what McBride left out was the part about the dope, the *cocaína. Motherfucker,* Roseman thought. *Led my ass into a drug deal and never told me. And now he's dead, and I'm probably gonna be.* He didn't feel quite so bad about the brown envelope he had clenched between his teeth.

It took him a half-hour, creeping through the darkness, to find the trail to the garage where they'd parked the rig, and another twenty minutes to retrace the tracks they'd made with the horses. Soaking wet and covered with mud, he squatted on the hard-packed ground within shouting distance of the ramshackle buildings and the two old Airstreams parked nearby. The Freightliner and trailer were gone, as he imagined they would be, probably already in a body shop across the river being altered and painted before the trip to Chihuahua or wherever the horses were headed.

There was a light on in the garage and for a few minutes Roseman debated showing himself. His best bet was that the Mexicans believed he lay dead somewhere in the ravine away from the truck. If, on the other hand, they were there waiting for him . . . but why would they be? They had the cocaine and the horses and the rig. True, he had the money, but how much was it? He had no idea. And then there was the fact that he was a witness. Or was he? He couldn't even say for sure who'd done the shooting. He was cold and dizzy and his shoulder was killing him. He couldn't think anymore. "Fuck it," he said. He stood up and walked around the corner to the front of the garage.

A girl with very short, straight brown hair and pale skin was lying on the hood of a nearly new Mustang GT convertible, her back propped against the windshield, smoking a cigarette and listening to a ZZ Top tape playing on the car's deck. She was wearing high-heeled boots, jeans, and a white sweater-coat with Indian designs on it that came down almost to her knees. Her mouth and fingernails were painted the same shade of dark red, and looked almost pur-

ple under the hooded fluorescent light. She turned her head
at the sound of his footsteps. Her eyes widened, but otherwise she showed no reaction to his appearance. She could
have been anywhere from sixteen to twenty-two. "Oh," she
said. "You ain't Wayne. I been waitin' for him for over an
hour. You seen him?"

"He the one drives the Nova?"

"Yeah, that's him. Mr. *No va.* Only he went somewhere
tonight, and without me." She was looking at him closely
now. "Jesus Christ, what'd you do, drive your dirt bike off
a cliff or somethin'?"

"Or somethin'."

"Where'd you see Wayne?"

"Right here, where you're sittin'. Workin' on his machine. Talkin' on the car phone." Roseman was fishing,
though he wasn't sure why. Whatever Wayne was up to
didn't change the fact that he had to get his ass out of there.
If he didn't hurry he was afraid he'd pass out.

"When you got here," he asked her. "When you came
back. Was there a rig—big ole tractor-trailer—parked out
behind his place?"

The girl eyed him suspiciously. "You and Wayne doin'
business?" she asked. " 'Cause I don't know nothin' about
that shit, and I don't want to. I told him I was done with
it and I meant it."

Roseman shook his head. He was afraid if he pushed it
she'd bolt. "Listen," he said, "I ain't in any kind of business. I need help. Can you take me to the nearest airport.
I'll pay you. I got money."

"The nearest airport? Man, there's this little ole no-count
one in Marfa. Nothin' there'll take you as far as you want
to go. You want a real honest-to-God airport, you gotta go
all the way to El Paso or Midland. That's a long haul, man.
Five hours, anyway, if you really get on it."

Roseman looked in the brown envelope for the first time.
There was a stack of bills inside, two inches thick, all hundreds. "I'll give you five hundred bucks in advance, you
take me to El Paso," he said. "I'll give you another five
hundred when we get there."

"I'll tell you where Wayne went," the girl said. "He
drove down to that whorehouse in Ojinaga. Get himself

high and fuck some chiquita. Come back here tomorrow struttin'. Think he's showed me somethin'. Give me the whole thousand up front, you got a ride. My name's Brenda."

He slept fitfully in the passenger seat, unable to find a comfortable position for his shoulder. At a full-service truckstop on the interstate outside Van Horn he took a shower. Then, wrapped in a blanket, he dozed in the car while she washed and dried his clothes in the all-night Laundromat. When he was dressed, she peeled off the bandanna he'd tied around his head and bandaged his wound. Ten miles down the road, she turned off the highway again and pulled up in front of a motel. It was quarter after four in the morning. "I can't keep my eyes open," she said. "I gotta get a few hours of sleep." He nodded. It didn't matter now. If anything was going to happen to him, it would happen in Orlando, not here.

Sometime later, how many hours he didn't know, she left her bed and slid in beside him. He had been having the dream about his father and the campfire, only this time McBride was lying there with them. McBride kept reaching for him from across the fire, burning his hand in the flames, and his father had the face of the tall, thin Mexican, Raimundo, the one with the awful smile, the one he'd seen someplace before.

"Take it easy," she said. "Relax. It's gonna be all right."

She was naked, her skin smooth and cool, her nipples erect, and she was wet. She touched his upper lip, wiping away beads of perspiration, and he could smell her, smell the finger she had used to excite herself while she lay in the other bed alone. She ran her hand down his belly, stroking him with the backs of her long nails, then taking hold of him, drawing him to her.

"Come to me," she said, her mouth against his ear. "Fuck me."

She slipped carefully under his injured body, both hands twined in his hair, undulating her hips slowly with him deep inside. Slowly, still slowly she moved, even when he held her tightly by the shoulders and she could feel him swelling and cried out, slowly even when he came, but gripping him then with her cunt, in short, quick spasms, coming with him at the end, saying "Now, oh now, oh now."

"I saw the guy take your truck," she told him. She was towel-drying her short hair, standing in a shaft of sunlight that streamed into the motel room where the heavy curtain on the bay window didn't quite close. Without her boots and the sweater-coat she looked tiny, frail almost, except for her full, pendulous breasts that bounced up and down as she rubbed her head. Naked before him, she was completely at ease, possessed of that kind of cocky toughness common to certain small people. Her eyes were wary, but she was without guile.

She was twenty, she told him, and lived in Shafter, up in the mountains, with her parents, who ran a fishing camp and hunting lodge. At eighteen she had married one of their clients, the son of an oilman from Odessa. The marriage lasted less than a year. She came home and had been there since. All she would say about Wayne was that sooner or later he was going to get his ass shot, and she didn't plan on being there when it happened. Outside, a procession of semis geared down for a long hill on the interstate.

"Was it a Mexican who took the truck?" he asked. "A real tall one in a long leather coat, or tall one with a gut?"

"It wasn't no Meskin," she said. "It was a white boy, pretty big, had long blond hair like a surfer. He never saw me. I was lookin' out the window of the Airstream, watchin' for Wayne, when he came roarin' up on his bike. Drove it right into the trailer. Fired up that rig and he was gone. That's what made me ask if you had an accident with a dirtbike. I thought maybe you and him were together."

"I was alone," he said. "By myself. Maybe I wasn't even there at all."

At two in the afternoon, Saturday, she dropped him at the El Paso airport. He had called from a restaurant and made a reservation, in the name of Fred Pultusker, on a three o'clock Continental flight to Houston, connecting to Continental's 6:05 to Orlando. With a little luck, he'd be at his barn by 10:30. He desperately wanted to see his horses, to walk into each of their stalls and let them know he was back. After that, he could sort out what to do next.

As he was about to get out of the car, Brenda leaned

over and kissed him. "What we did in the motel, that didn't have nothin' to do with the money," she said.

"I know," he told her.

"Here," she said, sticking a business card into the pocket of his vest. "It's got the number of the lodge on it, if you're ever, you know, back in Texas. I don't expect you'll be comin' down there to the river anytime soon."

"No, I don't expect I will. But I'd like to."

"Uh-huh," she said, and gave him a light backhand on the thigh.

"You watch yourself driving back," he told her. The night before, she had run the Mustang consistently at a hundred miles an hour.

"I better," she said. "This ain't even my car."

"So you fly on home with a bootful of money and rent the Lincoln," said Roland Troy. "Then what?"

"I get back here and I'm feelin' like homemade shit," Billy said. "I'm thinkin' about Myron . . . man, if he knew it was about drugs why didn't he at least bring guns? If we were armed . . ."

"They wouldn't 've worried about spookin' the horses," Troy said. "They'd 'a shot you as soon as you came out of the river. You were lucky."

"I was," Billy said. "Not Myron, though. Or that old Mexican. Why the hell did they kill him?"

"He was a witness," Troy said. "He was there. He'd fucked with 'em five years ago. Don't take much of a reason for people like that."

"What the fuck did Myron get into? What did I get into?" Billy sighed and shook his head. "I'm in the Lincoln, and I know I should get my head sewn up. I can feel the heat of that open wound. But I gotta see my horses. Make sure they're all right. So I go straight to the barn, and there's Nikki in my office reading a book, looking like something out of *Vogue* magazine.

"I'd never even touched her before. I never did more'n put my arm around her shoulder to say thanks for something she did. I thought about it. She was a beautiful woman, even in the raggedy old clothes she wore around the barn. And now there she was on my couch, in this sexy dress, looking absolutely gorgeous. Like every man's fantasy date. Sayin' c'mon, smoke some of this dope with me. One minute I'm being ambushed, then I'm in the sack with Mustang Sally, then that. Now this."

Billy hunched forward on the edge of his cot until his head almost touched his knees. He rubbed his temples with the ends of his fingers, sighed again, and looked up at Troy.

"So we smoked some dope," he said. "Then we made love. She was like . . . I wasn't ready for that at all . . . the kinkiness . . . wanting me to rip her clothes off and put my gun in her mouth. I was out of my mind by then. The weirdness of it . . . All the time she hung out at the barn it was a side of her I'd never seen.

"Anyway, that's all I remember. Next thing I know they got handcuffs on me and I'm in the back of a patrol car and they're saying I raped her and shot her and they're asking me what I did with her nipple . . . after . . . I mean Jesus Christ, Roland, she was my friend."

"Nikki the Raven," Troy said.

"You knew her?"

"I listened to her on the radio. I liked what she played and I liked her voice, but I didn't know her."

"Evidently I didn't either," Billy said.

VIII

◆

Nikki Waters would read to her listeners every night before she signed off. Maybe she'd have some Coltrane playing softly in the background, or some Wes Montgomery, or something off the Bill Evans Village Vanguard Sessions. For a week, she played Dr. John's solo blues piano. She liked that one particularly since nobody had any idea who it was, and when she finally told them—"And you thought all the man did was gris-gris. Guess I fooled you some, huh baby?"—a local record store sold 185 copies of the album.

She read poetry to them, Blake, Milton, Sir Philip Sidney, Robert Lowell. She read history. She read from a book called *Tales of Great Exploration and Adventure*. She read from a biography of Crazy Horse. She read Faulkner. It didn't matter. Her voice was one in a million, rich and resonant, yet soft and mysterious, swirling from the speakers like a deep, viscous river, felt as much as heard. "She sound like a nylon stocking sliding up a perfect leg," said Cool Babba Wisdom, the reggae man whose show followed hers. "Dat woman could read me de Ten Commandments and I be tossin' and turnin' all night."

She was on the air six nights a week, Monday through Saturday, eight to eleven. One night, she played "Rock Me Baby" by Muddy Waters. "Oh, Muddy!" she said when the song was over. "Muddy, baby! Don't stop now!" She played the song two more times before Parker Twitchel, the station manager, called her from his house. He believed someone who would actually read a poem over the radio about dead Yankee soldiers or trying to hold the wind in a net was at the very least unstable, and had more than once made it clear to Nikki that he thought she was totally insane.

89

"Hey," he said to her. "This isn't San Francisco or something. This is Orlando, Florida. Tupperware's international headquarters are here. This is where the Worldwide Campus Crusade just relocated its central office. The Magic Kingdom is here. Sea World, Shamu, fun in the sun. People here want stuff they can relate to. They want football scores. They want Inlet Charlie's surf report. They want to know where to go for a good, cheap Sunday buffet. They most definitely do *not* want someone to roll them like you'd roll a wagon wheel."

"Relax, Parker," Nikki said. "You're ranting."

Twitchel had recently taken his three children out of the public school system. They now went to a private academy run by his friend, Reverend Don Sheffield, a religious fanatic who lobbied ceaselessly against pornography. Sheffield raved at every opportunity about how pictures of naked people having sex caused rape, hideous forms of torture, and even murder. One of his proudest achievements was getting *Playboy* and *Penthouse* removed from the shelves of certain convenience stores. Referring to the mélange of soft rock and synthesized quasi-jazz the station played during the day, Sheffield praised Twitchel, publicly, in church, for his high-quality programming, his refusal to capitulate to those who encouraged fornication and devil worship in their music. The reverend obviously didn't do much listening after eight o'clock at night.

"Nikki, are you paying attention to me?" Twitchel said. "You quit playing that song."

"Blow it out your ass, Parker," she said, and hung up on him. She then proceeded to play Howlin' Wolf's "Backdoor Man" followed by John Hammond's version of the same song, and "Midnight Rambler" by the Stones. That night she closed with a few verses from Blake's "Marriage of Heaven and Hell."

Twitchel listened helplessly from the chaise longue beside his pool. What, after all, could he do? He had been told to hire Nikki Waters by Liberty Bell Media, the corporation based in Philadelphia that owned the station along with eighty more around the country. Twitchel endured Cool Babba Wisdom, whose show ran from eleven-thirty until three in the morning; he was rarely up that late and almost never listened to the Jamaican. Furthermore, there was hardly ever a complaint about Wisdom. Twitchel reasoned this was because the only people who understood what Wisdom said or the lyrics of the songs he played were his fellow Rastafarians.

Nikki Waters, however, was another story altogether. In addition to her reading selections and the brand of music she played, she refused to attend staff meetings right from the start, and absolutely would not make any public appearances nor do promotions for the station or anyone else. Twitchel, who had no idea where the directive to hire her originated, attempted to find out in order to register his displeasure. This was a calculated risk on his part, since he had been told Liberty Bell had some very influential friends in Washington. He knew he was in danger of stepping on powerful toes, but Nikki was driving him to distraction, so he forged ahead with abandon.

What he discovered was that no one at Liberty Bell Media could tell him anything. Neither could anyone at the Strong's Neck Savings and Loan Corporation on Long Island, which, he discovered, owned Liberty Bell Media. He was referred by the folks at SNS&L to the Winooski Holding Company in Shelburne, Vermont, where a pleasant-sounding young woman asked him to please wait one moment. After about five minutes, a man with a voice like a growling dog picked up the phone. The man did not identify himself.

"What's your problem?" he asked by way of introduction.

Twitchel, politely as he could, outlined the situation with Nikki Waters.

"She been late for work?" the man asked.

"No," said Twitchel.

"She say cocksucker or motherfucker or one of those words on the air?"

"No, sir, not to my knowledge." Twitchel was aware that he had suddenly become deferential to someone who for all he knew was sitting in his underwear on a farm.

"Your station's ratings have tripled in that time slot since she went to work there. She's running dead even with WDIZ, which according to what I've got in front of me here is the number-one adult rock station in your neck of the woods. And she's only been there two months. She must be doing something right."

Twitchel was dumbfounded. Who was this guy? Where did he get that information? *Why* did he have that information? "She's an embarrassment," he finally blurted out.

"To whom?" asked the man.

Twitchel was silent.

"You got anything else you want to tell me?" the man said.

"No, sir," said Twitchel.

"Good," said the man, and hung up.

After that Twitchel knew his efforts were useless, but every so often he got on Nikki's case anyway. He couldn't help himself; she was easily the most sensual woman he had ever been around, far more alluring than his wife.

Nikki Waters was of medium height and very thin, with long, sinewy limbs, prominent cheekbones, and a straight, narrow nose. She had full, pouting lips that curled back slightly, revealing perfect white teeth, large, hazel eyes, owl-like in intensity, and ash blond hair that hung over her shoulders and swung back and forth when she turned her head. But more than her actual beauty, it was her aura—the carnal electricity she carried with her into a room—that drove Twitchel crazy. When he saw her run her fingers through her hair, or arch her shoulders slightly and dig her vermilion nails into the arms of her chair as she brought her mouth up close to the microphone, the tip of her tongue running back and forth over her upper lip, he felt as though he were observing her in the throes of unrestrained passion.

Once, in the middle of a cerebral set featuring the Modern Jazz Quartet playing Bach, she put on Chuck Berry's "Wee Wee Hours." He watched through the thick glass of the studio window as she put her legs up on the desk, leaned back in her chair, lay a hand on top of either thigh, and moved her hips almost imperceptibly to the music. When the song was over, Twitchel's shirt was drenched with sweat.

And then, on top of everything else, she had that voice. It had been more than a year since Twitchel remained at the station when Nikki was on the air, but he was unable to keep himself from listening to her. Even when he was at church, on Wednesday nights, he would excuse himself from Bible study claiming he was just going to grab a quick smoke. For ten minutes he would sit in his car, hoping to hear more than music, hoping for her voice, aroused and filled with loathing for himself.

Her voice was the only connection she had to her listeners; since she never made public appearances on behalf of the station, none of them had any idea what she looked like. This was intentional. All her life, she believed, she had been valued only for her physical appearance. Finally, through a stroke of good fortune, she had been given the opportunity to enthrall people who couldn't see her. It was the next best thing, she imagined, to actually being invisible.

Neither did any of her audience know her name. She called herself "the Raven," which she understood to be the most intelligent of all birds, the bird of the gods, wise, yet tricky and even ruthless. It flew, she had read, simply for the pleasure of flight, rising to great heights, then diving toward the ground, showing off its remarkable acrobatic skill. She knew some American Indians believed the raven could will things to happen. She knew others believed it was the messenger of death. To be the Raven, to embody all of these attributes, so symbolic of great power, was a thrilling thing indeed.

There was a half-hour between the end of her show and the beginning of Cool Babba Wisdom's. During this time, the station ran national and local news, weather and sports, and a nightly fifteen-minute public-service interview program called "Central Florida Speaks." The interviews, with civic leaders, public officials, and activists representing various causes, were taped earlier in the day. When her show was over at eleven, she would usually share a cup of coffee with Cool Babba Wisdom in the station's small lounge before taking the elevator to the locked parking garage on the building's first floor. Her black Porsche 911 coupe had tinted windows, so even if someone waiting outside the garage suspected she was in the car, they could never be sure.

Occasionally, Nikki and Cool Babba would go up on the roof and have themselves a taste with their coffee, rolled from Wisdom's endless stash. Wisdom's dope was grade-A Jamaican, potent enough to paralyze the average smoker for hours, but Cool Babba could handle most of a good-sized joint, hit the mike's "on" button, and wail for three and a half hours nonstop, usually without ever sitting down. He was six-nine, weighed two-forty, and had dreadlocks hanging to his shoulders like the thrums of an enormous black mop. When he began to cavort, the whole studio would shake, but no one was about to tell him to relax.

"It run according to de arrangement of your genes," he told Nikki. "In former times, smoke geared I for sugary food and sex. Now, de significance of other things appear to I. Now, in de case of I, ganja produce de desire to play music and speak to my brothers and sisters. In de case of you, it produce de desire to reminisce. So now me do de show, you sit awhile up here and view de stars. Dat signifies things too. You de wise Raven, maybe dream up tricks to play. But be sagacious you. Don't fool de wrong one."

Someone, quoting Samuel Johnson, wrote below Nikki's picture in her high school yearbook, "It is better to live rich, than to die rich."

That was in Greenville, Mississippi, where she was born and raised. Her mother was a beautician there. She was a quietly furious woman who gave birth to four children before she was twenty-five, then hardened to granite before her husband, a tugboat pilot, who drank and beat her periodically. Nikki was her oldest child.

Nikki's father worked on the Mississippi, towing barges. She hardly knew him. By the time she was six or seven he rarely came home. He preferred to sleep on the boat, often with women he picked up in bars. Late one night, when Nikki was fourteen, he showed up at the house drunk and climbed into her bed while she slept. She awoke to a horrible burning pain between her legs and his hot foul breath on her face.

When he left, she lay there, curled in a fetal position on her fouled sheets, unable to sleep, unable to cry, staring wide-eyed into the darkness. In the morning, as soon as it was light, she took a bath, got dressed, and threw her sheets and the T-shirt she'd worn to bed into the washing machine. She was running them through for the third time when her mother awoke and asked her what the hell she was doing.

"I got my period early," Nikki told her. "I couldn't sleep so I figured I'd clean up my mess."

That night she said yes to a boy who'd been trying to sleep with her for six months. Within a year she'd slept with half a dozen others. Every one of them tried, in his way, to possess her, but she refused to be controlled. She quickly realized that her considerable sexual appeal could just as easily give her power over them, a situation she found far more to her liking.

From an early age, Nikki had been a loner, preferring the company of animals to people. When she was eleven, she began taking care of quarter horses at a local ranch in exchange for riding time. Young as she was, her remarkable, hypnotic voice could calm even the most recalcitrant animal. Before long, the owner of the ranch was giving her horses to break. The vet, too, took advantage of her way with animals. He would have her stroke their heads and talk to them while he conducted his examinations and administered drugs.

A week after her father raped her, she asked the owner of the quarter-horse ranch if she could move into the small apartment above one of the stables. Her mother didn't care, as long as Nikki stayed in school. It was one less mouth to feed. The owner, a man named Howard Hinshaw, who already pretty much considered Nikki one of his family, agreed. In addition to her work around the stable, she could baby-sit for the Hinshaws' three kids and help out around the house. In exchange she would get room and board.

Howard Hinshaw, the son of a wealthy natural-gas driller, had never worked a day in his life. He was a dilettante who originally built the apartment Nikki occupied as a studio for himself. For a time he painted landscapes there. Then, for a year or so, he did research for a book about Mississippi bargemen which he never wrote. The ranch itself was his wife Bonnie's idea. She was a psychologist.

Howard Hinshaw taught Nikki Waters about literature and art. He taught her about classical music, jazz, and the roots of rock and roll. He and Bonnie took her with them to New Orleans, New York, and Aspen. Nikki found traveling marvelous. Even with her baby-sitting duties, she got to visit Bourbon Street, hear the New York Philharmonic, and shop in Bloomingdale's, and she learned to ski. It was on a ski trip to Taos, during Christmas vacation of her senior year, that Nikki first slept with Howard Hinshaw. This was a very delicate situation for him, due to her age and the fear he had of his wife. For two years, he gave Nikki hugs, pecks on the cheek, and back rubs, all in an avuncular way, waiting for the appropriate moment to make his move.

During the trip to Taos the perfect opportunity presented itself: Bonnie's friend Stephanie Palmer twisted her ankle and the two of them decided to bag the skiing and spend a few days shopping in Santa Fe. After dinner, on the day his wife left, Howard asked Nikki to come to his room. He had something to show her, he said. In the room, he gave her a beautiful Indian necklace as a Christmas present and asked her to put it on. She was wearing a Saints football jersey and jeans, and he told her, his heart pounding in his ears, how much better the necklace would look against her bare skin. In the moment after he uttered the words he was so terrified his legs began to shake. He was convinced she would run screaming from the room and his life would be in ruins.

But Nikki didn't scream. Instead, she walked over to him, unzipped his pants, and wrapped her long, elegant fingers around his cock, all the while looking him directly in the eye. "Is this what you want?" she asked. "Is it? 'Cause if it is, you can have it, but it's gonna cost you some money, and baby, I'm not talkin' about no hundred bucks."

It took Bonnie Hinshaw six months to find them out. It was her friend Stephanie who put the idea in Bonnie's head, but once she did, Bonnie took it from there. Using her talents as a therapist, she wrung not only a confession from her husband, but a detailed account of his and Nikki's lovemaking.

She then attempted the same tactics on Nikki. The blunt, dispassionate, approach was best, she believed, to bring about a subject's acknowledgment of guilt and remorse. "I'm not going to ask *whether* or not you slept with my husband," she began. "I already know you did. What I want you to tell me is how it felt. Did you enjoy it more when you had oral sex or when you actually had intercourse?"

"You want to know if I like suckin' better than fuckin', you're gonna have to watch," Nikki said.

"How could someone who is so good with horses be so callous?" Bonnie asked. "We treated you like family. How could you bring yourself to go after my husband?" It sounded ridiculous to her the minute it was out of her mouth, but it was all she could think of. She had completely lost her grip on the situation.

"I didn't go after your husband," Nikki said. "He came after me. And he didn't even wait 'til I was eighteen. You know what the rap for statutory rape is in this state?"

Bonnie felt light-headed and was having trouble drawing a breath. They were sitting on the park bench Howard had placed beneath the giant magnolia that grew between the stable and the corral. She felt that if she didn't get out of the heat quickly she would pass out, but she couldn't move. "Would you get me a glass of ice water?" she asked Nikki.

"Bonnie, I don't live here anymore," Nikki said. She had just finished cleaning all her things out of the apartment; they were crammed into the back of the Chevy Blazer Howard had bought her in January. He told Bonnie it was an early graduation present. "I don't live here anymore, and I don't work for you anymore. You get your own goddamn glass of ice water."

"You are the most heartless human being," Bonnie said. "You're despicable."

"Right," said Nikki. Fucked if she'd tell Bonnie Hinshaw about the image of her mother she'd forever carry in her head. She had gone over to the beauty parlor one day the previous summer, just to say hello, maybe take her mom out for a cup of coffee and a piece of pie if she wasn't too busy. She was just inside the door, but her mother hadn't seen her yet. Her mother was washing a woman's hair. Her hands and wrists were covered with lather, her fingers working on the woman's scalp. "Betty, I'm just dyin' of thirst," the woman said. "Get me a Diet Pepsi out of the machine. There's money in my purse."

"Let me rinse you out first, Mrs. Richardson, then I'll be

glad to," Nikki's mother said. "It'll just be two or three minutes."

"Maybe I didn't make myself clear," the woman said. "I want a drink now, not in two or three minutes."

Nikki's mother rinsed the lather from her hands, took the change from the woman's purse and walked across the room to the soda machine. She stooped to get the can of Pepsi from behind the little plastic door, straightened, and saw her daughter. She waved and managed a smile, but not before Nikki saw the anguish and despair in her eyes.

Nikki sped from the Hinshaws' ranch, raising a cloud of dust all the way down the long driveway. She drove furiously for almost a mile before she turned off the road and parked in a pine grove where her Blazer could not be seen. She shut off the engine and rolled down the windows. Only then did she let go of the horrible, pounding knot in the back of her throat. Fucked if she'd let Bonnie Hinshaw see her cry.

"I don't want a divorce," Bonnie Hinshaw told her husband. "What I want is for you to pay that bitch off and get her out of my sight. Way out. I do not want to go into one of my favorite restaurants and see her sitting across the room. I do not want to go into a movie theater and see her standing there in the lobby. I do not want to go into a clothing store and run into her in the dressing room. I want her gone from the state of Mississippi, you understand me?"

Nikki went to New York. She knew her affair with Howard Hinshaw wouldn't last; she hadn't wanted it to. If Stephanie hadn't told Bonnie about them, she would have broken it off herself. She was out of high school now, and though she had formerly thought she would go on to college—she was accepted at Ole Miss as well as Bennington and Vassar, which had been Howard's suggestions—she now had a different plan. A photographer, working on a piece for *Vogue*, had approached her while she was watching the Hinshaw kids in the pool at the lodge in Taos.

"You ever do any modeling?" he asked her.

"Uh uh, never," she replied.

"How tall are you?" he asked.

"Five-seven," she said.

"That's a little short," he said, "but with your face they

probably would make an exception. Here's my card. Call me if you come to New York. I'm not gonna bullshit around with you. Pictures'll cost you a thousand dollars. But if things go as well for you as I think they will, it won't be long before you're making that much in an hour."

For a time it went well for her in New York. The money Howard Hinshaw put in her account was more than enough for a nice apartment, furniture, and clothes. She had photographs taken, sent her composite around, and was interviewed by several top agencies. She signed with one of them and soon began to get work. Wealthy men, wanting to be seen with her, took her to dinner, the theater, sporting events, and to the Hamptons and Vermont for weekends.

Her career as a top fashion model seemed inevitable. She was to be featured in a major national print campaign for a new line of lipstick and blush being brought out by a major cosmetics company. The president of this company had been spending a good deal of time with Nikki and had even taught her to fly his plane. Then, two days before the photo session for the cosmetics ads, Nikki got a call from Peter Pisciotta, the creative director of her agency, asking her to join him for lunch.

"I don't know how to break this to you, Nikki," he said, "but they've decided to go with another girl."

"What do you mean, another girl? Why? What the hell happened?"

"I don't know any other way to say this," he sighed. "It's your tits."

"My tits!" she screamed. "What the hell's wrong with my tits?"

"For God's sake, Nikki, keep it down," Pisciotta said. The restaurant had grown very quiet and people were staring at them. "They think yours are, you know, too small. They want a girl with lots of cleavage."

"Peter, this is an ad for lipstick, not bathing suits. What's going on? Why am I getting fucked over like this?"

"I don't know any more than I've told you," he said. "I'm sorry."

The day after Nikki got the news about her replacement, she showed up at the office of the president of the cosmetics company. She was wearing ripped jeans, an old gray

sweatshirt, and a New York Mets hat. A blue baseball
equipment bag with an orange Mets logo was slung over
her shoulder. The president's secretary was accustomed to
seeing her; for several months she had been a frequent visitor to his office. The secretary assumed Nikki's outfit was
part of some new promotion, especially since Nikki was
impeccably made up. Nikki smiled and held an index finger
up to her mouth. "It's a surprise," she whispered. She did
an exaggerated tiptoe around the secretary's desk, opened
the president's door, unzipped the bag and took out an aluminum baseball bat. "You told me you liked small tits, you
son of a bitch," she said, and started swinging.

By the time the security guards got there she had pulver-
ized three Tiffany lamps, a priceless Greek vase, and an
earthenware horse from the Tang Dynasty. She hadn't gone
after the president at all, only the antiques that had cost him
a load of money. No charges were ever pressed against
Nikki. As it was, the president was going to have his hands
full concocting an appropriate story for his wife, who had
collected the stuff.

Nikki still got work after that, enough, in fact, to make
an excellent living, but she was never going to be a star, a
supermodel bringing in a million dollars a year. Six years
went by. Several men asked Nikki to marry them; twice she
almost said yes, but at the last moment backed out. No matter what they told her, she was convinced they didn't love
her, that they only wanted to possess her, to display her like
a painting or a yacht. No man she had known ever dis-
abused her of that view. She came to terms with what she
imagined every man desired: she would be the woman they
hungered for, the incarnation of their secret lusts, but she
would never sacrifice her independence. When she met
Drew Parabrise in the summer of 1987, at a party on a
fifty-eight-foot Hatteras docked at the Seventy-ninth Street
Boat Basin in Manhattan, she was twenty-six years old and
had rejected the idea of marriage for good.

Parabrise had his back turned to her and was talking to
the man who owned the boat, a generous campaign contrib-
utor with vast real estate holdings both in Florida and New
York. A few weeks earlier, Nikki's youngest sister, twenty-
one and divorced with two children, had been killed in a

car accident and Nikki had flown to Mississippi for the funeral. At the cemetery, her father, who had been drinking heavily for three days, passed out in the hot sun. They used the hearse to rush him to the hospital. As Nikki stared at the coffin resting in the ground, she wished with all her heart it was her father lying inside. She wondered how many times he crept into her sister's bed before she ran off and eloped at sixteen. Since returning to New York, Nikki had been keeping to herself, working out at her health club and reading college catalogues. She was thinking of going back to school.

She had come to the party reluctantly with a friend who managed some of the boat owner's Manhattan property, and was telling the woman about some guys she knew in a Mississippi blues band currently playing in the Village. When Drew Parabrise paused in his discourse, he heard her speak. He turned and saw her standing there, leaning against the deck rail, in a white cotton tank dress, barefoot, her hair blowing in the stiff breeze.

"You have an incredible voice," he said.

"Thank you," she said. She knew who he was; he had been pointed out to her earlier in the evening and she had listened from a distance while he pontificated about better ways to achieve a balance of trade. Now she couldn't keep herself from laughing.

"What's so funny?" he asked.

"I was just thinkin'," she said. "Your voice reminds me of a bowling ball rolling down an alley. Every time you come to the end of a sentence I keep waitin' for this loud crash . . . you know, of the pins."

He flushed and bit his lower lip. "Do I really sound like that?" he said. She nodded. "Well, if you say so, then I guess I probably do. Maybe I've been hanging around in Washington too long. You like boats?"

"Yeah," she said. "I like boats."

"You like fast boats, I've got the keys to the one next door." He gestured with his thumb toward a fifty-foot Wellcraft Scarab moored alongside the Hatteras. "It's got three big ole turbocharged Chevy motors in it. Belongs to a friend of mine. I don't believe he'll mind if we take a ride."

"Can one person run a boat like that?" she asked. " 'Cause I don't know a damn thing about 'em."

"Ain't no problem runnin' one," he said. "The problem's affordin' one. That sumbitch cost my buddy the better part of a million dollars."

She had aimed for an immediate kill shot—this slightly overstuffed bozo's vanity—and thought she had been successful. Now she was sure. He was getting more grits and corn pone into his accent with every word. Senator Redneck himself. Next he was going to show her what a hardass he was piloting a killer boat. She was up for it. She'd never been for a ride in a drug-runner special before. A straight shot of raw horsepower. Clear her pipes. Get her blood circulating. She just hoped she wasn't about to get herself drowned. *He's gonna open this thing up and flip it over sure as shit,* she thought, as she buckled on a life vest. *In order to prove he's not an asshole he's gonna do us both in.* She could see the headline: FLORIDA SENATOR AND FASHION MODEL PERISH IN BIZARRE HUDSON RIVER SPEED-BOAT MISHAP—POLICE DO NOT RULE OUT FOUL PLAY.

But she was wrong; Drew Parabrise was as good at the helm of the Scarab as he had been loud on the deck of the Hatteras. She watched him as he brought the boat smoothly up to speed, his blond hair blowing straight back in the wind, his big hands gripping the wheel firmly but without tension. There was an easiness about him—the slight tilt of his head and relaxed balance of his athletic body, the way his eyes crinkled up at the corners, the insouciance of his rolled sleeves and flapping shirttail and bare feet below the cuffs of his expensive slacks—that somehow managed to combine recklessness with stability. In spite of herself, in spite of her general distaste for politicians, Nikki was drawn to him. The man who had pointed him out to her earlier in the evening said Parabrise would one day be president. *Yeah, sure,* she thought when she first heard him speak. *Him and every other good-looking blowhard in Washington.* Now, only an hour later, she was less skeptical.

They ran all the way down past the tip of Manhattan Island, almost to the Statue of Liberty, then doubled back to the boat basin, the guttural roar of the three racing engines

sucking her into a vortex of sound. She was hanging on too
hard and her eyes were tearing too much for her to look
over at the gauges to check their speed, but it was fast
enough to take her breath away and cause every part of
her—from the soles of her feet to her teeth—to vibrate.

By the time they returned to the slip and made fast she
had decided to sleep with him, to control this powerful senator with her body the way he controlled the boat.
"Where'd you learn to drive one of these things?" she
asked.

"I ran a patrol boat in the Mekong River for a year," he
said. "I raced boats for a while after I got back, but I didn't
do all that well. I'm probably better on the water at night
than during the day. What about you?" She didn't answer
him. Instead, she went forward into the cabin, closing the
door to the cockpit behind her. He stowed their life vests,
took the key out of the ignition, rechecked the mooring
lines and shrugged his shoulders to the stars. Then he
opened the door and stepped into the cabin after her.

She had found a small candle lantern in the galley and lit
it. In its dim light he could see her stretched across one of
the bunks, her dress pulled up around her hips. With two
fingers of one hand she held the silky material of her bikini
panties to the side, as though she were drawing back the
string of a bow, exposing herself, allowing herself access.
Her other hand moved between her legs in short, rapid
strokes, the fingertips a scarlet blur against the sparse pale
hair of her mound. Her mouth was open, and each time she
exhaled she moaned softly, tossing her head from side to
side. Then she was talking to him, whispering, so that he
had to bend close to her to hear.

"I want you in my mouth," she said. "I want you to
come in my mouth while I get myself off." Her head
stopped tossing and she looked up at him, her eyes wild
pinpoints of light. "Do it now," she said, her hand moving
faster. "Please do it now."

While he undressed, she took her panties off, then pulled
him to her with her free hand, running her tongue around
the tip of his penis, pumping him with her thumb and index
finger, using the same rhythm on him as she used on herself. "I'm your whore," she said, as he came.

When he made love to her an hour later, probing between her legs with his tongue, biting gently on her, he
asked her to say it again. "Talk to me," he said, kneeling
over her, sliding into her and watching her sinewy body
writhe beneath him in the shadows. "Say something you've
never said before."

At first she said nothing, as though she hadn't heard him.
Instead, she began moving quickly, thrusting up at him,
squeezing her nipples between her fingers. "I'm so hot,"
she said finally, "I'm so hot. I'm gonna take you in my ass.
You can have me in my ass." She felt him grow bigger as
she spoke, felt him ready to explode inside her. Then he
was out, searching with his fingers for the other opening,
wetting it for her, entering slowly. "Go ahead, baby," she
said. "I know you want me there. I know you want me in
the ass where it's so tight."

Before dawn she went topside and sat with her legs dan-
gling over the transom, staring across the river at the cliffs
along the Jersey shoreline. She wondered whether the barmaids her father brought to his tugboat talked to him the
way she'd talked to the man sleeping below, this man
whom she'd only just met but knew so well. The cabin of
the tugboat always stank of diesel fuel and rancid bacon
grease, and you could kill yourself tripping over coils of
moldy rope. The cabin of this boat was upholstered and
carpeted and smelled like the inside of a cedar closet. The
barmaids went back to the pissholes where they worked, to
the mobile homes where they lived with their mothers and
a couple of screaming kids. And what about her? Where
was she going, she wondered.

The barmaids got absolutely nothing from men like her
father beyond a few minutes of drunken sex. What would
she get from Drew Parabrise if she became involved with
him? What was it she wanted? For a while it had been
apparent to her that it was time to change her life, to set
out in a new direction. She wasn't sure yet what that direction might be, but there was no doubt in her mind that
Parabrise's connections and influence could help her im-
measurably. She wouldn't ask him for help right away.
Resolute in her determination to maintain her independence—to be in no man's debt—she decided she would

wait until he first asked for something from her. She was certain, however, that he would ask—that this United States Senator would want more from her than any of the other men she'd known. She knew that in her heart the minute she lay eyes on him. She knew it because under the cloak of political power and super-jock self-assurance that attracted her she saw weakness, the kind of weakness that preyed on people who were stronger and used them. The trick, she told herself, was to see it coming and use him back. It wouldn't be difficult. He was already convinced he had conquered her when in fact, as far as she was concerned, the reverse was true.

During the first year of their relationship, she began to cut back on her modeling. There was money in her bank account left from the sum given her by Howard Hinshaw, to which she had wisely added over the years. The total amount was substantial, but she still needed to work. The problem was she'd grown sick of earning her living posing for pictures. It got so she was ready to kill the next photographer who told her how marvelous she looked.

Parabrise asked her to move to Washington, but she refused. She found the people there insufferable, and anyway, she never wanted to run into Parabrise's wife. Instead, he came to her apartment in New York, or she met him at motels in Maryland and Virginia. She would rent the room so that he would not be recognized. Her Blazer, which she loved dearly and had named Winston, showed signs of giving up the ghost, so she sold it and bought a year-old black 911 Porsche coupe with 11,000 miles on it from a woman up in Larchmont.

Twice, Nikki flew to Orlando when Parabrise was there on business and they spent the night together on an old houseboat moored in a remote part of the St. John's River. When they couldn't be together, he would call her late at night. "Talk to me," he'd say. She could hear his breathing quicken and sense his level of excitement rise as she told him where she was touching herself and what she wanted him to do to her when they were together. Once, he asked her to pretend she was with another woman. That night she talked for less than thirty seconds before he came. She had never had sex with another woman. After she hung up and was lying alone in the dark she thought about what it would actually be like until she fell asleep.

During that first year, Nikki applied to a couple of colleges in the New York area, was accepted, but changed her mind about going. Something else far more intriguing began to take shape in her mind. The seed was planted by Parabrise, who told her over and over that he'd never listened to anyone with a voice like hers. He told her if she were a senator she could propose a bill making Cuba the fifty-second state and it would pass.

Other men had made similar remarks to her over the years, women too, but she never thought that much about it, probably because her looks drew so much attention. Now that she had decided to quit modeling, however, she began to think about it all the time. Why not earn her living with her voice? Every other model she knew wanted to work in movies or television. What she wanted, she finally decided, was something completely different. She wanted to get into radio. She would enroll in broadcasting school and do it right. Then she would get a job talking to people who knew nothing about her body or her face or her life. She would be a voice in the night, playing the music she loved—jazz, blues, baroque chamber music—stuff you never heard mixed together anymore. She would read poetry. She would be a spell-binder, a conjurer, the messenger of imagination. She had already decided she would be the Raven.

She was wise enough to know it would not be easy to get someone to set her loose like that. The kind of position she wanted, the lack of control she sought, barely existed in this age of prepackaged, demographically ordained radio formats, especially for someone straight out of broadcast school, no matter how good she looked. But she was not about to go through the rigmarole associated with obtaining a broadcaster's license in order to spend her days as an eye-in-the-sky traffic bimbo, waiting for an opportunity to move up to button-pusher for preselected Top Forty discs. Nor was she about to be the female foil for a couple of jokers doing morning drive-time. That kind of crap was worse than runway work in the garment district. The job she had in mind, the show she'd do any way she damn well pleased, already played with regularity in her head. She was convinced it would be her salvation. When the time was right, she would turn to Parabrise and he would help her get it.

She knew what kind of legislation his committee had jurisdiction over. She'd done some research in the library and read about his efforts to deregulate the communications industry, the same way he'd helped deregulate the airlines, the railroads, and interstate trucking. She knew he had powerful friends who'd been able to build huge chains of radio and television stations, to create virtual monopolies with his help. She'd even met a couple of them, though of course she'd played dumb and just smiled while they argued about whether Texas, Mississippi, or Georgia grew the best-looking women on the face of God's earth.

When Parabrise finally did approach her it was in January, on a bitter cold night, in a run-down motel outside of Rockville, Maryland, just after they made love. "Nikki, I have a very big favor to ask of you," he said. "It would mean a lot to me if you'd do it."

"That's what friends are for," she said. She got up and walked over to the chair where she'd left her handbag, took out a brush, and began brushing her hair. When her instincts proved correct it always filled her with incredible nervous energy and she couldn't lie still. "I just hope it's fun, this favor of yours."

"The thing is, I can't be the one to tell you about it," he said. "Someone else will have to do that."

"You mean it's so dirty you don't want to be involved, or you just ain't got the guts to spit it out?" She was glad they were in the dark. She was already sorry she'd betrayed so much with her voice and was sure the disgust was registered on her face.

"I can't be connected. That way, later on . . ."

This was not at all the way she'd envisioned it going down. For all her savvy, she had somehow naively assumed it would be something they'd do together, something concerning political pressure or subtle influence in which her presence would smooth the consummation of an arrangement. She hadn't believed he would use her so crudely. Now she felt her whole plan slipping out of control. "What the hell is this, some fucking arms deal? A bank job? You

want me to take somebody out? 'Cause, honey, that kind of
shit's way out of my league." He was even more of a cow-
ard than she'd imagined, and his paranoia was causing her
to panic. That had to be it. She would calm down and see
where it led. She took deep breaths and concentrated.

"All right," she said. "Tell me what you want me to do
and I'll listen. And then you're gonna listen to what I want
you to do for me."

The morning on which John Varney was to meet Nikki
Waters had not been a pleasant one for him at all. At quarter past six his wife, Kirsten, Miss Hawaiian Tropic
runner-up, several years removed, woke him with the star-
tling news that she was pregnant. An hour later, he received
a phone call from one of his assistants informing him that
a Hong Kong real estate deal in which Varney had a substantial interest had fallen through. Then, on the way to
meet the woman from New York, his brand-new Cadillac
Allante convertible suddenly stopped dead. Varney coasted
onto the grass at the side of the road, grabbed the car
phone, and called the service manager at the dealership.
"Bring a tow truck and have someone follow you with another car," he said. "And step on it. I'm late for an appointment."

John Varney's father started out as an inventor, but three
years of his work was stolen by a crooked partner. Crushed,
he took a job teaching chemistry at Valdosta State College,
in Georgia, where he remained for thirty-five years. When
his son was accepted at Princeton with a full scholarship,
the elder Varney gave him some advice. "Buy expensive
clothes, even if you have to borrow the money, and never
trust anyone. You're smart and you're mean. You'll figure
out the rest."

To the advice his father gave him, John Varney immediately added the importance of making the right connections.
Using those connections with cold-blooded cleverness, together with an innate ability to construct deals, he built a
considerable fortune before he was thirty. He got his start
by marrying the daughter of Mansel Oigarden, founder of
Oigarden Juice, the largest citrus processor in Florida.
Three months after the wedding, Mansel Oigarden provided

the loan guarantees that enabled Varney to take over his
first bank. It was a very small savings-and-loan institution,
but it was strategically located in Winter Haven, and soon
attracted many of the citrus growers' business. It didn't hurt
Varney any that these growers sold much of their product to
Oigarden Juice. When he divorced his first wife five years
later, Varney owned two more banks, a 6,000-acre citrus
grove, and the largest shopping mall between Jacksonville
and Miami Beach.

While he waited, Varney put the top down on the Allante
and lit a cigar. These were minor annoyances, really, that
had begun his day. The real estate deal had been shaky
from the beginning and he had all but written it off anyway.
His current wife would get rid of the baby, he'd make sure
of that. And the car? What the hell, his bank owned the
dealership. He could drive a new car every week if he
wanted to bother. The important thing was not to let any of
it get in the way of the business at hand, the woman from
New York, Parabrise's friend, another factor to be reckoned
into the equation.

When he met Drew Parabrise in 1976, during Parabrise's
first run for the U.S. Senate, Varney decided the time was
right to apply the same tactics that made him rich to his
next objective, the accumulation of power. In general, people did not like John Varney. He knew that and was not
bothered by it at all. It precluded, however, his running for
office. That didn't bother him either; the idea of speaking
to masses of voters made him sick. He'd simply connect
with someone people instinctively wanted to represent them
and go from there. In 1982, he managed Parabrise's successful reelection campaign. By 1988, he had moved into
the background, working as a fund-raiser, constructing an
ever-growing network of supporters, negotiating secret bargains, widening the sphere of influence that centered
around Drew Parabrise.

The wild card in all of this was Chotoku Nakama, the
mysterious Oriental, who seemed to have his own sphere of
influence, nebulous as smoke. Varney, who prided himself
on his ability to read people, to find their weak spots and
use them to his advantage, could find no weak spot in
Nakama at all. What he knew was that Nakama's empire

easily rivaled Mansel Oigarden's, though despite his efforts
he could never penetrate its shell. He knew too that when
Nakama spoke, no matter how obliquely, those he spoke to
listened. Nakama was the one connection with an incorrupt-
ible power base of his own. It might be that someday he
would have to have the Oriental killed, but for the present
Nakama was essential to Varney's plan. What John
Varney's prejudice kept him from understanding was that
Chotoku Nakama had an even more ambitious plan and
considerably more influence than Varney realized. At any
rate, it was Nakama who had suggested using Nikki Waters,
when Varney proposed his scheme involving Steakhouse
Papa, the horse he had recently acquired and syndicated. It
was Nakama who somehow knew all about this female
friend of Drew Parabrise, right down to her expertise with
animals. And it was Nakama who, through a messenger,
told Parabrise to approach her and arranged the meeting to
which Varney was now an hour late. Varney was also almost certain the Oriental owned the radio station in
Orlando where Nikki Waters was going to work.

John Varney entered the restaurant of a country club in
Longwood, north of Orlando, and saw Nikki Waters at the
far end of the bar. She was wearing a gray silk suit with an
exceedingly short skirt and open-toed, high-heeled sandals.
Her legs were crossed and she had the heel of one shoe
hooked over a rung of the bar stool. Her presence was
causing palpable tension in the room. He nodded to her and
she walked with him to a small table next to a bay window
overlooking the eighteenth green.

"Whatcha drinkin'?" he asked her when the waiter came
over.

"I'm having a Diet 7-Up," she said. "With a twist. But
you go ahead. You look like you could use a drink."

He ordered a double Stolichnaya on the rocks and stared
down at the three middle-aged women with skin like harness leather who were getting set to putt. When his drink
came, he finished it in three gulps.

"You'll love Orlando," he said. "It's historically unique.
First time in the annals of civilization a metropolis has been
built on the coattails of an amusement park. Of course, it
doesn't have the cultural attributes of a city like New York.

I know you're gonna miss all that, a woman of the arts such as yourself. But then . . ." He gestured out the window with his hand. "You can play golf twelve months out of the year. You like golf?"

"I haven't made the decision yet about whether I'm movin' here or not, John," Nikki said. She raised her eyebrows and licked her upper lip. This guy didn't just hate women, he hated everybody. "You don't mind if I call you John, do you? Or would you rather I called you Bubba. I mean are we doin' Princeton today, or is it gonna be the Georgia woods?"

"I didn't think there was a question as to whether," he said.

"That why you kept me sittin' at the bar for an hour? Don't be givin' me no caught-in-traffic bullshit. There's a phone in here, and I know a man such as yourself gotta have one in his car. By the way, I'm real hungry. You mind if I get myself somethin' to eat in here?"

"Be my guest," he said, signaling the waiter.

"No, John, I don't think I will. Be your guest, that is. I believe I'll buy my own lunch. I already looked at the menu," she told the waiter. "Let me have a turkey breast on whole wheat with lettuce, tomato, and mustard. And another Diet 7-Up. You havin' something, John?" He shook his head. "Well, then bring him another vodka."

When the waiter left, she leaned back in her chair, cocked her head to one side, and smiled. "If you'll excuse me for a minute I think I'll use the ladies' room." A number of the club members stopped eating to watch her as she walked by. Varney sipped his vodka and gazed out the window. The three golfers were gone and the green was empty except for two squirrels that were chasing each other around the pin. Parabrise had been right about her looks and her voice. He had been right about her fierce independence and her brains. What he had neglected to include in his description of Nikki Waters was that she was as tough as any man Varney had ever met. He was going to have to promise a lot more than a job at a radio station to get what he needed out of her. Who knows? Maybe somewhere down the road he'd find a place for her in one of his banks.

Nikki's food was on the table when she returned and she

ate it with gusto, only pausing to say "Mmm, good turkey, John. You want a bite?" Varney declined.

"You notice the black Porsche in the parking lot when you came in? The 911 Turbo?" she said when she finished and the waiter took her plate. "The one with the New York plates? The one I drove down here all by myself? I bought that car for cash, John, with my own money. Part of the money I earn as a well-paid model. The same money that pays for my clothes, my jewelry, my furniture, everything I own. The same money that pays for the motel rooms I stay in when I vacation in the area of Washington, D.C. Now then, our mutual friend, the venerable senator from this here state, whose name we're not gonna mention because of the delicacy of this situation, that person came to *me*, you understand, not the other way around. He came to me and he said, 'Nikki, I have a big favor to ask of you.' So now you tell me what the fuck it is y'all want me to do, and then I'll let you know whether I'm interested, or whether I'm gonna climb into the car that I bought with my money and drive on back to New York, with its cultural attributes and seasonal but nonetheless challenging golf."

"For starters, we want you to kill a horse," John Varney said.

Access to the stall was easy; she was part of the group traveling with the assemblage of horses to the race, moving in and out of the barn area with a hundred other people: grooms, drivers, owners, trainers, vets. She wore little makeup, kept her hair in a braid, and always wore her credentials, encased in plastic, pinned to the front pocket of her hooded jacket. When the time came she moved quickly, talking to the animal softly as she knelt in front of him. Expertly, she hit the vein, injecting fifty cc's of synthetic adrenaline into his bloodstream. Immediately, she left the track, driving fast to be as far away as possible when the race began.

She never looked into the horse's eyes. She couldn't bear to, knowing what she'd done, but she saw them anyway, the next day, in the paper. There'd been a photographer with a telephoto lens and a motor drive shooting the horses as they came down the back stretch where it happened. His picture, freezing the horror of that moment, was published around the world. He caught the sulky, pitching sideways, and the driver, Lambert D'Artigue, arms extended, flying through the air, about to crash into another sulky's wheel. He caught the horse, front legs buckled, his chest and twisted neck plowing furrows in the dirt. And he got the eyes, the eyes of Steakhouse Papa, looking skyward, wide with terror, filled with agony from his exploding heart.

IX

$\blacklozenge$

Billy Roseman returned to Orlando from up north the day Steakhouse Papa died. That night he got drunk and cried himself to sleep on the floor of his office. The next day he went back to work.

He met Nikki Waters six weeks later in front of his barn. He had turned his back on an ornery colt named Mr. Wiggler, and the horse had knocked him on his face in the mud. When he got up she was standing there in a sweatshirt and jeans, her hair tied up in a bandanna. "That'll teach you to work around horses in a pink shirt," she said.

"Horses are like people," he said. "Some of 'em are very sensitive. If you yell at 'em they'll fold up like a flower. This bastard here you gotta treat like he was the town bully. You turn your back on him he knocks you on your ass. But sometimes I forget."

"What's that got to do with working in a pink shirt?"

He wiped some of the mud off his face with his sleeve and studied Nikki more closely. Women came around the track all the time, but not too many who looked this good in work clothes. "I always wear pink shirts," he said. "Work. Play. It's an old family tradition. My name's Billy Roseman." He brushed his hand off on his jeans and extended it. "Sorry about the dirt."

"I'm Nikki," she said. "Nikki Waters." His hand was hard and callused, his smile a little roguish, but his eyes were sad. "I didn't mean to sneak up on you. I was just driving by and saw the barns. The gate was open so I drove on in. It's quite a place, right here in the middle of town."

"They keep threatening to close it, but there's still enough ole boys around who won't let 'em. Where you from?"

114

"Mississippi originally, but I lived in New York for years. I just moved here a couple of weeks ago."

"I gotta go up to the track," he said. "There's a filly I want to watch jog. Take a walk with me."

They sat on a bench in front of the white rail fence that bordered the mile oval of red clay and dirt. The morning was cool. Thick mist swirled around the track. Horses passed them going in either direction, some at a slow, easy jog, others at a faster training pace. The drivers, grooms, and other trainers, riding on training sulkies, or jog carts, sat huddled in parkas or hooded sweatshirts, talking softly to the horses. A few people with stopwatches sat on nearby benches or up on the topmost fence rail.

"Listen to their hooves," Roseman told her. "If it sounds like they're running across your living-room carpet, then the track is just right. If their hooves sound hollow, then it's too hard and they can hurt themselves. This track, it's never too hard. They keep it perfect. That's why it's the best place to train in the world. You know, these horses are just babies. They can get hurt real easy. They weigh what? Maybe twelve hundred pounds? But the bones in their legs are no bigger than yours or mine."

"I know that," she said.

"You been around horses?"

"I worked on a quarter-horse ranch for four years. I've been around horses since I was a little girl."

"Then you know about what I was tellin' you at the barn. About personalities. About a horse's individuality. That's the key to success in training a racehorse. That and havin' an eye for good ones in the first place. And luck. They get sick. They get hurt. Ain't nothin' you can do about that.

"See, there's six hundred and something horses training here at Ben White. A hundred or so will make it as racehorses. So that's less than twenty percent that even get to race. Maybe fifty'll make it as stakes horses—the ones that run for the real money. Me, I was always poor. I couldn't afford to support a stable full of horses that would never run for me. The ones I do buy I work with the way you'd work with a great pitcher or a quarterback. You can't ex-

pose them to too much too soon. You don't want to damage
their confidence. Why are you looking at me like that?"

"I never heard anyone talk about horses that way," she
said. "It's been a long time since I heard anyone talk about
their *work* like that, to tell you the truth. It's refreshing. I
used to be a model. I was only in it for the money. Now
I have this new job and I think I feel about it like you do
about yours. I *want* to feel like that about it."

"What do you do?"

"I don't want to tell you now. Maybe when I know you
better."

"What are you, a hooker? A dope dealer?"

"Gimme a break," she laughed. "Tell me more about these
trotters."

"Well, for one thing, they ain't all trotters. Trotters hit
the ground with the front foot on one side the same time
they hit with the back foot on the other. That's called an al-
ternating gait. Most of these horses are pacers. Their front
and rear feet on the same side hit the ground together. Pacers are faster and race for the big money, the big-stakes
races. Trotters are more elegant and harder to train."

"Which kind do you have?"

"Almost all of mine are pacers. It's the economics of it.
Aristocrats can afford to train trotters. If their horses don't
make any money, what the hell do they care, at least they
look good. People like me, we don't get to the big show
pretty soon we disappear altogether."

"You get to the big show a lot?"

"I told you how many of these horses ever get to race.
I get seventy-five percent of mine to the track, and that's no
bullshit. I mean, I know that sounds like braggin', but it's
true."

"How many do you have here now?" she asked.

"Oh, baby, that's a sore subject with me right at the moment. I went out and got thirty-seven yearlings this season.
Fifteen I own outright. The rest I own a piece of with other
people—investors—guys who call me at all hours of the
night and drive me nuts. It's the most I've ever trained,
'cause I thought I was a millionaire." He laughed and
scratched his head. For a minute he stared out across the
track. "Well, I *was* a millionaire, on paper. Now I'm not so

sure. My future's in the hands of the insurance company. And this guy who owns a bank. Or a couple of banks. He's hard to pin down. You can't imagine how much money I owe. See, I had this horse who died ... Of course you never know, one of the ones in my barn now might be a winner, but not like him. I'll never get another one like that. Not in this lifetime."

She still had no idea who he was. John Varney had never mentioned Billy Roseman's name to her, nor, in her several trips to Orlando, had Drew Parabrise ever spoken to her about this track. She was out for an early-morning ride, checking out the town, her new home, when she stumbled on it, down off Lee Road. It was in the middle of a bunch of fast-food restaurants and liquor stores and automobile repair shops, where you'd never in a thousand years expect to find rows and rows of barns, and old guys in tweed caps with stopwatches, and dozens of horses circling a track in the mist.

She was stopped at the traffic light next to the main gate. As she sat there, she could hear the horses snorting and whinnying to each other. When the light changed she drove on by. She didn't want to turn in. She was afraid to see the horses' eyes. But something pulled at her, some indefinable longing to be near the animals, to smell them, to listen to their clamor in the stalls, so she made a U-turn and went back. Then she had been attracted to his barn, to the outrageousness of the blue-and-yellow awning running the length of it, shading the stalls, and by the logo on the side, the horse wearing a holster and a six-gun above the words QUICKDRAW STABLE. She knew nothing about standardbreds. She had only been to a harness racing track one time, six weeks before.

She walked back to the barn with Billy, listening to him talk about his horses. He was totally without pretense, oblivious to the dried mud that caked his shirt and jeans and flecked his hair. *This guy's all right,* she thought. *I could use a friend like him in this new place.* The trepidation she had felt on her arrival at the track was gone. What she had done, what she had destroyed, was for the moment as indistinct as the far side of the mist-shrouded track. Then they walked into his office and she saw the poster, three feet by four feet, hanging over his desk. In it he was standing next to the horse, grinning, with his arm draped over its neck. In his other hand he held a gold-plated revolver, pointed to the sky. "Quickdraw Stable," it said across the poster's bottom. "Billy Roseman, owner, trainer, driver. Steakhouse Papa, World Champion Two-Year-Old Pacer, 1988." The horse's bearing was regal, his eyes were clear and defiant. He was the best and he knew it.

She was back the next day. "I think you could use another hand," she said. "I work cheap. Buy me a beer and a pizza on Sunday night."

Two, sometimes three days a week she showed up at his barn. She bathed horses for him. She hot-walked them when they came off the track. She cleaned out stalls. Because of her schedule at the station, she rarely got to the barn before nine in the morning, but even at that hour there were horses in his stable that still needed to be jogged, and soon she was doing that as well. Within a month she was helping him with his books, which were a complete mess.

She refused to take a penny from him. "Look," she said, when he tried to pay her. "Grooms make forty bucks a day, so that's what? Eighty a week you'd have to pay me? I have plenty of money, Billy. I saved a ton from when I was modeling and I get a good salary now. You need the eighty a whole lot more than I do."

Almost every Sunday night, though, she was there at his barn around seven o'clock when he would come to check the horses. She'd let him buy them beer and pizza and they would sit in the office, or out in front of the stalls if the weather was nice, and eat and drink and talk. She told him about Mississippi, about the river and the Delta blues bands she loved. She told him about modeling in New York, how she almost made it to the very top, and about this very important man, high up in the government, she saw from time to time, though she never mentioned Drew Parabrise by name. She swore him to secrecy and told him about her job at the radio station. "I won't ever say a word to anyone," he told her, "but I already knew. I hear you talk enough."

She asked about his wife. "My wife," Billy said. "Beverly my wife. I knew her for three years. She's very pretty. Period. She taught aerobics at this gym where I train sometimes. She wouldn't even go out with me. So of course, being a typical asshole, I fell madly in love with her. So then Steakhouse won and I went nuts and bought all this shit, the house, the condo, the cars, and one night I show up at the gym with the Ferrari and now she's talkin' to me. She says, 'Take me for a ride in it.' I say, 'Hop in.' It's like, you know, my dream come true. Cowboy Billy in his Ferrari with Miss America. I say, 'Where you want to go?' She says, 'Honey, we can go wherever you like.' So we drove to Las Vegas and got married. Now she lies out by the pool at the house and watches the soaps and teaches aerobics. She doesn't come here much. Only when she needs money to go shopping. She says she doesn't like the smell of horseshit. My mother met Beverly once and said if she had any brains she'd be dangerous. She said as things stood I didn't have to worry; as soon as Beverly got done spending all my money she'd go away."

"You drove to Las Vegas? From Orlando?"

"Yeah. Nonstop. Spent one night at Caesar's Palace and drove back. I had a week with nothing to do . . . before I went and spent even more money I didn't really have at the yearling sale in Lexington. So, what the hell, you know? Drive to Vegas and get married. It seemed logical, given my state of mind at the time."

"Why'd you name him Steakhouse Papa?" It was the first time she had mentioned the horse. As she asked him she could feel her throat go dry and the words catch, but she had to know. It was May. In a week he would be shipping horses north for the racing season. Unless she flew up to one of the tracks to watch him drive, she wouldn't see him for six months.

"Why'd I name him Steakhouse Papa?" He sighed. They were sitting in front of the barn in a couple of old lawn chairs. An owl flew over and perched on a high branch of a pine tree. A full moon hung over the track and they could see the outline of the owl's body in the moonlight. Billy rapped the heels of his boots a few times on the concrete to clean off the mud. "Owl watchin' you's good luck. Or is it bad luck? I forget," he said. "So. The naming of Steakhouse Papa. Good story.

"As usual I was broke. This is a year and a half ago,

we're talkin' about, at the time of the yearling sales. But I
went to the sales anyway because ... well, bein' broke in
the horse business is like bein' broke in the oil business—
there's always a chance you can find a backer. Anyway,
I'm stayin' far away from the high-priced horses, seventy-
five grand and up, seein' if maybe I can spot a good one
among the bargains. I walk here, I go there, I nose around,
nada, zilch. This goes on for a couple of days. Then I see
this colt, not very big, but he's put together, his proportions
are right, and I get a feeling. They wanted forty-eight thousand for him. Me, I'm forty-eight thousand light, but I buy
him anyway. Now I have twenty-four hours to come up
with the money.

"I go to Worthington Wadhams, one of the Wadhams
brothers, owners of the second-biggest standardbred stable
in the country. Partners with Barbara Gunderson in Iroquois
Farms, the largest breeding farm of standardbreds in the
world. 'Worthington, I've found a wonderful colt,' I tell
him. 'I need fifty thousand worth of credit. You know I'm
good for it.' 'Billy, you've always paid your debts,' he
says, 'and I respect you for that. And I know you're a man
of your word. I'll extend you credit for twenty-five thousand.'

"The man's worth a hundred million, I could have spit in
his eye, but I smile and say, 'Thank you very much, sir.'
Twenty-five's better than zero. Now I'm on the phone like
a lunatic. I'm callin' every son of a bitch in America I ever
did a favor for, every person who might remotely want to
invest in a racehorse. And I'm striking out. Then I get a
bright idea.

"When my mother moved here to Orlando from Texas
she was seventeen. I was a baby. We lived with my uncle
Marvin who owned the restaurant at this track, the café
over there by the maintenance building. My uncle Marvin,
may he rest in peace, owned a lot of other things besides
the restaurant, but that was his first love, that's where he
hung his hat. In the old days it wasn't just a horseman's
joint, it was the hub of political movin' and groovin' for
this whole town. Everybody who was anybody ate in there.
Seven-thirty any weekday morning you could'a dropped a

bomb on it and there wouldn't have been anyone left to run Orlando.

"One of my uncle's friends was a man named Charlie Zonderman. Charlie Zonderman owned the kosher butcher shop in town. Now, in those days, there weren't a whole lot of Jews in Orlando. Charlie Zonderman was lucky if he made ten grand a year. He drove a car that was so old it had a rumble seat. One day, this is like nineteen sixty-two or sixty-three, Charlie comes to my uncle with a plan he's developed to do a little better financially. He wants to open a restaurant. He's got an idea for a place where you can buy one thing: steak. No ribs, no chops, no chicken, no shrimp, just steak. You can have a baked potato, salad, and steak. The best steak in central Florida. For dessert you can have three things: apple pie, ice cream, or apple pie *and* ice cream. 'Marvin,' he says to my uncle, 'it can't miss. And get this. I got a deal on a lease out on Colonial. I sign for five years, I get the first year for nothing.'

"Charlie isn't finished. He hits my uncle with the kicker. See, I never knew my father, so I always called my uncle 'Papa.' People comin' into the restaurant, they thought it was cute, so pretty soon everyone got to callin' him 'Papa' too. That was his nickname. 'Lend me fifteen thousand dollars to get started,' Charlie Zonderman says to my uncle, 'and I'll name the place after you. I'll call it Papa's Steakhouse.'

" 'Tell 'em you'll sign for seven years,' my uncle says to Charlie. 'If they give you free rent for two.' I think Charlie eventually quit opening new branches when he got to nine or maybe ten. Five years ago, General Foods bought him out for twenty million.

"My bright idea was I called Charlie Zonderman, who is now eighty-one years old and lives in Israel, and I said, 'Charlie, how about you lend me twenty-five grand so's I can buy this horse that's gonna be champion of the world. I'll name him after your restaurants. I'll call him Steakhouse Papa.' See, I figured that sounded a little tougher than Papa's Steakhouse. 'It'll be like we're honoring my uncle Marvin in a way, too.' "

* * *

They never made love, never kissed, never even held hands. All they did was talk. She thought about what she would do if he made a pass at her. She rehearsed the words she would still him with at first. "Wait," she would say. "Wait, there's something I have to tell you before we do anything. There's something you need to know."

But he never made a move. "Don't you want me?" she screamed at him in her mind. "Don't you want to pull me into the dark horse smell of an empty stall and take me standing up against one of the walls? You could do that to me. You could do anything you want, after I tell you."

When he left to go north, when all of the harnessmen were gone and the long rows of barns were empty and the track itself was rutted and grooved from the summer rains, she still came there, now and then, in the early morning, and sat alone in his office, staring at the poster above the desk. She looked at Billy in that picture, triumphant, his long, lanky body leaning against Steakhouse Papa, smiling like he didn't have a care in the world, and thought about him now, with his melancholy eyes and his self-deprecating wit.

"I wanted to be the high-plains drifter," he had told her, "but instead I sold out to the dude who owned the bank. I fuckin' blew it, Nikki."

"Yeah," she had said, "but you still come to work every day, you treat every one of your horses like a winner, and you haven't lied to a single person who's invested in your stable. Not even the ones who lie to you. You have integrity, Billy. I can't say that about a whole lot of people I've met."

It was that honesty, that commitment to a code of honor in spite of his misfortune, in spite of his shattered dreams, that drew her to him in a way she could never be drawn to a man like Drew Parabrise, powerful as he was. There was a purity to Billy Roseman, a total lack of guile, that a man like Parabrise wouldn't even understand.

Once or twice that spring she almost told him what she had done anyway, even though he never touched her, but she stopped, unable to speak, horrified by the words herself. When he returned to Florida in the fall, his stable was only a fraction of the size it had been the year before and he really didn't need her help. Just the same, she resumed where she'd left off, showing up at the barn twice during the week to bathe and walk the horses, and on Sunday nights to eat pizza and talk. Nikki thought constantly about confessing and about telling Billy she had fallen in love with him—something she had never told a man before—but Billy's wife had left him by then, the few horses he had didn't look all that promising, and Billy was despondent.

"I'll wait until things smooth out a little for him," she thought. "In the meantime I'll just be there for him. As a friend."

In truth, she didn't tell Billy about Steakhouse Papa because she knew he would never forgive her.

X

Roland Troy's models were all mounted on sheets of half-inch plywood that slipped perfectly into the bed of his El Camino. The bed had a custom-fitted tonneau cover completely sealing it from the elements, so even if Troy were caught in a severe thunderstorm while transporting his work, the model always remained dry. Troy brought his models to the rear of the county courthouse, backing the El Camino into the same drive-in entrance used by the sheriff's department to deliver prisoners from the county jail. There, the routine never varied. Harold Freeman, the security guard stationed at the rear entrance, gave Troy a snappy salute, said, "Mr. Roland Troy, a pleasure to see you again," and turned the key activating the automatic opener for the bulletproof-steel overhead door. Once inside the building, Troy shut off the El Camino's engine, climbed out, and with Freeman's assistance loaded the model onto a collapsible metal table with wheels. Next, Troy took a Polaroid camera from his vehicle and snapped a picture of the model with Harold Freeman standing next to it, holding a card on which the model's identification number was written. Harold Freeman then gave Troy a receipt for the model, Troy thanked him, and left. Harold Freeman, he knew, would immediately lock the model away and let no one near it until it made its debut.

The reason for this elaborate process was that one of Troy's early models somehow disappeared before the trial in which it was to be used. It was a model of the exterior of a motel with twenty-four units along with the interior of one room where a forty-year-old drug dealer and his fifteen-year-old girl friend had been gunned down. Fortunately, the loss was discovered in time for Troy to make a duplicate, but there was no record of the first model having been received at the courthouse, and, despite the entreaties of Teddy Chambers, the state attorney and Roland Troy's old and trusted friend, Troy refused to be paid twice. "Don't sweat it, Teddy," Troy said. "I ain't doin' this for the money anyhow. We'll just devise a simple tracking system for the boogers so it won't happen again." Chambers had relented, but insisted on at least buying Troy a good dinner.

"You got anything coming in?" Troy asked Harold Freeman.

"Not this afternoon, no, sir. Not that I'm aware of," said Freeman. "Why?"

" 'Cause if not, I'll just leave my car where it is," Troy said. "Otherwise I'll pull it outside. I'm going upstairs for a few minutes."

Harold Freeman raised his eyebrows but said nothing. Something big must be up, but it was none of his business. In all the years Roland Troy had been bringing his models to the courthouse he hadn't once gone up into the musty old brick building filled with courtrooms, judges' chambers, offices, and rooms lined floor to ceiling with files. Every time, after the two of them loaded the model onto the rolling table and took the picture, Troy got back into his El Camino, said adìos amigo, and drove away. In the old days he was up there all the time, rumbling around, taking care of business, but not anymore.

Freeman had heard the story about Troy's last appearance upstairs several times, once from the bailiff who witnessed it. It had been at the arraignment of a man named Timmy "Big Bull" Hammond, a six-five, 280-pound logger from Defuniak Springs, up in the Florida Panhandle. In addition to logging, Hammond ran a bootlegging business and had killed at least three men, but was never convicted since no one could ever be found to testify against him. He came to Orlando with his girl friend, intending to commit a couple of robberies so he could buy a bar. In the space of a week, Hammond's girl friend, a very pretty young woman named Rita Boland, lured two well-to-do men she met in bars into the woods with the promise of sex. Hammond, who had followed Rita and the men in his own car, robbed them, then shot them dead.

Roland Troy was the chief investigator for the sheriff's department back then, a legendary homicide detective who operated alone and had solved nearly two hundred murders in just over ten years. He sat quietly in one of the court-rooms and listened as Orin Whitman, the former state attorney, told the presiding judge there wasn't enough evidence to warrant a charge of first-degree murder. "Your Honor," Whitman said. "The State moves that Timothy Hammond be charged with one count of manslaughter."

This was the fourteenth case in a row he brought to Whitman—all, in Troy's opinion, unquestionable first-degree murders—in which the charges had been reduced to manslaughter, or at best murder in the second degree. "There isn't enough evidence for a first-degree indictment," he told Troy in every instance. Orin Whitman made no bones about his desire to become governor of Florida, and held up his admirable conviction rate as an indication of his suitability for the job. To Roland Troy, Whitman was nothing more than an opportunist, and a cowardly one at that.

It had taken Roland Troy fifteen months to find Big Bull Hammond and compile the evidence needed to convict him. At one point he had gone undercover in Defuniak Springs, hanging out at Hammond's bar, a road-house called Bull's Run. The bar was filled with all manner of cutthroats and desperadoes who would think nothing of shooting a cop and dumping his body in the swamp. While undercover, he risked his life by confiding in Rita Boland, who had become pregnant. Convinced by Troy that the only hope she had of raising her child in freedom was to testify against Hammond, she agreed to turn state's evidence. Troy promised to relocate her once the trial was over.

"One minute he was sittin' there quiet as could be, ob-serving what was goin' on," the bailiff told Harold Free-man. "Next minute he's got this snub-nosed thirty-eight stuck in Bull Hammond's ear. He must've had the gun strapped to his leg. 'Don't even think about goin' for it,' he says to me. 'Don't anybody in here think of moving.' Then he looks up at the judge. 'Two young men this man mur-

dered, Your Honor,' he says. 'Two decent young men in
this here community. Murdered them in cold blood. How
would you feel about a charge of manslaughter if one of
them had been your son? Your son was in the same bar as
one of the victims, you know that, don't you? What I ought
to do is blow his fuckin' brains all over this courtroom. Do
the state a favor. Do humanity a favor. But I won't. I
changed my mind. You and this chickenshit state attorney
can dance with him. He'll be out in two years. Never know,
he might decide to kill you next.'

"He stuck the snubby in his pocket and walked out," the
bailiff said. "I wasn't about to go after him. Not me. Not
after that boy. Way I heard it, he turned in his badge the
next day. They never did nothin' to him neither. State attorney was gonna run for governor and didn't want no big investigation of his office. Six months later Whitman was
gone and Chambers came in. Six months after that, Troy
started buildin' those models. But he don't ever come upstairs. You 'bout the only dude around this place ever gets
to see him. He was somethin' else, that Roland Troy, back
when he was investigatin' murders. Man could track a
mealworm through a silo full of rice."

"It's good to see you, Roland," Teddy Chambers said. He
was sitting in his shirtsleeves with his feet up on the desk.
Troy leaned over the desk, shook his hand, and sat down in
the leather easy chair across from him.

"Nice suspenders," Troy said.

"They were a Christmas gift from Maxine. I've worn
'em 'bout every day since, but she still says Daddy do you
really like 'em every time I come down to breakfast. Ain't
as easy convincing teenage girls as it used to be."

"I don't remember it used to be," said Troy. "Not for you
or me. Unless you knew some you never told me about."

"I figured you'd be calling me, maybe come over to the
house," Chambers said. "I never thought you'd come up
here." He shook his head, sighed, and shrugged his shoulders. "It's Clara I feel bad for. Smitty told me he ran into
her down at the jail. That kid of hers. He could train the be-
jesus out of a standardbred, but sooner or later he was

bound to step into something with no bottom. Never figured him for murder though."

"Clara says he didn't do it," Troy said.

"And you never heard anyone say that before, huh? 'Cept about two hundred thousand times."

"I just came from the county jail."

"And Billy says he didn't do it either," Chambers said. "What a surprise."

Teddy Chambers was one of the smartest men Roland Troy knew, as well as one of the most scrupulous. He was a small, compactly built man who still trained regularly at a local boxing gym. He presented himself with good-ole-boy simplicity, but had religiously read at least a book a week for the past twenty-five years. He had also written three of his own—a history of the Seminole Indians, a book about the various pirates who frequented the Florida coast during the eighteenth and nineteenth centuries, and a highly regarded volume on the techniques of criminal prosecution. He and Troy had been close friends since they were twelve and could communicate perfectly with very few words. Chambers's father and Roland Troy's had gone off together to be pilots in World War Two. Teddy Chambers's father had come back.

"I'm gonna see what I can do to help them," Troy said.

"Well, you got your work cut out for you."

"I'm goin' down to the track. Do some research for a model."

"No problem there."

"What if I want to ask questions? Check things out. Go visit a few people."

"Talk to Smitty. I can't go around him, Roland. Not even for you."

"You lookin' for the death penalty?"

"If he did what they say he did I'm gonna have to."

"And . . ."

"And it looks like he did. The fuck." Chambers shook his head again. "It's his poor mamma I keep thinkin' about. Her and the dead girl. Raped and then had her fuckin' brains blown out. Lord have mercy, Roland. Twenty-three years and I'm beginning to think maybe I've had enough. I've had two offers in the past year to teach law school. I

may just take one of 'em. You know, I already go[...]
from my buddy Hugh Drummond up there in Flag[...]
County. Him and that fire-breathin' preacher got 7-Eleven
to stop selling *Playboy* and now he thinks he's God's personal state attorney. He's willing to bet me Billy Roseman's
a porno freak. What an asshole. He actually told me one
time that the Devil founded the A.C.L.U. You eat lunch
yet?"

"I want to get down to the track. I'll eat somethin' in the
car on the way," Troy said.

"Fruit. I bet you got fruit. And a piece of homemade
bread. Am I right?" said Chambers. Troy nodded. "Lucky
you, you'll live forever. Me, I'm goin' across the street for
some barbecue. You still smoke cigars though. Here, take
one of these. Fidel's finest. Christmas present from J. W.
Register. That old bastard must be eighty at least and he
told me he still smokes six cigars a day. I ran into him and
Jimmy Swinton at the Backstretch Café, speaking of the
track. Them and the Trigg brothers, couple of others,
Johnny Wallace, they're all that's left of the old-timers.
Man, those guys were just as crooked as the new ones
but they had more style. Town's gonna wind up being run
by lawyers from New York and Chicago. You know what
J. W. Register says to me? He says what's black and brown
and looks good on a lawyer? I look down at my pants.
We're at the track, I think maybe I got splattered. I say I
don't know, J. W. What is black and brown and looks good
on a lawyer? A rabid Doberman, he says. Then he gave me
the cigars."

The room was cold and still held the acrid smell of violent death. Sheridan Halpatter told Roland Troy the Indians believed one who was in tune could feel the dead soul's
unrest in such places. Troy told Halpatter violence hung in
the air for weeks. He could taste it, Troy said. It was me-
tallic and bitter, like particles of smoke-tainted dust in a
burned-out building. Halpatter was the only person Troy
mentioned this to. He was afraid his other friends, even
Teddy Chambers, would think he was crazy.

Troy walked around behind the old oak desk in the far
corner of Billy Roseman's office and sat down in the swivel

vantage point he could see the door, the
erstuffed easy chair with the rip on one arm,
the low coffee table in front of it, and the
the couch, stained and speckled with dried
what once had been inside Nikki Waters's head.
his less critical role of model maker, Troy would
study a crime scene intensely before drawing sketches on
his pad, taking photographs with his thirty-five millimeter
camera and taking the precise measurements he needed to
create his models. Now, however, he reverted to the days
when he investigated homicides and sat quietly for an hour,
absorbing the feel of Billy Roseman's office until he could
close his eyes and recreate the space perfectly in his mind.

Finally, he rose from the chair, crossed the room, and
stood next to the coffee table. It was Wednesday afternoon,
two days since the crime-lab technicians had scoured the
office for evidence. All that remained from their visit were
a gouge in the wall where they had no doubt dug out a bullet, and two outlines done in colored chalk, one of Nikki
Waters's body on the couch, the other, on top of the coffee
table, of Billy Roseman's revolver, the Wyatt Earp commemorative single-action forty-five. Troy removed a ten-
foot Stanley Powerlock tape from his pocket, measured the
length of the Colt's barrel, and whistled. He looked slowly
around the room, scratching pensively at his beard, went
back to the swivel chair, and rapidly took several pictures
with his camera. Then he got up, took a few shots from different points around the room, and was about to leave when
something occurred to him, something about the outline of
the gun. He walked back over to the coffee table, took a
photograph of the chalked outline on its surface, packed his
camera gear into the canvas shoulder bag he carried with
him, and left the office.

"You're wasting your time, Tooth," John Smith said. He
took an enormous bite out of his hamburger and stuffed a
few French fries into his mouth as well. He washed it all
down with a swig of Coke, set the burger down on a napkin
spread open on his desk, and belched. "Excuse me," he
said, and drank some more Coke. "This one's open and
shut. Wham bam thank you ma'am. Roseman did it."

John Smith held the rank of captain and was the head of the homicide division of Orlando's Metropolitan Bureau of Investigation, an elite organization comprised of officers from local sheriffs' departments and police forces. Before that he had been chief homicide investigator for the sheriff's department, the position from which Roland Troy resigned in 1979. He was the only man left in the department who called Roland Troy "Tooth." It was an indication of his fondness for Troy, as well as his respect.

Schools in Florida were still segregated when Roland Troy went to Micanopy High. John Smith, who was the same age, attended Carver, the black high school in Sanford. Smith was the only wide receiver in central Florida Troy consistently had trouble covering, and the only sprinter who regularly beat him in the hundred and two-twenty. After high school, Smith spent four years at Florida A&M, followed by four seasons with the Kansas City Chiefs. When his pro career was cut short by a severe knee injury he tried coaching but found football boring unless he was on the field, so he went home and became a deputy sheriff, the first black man in central Florida to be given such a job. He was working as a deputy when Roland Troy solved the case that got him the nickname "Tooth."

It happened in 1971. Two little kids walking on the shoulder of a country road had been killed by a hit-and-run driver. A witness to the accident who knew something about high-performance cars remembered seeing the numbers "409" on the side of the front fender as the car sped away, and identified the vehicle as a white 1963 Chevrolet Biscayne with a 409 motor. Only twenty white 1963 409 Biscaynes had been sold in all of Florida, and eventually, after searching for several months, detectives found what they believed to be the vehicle involved in the accident. There was a problem, however. The car had been completely rebuilt and was no longer owned by the man police believed responsible for the children's deaths. Despite a thorough investigation by the department's forensics division, nothing could be found to positively link the Chevy to the accident. The new white paint didn't match the paint on the dead bodies, and not even a single thread of the children's clothing could be found on the car. Since no

witnesses had written down the license plate number, the
former owner of the car was not charged.

Roland Troy had gone to school with the mother of the
dead children, and since technically the accident was a
homicide and therefore not subject to the statute of limitations, he decided to check into it. When he went to look at
the car, the new owner told him he had wrecked it. The car
was too fast for its own good, the man said, because it
didn't handle worth a damn. He had rolled it over and felt
lucky to be alive. His insurance company considered it to-
taled, and it had been carted off to a junkyard.

Troy was certain the man who bought the 409 from the
insurance company would never put it in the crusher. He
was right, but unfortunately the junky had traded the
Biscayne to another junkyard operator at an auction and
had no record of that man's name or address. Troy called
a few bootleggers he knew, a couple of stock car drivers,
and a man who built racing engines in Daytona, all of
whom kept their eyes open for high-performance wrecks.
He told them to ask around about 409 Biscaynes, but nothing surfaced. A year went by and the case was all but
forgotten when Troy got a call from a man who ran a
junkyard in the mountains of north Georgia. "You Juny
Pocock's friend?" he asked.

"Yeah," said Troy. "Who are you?"

"I'm the guy's got the 409 you're lookin' for," the man
said.

The car, or what was left of it, was under a sheet of plastic in an old barn. Troy rigged up two powerful spotlights
for illumination, then spent a day and a half going over every inch of the remaining sheet metal. Like the forensic
specialists before him, Troy was about to concede defeat
when his eyes fell on the rubber grommet that circled the
hood latch just above the Chevy's grill. Despite the body-
work that had been done to the car, the grommet appeared
to be original. Troy took out his pocket knife and pried it
up. Wedged under the grommet and protected for nearly
two years from the weather, a paint gun, and an accident
that had crushed the car's roof, was a tooth. Subsequent lab
tests proved it belonged to one of the dead children. The

presence of that tooth convicted the car's original owner of manslaughter.

"I knew you were coming to see me," John Smith said. "Chambers called me and told me you would be. I even know why. Nobody had to tell me that. The question is, what the hell am I going to do? See, man, I got shit flyin' off the fan at me from every direction, and I ain't just referring to the Nikki Waters murder.

"Like I have this deputy assigned to MBI, this woman, this good-looking woman. They *tell* me she's very intelligent. They *say* she's a police officer with highly superior qualifications, which is why they assigned her to MBI, right? So listen to this. She's off duty. Some guy she doesn't even know comes up to her in a supermarket parking lot, tells her his car broke down, and could she please take him to the bank so he can make a withdrawal. That way he can pay to have the car towed to the shop. She says sure. What the hell, she isn't worried, she's armed and he looks like a decent guy. So she drives him to the bank and sits outside while he goes in to make his withdrawal. Then she's driving him back to the parking lot when about four patrol cars come on her with their lights flashing and their sirens blowing. Dude made a withdrawal all right, but what he failed to tell my deputy with the highly superior qualifications is that he made it by sticking a three-fifty-seven in the teller's face, and now she's in jail for driving the getaway car. And wouldn't you know, this guy's claiming the robbery was her idea, she put him up to it, threatened to have him arrested if he didn't do what she told him. You want to hear more?" John Smith took another bite of hamburger and drink of Coke. "That's only the beginning," he said.

"I want to know why I'm here," Troy said.

"What?"

"You said you didn't need anybody to tell you why I was here."

John Smith turned in his chair and pointed to a three-by-four-foot framed poster hanging on his wall. "You know who that is?" he asked. "That's Bat Masterson. The picture was taken in 1877, right after he was appointed sheriff of

Ford County, Kansas. Ford County was a big place, a hundred miles east to west, seventy-five miles north to south. Bat traveled all over that territory in a horse-drawn buggy with two ivory-handled Colt Peacemakers stuck in his belt, and nobody gave him any shit because he had already proven he knew how to use those guns. But that's not why he's hanging on my wall. He's hanging on my wall because he knew when to pack it in. Before some young son of a bitch with a fast hand shot him dead in the street he moved to New York City and became a sports writer. Teddy Roosevelt tried to get him to go back out west and be the U.S. marshal in the Oklahoma Territory, but ole Bat wrote a letter to Roosevelt saying no thanks. 'I have taken my guns off, and I don't ever want to put them on again,' was how he phrased it."

"He's buried in the Bronx," Roland Troy said.

"Bat Masterson? How do you know that?"

"When I was nine years old I ran away from home and took the subway uptown to look at his grave. It was, you know, one of those little mausoleums with doors. I thought about breaking in and stealing his guns, if they buried him with 'em, that is. But the doors were real heavy steel. I'd 'a needed explosives."

"C'mon. What kind of bullshit you handin' me?" John Smith said.

"It's true, John," said Troy. "I lived in Manhattan with my mother and her parents until I was ten. The second time I ran away I was more ambitious. I took a crosstown bus to the freightyard way over by the Hudson River and climbed into a boxcar. I wanted to visit Tombstone, Arizona, see if I could find the O.K. Corral. Of course they caught me before the train ever started moving. My mother sent me to live here with my grandparents right after that. So you think I'm here to strap my Peacemaker on again, and you're tellin' me it's a mistake. Is that it?"

"You never heard any of this from me," John Smith said. He ate the rest of his hamburger, weighing what he was about to tell Troy. "You understand, by all rights the Nikki Waters killing should be a county case," he finally said. "They threw it at me so it wouldn't get fucked up. There was rape. There was murder. There was dope. The both of 'em had a head full of grade-A Jamaican weed. There was more of it laying around Roseman's office. He says he was down in Mexico on some kind of horse-trading expedition. He says his buddy, some dude named McBride, the guy who set up the Mexican deal, got himself shot down there, right near the Rio Grande, but Roseman can't even tell us where they crossed the river."

Smith paused, ate a single French fry, and licked the grease off his fingers. "But you already know all that," he said. "Am I right?"

Troy shrugged. He knew they'd call whoever was in charge of the case from the jail as soon as he showed up to see Billy.

"We traced his trail back as far as El Paso, where he got on a Continental flight to Orlando, so we know he was somewhere in the vicinity," Smitty said. "The Mexican authorities are no help. No dead gringos floating downstream in the past week or so. Then there's the missing tit. Billy mention that to you?"

"He told me they asked him what he did with the nipple. He didn't elaborate," said Roland Troy.

John Smith ate another fry, all the while watching Troy, studying his face. "Part of Nikki Waters's left breast was cut off," he said. "The nipple and about an inch and a half of flesh behind it, judging by the size of the other one. You see, Tooth, my man, I may be accused of taking the simplistic approach, but what it really all boils down to is that we got the makings of a circus here. Beautiful blond ex-model, horse racing, drugs, perversion, big money. Roseman was involved with John Varney, the millionaire banker, the wheeler-dealer. Sold Varney that world champion horse he had. Those in command don't want a circus. They don't want Nikki Waters's face sitting there next to every supermarket checkout counter in America. They don't want all the lovely housewives of the world thinking they're gonna get their tits cut off if they come to spend their vacation at Disney World or Universal Studios. So they gave the case to me. No side show. Assemble all the evidence, bring it to the state attorney, let him present it to the court. Wham bam thank you ma'am, as I said earlier. What they're gonna do when it comes to trial I don't know, but that is not my problem. My problem is to keep the ship sailing with the wind right now, not get blown off course, so to speak."

John Smith paused to chew a couple of the little ice cubes from his plastic Coke cup. Roland Troy sat quietly, waiting for Smith to continue.

"We got Roseman's prints all over that forty-five," Smith said. "We got his prints all over the woman's body. We got his sperm in her pussy. We got her fingernail scratches up and down his arms. We got him admitting he fucked her. We even got him admitting he put the gun in her mouth, although according to him that's the way she liked it. He says it was her idea for him to tear her dress off. He says she put his hands on the buttons and told him to rip it. We found *him* in a rental car, a big fuckin' Lincoln, sixty feet from his office. He was in the back seat, door open, out cold. At first, the deputy that found him thought he was dead too. The knife that cut her tit off was on the floor of the car next to Roseman. No prints on the knife. It was wiped. But there was blood on the cuff of Roseman's shirt. A-negative, same type as Nikki Waters's. Roseman's is O-positive.

"And then there's the money. Damn near thirty grand in hundreds stuck in a envelope in the trunk of the Lincoln. Roseman claims it was in payment for the horses he helped deliver to Mexico. That's wonderful we say, only the lab turns up traces of cocaine in the bottom of the envelope. That ain't gonna help his case a whole lot now, is it? And the reason I'm telling you all this is so you get the whole picture—so you know what you're dealing with when you go marching out of here to try and prove that Roseman didn't do it. That is what you intend to do, isn't it?"

"All I want to do is ask some questions," Troy said. "I didn't want to step on your toes. I came here to ask your permission."

"Man, you don't need my permission," Smith said. "You and me go back too far for that shit. You're a special investigator for Chambers's office. You're gonna be making a model, aren't you? You need some information, you ask. Anybody calls me, I'm gonna tell 'em you're just doing your job. But don't stretch it. Don't get theatrical on me. Remember, I was there when you brought the whole front end of that Chevrolet into the courtroom so you could show the jury that little boy's tooth. Those days are over, Roland. What they want now is to keep all the special effects in the theme parks. They want all the cowboys there too."

Roland Troy stroked his beard and considered what John Smith was saying. Smitty was a good cop, an intelligent, sensitive man who had spent his career being pulled apart by other people's expectations. The black community expected him to become the first black police chief of Orlando, or better yet, the mayor, two nearly impossible goals, at least for the remainder of the twentieth century. On the other hand, the white power structure, the men who belonged to the exclusive Pelican Club, expected him to fall flat on his face, confirming their deep-seated belief that black people were genetically incapable of handling positions of authority.

John Smith had laid it out clearly for Roland Troy many years before, when he was a deputy and Troy was a homicide detective. The two of them had gone fishing together on Lake George. Neither of them was catching many fish, but they were having a fine time drinking beer and telling football stories. Roland Troy's voice was by then almost a duplicate of Bear Bryant's growling bass. After they'd split a six-pack, all he had to do to set Smith to howling was say, "Boy, you here to play football or scratch your ass." Suddenly, in the middle of one of these paroxysms of laughter, Smith stopped as though he'd been kicked in the stomach.

"Tooth, I gotta tell you what happened to me last week," he said. "I busted these two black guys. Caught 'em with a load of dope. Right away they started calling me Brother. Brother this, Brother that. When they see I'm really taking them in, they get real quiet. I'm driving 'em to jail, right, and one of 'em starts talkin' again. Brother this, Brother that. Other one says save your breath, he's nothin' but a house nigger. I get 'em booked and Chatsworth calls me into his office. He says, 'What'd you get those two monkeys for?' I pretend I don't hear monkeys and I say, 'I got 'em for possession, sir.' He says, 'Possession, what the hell am I gonna do with possession.' He says, 'Those fucks are dealers. Now they're gonna walk.' I say, 'Sir, they weren't dealing. I've been watching them for two weeks and possession's the best we can do.' He says, 'Don't hand me no "we" shit. You might as well have bought 'em a couple of tickets to the Bahamas. I'd 'a shot 'em.' "

When John Smith finished the story Roland Troy, who'd been looking out over the lake, glanced at him, but quickly looked away. The black man had put down his fishing pole and had his hands clasped in front of him as though he were praying. There were tears running down his face. "It's okay," Smitty said. "I don't care if you see me cry. Man ain't no different than a pressure cooker. That water don't come out, sooner or later the top's gonna blow off. Don't worry. I'm cool. Ain't none of 'em gonna get the best of me."

For twenty years, John Smith had managed to withstand the pressure and had risen through the system by playing everything precisely by the rules, sublimating any decision based on emotions, suppressing any inclination to grandstand. Bat Masterson hanging on the wall of his office was the closest he would ever come to revealing an unconventional point of view.

"I appreciate what you're doing for me," Troy said. "Don't think for a minute that I don't."

"Oh, I know, I know," Smith said. "You don't have to tell me. You might tell me what you have though. Long as you're being so appreciative and all."

"What I have?"

"Tooth, you got *something*. I don't care how badly you want to help your friend. I know you better than that. You ain't about to run your ass all over hell and back unless you've got something that at least *suggests* to you that Billy Roseman didn't do it. I don't want no surprises."

"You want a cigar?" Roland Troy asked.

"Sure," said John Smith. Troy took two from his shirt pocket and tossed one to Smith. They lit up and smoked in silence for a minute, watching each other.

"One you've got's from Havana," Troy said. "Chambers gave it to me."

"You know, back when I played with the Chiefs there was one corner always gave me fits," Smith said. "Hubert Howell. Remember him? Played for San Diego. He re-

minded me of you, in fact, just a little bit quicker." Smith
took a puff on his cigar and smiled. "No offense, man.
Dude ran in the Tokyo Olympics in sixty-four, you understand. Got him a bronze medal in the two-hundred-meters.
Anyway, I'd put moves on that boy hadn't even been invented yet. I'd get done with my thing, there he'd be, every
time. I never knew how the fuck he did it. It was like I'd
sent him a map of my pass routes. I caught a few on him,
but only if the ball was thrown high. I could outjump him,
you see. Well, couple of years ago I ran into him out in
Houston at a golf tournament. They got a bunch of old
players from the AFL together, had this deal for charity.
We're sitting in the clubhouse after a round and I say,
'Hubert, c'mere and let me ask you something.' He walks
over to my table and sits down. 'What's on your mind, Rufus?' he says. He called every receiver Rufus. I say,
'Hubert, all these years it's bothered me how you knew exactly where I was going on a pass route. How *did* you
know?' I'm thinkin', hey, we're a couple of old fucks now,
old comrades in arms, sitting around the campfire. Time to
reveal all secrets, understand what I'm saying? That
motherfucker looked me in the eye, just like you're doing
now, and you know what he says? He says, 'Houdini never
told anyone how he did his tricks and neither do I. Here,
Rufus, have a cigar.' His weren't even from Havana."

The gun used to kill Nikki Waters, the single-action, .45
caliber, gold-plated Wyatt Earp Commemorative with the
twelve-inch barrel, weighed nearly three and a half pounds.
Had it been thrown onto the coffee table in Billy
Roseman's office, it would have gouged the surface, but
Roland Troy had seen that the surface, gleaming from an
obviously recent refinishing, was unblemished. Even within
the chalk outline of the gun, the teak was without a scratch.
That meant the revolver had been placed on the table with
care. The chalk outline revealed the gun was resting on its
left side, the way a right-handed person would set it down,
but Billy Roseman was left-handed. Troy remembered that
clearly. He remembered buying Billy a little rubber football
and showing him how to pass it, remembered placing the

ball in Billy's tiny right hand and hearing Billy say "No, dis one, dis one," moving the ball to his left.

In itself it was weak proof. Measured against what John Smith just told him, it was close to nothing at all. The gun could have been shifted from one hand to the other after the shot was fired. Roseman could have fired it with his right hand. He would have to look at the fingerprint report to see whether that had been the case. There were a couple of other things he needed to check out at the lab as well. But all that stuff aside, he was operating on feel here, and his feelings told him Billy Roseman didn't do the shooting. Why not? *Why didn't he?* Troy asked himself. *I don't know,* he answered.

Maybe it was the gun, presenting itself so conspicuously, so neatly, amidst the chaos of unbridled violence—the torn dress, the scratches, the stains on the couch cushions and the wall, the knife, what the knife had done. It was almost as though the gun were an offering, a centerpiece, order within disorder.

Maybe it was only his wishful thinking prompted by a desire to set things right with Clara after all these years, a desire to do something for her, to demonstrate—and this was the hard one to admit—that he and only he could pull her tragedy out of the fire. She had come to the right person for help, he told her. *A little hubris there, Roland,* he thought. No question about it. But then, it was true. No one else would run with it like he would. No one else cared. If self-interest was a motivating factor, his was the only self-interest that could possibly help Billy Roseman. The rest— John Smith, the men Smitty referred to as "those in command," even his friend Teddy Chambers—would just as soon see Roseman fry.

He rolled down the windows of the El Camino and gunned the car up the on-ramp of the interstate. A good highway song, "Hard to Be," by Stevie Ray Vaughan, came on the radio, followed by his brother Jimmie singing "Good Texan" off the same album. You never know when it's coming, he said to himself, thinking of Vaughan's untimely death in a helicopter crash, thinking how many close calls he'd had in helicopters, thinking of the time he'd been shot and left for dead. He was ahead of rush hour and the road was relatively empty. He turned up the volume and tromped on the accelerator, running the El Camino up to seventy-five.

It was smart that he'd said nothing to Smitty about his suspicions. He would say nothing to Teddy Chambers either, nor to anyone else. Smitty hadn't really given him shit; the stuff he told him Troy could have found out from the guys at the lab or one of the deputies on the scene. Hell, he could probably get it from Roseman himself. All that stuff about cowboys, Smitty's homilies, it was a smoke screen, a lube job to find out what he knew. Dude must think he'd gone senile. *What does he really know?* Troy wondered. *What's he hiding?*

Troy left the interstate and headed north along the same road Nikki Waters took to meet Drew Parabrise on the night she died. He drove by the narrow, weed-choked path through the pine trees, where she turned off the main road, and continued on for several miles, making a left onto a less traveled paved road and then another left onto the dirt road leading to his land. The radio station had switched to a set by Bonnie Raitt. They played two cuts from her new album and then "Everybody's Cryin' Mercy," a Mose Allison tune she recorded way back in 1973. "A bad enough situation is sure enough gettin' worse," she sang. "Everybody's cryin' justice, just as soon as they get theirs first."

"Ain't that the truth," Troy said out loud. "Ain't that always been the truth." The fact is, he wouldn't have told John Smith what he suspected even if he didn't believe Smith was holding something back. Roland Troy didn't trust Smitty. It was nothing personal, absolutely nothing racial. Roland Troy simply didn't trust anyone other than himself. He pulled into his front yard, killed the El Camino's engine, and sat for a few seconds, listening to the snap and ping of contracting metal underneath the car's hood. Clara Roseman's car was not there.

XI

♦

There was a note taped to the front door of Troy's house. "Dear Roland," it said. "Well, I went and checked out of the Park Suite and drove back up here with all my stuff but I couldn't get myself to bring it into the house. I felt foolish going back and checking into the Park Suite again, so I decided to stay at Billy's after all. The place is a complete mess, which is good in a way because cleaning it up will give me something to do. By tomorrow I should have Billy's place enough in shape to fix you a nice vegetarian dinner. Please call me. Clara." Under her signature was the phone number at Billy Roseman's house.

He called the lab first. "Pathology," said a young man with a nasal whine.

"Lemme talk to Dr. Pizer," Troy said.

"I'm sorry, Dr. Pizer's left for the day," said the young man. "You want to leave a message?"

"Tell him it's Roland Troy."

"Mr. Troy, I told you, Dr. Pizer's left for the day."

"Pizer ain't left that place before six o'clock three times in the last fifteen years," Troy said. "Tell him who it is." The young man put his hand over the mouthpiece but didn't cover it completely. Troy could hear Ronald Pizer say something in the background and the young man mumbling his name.

"Roland, for Chrissake, what a surprise. Why didn't you say it was you?"

"I did," Troy told him.

"Oh," said Pizer. "Well, here I am. Have to be very careful. They drive me nuts, you know."

Troy was about to ask who "they" were but thought better of it. As far as he could determine Ronald Pizer had been nuts for a long time. Probably, Troy assumed, it was from the combination of breathing the horrible smelling chemicals he used for so many years and never dealing with a live patient.

"I need some help, Ronald," Troy said. "A piece of information."

"Oh," said Pizer. "What is it you need to know?"

"It's about Nikki Waters. About the missing part of her breast. I need to know whether it was cut left to right or right to left."

"I'll have to check. Hold on a minute." In less than thirty seconds Pizer was back. "What's this got to do with building a model?" he asked.

"It doesn't," Troy answered. There was no point in being evasive with Ronald Pizer. He was crazy, but far from dumb. "This is personal. You're doing me a personal favor. Maybe saving somebody's life, if you know what I mean."

"Ah," said Pizer. He was silent for a bit, thinking it over. "Right to left," he said finally. "Cut by a very sharp knife held in the right hand. I hope that helps."

"It does," said Troy. "It helps a lot."

"If you save somebody's life, let me know," said Pizer. "One of the drawbacks to this work is that I don't get to do that. At least not directly. You know, I used to listen to her on the radio, Nikki Waters. She was the Raven. She had a voice from heaven."

"I listened to her too," Troy said.

"They told me she was very beautiful," said Pizer. "I have to go now, Roland. Stop by when you have a chance."

A friend of Troy's in forensics told him the gun was definitely fired by someone holding it in his left hand. There was a left index fingerprint on the trigger, and prints from the third, fourth, and fifth fingers of the left hand on the right grip, where the hand had been wrapped around the revolver's butt. The prints were all unquestionably Billy Roseman's. A test for gunpowder residue had proven negative, but they'd expected that. Billy had slipped getting out of the Lincoln and covered both his hands with mud.

Troy was about to call Clara when something occurred to

him that he'd totally forgotten to ask John Smith. He dialed Smitty's number, hoping he hadn't left for the day.

"This better be important," Smitty said. "I got Magic tickets. I gotta go all the way home, get my kid, turn around, and be back at the arena by seven-thirty."

"I forgot to ask you if you found the tit," Troy said.

"The tit," said Smitty.

"The part that got cut off Nikki Waters."

"Yeah, I know which tit you're talking about."

"Billy didn't walk no more'n fifty, sixty feet from the barn to the Lincoln," Troy said. "If you can't find it, where do you imagine it went? You don't think Billy ate it do you?"

"Roseman ... see, Tooth, this is *exactly* what I don't need, man. This is the kind of thing that can turn into a feeding frenzy for the tabloids. The case of the missing tit. Roseman claims he doesn't know what the hell we're talking about. He was so fuckin' stoned it took twenty minutes to wake him up. Maybe he dropped it out in the mud there where an animal could get it. It's not like it was an arm or a leg. It was a small piece of flesh. A rat could have carried it off. A raccoon. What's the difference? We got the knife. We got the dude's prints on the murder weapon and everything else. You know all that."

"What-all do *you* know about Nikki Waters?" Troy asked.

"What do you mean, 'what-all do I know'? What are you driving at? Gimme a fuckin' break. She was a good-lookin' piece of ass. A disc jockey. A former model, they tell me. You got a conspiracy theory for me? You think she was a spy?"

"Don't get so excited, Smitty," Troy said. "I ain't got nothin' on Nikki Waters for you. Not yet."

"Yeah, well you come up with anything you be sure to let me know. Now I'm going to the ball game."

On the Saturday night Billy Roseman returned to Orlando from El Paso, on the day after Myron McBride was killed, on that night, when her radio show was over, Nikki Waters was to meet Drew Parabrise. She played a cut from

Miles Davis's *Kind of Blue* album while she read from Shakespeare's sonnets a poem about lust:

Mad in pursuit, and in possession so; Had, having, and in quest to have extreme; A bliss in proof, and proved, a very woe; Before, a joy proposed; behind, a dream. All this the world well knows; yet none knows well . . . To shun the heaven that leads men to this hell.

"Can *you* shun it?" she whispered into the mike. "Be honest with the Raven now. Can you? Maybe someone brushes up against you in a crowded bar and when you watch 'em walk away you feel that chill. Or maybe you're driving in your car, and you stop for a light and look over at the car next to you just when someone in that car looks at you. Or maybe you're in an airplane, just a few passengers on a long flight at night, and it's dark in the cabin, and there's someone across the aisle, partially wrapped in a blanket, who looks real good. Don't you want to lift that blanket up and get under there with 'em? Don't you think about it? Can you *really* shun it? I know I can't.

"Lord knows I've tried in my life. Lord knows the Bard was right—it's bliss, but once it's over it's a woe. No matter. *My* baby's waitin', and I'm gonna fly right to him . . . tonight. I sure do hope there's someone out there who's waitin' just for you, too. You know I do. I'll catch y'all on Monday and we can talk about it some more. 'Til then, *vaya con Dios.* Peace."

"You lookin' fine dis night," Cool Babba Wisdom said. "In dat tight dress and so high-heeled shoes. You in a rush."

"Yeah," Nikki said. "I got a hot date."

"In dat case, take dis along," said Cool Babba. He handed her a Baggie filled with buds of dark brown grass mottled with streaks of amber. "Watch yourself wit dis. Dis be ganga of de utmost kind. You t'ink you seen brother lust, like Shakespeare say, but dis show you a new aspect of de animal of raw desire. You get down on dis in ways beyond your dreams. Time for I to wail."

Before leaving the studio, she looked in her mailbox. Sometimes she would talk to people who wrote to her, but she never answered any mail in writing sent to her at the station. It was the first time she'd checked the box in over

a week. There was a stack of letters addressed to the
Raven, which she put back in the box to open on Monday,
an application for a gold MasterCard in the name of Ms.
Raven, which she trashed, and a note from Wanda
Donnerstag, dated ten days earlier, which she sat down to
read.

"Dear Nikki," the note said. "How did I find you there?
I've known all along. The first time I heard your voice on
the phone I knew it was the same voice I listen to at night
on the radio. I didn't say anything because I didn't want to
intrude into that part of your world, as you didn't intrude
into the other part of mine. But you haven't answered my
calls, or the letters I sent to your house, so I'm writing to
you at the station. I miss you terribly, my Raven, and can't
believe you don't miss me too. I hear your voice on the air
and know you're talking to me. I can feel it. I think about
you constantly and think I will go mad if I don't see you.
Please call me. OK? In case you're wondering, there's been
no one else since you. I need you. Wanda."

Below Wanda's signature was a postscript. "I know far
more about you than you realize," it said. At first the line
sounded to Nikki like a threat, but after she read it a second
time, and then a third, she'd convinced herself it was nothing more than a harmless reference to what Wanda thought
she heard in Nikki's radio voice.

Wanda Donnerstag was an editor at the daily newspaper
in Orlando, the *Journal-Express*. She was a driven woman,
obsessed with her job, who routinely put in seventy-hour
weeks running the paper's life-style section. Were it not for
her petulant mouth and the shapeless clothes she wore, she
would have been quite attractive. She had dark, haunted
eyes, made darker still by gray eye shadow, a narrow, aq-
uiline nose, and pale, almost translucent skin, dusted with
blush along the cheekbones so that she always looked
slightly feverish. She was tall and lean, bony almost, and
wore her thick, straight black hair in an asymmetrical cut
that gave her the aspect of a plainswoman, standing alone
on the prairie in a strong crosswind.

It was assumed by the writers and assistant editors who
worked under her that Wanda Donnerstag was sexless, a
woman with no personal life at all, and that she would be

happiest if they had none as well. She dealt with these people in a remote, imperious manner, and was feared like no one else at the *Journal-Express*, not even Byron O'Reilly, the bombastic editor-in-chief. Prosaic though her section was, Wanda Donnerstag got more column-inches out of fewer staff members than any other department head at the paper. She also saw to it that the stories written by Allison Smith, O'Reilly's mistress, were always impeccably edited and regularly sent out on the wire for national consumption. It was not surprising, therefore, that Donnerstag had O'Reilly's complete support. When she emerged from her office in the corner of the large bull pen occupied by life-style, and stood with hands on hips, some pages of hard copy crumpled in her fingers, every soul in the room looked as though he were ringed by a brush fire with nothing to climb.

Nikki Waters knew a far different Wanda Donnerstag, the one whom she met through a telephone dating service. During an extended period of absence from Drew Parabrise, Nikki called this service out of curiosity and boredom one afternoon in the middle of a steaming late-August heat wave. After listening to a series of instructions, she first pushed the designated number on her phone for women wanting to hear messages left by men. The nasal recorded voices were tentative and uneducated, obviously a bunch of dumb, frustrated husbands looking for something on the side. She returned to the main menu and hit the button for women wanting to hear messages left by other women. They were only recordings, but she felt nervous and was slightly out of breath.

The first few were no better than the men—old dykes cruising the phone lines for young girls, women with barmaid rasps claiming they'd never done this kind of thing before—but then she heard a voice that was completely different. It was soft and cultured, yet held the throaty, wanton promise of complete abandon. The woman said her name was Grace. She gave a post office box number in Lake Mary for anyone who wanted to contact her.

"I was with a woman," Nikki told Drew Parabrise. "We were together twice." She had flown to Richmond, rented a car, and driven to Fredricksburg to meet him. He had been on a fact-finding trip to various railroad facilities around the country with other members of his committee and then on vacation in Europe with his family. It was the first time they'd seen each other in two months. They were in a cheap motel right off I-95. The anonymity of places like this, the feeling of transience, excited her.

"Tell me about it," he said. They were undressed, but at her insistence had yet to touch. He was sitting in a chair; she stood in front of him, still wearing her heels and jewelry—a gold chain necklace and gold bracelets on either wrist.

"This is how I looked, with just my shoes on," she told him. "I kept them on both times for her. I lay down on the bed and she walked over to me, just like you're doing. She had on this long, full skirt and this baggy blouse so you couldn't tell what her body looked like underneath. She stood next to the bed and took her clothes off and she was thin with very smooth skin. She's thirty-three but her skin is tight all over. She has little tits like me and a high, firm ass. She stood over me and put one leg up on the bed and fingered herself while I watched." She took his head in her hands and pulled his face between her legs. "Then she licked me like that, and like that, and she put her hands on my breasts like this, and moved her tongue real fast back and forth until I came. Like I'm coming now, like I'm coming for you now.

"You want me to tell you about the second time?"

"Yes," he said. "Please tell me."

"I want you inside me first," she said. "I want to sit on you. That's it, just like that. Don't move until I tell you to. Can you keep from moving? The second time was at my house. We were both naked, in my bedroom, but we hadn't touched each other, like you and me, before. She said, 'I want you to fuck me. I brought something for you to use.' She took this wooden penis out of her bag and it had leather straps on it. She buckled them around me so the penis stuck straight out, and then she covered it with Vaseline."

She was silent for a moment, moving up and down above him, her breath coming in short, quick gasps. Her hands were on her belly, fingers splayed. He rose to meet her, watching her face, watching her bright red nails slide upwards to her breasts. A bead of perspiration trickled down her neck and disappeared behind her wrist. "Now get on top of me," she said. "I was on top of her and I was going real hard like you are. Oh, baby, you like that, don't you? You want me to tell this to you, don't you? Go harder now like I did. I went so hard into her, in and out of her. She was shaking all over, and when she came . . . when she came she screamed, 'Oh God, Oh God, don't stop. Keep it in. Keep it in.' "

After they made love he would talk to her about his work. Was it because of her dominion over him in bed? Was it because with her words, or gestures, or the articles of clothing she demanded he rip from her body, she controlled him so? Was it because there, in the musty rooms where they coupled, the impersonal rooms she chose and paid for along anonymous highways, she found him out and he was powerless?

He had recently joined another Senate committee, the Energy and Natural Resources Committee, and was developing legislation governing the extraction of minerals from the ocean. This coincided with the oceans-policy legislation he was involved in on the Commerce, Science, and Transportation Committee. Between the two committees, he told her, he himself would ultimately control the leasing rights to the waters off the American coast. He would be like Neptune, the god of the sea. She listened, on this night, as he stirred for her his stew of political intrigue, the promises and threats he'd had to make, the bargains that were struck, the stack of markers he'd accumulated, all in the name of carving up the ocean for him and his friends.

Before leaving the station on that cold January night, Nikki Waters threw away the letter from Wanda Donnerstag. She thought about a line in the sonnet she had just read to her listeners: "Before, a joy proposed; behind, a dream." She never wanted to see Wanda again, not even for a cup of coffee. The woman was definitely unstable, if not completely insane. Nikki drove north that night on a

winding country road to meet Drew Parabrise, the windows
of the Porsche opened just a little to let in the chilly air.

The road she was on outside Orlando once ran for miles
through cypress swamp, through a dense forest of pine and
oak, and through occasional stretches of lightly wooded
pasture. Almost all of that had disappeared, replaced by one
luxurious subdivision after another. Where bear and deer
and wild hogs used to run, where red-tailed hawks and bald
eagles hunted, huge, sprawling homes loomed beyond high
brick walls. Behind man-made hillocks bordered by split-
rail fences, walkways, lit at night by quaint streetlamps,
threaded through what remained of the trees. The walkways
led from the homes to private golf courses and tennis
courts, to health clubs and riding stables, all unseen from
the main road. It was at the restaurant of one of these golf
courses, in fact, that Nikki first met John Varney on a day
in January two years before. Access to these places, these
enclaves of wealth and prestige, was gained through electronic steel gates guarded by humorless armed men seated
in turret-shaped enclosures.

For the most part, but not entirely, that was now the way
it was in this area north of the city. There were, however,
pockets of wilderness not far from the clusters of million-
dollar homes, tracts of nearly impenetrable swamp and
thick woods through which snaked a murky river. This land
was untouched as yet by the developers who coveted it the
way a despot covets tribute. There were people on this
land, but no one knew how many. It was rumored that alligator hunters, moonshiners, and itinerant pot growers lived
there, dwelling in old, decrepit panel trucks, ancient trailers,
tents, and shacks made from rotting wood. It was said that
there were renegade squatters hiding back in the swamp, on
the run from who-knew-what, and mystics who communed
at night with the river, perhaps even a few Indians, no one
knew for sure. Every now and then a few of them would
appear, in the early hours of the morning at an all-night supermarket, buying supplies—fatless, bearded men with
leathery skin and wild eyes; tanned women with long hair
and tattoos, wearing snake boots; occasionally a barefoot,
feral-looking child. They drove rusted-out pickups or old
cars with no back seat, guarded by mongrels chained to the

steering wheel. What was known was that those who held
the deeds to the wild country where these people lived refused to sell, in spite of the incredible sums they were periodically offered.

Someone following Nikki Waters that night would have
automatically assumed one of the fancy neighborhoods
along this country road was her destination, that her
Porsche would pull up to one of the dozen guardhouses and
she would be waved through. But that was not where she
was headed. Instead she turned off onto a barely visible,
narrow dirt lane overgrown with weeds, that disappeared
within a few yards into a stand of slash pine. She stopped,
cut the engine, turned off the lights, and lowered the windows all the way. For a minute or two she sat this way,
breathing the night air, shivering slightly, not from the cold
but in anticipation of her lover, who was to meet her in an
old cabin owned by a friend of his and located near the
river. She had met him there several times before and was
familiar with the way.

The land she was on was shaped like a lollipop. When
she restarted the Porsche she proceeded very carefully between the trees along a natural causeway no more than
twenty feet wide that dropped off on either side into the
swamp. As she drove, she could hear grass and low-
growing bushes scrape along the underside of the car. In
less than a quarter of a mile she came to a circular point of
land—a clearing—surrounded by water. Directly in front of
her, an old wooden dock jutted out into a portion of the
swamp where the water deepened, and to her right, partially
obscured by a tangle of saw palmetto, was the cabin, which
was dark.

Drew Parabrise was staying at an estate a mile or so up-
river from the threadlike branch that ran from the main
flow to the cabin. He would be coming downriver in a
small boat with less than two feet of draft. Few people
knew the way from the river to the cabin over water, but he
was one of them. As a boy he had made the trip many
times at night with his friends. Tonight, he would tie up at
the dock and walk to the cabin where he would find Nikki
waiting for him in the dark. It would be warm in the tiny
cabin; he would hear the hiss of the kerosene heater she

had lit and see its glow. He would smell her perfume and see the outline of her naked body on the bed. This is the way it would be because she had written it in a letter to him that he read and immediately burned.

She turned on the vanity light in the Porsche to check her makeup, pivoting the rearview mirror and leaning forward slightly to better see her face. She held a cosmetic brush in her hand and had just made several quick passes at either cheek when something made her stop, made her pause in mid-stroke, the small brush with its silver handle held expertly in her hand, poised above her cheekbone. She had the intuitive, primal feeling that she was being watched, not by her lover (she would have heard his boat) but by someone else, by eyes she didn't know. She turned, her neck and shoulders still arched toward the mirror, her freshly painted lips parted, her eyes wide and questioning. She stared this way out the passenger window for several seconds but saw nothing in the darkness, yet she was sure someone was there.

She turned the light out in the car, locked the doors, and closed the passenger window, but left the driver's window partly open the better to see into the night. For several minutes she sat motionless, her eyes adjusting to the darkness, listening, afraid to go inside the cabin. Then she heard a sound, a rustling, barely audible, in the leaves beside the cabin, and saw something move between two trees several feet from the cabin wall. A chill ran up her spine and she shuddered. *Oh, Jesus, somebody's waiting for me,* she thought. *Someone is waiting for me to get out of my car.*

She knew she should get away from there at once, but she was suddenly paralyzed with fright, unable to move her right hand from the steering wheel to the ignition key. Who the fuck was after her, she wondered? Who had she underestimated? What mistake had she made? Had Cool Babba been trying to tell her something with his warning not to fool the wrong person? The pale, haunted face of Wanda Donnerstag flashed through her mind. Wanda, who claimed to know more about her than she realized. Wanda, who kept a .22 automatic beside her bed in a hollowed-out Modern Library edition of Plutarch's *Lives*. Did Wanda know about Drew? Had she followed her from the station in a crazed fit of jealous rage? Or was it someone sent by that scumbag Varney? Was that who was lurking out there in the woods?

She saw motion again between the trees, heard a twig snap, and then another sound, this time from the creek, where something—a boat, an animal, a person—had broken the water. Her legs were shaking now and she could feel a rivulet of cold sweat run from her neck down between her breasts. *Maybe it's Drew,* she thought desperately. *Maybe he's here after all.*

She was about to cry out to him, to shout from her car for him to hurry, that she needed help, when it came to her, as clearly as her sense of being watched, that Drew Parabrise was not going to show up. "You bastard," she said aloud. "You spineless motherfucker. So this is how it ends."

Breathing audibly through her mouth, fogging the windshield with her breath, she forced her hand from the wheel, started the engine, spun the car wildly around in the clearing, and raced back down the path. When she reached the highway, she hit the gas so hard she fishtailed for fifty yards down the road, leaving thick black tread marks on the asphalt. Even if she had looked, she would not have seen the car, hidden in the grove of slash pines, where the narrow path began.

At six in the morning, after a sleepless night, Wanda Donnerstag showered, dressed, and drove the two miles from her house to the paper, seeking the comfort of her office, the cocoon of her work. It being Sunday, there were only two other people in the entire newsroom—a young intern monitoring the police scanner and a writer in sports checking the overnight wire for late basketball scores from the West Coast. Paying no attention to either of them, she went into her small office, closed the door, and began to dig through the stack of potential articles for the life-style section sitting in two foot-high piles on her desk. Within minutes she was adrift in a phantasmagoria, each part of which assumed a brief, intense reality only to fade away and be replaced by another, much like an orchestrated display of fireworks against a pitch-black sky.

For a short time she was consumed by the plight of unmarried women who decide to have babies, then captivated
by a group of former secretaries who found they could earn
five to ten times their former salaries running roadside hot-
dog carts while wearing spike heels and spandex mini-
dresses. This was followed by the importance of exercise
programs for the elderly, the hidden perils of cosmetic sur-
gery, and the twenty-year fight of a famous movie actor
against drug and alcohol addiction.

Several more people drifted into the newsroom, but
Wanda Donnerstag was oblivious to their arrival. She did
notice, however, when a commotion took place around the
scanner a little after nine o'clock, and came out of her office to see what the fuss was about. A woman had been
found brutally raped and murdered at the Ben White Raceway, someone told her. A suspect had already been arrested.
A reporter at the scene had called in with information that
the victim was the Raven, the popular radio personality.
Wanda listened impassively to the chatter for a few more
minutes, saying nothing. Then she returned to her office
and resumed her work. Finally, at quarter to eleven, her
eyelids began to feel heavy and her head started to nod.
She hurriedly threw several more articles into her briefcase,
buckled it, and left her office, giving only a cursory nod to
the assistant editor who looked up from his desk as she
walked past him on her way to the stairs.

She drove home quickly, and once inside her house undressed as rapidly as she could. She felt sleep coming over
her at last, but didn't want it to happen yet. Naked, she
walked into her study and removed a picture from a manila
folder on her desk. She walked back into the bedroom
carrying the picture—a full-page color photograph that had
been clipped from a French fashion magazine—and four
push-pins which she used to tack the photo to the wall just
above her pillows.

The photograph was an advertisement for a hotel on the
Riviera. It was taken at sunset, with the hotel in the distant
background. In the foreground, a woman with long, silky
blond hair sat in a wicker chair at the edge of the ocean,
her legs outstretched into the shallow waves, a glass of
wine in her hand. The woman, whose face was visible in

profile, wore a filmy, see-through gown. Her body was positioned in such a way that through the material of the
gown, one of her breasts and the shadow of her pubic hair
could be seen. The woman in the advertisement was Nikki
Waters.

There were other pictures in the manila folder. There was
one of Wanda in a cap and gown, taken when she graduated, summa cum laude, from Wellesley. She was only
twenty, but already her mouth turned down cruelly at the
corners and there was madness in her eyes.

There was another of Wanda and her mother taken on
Wanda's fourteenth birthday. Wanda was dressed in the uniform of the private school she attended in Connecticut—the
school where her father served as chaplain. Her hair was
cropped short, like a boy's the way her father insisted she
wear it, and her face appeared ghostly pale since he had
also forbidden her to wear any makeup. It was the only
photo she had of the two of them. A year later, her mother
pulled out a gun at the dinner table, placed the barrel in her
mouth, and killed herself. After the funeral, her father destroyed every other picture of his wife in the house.

There was also a shot of a very pretty girl with long
blond hair—a girl who looked somewhat like a young
Nikki Waters—dressed in the same regulation jumper and
blouse of the private school. The girl's name was Ellie
Daniels, and while the uniform made Wanda appear drab
and sexless, on Ellie the outfit was transformed into the en-
semble of a vamp. Ellie Daniels had been one of the most
popular girls on campus, and though she was a year ahead
of Wanda, they were in the same French class. Wanda,
timid and withdrawn, silently worshiped her older class-
mate, who exuded supreme self-confidence. Wanda would
stand in front of her mirror, trying over and over to imitate
the insouciant way Ellie tossed her head, but without Ellie's
long, flowing hair she always seemed to look like someone
with a tic.

Wanda, however, was a far better student than Ellie Daniels, a fact that was not lost on Ellie, who also sensed
Wanda's infatuation. One day she asked Wanda to help her
with a French assignment knowing full well Wanda would
agree. A week later, Ellie asked Wanda to correct a theme

for her and once again Wanda obliged, basically rewriting the essay. When Wanda delivered it to Ellie's room, Ellie invited her in. "You're so sweet to help me with my work," she said, kissing Wanda on the cheek and stroking her neck. "I've seen the way you look at me in class. Let me do something for you."

Her relationship with Ellie had been going on for a month when Wanda walked into Ellie's room and found her in bed with another girl. "Don't look so shocked," Ellie said when she saw Wanda's face. "She helps me with my English. Tonight's her turn."

At first Wanda was going to burn the snapshot she had taken of Ellie Daniels, but she changed her mind and decided instead to keep it forever. She had learned a great deal from Ellie, considerably more than the smattering of French Ellie had learned from her.

By the time Wanda Donnerstag had tacked the page from the magazine to her bedroom wall, she was breathing heavily. She lay down with her head toward the foot of the bed, her legs resting on the pillows, her feet locked behind the vertical brass bars of the headboard, and began with her left hand to gently play with her breasts. In her right hand she held a six-inch vibrator that she turned on with the press of a small button and placed between her legs. Her eyes riveted on the picture, she began to gasp, then moan. Her cries were soft at first, almost as though she had stepped into a deliciously hot bath, but soon they grew louder, then louder still, so that at last, when she came with both hands moving in spasmodic bursts, the vibrator's hum was completely drowned out by her screams.

Wanda slept after that, so deeply that even the mewing of her hungry cat didn't wake her until Monday morning at five o'clock. She rose from her bed, gave the cat a can of food and fresh water, returned the picture of Nikki Waters to the manila folder, and took a long shower. Emerging from her bathroom, she pulled on a wine-colored silk robe and sat before the mirror attached to her dressing table. She opened the drawer of the table and took out another picture of Nikki Waters, this one a close-up of Nikki's face used in an ad for eye shadow.

For several minutes Wanda studied the picture, staring at

it with such intensity it would have seemed to someone
watching her that she was in a trance. Then she gave her
head a quick shake and began to make herself up, working
carefully to create the allure and mystery, the wanton avail-
ability, that Nikki Waters conveyed on the page before her.
In all things Wanda Donnerstag was a painstaking woman,
so this process, with which she was not particularly familiar, took her more than half an hour, but when she was finished the transformation of her face was truly remarkable.
Coldness and sterility had been replaced by fecund heat.
She let the robe slip from her shoulders, cupped her breasts
in her hands, and looked at herself once more in the mirror.
Slowly she licked her upper lip with the tip of her tongue,
the way she remembered Nikki Waters licked hers. She
smiled slightly, affecting at the same time her memory of
Nikki's sensual pout. Then she lifted the photograph from
the dressing table and kissed it, leaving on the glossy paper
the imprint of her freshly painted scarlet mouth.

She felt certain they were looking at her as she strode
past their desks to her office, but she never let her eyes
wander. In her mind she saw Nikki Waters walking with
cool elegance down a runway flanked by fashion editors,
clothing buyers, and photographers. That was the image she
would project. She would teach herself to walk like that.

She reached her office, opened the door, and went around
the desk to sit in the well-cushioned, high-backed swivel
chair—an editor's perk she particularly relished—that faced
the large bull pen where the other members of the life-style
section passed their days. A wide window next to her door
allowed her to observe the entire space populated by those
in her charge.

In the center of the large room was a horseshoe-shaped
cluster of desks where the copy editors pored over the stories that would appear in the paper the next day. On either
side of this central work station were the desks of the various writers: the food, television, and drama critics; the
fashion editor, originally from Australia, who dressed like
the Church Lady on "Saturday Night Live"; the movie
critic who was so fat he needed two seats in the theater;
Wesley Stoyer, the brilliant, sharp-tongued music critic

whom Wanda would fire in an instant if he gave her half an opportunity; Jasper Deputy, the redneck cartoonist, the shit-kickers' answer to Garry Trudeau; Scott Berger, the assistant editor who was so fearful of Wanda's wrath he began to sweat the minute he entered her office; the general-assignment reporters and the young interns; and of course the long-haired Allison Brown, the unassailable Allison Brown, Byron O'Reilly's Allison Brown, whose stories, that ran on for page after page, were edited by Wanda herself.

If any of these people noticed something different about Wanda Donnerstag, none showed it. No one was watching her. As far as she could tell, business seemed to be going on as usual. Good. That was the way she wanted it; no way would she allow her new persona to influence her devotion to her job. No way would she countenance any erosion of the absolute authority she maintained in her tiny kingdom. She looked out once more at the busy people under her control, smiled contentedly, slipped on her reading glasses, and went to work.

Wanda remained working at the paper until almost eight o'clock that night. Several times during the day she broke from her dogged attention to the life-style section to read the day's front-section story about the gruesome murder of Nikki Waters. She studied the pictures of Nikki as a model, Nikki covered with a sheriff's department blanket on the couch where she died, and Billy Roseman, the trainer accused of Nikki's murder and rape.

The life-style section bull pen was nearly empty when Wanda closed and locked her office door, descended one flight to the ground floor of the *Journal-Express* and walked to the parking lot across the street. She drove slowly from the lot, stopping to say good night to the attendant, but once on the road hurried to her house. She made herself a tuna salad sandwich and a cup of coffee and took it into the living room. There, she flipped the switch of her stereo receiver to the FM setting and adjusted the dial so that the station where Nikki Waters had worked came through clearly on her Bose 901 speakers. She placed her sandwich and coffee carefully on the glass table in front of the couch, positioned herself midway between the speakers to get the best stereophonic effect, and waited.

"Tonight we be jammin' in sadness," Cool Babba Wisdom said. "Tonight we grieve for de Raven who no more flies among us, who no more coax us wid her perfect voice. You must please excuse Cool Babba if any extra t'ings he doesn't say. Tonight we play de music Raven loved and save de talk for other times. Peace, Raven, wherever it is you be."

XII

♦

When Byron O'Reilly strode into the policy room of the
Orlando *Journal-Express*, the members of the paper's editorial board knew immediately what was in store. "Bombast
blue," Ethan Peoples whispered to Dick Broome, the managing editor. Peoples, the laconic metro editor, was referring to O'Reilly's dark-blue pinstripe three-piece suit.
During his three-year tenure as editor-in-chief of the paper,
O'Reilly's moods had become easily identifiable by the
outfit he was wearing. His loden-green corduroy suit, for
example, signified smooth waters, a general sense of satisfaction with the paper's performance. His dark-gray suit—
his "banker's git-up," Peoples called it—presaged a tirade
on belt-tightening. Occasionally O'Reilly showed up wearing khaki pants, a tattersall shirt with the collar unbuttoned
and a loosely knotted tie, an outfit meant to convey his
identification with the rank and file. On those days he
would meander through the newsroom, stopping here and
there to sit on the corner of a reporter's desk to chew the
fat, a fully terrifying experience to all but a few of the old
timers who looked up at O'Reilly with the flat-eyed indifference of a fifteen-dollar whore.

O'Reilly's blue suit signaled the trumpeting of a cause
and foreshadowed speechifying on a grand scale. It also
meant the editor-in-chief had probably added a few extra
lines to his usual wake-up dose of cocaine and would brook
no disagreement to whatever course of action he was about
to outline. He took his seat at the head of the long, oval table, removed a pack of Camels from his vest pocket, tapped
a cigarette from the pack, and slapped the pack down on
the table. The snick of his Zippo lighter was the only sound
in the room.

O'Reilly took three long drags on his Camel. For years he had secretly studied the oratory of Adolf Hitler and found the German leader's technique of prolonged silence before a harangue particularly effective. Like Hitler, O'Reilly would usually begin talking quite softly, working his way up to a frenzied crescendo, unless, that is, he was particularly angry at someone. Then he would dispense with drama and simply begin screaming at the offending party the moment he lay eyes on him. Often, this display of wrath took place in the middle of the newsroom and became the verbal equivalent of a public flogging.

Today, O'Reilly wasn't angry. He leaned back, pointed his cigarette at Rebecca Vosburg, and smiled. "Damn fine editorial, Becka," he said. "Damn fine. Now what we need's a follow-up. Hit the violence-against-women aspect. You know, soft on crime means hard on women, something along those lines."

Rebecca Vosburg was the chief editorial writer for the *Journal-Express*, the newspaper's paradigm of social and political rectitude and a particular favorite of Byron O'Reilly, since she was very skillful in seeming to address the important issues of the day without offending either the paper's major advertisers or O'Reilly's political friends. She had made quite a reputation for herself championing the cause of migrant workers, deploring their squalid living conditions and their indentured servitude to the men who brought them across the border, but she steered clear of leaning on Florida's sugarcane and citrus industries to recognize the United Farm Workers Union. Florida was a right-to-work state and the non-guild newspaper she worked for wanted it to stay that way.

Of late she had taken up the banner of the Arab League, writing a series of scathing anti-Israeli editorials. When Sandra Michaelson, the fashion writer and a staunch feminist, pointed out to Becka (as she preferred to be called) the deplorable position of women in the Arab world as compared to that of women in Israel, Vosburg uttered something unintelligible and stomped off.

"What did she say?" Michaelson asked Wesley Stoyer, the music critic. "I never understand what she says. It sounds like she's talking with a mouth full of motor oil or something."

"She said may your first-born have the brains and good looks of a camel," Stoyer said. "I was you, I'd start sending out my résumé."

O'Reilly turned his attention to Ethan Peoples, raising his voice somewhat, but still not intolerably in the small room. "Ethan, I want more out of metro on this," he said. "Much, much more. I want this story milked like a six-titted cow. You understand me? Get a piece on that horse track. Who knows but maybe there's dead bodies buried all over the place. Three quarters of this fuckin' town doesn't even know it's there. Get some history on the Roseman guy. Put some fuckin' spin on it. You know, the time-bomb angle. Find a couple of his childhood friends who always thought he was a wacko. See if there's a girl friend some-place he slapped around." O'Reilly was warming to his subject now and began to shout in short, clearly enunciated bursts.

"I understand there was mutilation. Mu-til-a-tion. You know what that means? Those four college girls. Tampa. We could be looking at a tie-in. Maybe this character's a serial killer. Get somebody to check it out. Get something on the radio station. Get reaction from the dead woman's listeners. The Raven. She was the Raven. Can you believe the symbolism in this thing? The death of the Raven. The *murder* of the Raven. Edgar Allan Poe. Norse mythology. Is there a raven in the Old Testament? Somebody find out. Do a reader survey on the death penalty. Broome, soon as I'm through here, you haul your ass over to sports. Get some-thing going on Roseman's career as a trainer. Tell Jackie we're going to run it in a special Saturday section, not in sports. Wanda. Wanda, are you alive over there?"

Wanda Donnerstag stared wide-eyed at O'Reilly. Under her carefully applied makeup she was pale as alabaster and sat absolutely motionless, as though she had been turned to stone. Her asymmetrical coiffure, even more pronounced than usual, made it appear as though O'Reilly's bellowing had blown all the hair to the far side of her head. "I want Allison in New York, Wanda," O'Reilly shouted. "You got that? The Big Apple? I want a piece on the dead woman's modeling career. With pictures. Send fucking what's-his-name. The Cuban."

"Ramirez," said Ethan Peoples.

"Right. Ramirez. Send Ramirez."

"With all due respect, Byron, what do we need a photographer for if the woman's dead?" asked Dick Broome. He had already assigned Ignacio Ramirez to cover the county jail where Billy Roseman was being held, and the courthouse where he would be indicted and eventually tried.

"You dumb fuck," O'Reilly roared. "I don't want pictures of the woman. I want the apartment building she lived in. I want the bars where she hung out. Anybody who knew her way back when. I want . . ." He threw his hands up into the air. "I want . . . I want someone along in case Allison digs something up. I do not want her without photographic backup. You got that?"

For several seconds the room was deathly still. Finally, Foley Frazier said something barely audible that sounded like "What a hippie."

"Foley, what the hell did you say?" O'Reilly screamed. "What did you call me?"

"Nothing, Byron," Foley squeaked. "I didn't call you anything. I just said, 'What about Mississippi?' "

"What about Mississippi? What the fuck is that supposed to mean? We're sitting here in the middle of a murder that's a newspaper reporter's dream, a goddamn cornucopia of violence and perversion, with a mystery woman for a victim, and you ask me about Mississippi. What kind of jackasses are you people?"

"Mississippi's where the dead woman comes from," Foley Frazier said.

O'Reilly paused and lit another cigarette. "Well, all right then," he said. "Send somebody to Mississippi. What I don't want—and I can't emphasize this enough—what I don't want is to have the fucking *Miami Herald* or those turkeys in St. Petersburg scooping us on this. This is our story and it better stay that way."

"Aren't we coming on a little strong here?" Ethan Peoples said. Peoples rarely spoke at editorial meetings. In fact, Ethan Peoples didn't speak much at all, but when he did he almost always had something of value to say. Among the reporters at the *Journal-Express* he was considered the paper's finest editor, thorough and demanding, but sensitive to a writer's individuality and always willing to praise good work. He came from a very wealthy old New England family, and while he caught his share of Byron O'Reilly's vituperation, O'Reilly was too much in awe of Peoples's patrician background to threaten him the way he did other members of his staff. "I mean all the background stuff is fine and dandy, but shouldn't we take care not to convict this man in the press before he's had a fair trial?"

"Peoples. Peoples. What is this, your first week on the job, for Chrissake?" O'Reilly said. "You haven't heard of the word 'alleged'? The word 'suspect'? I'm not suggesting we say he's the killer. We just say he's the number one, prime, grade-A suspect. Son of a bitch like him's gonna say he can't get a fair trial no matter what we print, so what we're going to do is print it now and worry about the fair trial bullshit later. Now, I have an important meeting to get to, so unless somebody here has a life-or-death situation to present, we're outa here. Anybody? Good. Get to it." Byron O'Reilly stuffed his pack of Camels back into his vest and left the room.

With O'Reilly's departure, the tension in the room lifted. Chairs tilted back. Foley Frazier lit his pipe. Becka Vosburg leaned over and whispered something to Dick Broome, who released a dump-truck load of pent-up nervousness with a whooping laugh. Only Wanda Donnerstag remained unchanged, as rigid and pale as she'd been throughout the meeting. "Wanda, you all right?" Ethan Peoples asked. Her acute distress had been tangible from the moment she sat down across from him, and several times during the meeting he had actually imagined she was screaming hysterically, even though she hadn't made a sound.

"I'm fine, I'm fine," she blurted out, as though Peoples had awakened her from a deep sleep. "Well, no point sitting around. I've got work to do." With that she jammed her pen and note pad into her shoulder bag and departed. Ethan Peoples watched her go. He turned to Dick Broome and was about to say something but changed his mind. Peoples was one of those rare individuals who, having made an observation, needed no corroboration from his peers.

Newspaper people work late, so Byron O'Reilly had no trouble rounding up the entire editorial board of the *Journal-Express* when he called another meeting at six-thirty that evening. No one was unduly surprised. O'Reilly would often go two weeks without holding a board meeting and then gather the editors together three times in one day.

"Why do you think he works that way?" Dick Broome once asked Ethan Peoples. "Auto-erraticism," Peoples said, inhaling loudly through his nose three times in rapid succession.

"I know it's late, so I'm going to make this very quick," O'Reilly said. "I've given considerable thought to what Ethan said this morning, and I've decided to change our tack in regard to the murder. We're going to low-key it. I don't want it ever to be said that my paper hindered the conviction of a rapist and a murderer. All we're going to run is a calm, A-section recap including any new developments. Period. No special Saturday section. Allison's not going to New York. She can do a tasteful little story from right here about the woman's career as a model and her popularity as an innovative deejay in Orlando. One small black-and-white of the woman's face. No Mississippi. No Tampa college girls. No serial killer. Cops say the M.O.'s different anyway. Becka, forget the second editorial. Your first one nailed it, let's leave it at that. Any questions?"

A number of exasperated looks were exchanged but nobody said anything. It wasn't the first time Byron O'Reilly had issued a sweeping directive only to turn right around and pull the plug on it. At least this time he'd reversed himself soon enough to spare everyone a lot of unnecessary work. "Well, see you all tomorrow," he said. "Cheerio."

"Where's Wanda?" Ethan Peoples asked Dick Broome after O'Reilly departed.

"Wanda is in her office, consumed by her work," Broome said. "Wanda is always consumed by her work, you should know that. She's never missed a day of work since she came to this paper. She's never missed a minute of work, I should say. I know a woman who went to school with her at Wellesley. She said Wanda never cut a class in four years.

Thirty-three years old, Wanda Donnerstag is, and I believe she's already put in enough time on the job to draw social security. Although I will say she looked kind of sexy today. Weird, but sexy. Maybe she's finally gone into heat. You think she's ever been laid?"

"I think Wanda Donnerstag is a very bizarre person," Peoples said.

"Yes, I know she's bizarre," said Broome. "She's bizarre, Machiavellian, and cold as the bottom of the Labrador Sea. But has she been laid?"

"Why is it whenever I talk to you I feel as though I'm back in my high school lunchroom?" Peoples said.

"Why is it whenever I talk to you I feel as though I should be asking for absolution?" Broome said.

"You tell me," Peoples said. "At least Wanda Donnerstag gets her job done."

Ethan Peoples sat in the tiny cubicle that was his office, doodling on a yellow legal pad and thinking. It was eight-thirty, on the other side of his office window the newsroom was nearly empty, but the hour was of no importance to him. He was unmarried and lived according to his own timetable, often remaining at the paper until ten or eleven at night. Peoples was a thin, scholarly looking man of thirty-two with a mop of thick straight hair and piercing blue eyes that peered out from behind wire-rimmed glasses. He had been the captain of the cross-country team at Colby College in Maine and continued to run after graduating, competing in two or three marathons a year. Long-distance running suited him; he was a ponderer, a ruminator, a frugal Yankee who conserved everything and never acted impulsively. Though he could easily afford a BMW, he drove a Honda Civic. With a single telephone call to one of several family friends he could have a job at the *Boston Globe*, the *Washington Post*, or the *Wall Street Journal*. He preferred, however, to remain where he was, in Orlando, not from lack of ambition, but because he had earned his position at the *Journal-Express* without using his family's considerable connections.

Peoples had the true newspaperman's feel for a good story. As an editor, he could read through a reporter's rough draft and ask the single question that would help the writer hone in on the heart of his piece. Now, as Peoples doodled, he was troubled. "Never back away," he always told reporters. "Confrontation is the essence of newspaper work."

Something wasn't right about the handling of this murder at the harness-racing track. Peoples was sure of it, but couldn't say what the problem was. He didn't for a minute buy Byron O'Reilly's reason for pulling the plug on the paper's extensive coverage. Peoples despised O'Reilly. He considered the editor-in-chief the most venal of men, totally incapable of acting in a humane manner, and had thought about leaving the *Journal-Express* when O'Reilly was brought in. Peoples remained at the paper primarily because the notion of being driven from a place by someone like O'Reilly appalled him, and also because he was certain a man with O'Reilly's temperament would eventually self-destruct. *He was warned off the story,* Peoples thought. *But why? And by whom?* There was no way he could send a reporter out on a digging expedition. Peoples knew what O'Reilly would do if he got wind of it, and while he wasn't afraid for himself, he would never wittingly place a writer in such a perilous position. He doodled on, drawing pictures of horses, returning again and again to the only possible course of action. Quietly, without attracting any unnecessary attention, he would do a little digging himself. The idea excited him. It had been five years since he had stopped reporting and begun editing, and even an inveterate distance runner can get bored.

XIII

◆

"I didn't know if you would call," Clara said. "I figured if you got back real late you wouldn't see my note in the dark."

"I saw it," Troy said. "I'm disappointed. I was hoping you'd stay here."

"Oh," she said. She sounded surprised. "Did you find anything out?"

"I don't think Billy did it," he said. "In fact I'm sure he's tellin' the truth, but I can't prove it. Not yet. I'll tell you what I know tomorrow when I come for dinner."

"I'll be up 'til midnight at least," Clara said, "if you want to stop by tonight for a cup of coffee or a mug of tea. We could talk, build a fire. There's some wood in the garage. Let me tell you how to get here."

Her voice was husky. Its tone, lower than before, was almost seductive, as though she were directing him to a clandestine rendezvous. He had taken the portable phone out onto the porch and was sitting where they'd been when they talked earlier in the day. The hint of her perfume still clung to the chair where she'd been sitting, and as he listened to her he became aroused.

Probably she was just lonely and upset and wanted company, someone who could calm her down, tell her things were going to be all right, reminisce. But maybe not. Maybe she was sitting there in nothing but her bra and panties as turned on as he was, her passion heightened by the maelstrom of emotions whirling inside her for the past couple of days, waiting for him to burst through the door and make love to her on the living-room rug. He tried to imagine what her body looked like after all this time, then was immediately ashamed. The poor woman was distraught, he told himself, not horny.

"I'm going to get some sleep," he said. "I want to get an early start tomorrow—go over and see Halpatter—get him to check around with the squatters. Some of them might have connections with grooms at the track. You never know what could turn up. But don't burn up all the wood. We'll make a fire tomorrow."

"Okay," she said. "Tomorrow's probably better anyway. I have people coming to fix the leak in the roof and clean the carpets. The place won't smell so bad by then."

He shivered and pulled his elbows in close to his sides. The sun had gone down behind the trees on the far side of the pond and a breeze began to blow out of the northwest. It was going to be a cold night, down into the thirties for sure. He walked inside with the phone and plopped himself down on the couch.

It was folly, thinking of Clara that way, Troy told himself, the result of his own sensory overload. What he needed was light, impersonal diversion unencumbered by thirty years of emotional baggage. After a meal of salad mixed with whole-wheat noodles, homemade bread, fruit, and herbal tea, he drove six miles to the nearest video store and rented a copy of *Hail, Hail, Rock and Roll*, a documentary about the career of Chuck Berry. The movie was exactly what Troy had in mind; he was immediately caught up in its music, especially the hard-pumping rhythm and blues of Johnny Johnson, Berry's longtime backup piano player. Then the film shifted to Chuck Berry inside an enormous garage on his estate.

Many years earlier a car dealer had apparently attempted to rip Berry off when the musician brought his hardly-used Cadillac in to trade for a new model. Berry decided to keep the car rather than accept the dealer's offer. He kept his next car too, and all those that followed, until he now had a barn full of low-mileage, carefully preserved, Chuck Berry–owned Cadillacs, presumably worth a small fortune. It was a poignant scene, symbolic of Berry's lifelong war against exploitation by the white man.

The barn filled with dust-covered old Cadillacs had additional meaning for Roland Troy. Throughout the rest of the

movie and afterwards, while he drank another mug of
herbal tea, did his stretching exercises, and lay in bed waiting for sleep, his head was filled with the image of a young
woman driving through the small-town streets of Orlando
in a gold Eldorado, her dark hair blowing in the wind.

What ever became of that car? he wondered. *She said
she'd never sell it. She said she'd drive our grandchildren
in it. She said the two things she would never part with
were that Cadillac and me.*

The following night, Roland Troy sat in front of the
dying fire in Billy Roseman's house, sipping hot apple cider, watching Clara poke at the logs with a tire iron, the
only implement to be found in the garage. Troy had spent
the morning with Sheridan Halpatter and Tom Waxe, questioning people in the swamp. He spent the rest of the day
at the track, first talking to the horsemen, then sitting once
again by himself in Billy Roseman's office. He learned
nothing new, but was not disturbed, the urgency of the situation tempered by his inherent patience.

The frigid air lingered over central Florida; it was only
ten o'clock and the temperature was already down in the
thirties. The National Weather Service was warning of a
possible hard freeze in the outlying areas, and citrus growers, reeling from three devastating freezes in less than ten
years, were frantically lighting smudge pots in their groves
and spraying water on their trees, trying to minimize the
damage. Troy had been watching the weather channel off
and on and had seen it was colder still in southwest Texas,
where he had decided to begin his search for the killer of
Nikki Waters.

"Look at this," Clara said. "I almost forgot. Look what
I found in Billy's dresser."

She reached into the pocket of her shirt and pulled out a
worn photograph of a lean, tough-looking young man sitting on the fender of a Corvette. He had on jeans and chaps
and a pink shirt with pearl buttons. "It's Burt, just before he
got killed," she said.

She handed the picture to Troy, who turned on a small
lamp the better to see it.

"I always figured that was why Billy drove a 'Vette," he

said. "Now I understand the pink shirts. Just wanted to be a cowboy like his daddy, huh? Be a buckeroo. Well, he sure drove the hell out of that Steakhouse Papa. Champion of the world. World record. Ain't too many people can say something like that, now, can they?"

Clara sighed and turned back to the smoldering logs. "This would be a whole lot easier if I had some regulation fireplace tools," she said. "I don't believe that son of mine has ever built a fire in here. I know for a fact that wife of his, or ex-wife, or whatever she is these days, never did. I saw her, you know, when I went over to the track to make sure Billy's horses were being cared for. She was with some fat slob of a groom. She saw me coming and turned her back on me, not that it matters any. Aerobics instructor. Jump up and down and say whoo, whoo. They invented the profession for gum-snappers like her. Thank God this house is in his name. I'm having all the locks changed. Billy wouldn't do it, but I am. Tomorrow morning. Damn. A tire iron just does not take the place of a good pair of tongs."

Despite her complaints she quickly repositioned the logs and shortly had the blaze roaring again. Troy studied her back, still lean and supple, and the graceful curve of her narrow shoulders—much stronger than they looked—over which swung her long dark hair. He remembered the day thirty years before, a lifetime before, when he watched her from behind for the first time as she paddled in the bow of his canoe. Her hair was so long the ends had dragged in the water, but he had been too entranced to tell her. Even stoking a fire she exuded elegance, just as she had at seventeen, whether she was driving through the streets of Orlando in her Eldorado, flipping hamburgers in the café, or changing her son's diaper.

Elegance and strength of character. She'd been born with it and it hadn't gone away, though he could see by the lines around her mouth and the tiredness in her eyes that thirty years fighting to keep a grip on it had cost her dearly. Even so, she could smile. Even so, she could laugh at herself as she had earlier in the evening when her homemade bread failed to rise and the lentils she made turned into a brown, glutinous paste that reminded her, she said, of the stuff they used to use in the library to repair book bindings.

Clara pulled the metal screen across the fireplace opening, sat down on the hearth, and hugged her knees. "That's a proper fire," she said. "Now I'm gonna go in the kitchen and fetch us some marshmallows. Don't you shake your head. You don't want one, don't have one. Me, I want a roasted marshmallow."

Elegance and strength of character. Stood on the deck of a drilling rig and shot the man who'd killed the man she loved. Buried her husband and father on the same day. Bore a child alone in a hospital room with only a nurse to hold her hand, and drove with that child in her dead father's Eldorado to Florida to start a new life at seventeen. All these years and he had never fully appreciated who she was, this woman who was here to try and save her son. There was nothing in the world that could make a woman like Clara Roseman fold her hand, of that Roland Troy was convinced. *What a fool I was to let her go,* he thought. *What a prideful, vengeful jerk.*

The woman he had married, the woman who bore his only child, had been elegant too, but weak and cold as the winters in northern Denmark, where she was born and where she returned after living with him for five years. Lona was her name, and when she left, saying she was tired of the Florida heat, tired of America, tired of him, she left their daughter as well, for him to raise alone as best he could. She was an artist who painted geometric shapes set against ghostly, lifeless landscapes. Fortunately, their daughter Katherine, a robust, outgoing marine biologist, was nothing like her.

"Close your eyes and open your mouth," Clara said.

He had told her what he knew about Billy's fateful trip to Texas while she roasted and ate three or four marshmallows. Now she removed a particularly gooey-looking one from the end of the shish kebab skewer she was holding and placed it between his lips. "I'm going to Texas with you," she said, as she wiped strands of marshmallow from his beard. "Don't try and talk me out of it, my mind's made up."

"These are bad people, Clara," he said. "They already killed Billy's friend. Anyway, you stay here you can help Tom Waxe."

"Tom Waxe slithers around in the swamp better than a water moccasin. If somebody in there knows anything, he'll find out without any help from me. You, on the other hand . . . what if you need a gun? I have friends all over the state of Texas."

"Guns are not my problem," Troy said. "I have a federal permit to carry. Anywhere in the U.S. of A., including airplanes."

"Airplanes," Clara said, "which I know how to fly and you don't. We need to get someplace in a hurry, we can rent one. What the hell are you doing with a federal permit anyway?"

"It was one in a series of gifts from the man who sent me off to war without informing me beforehand. He said we were going off on an adventure. Like everyone else, he assumed I died until I showed up at the kitchen door of his house in Virginia. He about shit a brick. The permit was part of a deal we struck. A deal that's been good for him and for me."

"You never told me about any of that," said Clara. "I told you about Drew Parabrise, but you never told me what happened."

"I never told anyone," said Troy. "I'll tell you now though. I figure that's the least I owe you. But not tonight. Tonight I have to get ready for Texas. And I'm going alone. I know you want to help, but I can't be worrying about anyone else. Go see Tom Waxe. *He* could use some help. He's gettin' old, Clara. He don't slither like he used to. He gets lost sometimes."

"How do *you* even know where to go, once you get to Texas?" she said. "Billy told me he couldn't find the place they crossed the Rio Grande again in a hundred years."

Troy took out his wallet and removed a mustard-colored business card with brown printing on it. He handed the card to Clara. "Monte Zorro Lodge, Shafter, Texas," the printing on the card read. "Brett McCrosson, registered hunting and fishing guide." There was a telephone number under McCrosson's name. "Billy don't know where he crossed the river," Troy said. "But the girl who gave him that card does."

XIV

$\blacklozenge$

After sitting at the end of the bar for an hour, Ethan Peoples thought he had the wrong place. He took the scrap of paper out of his shirt pocket, unfolded it, and read what he had scribbled down: "Pumpers—3rd Ave. betw. 72nd and 73rd—9:30 Fri. night." He'd walked up and down both sides of Third Avenue twice and seen no sign of a bar called Pumpers or any sign with a name that remotely sounded like it. On a hunch he picked the one he was in, Joe's Tavern. It was full of young women who looked like models, or were trying to look like models, and middle-aged men trying to hustle them. He checked his watch and ordered another beer. It was ten after ten. He'd give Melissa another half-hour or so and then go back to his sister's apartment and get some sleep. What the hell, he thought. It was good just being in New York for a change of pace, even if it was twenty degrees outside with a northeast wind blowing hard enough to skid bricks.

At ten forty-five Peoples had finally decided to leave when he saw Melissa come through the door, all six feet one of her, red hair blown around her face by the wind.

"Ethan, is that really you?" she said. He stood up and she bent gracefully to kiss him, obviously accustomed to greeting men who were shorter.

"God, you look so old," Melissa whispered in his ear. "Oh, man, I didn't mean that the way it sounded. I meant you look so . . . distinguished. Or scholarly, that's it, scholarly. It must be your glasses. You're still in good shape." She poked him in the stomach with a finger. "For an old guy, that is. C'mon, let's get a table."

"It's so weird that you called me," she said after they worked their way to a small table in the corner and sat down. "I just saw Roberta like last week and asked about you, how you were doing and all that, and she told me you were an editor at your paper. Man, it seems like it was yesterday I was this little kid hanging out with Roberta at you guys' house and you were like, you know, her older brother who never talked to us, basically. I always dug your stomach muscles. You must've done a million sit-ups, huh?"

"At least a million," Peoples said. "How's modeling?"

"I love it. Ethan, I absolutely love it. I'm up to seven-fifty an hour. Seven hundred and fifty smackeroos for dressing up and making faces. Can you believe it? Me? Gretta Gawk? My agent says I keep doin' like I'm doin' I'll be up to a thousand in six months. It's obscene, if you want to know the truth. My *father* doesn't make that much, and he had to study all those years to become a doctor. Crazy place, this world, but who am I to complain? Right? I found out what you want to know, by the way."

Peoples held both hands, palms up, above the table and smiled. "Lay it on me," he said.

"This did not come from me, right?" Melissa said. "I mean . . . you know what I mean."

"I would never reveal a source," said Peoples. "Never. You can trust me."

She smiled. "I know I can trust you. Roberta told me once you never lied. Not even about the time you and Chipper Thompson stole his father's boat."

"We didn't *steal* it. We borrowed it. What did you find out?"

Melissa leaned over the table and propped her chin on her hands. She had the largest eyes of any woman Peoples had ever seen. They were the deep blue-green color of a spruce tree. He imagined her naked, all long limbs, incredibly long limbs, and huge eyes, like a red-headed owl.

"She was a wild one, Nikki Waters," Melissa said. "This dude fucked her over, some big shot in the cosmetics industry, and she took his office apart with a baseball bat. That's a fact. The photographer who told me, he's like you. Never lies. But that's not the good part, the part you're looking for." She tapped the table with a fingernail. "The good part is she was fucking a United States Senator. From the state of Florida."

"Parabrise?" Ethan asked. It had to be him. The other Florida senator was too dumb to make change, much less figure out a way to fool his ball-busting wife. "Nikki Waters was sleeping with Drew Parabrise? Are you sure? I mean, Melissa, that's serious business, given the present circumstances."

"My roommate knows this model, Karen Brayne. They've been on shoots together, seen each other around, like that. Karen Brayne was at a party on a boat, like three years ago or something. It went on all night. So she's standing on the deck at about five in the morning, watching the tugboats go by in the early-morning fog, and she hears a noise from the boat next door. She looks over the side. See, the boat she's on, the party boat, is taller, higher, so she's looking down at this other boat which is a speedboat, like a *Miami Vice* boat, okay? And she sees Nikki Waters come out of the door to the cabin, and then a couple of minutes later this big blond dude comes out after her."

"Wait a minute," Peoples said. "You're losing me. Karen Brayne told you this?"

"No, Ethan. I don't know Karen Brayne. She told my roommate. Listen, relax. Drink your beer. You asked me to see what I could find out, right? Now I'm telling you, so let me finish."

"Sorry," he said. "It's been a long day."

"So where was I? Right, the boat. Karen Brayne didn't know who the guy was, but she recognized Nikki, 'cause Nikki was like a legend with the younger models. You know, like she might not have been getting the best jobs, but she was her own woman, never took any shit, lived alone kind of thing. She was cool. And she was gorgeous. I mean there's models and then there's models, and Nikki Waters had it. She was like, I am who I am and I know it and you know it and if you don't like it fuck you.

"So one day Karen Brayne and my roommate are on this shoot together in Aruba and Karen's reading *People* magazine and she sees this story about this senator who's working with the environmentalists to save the oceans, and she looks at the senator's picture and who is it but the big blond dude from the speedboat. She's positive it's him because of the way he wore his hair, real blond and floppy

like Dennis the Menace but with an old guy's face. He's
there in this picture with his family, right? Standing by the
ocean. Wife's wearing a long denim skirt, crew-neck cotton
sweater, Wendy-the-Wasp deck shoes. Daughter's at Smith,
son's at Exeter, la, la, la.

"Karen Brayne gets pissed. I never met her, but like she
was a *Sports Illustrated* swimsuit model and she's worked
with all these outdoor photographers, gone on shoots in remote locations, you know? So she's really become avid
about the environment. She turns to my roommate and
goes, 'So that's who Senator Parabrise is. I know all about
that motherfucker. He's full of shit.' My roommate is eighteen years old at the time. She's just getting started, just got
her first contract with Eileen Ford. She's like who? what?
where?

"Now comes the good part. Karen Brayne's big-time.
She's making like almost a million a year. So this guy she
knows, this investment banker, he's trying to get her into
bed by telling her how he can do all these wonderful things
with her money. He doesn't know from anything about her
being avid about the environment, right? So he tells her he
wants to get her into this holding company that's buying up
offshore oil and gas leases that aren't worth anything at the
moment because you can't drill where they are.

"That's how they talk, these investment guys. They're
going to get you into this, get you into that, you know? I'm
sure you've met 'em. This one, he tells Karen Brayne, to
show her how cool he is, that he personally knows the senator who is the head of the committee that's gonna open up
large sections of the ocean for oil and gas exploration. This
senator's gonna make it *look* like he's the biggest friend the
environmentalists ever had in Washington, but don't worry,
the legislation will get passed, and when it does, this holding company's stock will go through the roof.

"Karen Brayne tells the guy to get fucked. She forgets all
about his spiel until she sees the *People* story and then she
gets all incensed and goes on and on telling my roommate
the whole thing and how it's guys like this senator who are
raping our country, etcetera, etcetera, da da da da da."

"That's it?" asked Peoples. "That's the end?"

"Uh, uh. Not quite," said Melissa. "When you called me,

I asked my roommate if she knew anything about Nikki Waters because like I told you I didn't. So first she told me what I just told you, and then she gave Karen Brayne a call because like she didn't know any more than what Karen had told her when they were in Aruba. My roommate tells Karen about Nikki getting murdered and Karen says holy shit and tells my roommate another story." Melissa stopped talking and looked around for a waitress. "I need something to drink," she said. "All this talking's making me thirsty."

"Don't move," Ethan Peoples said. He got up, walked over to the bar, and ordered another beer for himself and a Diet Pepsi for Melissa.

"Where was I," she said when he returned to their table. "Oh, yeah. Karen Brayne. Karen Brayne got sick of modeling and got into acting. She was in this comedy-horror movie they were shooting at the new MGM studio down in Orlando. Karen rents this Porsche convertible from a dealer there but it breaks down the first time she drives it. The dealer says no problem, bring it back and he'll give her another one. So she goes over to the dealership and who does she run into but Nikki Waters, who's having something or other done to *her* Porsche.

"They talk, what are you doin', how've you been, what's new kind of thing. Nikki tells Karen she's quit modeling for good and has this radio show there in Orlando, she loves it, she thought she'd mind the Florida heat but she doesn't, la la la. Then—get ready for this. Then Karen asks her if she's still seeing that senator, Parabrise, 'cause Karen's like a dog with a bone my roommate says and she can't let go of that time she saw them on the speedboat because she's like gotten even more involved with the save-the-ocean people and she really hates the guy. So she comes right out with it, you know? I mean imagine it? She sees them together once and fixes on it like that. 'You still seeing that senator?' " Melissa paused, drank the rest of her Pepsi, and sucked on an ice cube.

"It was like Nikki Waters had seen a ghost, Karen said. That's how pale she got. And then she took hold of Karen's hand, my roommate said, and squeezed real hard. And she looked Karen right in the eye and said 'It's like I'm two people. One of them sees him and the other one wants to die.' "

"Karen Brayne told this to your roommate?" Ethan Peoples said.

"Yup. Word for word," Melissa said. "Karen remembered that time in Orlando really well 'cause she'd always idolized Nikki. Kind of like Nikki was this free spirit who wasn't controlled by people the way a lot of models are. But then she saw it wasn't true. It really freaked her out."

"Do you think Karen Brayne would talk to me?" Peoples asked.

"No way, man. When my roommate told her Nikki was murdered she got like real paranoid. I mean she made my roommate swear she didn't have a tape recorder attached to the telephone. She's big into conspiracies and shit. *You* don't have a tape recorder hidden on you or anything?"

"No. No tape recorders."

"Listen, Ethan. I trust you or I wouldn't have done this, but don't forget, you promised . . ."

"Don't sweat it," Peoples said. "We never had this conversation."

It was Saturday night, and as usual Byron O'Reilly was holding forth at Taylor's, a bar in Winter Park, thickly carpeted and decorated with rich, dark wood. It was the tavern of choice for the new power brokers in town. Men like J. W. Register, the Trigg brothers, and Jimmy Swinton, men who spent their lives making deals in Marvin Lodish's café at the Ben White Raceway dressed in jeans and Western shirts with pearlized buttons, wouldn't be caught dead in the place.

Ethan Peoples found Byron O'Reilly in Taylor's back room, seated at a large round table with two other men and three women. Peoples recognized only one of them, Allison Brown, who was snuggled up close to O'Reilly. The rest were not from the paper. If O'Reilly saw Peoples he gave no sign, but continued on with a story he was telling. "There's a rattlesnake, Saddam Hussein, and a lawyer in an elevator together," O'Reilly said. "A guy gets on the elevator with a gun, but he's only got two bullets. What does he do?" O'Reilly paused for a couple of beats while the others waited in anticipation. "He shoots the lawyer twice," he said. Everyone laughed loudly and Allison Brown gave O'Reilly a quick kiss on the ear. "Oh, Byron, you're so funny," she said.

Peoples circled around and came up behind O'Reilly. "Byron, excuse me," he said. O'Reilly turned and looked at Peoples, encompassing him in the bonhomie of the moment with the broad smile plastered across his tanned face. "I need to talk to you for just a second. It's important."

"It better be," O'Reilly said in a low voice, still smiling.

Peoples leaned over O'Reilly's shoulder. "It's about the Nikki Waters murder," he whispered. "I've gotten hold of some important information." During his flight back to Orlando Ethan Peoples had debated what to do with Melissa's disclosure. He ruled out going to the police or confronting Parabrise directly. The cops would say, so what? Parabrise was nowhere near Orlando when Waters was killed, and anyway all Peoples had was a third-hand story that came from some model he didn't know from a hole in the wall. Parabrise, if Peoples could even get to see him on short notice, would laugh in his face for the same reason. The only alternative, Peoples reasoned, was to investigate further the senator's connection to the dead woman. To do that he knew he would have to have the approval of the editor-in-chief.

"Excuse us for a minute," O'Reilly said to his friends. He got up, put his arm around Ethan Peoples's shoulder, and steered him away from the group. O'Reilly turned so that no one in the room could see his face but Peoples. His expression had changed from good humor to pure anger. "What information?" he said.

"I have reason to believe Nikki Waters was involved with Drew Parabrise," Ethan Peoples said. "I want to check into it."

"You have reason to believe? You have reason to believe?" O'Reilly snarled. "You got pictures? You got motel receipts? What the hell do you have, you little fuck? I thought I gave explicit orders to leave that story alone."

"I have confidential information. I have enough to light a fire under any self-respecting editor," Peoples said.

"So you want to start making accusations about a United States Senator based on your confidential information?"

"That isn't what I said. I only want to investigate it further. I'm not accusing anyone of anything yet."

"You listen to me, you son of a bitch," O'Reilly hissed. "I don't care who you are. I don't care what kind of family connections you've got. You go up against me and I'll break you in two."

"Who warned you off it, Byron?" Peoples said. He had prepared himself for this kind of reaction from O'Reilly. He was scared, but O'Reilly's behavior was unconscionable and Peoples's sense of outrage spurred him on. "Who's jerking your chain? Is it Parabrise or his handlers? Because something's going on here and I intend to find out what it is, either for the *Journal-Express* or for someone else."

"Talk to me Monday morning," Byron O'Reilly said. "We'll work something out."

"I'm serious about this, Byron," Peoples said. "Don't try to sandbag me."

"Hey, you're a good newspaperman." O'Reilly's smile had returned and he clapped Ethan Peoples on the shoulder. "I just don't want to go off half-cocked on this thing and wind up being accused of fucking up the police investigation."

Peoples stared at O'Reilly. He lived a life far removed from the drug scene and was unfamiliar with the instantaneous mood swings of a confirmed coke freak, but he knew enough about human nature to realize the man now grinning at him had nothing but ill intentions in his heart.

"Sure, Byron," he said. "I'll cool it until Monday. Then we'll talk."

"Good, good," said O'Reilly. "Remember, we're on the same team. Now I have to get back to my friends over there before they think you and I have something going on." He laughed somewhat too loudly and returned to his table.

By nature Ethan Peoples was not a crusader. As a journalist, he tried to uphold his belief in a noble tradition by quietly adhering to what he thought was just and honorable. Like most members of his profession he was no war corre-

spondent, no jungle crawler or infiltrator, and so had been
able to do this in a detached way, without ever becoming
embroiled in situations that were personally threatening.
This was even more the case when Peoples stopped reporting and became an editor, working in a world as cloistered
as that of a university professor. Now, unexpectedly, he had
stepped over the line, his desire to do the right thing yank-
ing him into the world of peril. This became clear to him
the following day when he went for his customary early
Sunday-morning jog.

Ethan Peoples looked forward all week to running early
on Sunday morning. He would set out in College Park, the
neighborhood where he lived, letting his muscles warm
along the shaded cobblestone streets lined with two-story
colonial-style homes interspersed with smaller one-story
wooden bungalows. He would run two miles until he came
to a small lake. Circling the lake on a dirt path added almost another mile, at which point Peoples left College Park
and began a ten-mile leg up and down a highway that ran
east and west through Orlando. During the week, and even
on weekend afternoons, this highway was jammed with
traffic, but when Peoples took his Sunday-morning run the
road was usually empty.

On the Sunday following his confrontation with Byron
O'Reilly, Peoples had covered five miles on this highway
and was about to turn around when he saw the truck. It was
a jacked-up four-by-four Chevy with mud tires that
hummed in the early-morning stillness like a hundred thousand bumble bees. It passed him going in the opposite direction and he paid it little mind, but then instead of fading
away the sound of its tires and loud exhaust pipes seemed
to be approaching again from behind. He looked over his
shoulder and the truck was there, fifty yards from him and
closing fast. In that instant, Ethan Peoples was certain the
truck was going to try to run him down. He had no time to
think, no time to look for an escape route, only a split-
second to react, and in that split-second he dove as hard as
he could into a ditch filled with tall grass and all manner of
debris hurled from the windows of a month's worth of
passing vehicles. He lay there on his stomach, his left arm
resting on an empty, flattened can of Miller Lite, watching

the truck roar down the road, waiting for it to make another U-turn and try again. But it didn't. He could hear it winding through the gears, picking up speed, and he could see it disappearing in the direction from which it had come. He put his head down and listened until he couldn't hear it anymore, and then he stood up. There was no sign of the truck; the only vehicle in sight was an old Toyota station wagon towing a small Boston Whaler.

Ethan Peoples had never experienced pure terror before, but it struck him now, first in the form of a numbing pain in the pit of his stomach, and then in wave after wave of nausea. He bent over, rested his hands on his knees, and retched over and over again into the ditch, bringing up nothing but some phlegm and bitter-tasting liquid he assumed was bile. Finally, after about ten minutes, the nausea subsided, and though he was in no shape to resume running, Peoples could at least walk. A half-mile from where he encountered the truck he found a pay phone, decided not to wake one of his friends, and called a cab, thanking the gods he had the good sense to carry a quarter in the tiny pocket inside his running shorts. By the time the cab arrived, Peoples had rejected the idea of going to the police, at least not right away. He had no tag number for the truck and no proof there was even a connection between his close call and the information he'd given Byron O'Reilly. It seemed to him, as he stood shivering inside the phone booth, weighing his options and trying to keep out of the wind, that for the time being there were better people than the police with whom to share what he'd found out about Nikki Waters.

"You got a visitor," the guard said. "Some guy from the paper."

"Tell him they already hung me," Billy Roseman said. "I ain't talkin' to no reporter."

"He said it ain't about no interview," the guard said. "He said to tell you he has important information. You don't want to see him, that's fine with me. I don't really give a shit one way or the other."

"Yeah, okay," Roseman said. "I'll see him."

The room where the guard brought Roseman had nothing

in it but a small table and four molded plastic chairs. The guard stood in one corner; Roseman sat down across the table from Ethan Peoples, who was in the room when Roseman arrived.

"You got ten minutes," the guard said.

Ethan Peoples had gone home, showered, and cleaned up the bruises on his arms and legs before driving over to the county jail. There was an Ace bandage on his left wrist and a Band-Aid on his cheek covering a cut he received when he landed face-first in the ditch. Roseman could see that Peoples's hands were shaking. In as low a voice as possible, he told Roseman what he knew and what had happened to him.

"A senator," Roseman said when Peoples was through. "I'll be a son of a bitch. She used to talk about this powerful dude she'd been involved with, but she never said who it was. You think he killed her?"

"I haven't the slightest idea," Peoples said. "But I know the cops in this town. I'll tell them about Parabrise, O'Reilly, and the truck and they'll say, 'Yeah, yeah, we'll check it out,' and write me off as a paranoid conspiracy freak. Especially with the case they already have against you. I thought if you put me in touch with your lawyer he might be able to help."

"Fuck my lawyer," Roseman said. "He's already given me up for dead. I got somebody better for you to talk to. Somebody I trust. Somebody who believes I didn't do it. You got a pencil and paper?"

Peoples shook his head. "They took everything away from me at the front desk," he said.

"How's your memory?"

"Not bad."

"Call the number I'm gonna give you. If anybody answers it'll be my mother. She'll tell you what to do."

"What if she isn't there?" Peoples asked.

"Lay low and keep calling," Roseman said. "You'll reach her. And thanks, man. I really appreciate what you're doing."

"For what it's worth, I think you're innocent too," Peoples said.

"Well, the list is short but at least it's growing," Roseman said. "Hopefully that's a good sign."

XV

✦

Wanda Donnerstag got the idea for the tattoo in Victoria's Secret at the Altamonte Mall. She had begun frequenting the various malls around Orlando a week or so after Nikki Waters's death. On her first trip, she bought a bottle of Opium, the perfume Nikki wore. Several nights later, she purchased some cosmetics and stopped to have a slice of pizza and a Diet Coke at a little restaurant that occupied a corner at a busy indoor crossroads. Wanda had heretofore eschewed malls, thinking them far too pedestrian, far beneath her tastes, but as she sat and observed the people walking back and forth in front of the pizza restaurant she began to undergo a conversion. The mall was climate-controlled. It was safe—free from the panhandlers and muggers who had become all too frequent on the downtown streets near the *Journal-Express* at night. This one had recently been renovated and had high, skylighted ceilings, fountains everywhere, and wide, pastel-colored walkways. It was also full of every type of suburban human being currently in existence. True, there were plenty of sloppy-looking, unattractive characters, but among them Wanda saw chic, athletic women walk by along with sexy department-store models and hot-looking teenage girls dressed in the latest styles. The mall, she suddenly realized, was the perfect place for the new Wanda, the Nikki/Wanda, to refine her act anonymously, since no one she knew ever went to one.

If she saw a high-heeled shoe, for example, that set off the ankle and calf in just the right way, and clicked on the hard tile floor of the walkway with a sound that grabbed her, there were a dozen or more stores within two minutes of where she sat in which she might find a similar pair. The same held true for blouses and skirts, for nail polish and lipstick, and for jewelry. In an hour, while she sipped coffee or drank a glass of wine or ate a snack, she could observe a moving fashion show that was far better than thumbing through the stack of magazines in her office.

One night, a whip-thin redhead wearing a mini-skirted linen suit over a T-shirt sat down at the table by the fountain next to hers. "Excuse me," Wanda said. "I hope I'm not disturbing you, but I was admiring your suit. Would you tell me where you got it?"

"Oh, no problem," the woman said. "I got it right here at Victoria's Secret. I think it might even be on sale."

The saleswoman thought Wanda looked smashing in the suit and Wanda agreed, though she didn't say so. The aerobic exercises and the early-morning jogging she was doing were beginning to pay off. Wanda told the woman she would take the suit and also a lavender Chancery Lace bra and matching panties. The saleswoman placed the suit, the bra, and the panties in a box, took Wanda's credit card, and gave her a warm, conspiratorial smile. "Lucky man," she said.

When the woman leaned over to run the card through the machine, Wanda noticed a small tattoo of a rose on her left breast. "I like your tattoo," she said.

The woman looked up and smiled at her again. "Thank you," she said. "I just got it a month ago."

"Could you tell me where?" Wanda asked. An idea had come to her that was so thrilling she thought she would have to sit down.

The woman finished with Wanda's card and handed it back to her. As Wanda stuck the card into her wallet, the woman wrote something on one of the business cards she took from a glass container next to the cash register. "Here's the guy's address and phone number," she said. "You should definitely do it. My boyfriend ... when he saw it ..." The woman smiled for the third time. "You'll find out," she said. "It drives them nuts."

"I want a raven," Wanda said. "I want it with its wings spread, but I don't want it to be too big. Here. I brought a photograph to give you an idea of what I have in mind."

"That's cool," the man said. "I can do it exactly like the picture." His name was Sailor Steve. He wore a white short-sleeved knit shirt, tan pants, and horn-rimmed glasses. If it weren't for the tattoos that covered his arms, he would have looked more like a college professor than a man of the sea.

"Where do you want it?" Sailor Steve asked.

"Right here," Wanda said. She lifted her skirt and touched a spot on the left side of her belly, just above the dark wispy hair of her mound. "Can you put it there?"

"Without a doubt," Sailor Steve said. "You lie yourself down on the table and we'll do it. What kind of music do you like?"

XVI

♦

From somewhere far, far away, Wayne Boudrie could hear his name being called. It couldn't be Frank and Betty. They were gone all the way to San Angelo to a wedding. It could be Calder or Butch, but it didn't sound like either of them. Wayne opened his eyes and heard the voice again, along with a knocking on the door of his Airstream.

"Who the hell is it?" he croaked.

"Wayne, you in there?" the voice called. "I got a message for you. It's important."

"Hold on," Wayne said. He looked at his watch. It was ten after seven. He sat up and pulled on his jeans, thinking what he didn't need was company, what he needed was a hot cup of coffee and a fix. He stood, a bit unsteadily, and walked from the back of the trailer, where he slept, to the door, pausing to grab the .38 Chief's Special from one of the overhead cupboards above the sink. No point in taking chances.

"What kind of message?" Wayne asked. He peeked out the window next to the door and saw it was a tall, thin guy with shaggy hair and a beard. He'd never seen the man before.

"It's from Villegas," the man said. "Open the damn door. I'm freezing my ass off out here."

"Villegas?" Wayne said. "I just talked to him two days ago. What the hell's he doin' sending messengers in the middle of the night?" He opened the door and a gust of wind caught it. He leaned forward slightly in a feeble attempt to keep the door from slamming against the side of the trailer, and as he did the tall man grabbed his gun hand and punched him hard in the stomach, twice. Wayne tumbled down the aluminum steps of the Airstream and landed

188

on his side in the dirt. The man kicked him just below his rib cage and he passed out.

"Looks to me like you been dipping into that Mexican brown pretty good, huh, Wayne?" Roland Troy said. Troy had cuffed Boudrie's hands behind his back, bound his ankles, and sat him on his bed inside the Airstream. Troy was sitting in a canvas deck chair in the narrow corridor running down the middle of the trailer. He had his .45 pointed at Boudrie's chest.

"Whatever it is you're doin', you ain't gettin' away with it," Wayne said. His nose was running slightly and his shoulders had begun to twitch. He gave a quick glance out the window next to his head.

"You're thinkin' about your two buddies over across the way there," Troy said. "I already been to see them. I'm afraid they ain't gonna do you no good at all."

"What do you want?" Wayne asked.

"I want to see Raimundo Villegas by ten o'clock this morning," Troy said. "You call him up and get him here or I'm gonna shoot you just like I shot your two friends in the other trailer."

"What the fuck . . . I can't do that," Wayne said. "He's all the way down in Chihuahua." He sniffed and looked out the window again. "You shot 'em? Why'd you shoot 'em? Who the hell are you? I thought Villegas sent *you*."

"Wayne, you ain't payin' attention," Troy said. "Now you call Villegas up and you tell him whatever it takes to make him hop in his plane and fly on up here and land it out there where it's been landing for quite a while, judging by those tracks. Otherwise, if I have to go down to Mexico to find him, I'm gonna tie you up real good and leave you all by yourself to go cold turkey. Then when I get back I'm gonna shoot you."

"How am I gonna call Villegas with my hands cuffed behind my back?" Wayne asked.

"Now we're gettin' somewhere," Troy said.

Roland Troy waited just inside a line of brush and low-growing trees for the plane of Raimundo Villegas. He lay on his stomach, insulated from the cold ground by the four-

ounce Space Blanket he had carried with him in the pocket
of his dun-colored parka and unfolded, reflective side
down, so that it would not be noticeable from the air. In
addition to the lightweight parka, he wore tan corduroy
Levi's, a pair of Vasque lightweight trail shoes made of
rough-out tan leather, and an old brown baseball cap, all
designed to reduce his visibility, to help him blend in with
his surroundings. He uncapped the Leupold 3 x 9 scope
mounted on his bolt-action Browning High-Power .270 rifle, chambered a round, and lay the gun back down beside
him, taking care that no sunlight reflected off its metal parts
or the glass of the scope. Satisfied he was adequately concealed, he regulated his breathing, slowing it, eliminating
any unnecessary motion of his body, so that if his pulse had
been taken at that moment it would have registered no
more than forty beats per minute.

Becoming one with the landscape was something he had
elevated to the level of an art form when he was cast into
the jungles and mountains of Southeast Asia. To remain
alive there, he had become so adept at composing himself
as part of the terrain, at tuning in, as he called it, that he
was no more distinct, no more obvious, than a fallen tree
limb or a pile of rocks. Once, in Laos, in the mountains
north of the Plain of Jars, a column of North Vietnamese
soldiers had marched along a trail ten feet from where he
stood leaning against a tree, and though several had looked
in his direction, not one of them had seen him.

By his estimate, Troy had an hour or so to wait for
Villegas, but waiting was another art he had perfected. In
this semi-meditative state of decreased respiration, his mind
clear, his nerves calm, an hour was nothing; as a sniper he
had once waited an entire day behind a crumbling stone
wall with only a few rice balls and a container of water for
sustenance until his target appeared. Like Raimundo
Villegas, the man he had waited for behind the wall arrived
by plane. He was a member of the Royal Laos Air Force
flying a T-28 North American Nomad, supposedly cutting
off North Vietnamese supply convoys on the Ho Chi Minh
Trail but actually relaying the locations of U.S. Special
Forces teams to the enemy. Troy had shot the man as he
climbed from the cockpit of the T-28, taking care not to

damage the plane. That had been twenty-five years ago, but as Troy lay there on that desolate piece of southwest Texas ground, calculating as precisely as possible where Villegas's Cessna would taxi to a halt, gauging the distance from that spot to his position, it seemed as though he were reliving an event that had happened last week. "Go to Okinawa, Roland," his karate teacher Ansai Shima said to him. "You will find peace there. You will come home a very different man." Shima had been right about the second part.

It was over a hundred degrees with total humidity on the September afternoon in 1963 when Roland Troy landed in Naha, the capital city of Okinawa. He walked from the plane across fifty yards of tarmac, wondering who would meet him in the terminal. There had been no one. He handed the scrap of paper on which Shima had written the address of *Sensei* Miyazato's *dojo* to a taxi driver, threw his duffel bag into the trunk of the tiny diesel-powered Datsun, and climbed into the back seat, too tired and dizzy from his long journey to be angry or upset.

The taxi deposited him in front of a small building on a narrow, winding street of little shops and rickety dwellings a couple of blocks from Koksai Dori, one of Naha's main thoroughfares. He climbed from the cab and was struck at once by the incredible stench of raw sewage. He cursed softly, wondering what he had gotten himself into, thinking that had he not been so determined to get away from everything reminiscent of his grandparents he could be floating down the calm Coacoochee instead of standing halfway around the world amidst the unremitting smell of shit. But there he was, and being the person he was he slung the duffel bag over his shoulder and walked into the *dojo* of Gishin Miyazato, determined to make the best of whatever lay in store.

He was standing in a short hallway. To his right was a large room he recognized at once as the *dojo*. It had a highly polished hardwood floor, various weapons mounted on one wall, pictures of a dozen or so karate masters along another, and a small, raised platform at one end on which rested several folding chairs. The *dojo* was empty; the only motion in the room was the slow rotation of an overhead fan mounted in the center of the ceiling.

On the other side of the hallway was an office where a small, compactly built man of about fifty sat behind a desk piled high with paperwork. He wore a white dress shirt with the sleeves rolled up and gray slacks. A pair of reading glasses were perched halfway down his nose.

"*Sensei* Miyazato?" Troy said.

"*Hai?*" said the man. "Yes?"

"I am Roland Troy," Troy said. The man looked at him with a blank expression. It occurred to Troy that he knew no English. "Shima," he said. "Shima my *sensei*."

"Shima?" Miyazato said. He shook his head. "No here. No Shima."

Troy's heart sank. Shima had told him Miyazato knew he was coming. Where was the welcome Shima had told him he could expect? The overpowering smell came in off the street through the office's open window and Troy thought he was going to be sick. He set his duffel bag down on the floor. The man behind the desk looked quizzically from Troy to the duffel bag and back to Troy. He said something in Japanese and made a circular motion with both hands, as though he wanted Troy to hurry up and open the bag. Troy was stymied; obviously Miyazato had no idea who he was. As a last resort he unbuttoned his shirt and took it off. "Shima," he said again, pointing to the prancing tiger tattoo.

"Oh," said Miyazato, a broad smile coming over his face. "You Roland-san." He nodded vigorously and stood up, motioning Troy to an old cloth-covered armchair in the corner of the office. "Good, good. You sit. You wait." Miyazato moved with short, rapid strides across the room and was gone before Troy could respond.

In twenty minutes Miyazato returned with a thin young man also wearing a white shirt and dark slacks. "Higa-san," Miyazato said, pointing at the young man. "Roland-san," he said, pointing at Troy. "Talk you. Good, good." He sat down once again behind his desk, smiled at them, and nodded.

Higa straightened everything out. He was a *sho-dan*, a first-degree black belt like Troy, who trained in Miyazato's *dojo* and was also an English teacher at the local business college. He explained to Troy that *Sensei* Miyazato had thought Troy was coming in December, not September, and was very sorry he had not met him at the airport. Miyazato, who ran a freight-forwarding business in addition to a karate school, thought Troy was delivering something from the U.S. military base in Kadena. Now the three of them—Miyazato, Higa, and Troy—would go out for a nice meal at Miyazato's favorite restaurant while Miyazato's wife prepared the room where Troy would live. "*Sensei* Miyazato says his friend Mr. Shima spoke very highly of you," Higa said. "*Sensei* says he is happy to have you here as his student. Oh, yes, *Sensei* says one other thing. He says if at all possible, keep your shirt on, except of course when bathing. He says you will know what he means."

"Does *Sensei* Miyazato know where Shima is?" Troy asked.

Higa turned to Miyazato and spoke to him in Japanese. The smile faded from Miyazato's face and he was silent for a moment. "No Shima. Don't know," he said, shaking his head.

Troy's room, small and tidy as the cabin of a ship, was just off the *dojo*, with a window that looked out on the street. The first couple of nights the smell was excruciating, but within a week he was not bothered by it at all. Nor did he mind any longer the sounds of the street, only a few feet from his bed, that drifted into the room at all hours.

At first he wondered what Shima was thinking when he said Miyazato would be good for him, inasmuch as the karate master did not speak English. But as his life in Okinawa became a series of regularly occurring events, a rhythmic pattern, much like the *katas* he practiced over and over, he understood. Every day during workouts Miyazato would be at his side, adjusting his stance, making him repeat moves again and again, sometimes talking so softly Troy could barely hear him, sometimes barking commands with the shrill cadence of a drill sergeant, working Troy so hard he often found himself splashing in a puddle of his own sweat.

Troy's routine rarely varied. Monday through Saturday he trained twice a day—two hours in the early morning, two more at night. In between, he and Miyazato's oldest son, Itoman, who was twenty-two and spoke halting English, delivered freight in Miyazato's truck. On Sunday there was no work, but Miyazato held a morning class from ten until twelve for *katas* performed with weapons—*nunchaku, bo,* and *sai.* Afterwards, Troy usually spent over an hour soaking in the public bath, ate an enormous meal at a neighborhood restaurant, went for a long walk into the hills on the outskirts of Naha, and returned to his room to read and sleep for the rest of the day.

It was on Sundays, when he had time to himself, that he thought most about Clara and reread the letters she had written. In one she told him she was spending weekends at his house. He would lie on his cot in the *dojo* picturing her with Billy in his canoe on the Coacoochee, sitting on the porch beside the pond, or lying naked in his bed, her long, dark hair hanging down around her breasts. Now and then, on his walks, he saw American women shopping in the market. A few were young, around his own age, and he'd been tempted to stop and talk to them, but thus far he had refrained. He wondered whether Clara had gone out with anyone to a movie or for a cup of coffee. He told himself that if she did, he would understand, that he couldn't blame her if she was lonely and wanted company. He told himself the separation would be a good test of their love.

Weeks went by, one the same as the next, the only change being the weather, which slowly turned from oppressive heat to warm days and cool, damp nights. Troy, totally immersed in his karate training and daily chores, paid no attention to the calendar and was only vaguely aware that Thanksgiving was approaching. He would always remember, however, that he was eating breakfast with Miyazato and his family early in the morning of November 24, 1963, when Higa came rushing in to tell him the President of the United States had been assassinated. He excused himself from Miyazato's apartment, went down to his room, and lay on his bed, staring at the ceiling. It was the first time since he had arrived in Naha that he desperately wanted to talk to someone. Since that was impossible, he got out a paperback volume of great American poetry Clara had given him before he left Florida and read from Walt

Whitman's *Leaves of Grass* until it was time for the morning workout.

For several days he felt strangely disconnected from everything, but seeing no alternative, threw himself even harder into his training. He had come to see himself as a samurai, a lone warrior, come to a foreign land to dedicate himself to his art, and made up his mind he would achieve *mushin*, the state of mind free from all trepidation, in which the *kata* performs itself.

One day Higa came to Troy's room and said that Miyazato wished to speak with him. Troy followed Higa upstairs to Miyazato's apartment, where the two of them sat with their teacher on tatami mats around a low table on which a teapot and china cups had been set.

"*Sensei* says Mr. Shima wrote to him that you are an expert at finding your way in ... I am not sure of the exact word ... in, I think, wild places," Higa said. "In the jungle, perhaps?"

"Tell *Sensei* Miyazato that it is true I spent a great deal of time in the woods ... in the forest ... and on the rivers, where I lived in Florida," Troy said, thinking how curious it was that his English always became very formal during these dialogues with his teacher.

"*Sensei* says also he remembers Mr. Shima mentioned you were an excellent tracker," said Higa. "He wishes you to teach these arts, the finding of your way and the tracking, to the black belts. He believes this would be very beneficial to them. It would be survival training. Would you agree to do that, he wonders?"

"Tell *Sensei* Miyazato I would be honored to," Troy said.

Higa relayed Troy's words to Miyazato, who smiled broadly and nodded. Then he said something else to Higa, who laughed loudly.

"*Sensei* is very happy about this," Higa said. "You will begin next Sunday afternoon, and we will do this in the jungle once each week. *Sensei* also says maybe if we are lucky one or two of the black belts whose names he will not mention will get lost in the woods and not come back. *Sensei* is joking, of course."

"Of course," Troy said.

Although the vegetation was somewhat different, the

terrain much hillier than Florida, Troy found himself immediately at home in the Okinawan jungle and welcomed the opportunity to be of more use to Miyazato than simply a delivery boy. Using Higa and Itoman as translators, he taught Miyazato's students the basics of orienteering— the use of a map and compass—how to move safely in the woods, and how to recognize the signs of wildlife. Within a few weeks he organized the black belts into two teams competing to see which one could reach an objective more quickly. Miyazato, finding Troy's program working even better than he had originally hoped, increased the jungle training to twice a week, and Troy soon included orienteering at night as part of his tracking instruction.

"I think a true student of karate should be able to feel his way through the jungle the way a Zen archer can feel the target without actually seeing it," he told Miyazato, hoping he wasn't being too presumptuous.

"I agree," Miyazato replied. "That is what I envisioned when I first decided to have you do this. Shima was right about you. You are an unusual man, and you are still so young. I am glad he sent you here to study in my *dojo*." This compliment from Miyazato was highly unusual. He did not often dispense words of praise, and Troy was embarrassed. He was afraid Higa, who had to translate what Miyazato said, and the other black belts, who would surely hear about it from Higa, would now resent him, especially since he was American, not Okinawan. Years later, when Troy looked back on what happened to him in Southeast Asia, he realized that his fears had not been unfounded.

On the Saturday after Higa translated Miyazato's compliment, he approached Troy at the end of *kata* class. "Come with me and Tada tonight," he said. "We will show you an adventure." Troy willingly accepted the invitation and out of courtesy did not ask where they were going. Although the black belts obediently followed his directions in the jungle and treated him with proper respect, this was the first time he had been invited to join any of them, other than Itoman, outside the *dojo* and he did not want to say anything that might be construed as impolite. Perhaps, Troy thought, he was wrong about Higa and the others. Perhaps this was their way of showing him he was now accepted as one of them.

There was no free-style fighting—no *kumite*—in Miyazato's *dojo*, only controlled sparring, since Miyazato believed that the intense study of *kata* over a long enough period of time would prepare a man for any self-defense situation he might encounter. Still, two or three of the younger black belts were anxious to test their fighting ability, so occasionally, on Saturday nights, they journeyed north to Kadena, to the karate *dojo* of *Sensei* Uesu, where they were welcome to join Uesu's students in bouts of full-contact *kumite*. It was to Uesu's *dojo* that Higa and Tada took Roland Troy, Higa first cautioning Troy to say nothing to Itoman. "And don't forget to bring your *gi*," Higa said.

"Higa-san, I don't need a *gi*. I don't want to fight," Troy said. Combat didn't scare him; in fact he was curious to find out how effective all his training had been, but he was afraid Miyazato would somehow discover what they had been up to and be angry with him.

"Whatever you like," Higa said. "But you will be sorry you left it in your room. Just wait and see."

There were about twenty men in the *dojo*, a dank, poorly lit, high-ceilinged building on a darkened street in a run-down section of Kadena. A couple of the men, Troy noted, were tough-looking, crew-cut Americans, obviously marines from the base a few miles away. For over an hour Troy sat on a low bench against the wall of Uesu's *dojo* watching the matches, that lasted about three minutes each, between competitors randomly selected by *Sensei* Uesu. Uesu himself sat against the wall opposite Troy on a high stool, focusing intently on the action taking place in the center of the room.

There was a good deal of blood, mostly from kicks or punches to the nose and mouth, and twice men were knocked out. When that happened, *Sensei* Uesu signaled with his hand to an assistant who revived the unconscious man by dumping a bucket of water over him. To Troy, the brutal atmosphere was in complete opposition to everything Shima had taught him about karate, though he remembered Shima warning him about men such as *Sensei* Uesu.

Both Higa and Tada fought inconclusive matches,

although Tada got clipped below the left eye with a back-hand punch that raised a substantial welt. After their fights, the two of them came over and sat down next to Troy. By this time he had seen enough and was about to suggest they leave to get something to eat when *Sensei* Uesu stood up and pointed to him. "You," he said, motioning to Troy. "Curly hair. Come here."

Troy walked slowly across the *dojo*, aware that the other men who were sitting on the floor with their backs against the wall were all watching him. "You have *gi*?" Uesu asked.

"No, *Sensei*," Troy said. "I didn't come here to fight."

"You afraid?" Uesu asked.

"No, *Sensei*," said Troy. "It's just that *Sensei* Miyazato has instructed me not to engage in *kumite*." He heard two or three snickers, no doubt from the marines who were able to follow the conversation.

"But you here, you not in *Sensei* Miyazato's *dojo*," Uesu said. "Why you here, you no want *kumite*?"

As Troy was considering how to reply, a white cloth bundle hurtled across the room and landed at his feet. "Now you have *gi*," Uesu said. "You fight or you go."

"I reckon I'll go, *Sensei*," Troy said. He was not yet twenty-one, but had already acquired the habit of slowing his deep voice to a measured drawl when he was very angry so that it sounded like a recording played at a slightly reduced speed, as though by speaking this way he could slow down his raging emotions as well.

He turned his back on Uesu and the *gi* lying on the floor, strode back across the room, and pulled on his desert boots, which had been underneath the bench. Without a word to Higa or Tada, he walked toward the door, never even considering whether or not they were coming with him, wanting only to get away from that place as quickly as he could, but when he reached the door his path was blocked by one of the marines.

"You're giving white folks a bad name," the man said. He was about thirty years old, an inch or two taller than Troy and a good fifty pounds heavier, with a thick neck and a red, beefy face.

"Get out of my way," Troy said.

"I ain't movin', Slim," the man said. "You gonna have to go through me. *Gi* or no *gi*, we're gonna see what you got."

"*Karate ni santinash,*" Shima had said to him many times. "There is no first move in karate. The question is, what constitutes the first move? It isn't necessarily a punch or a kick."

"So, how do I know what it is?" Troy would ask him.

"Oh, don't worry, when the time comes you will know," Shima always said.

It was very quiet in Uesu's *dojo* when Roland Troy hit the marine with a blow whose power derived not only from Troy's arm and shoulder but also from his twisting hips and torso. It was delivered with lightning speed in a straight line from just under Troy's right armpit to the center of the marine's chin, and sounded, when it landed, like the crack of a bullwhip. The marine was out cold before he hit the floor, where he lay twitching, his face drained of color. Blood ran from his mouth, a couple of his teeth were gone, and another hung between his lips by just a thread of gum.

It took Uesu and his assistant ten minutes to bring the big marine around, but Roland Troy was unaware of that. He left the *dojo* immediately, walked down the long winding street that ended at the main highway between Kadena and Naha, and stuck out his thumb, hoping to somehow catch a ride back home before Higa and Tada came after him. Feeling that he had been set up, he had no desire to see either of them. In his heart he was convinced their intention had been to have him soundly beaten in a fight, to show him he wasn't such hot stuff, no matter what Miyazato might think.

Because of the late hour traffic was very light, but in less than five minutes Troy saw an approaching car slow down and signal that it was pulling over. It was a white Austin-Healey, a strange enough sight in itself in Okinawa, but when Troy opened the door on the passenger side he was so startled he was transfixed.

"You gettin' in or what?" the woman said. She had a southern accent, short blond hair, and was wearing a skimpy dress, either black or navy blue, Troy couldn't tell in the dark.

"I'm gettin' in," Troy said. He worked his way into the seat and let out a long sigh. "It's been a long evening," he said.

"For me too, honey. I fought off a major for three hours. He's married. I told him beforehand, 'Look, I'll let you buy me dinner, but that's it. I don't mess around with married men.' Naturally, he figured he was the exception. Where you headed?"

"Naha," he told her.

"You aren't a marine. Your hair's too long. What the hell you doin' in Okinawa?"

Troy told her. "Well that's gotta be a first," she said. "An American coming to Okinawa who didn't have to. My name's Janine. I'm from North Carolina, originally. From Ashville. I work for the Defense Department. I'm an elementary school teacher. They sent me over here to teach the servicemen's kids at the school on the base in Kadena. One more semester and I'm goin' home, thank the Lord. Only good thing about this whole deal is I bank almost everything I make and I get to bring this car back to the States for free. It's hell in a rainstorm, but hey, you were impressed, right? I bought it from a colonel who was shipping out to Vietnam. I'm twenty-four. How old are you?"

"Twenty," Troy said. "I'll be twenty-one in April."

"You seem older," she said.

He had never met a schoolteacher who talked or drove like this woman. She was running the Healey through the gears on the deserted highway like a racing driver, double-clutching when she downshifted, keeping the revs up so that they had to shout to hear each other over the noise and vibration of the engine. When she pulled up in front of Miyazato's *dojo* and shut the engine off, the sudden stillness felt like swimming underwater.

Years later, when he thought about that night, he could never recall which of them reached for the other first. What he remembered were her hands caressing him, how alone he had felt, far from home, betrayed by the other black belts, and how hungrily he had clung to her in the closeness of the small car. They made love on his cot in Miyazato's *dojo*. Afterwards, he fell asleep and when he awoke at daylight, she was gone. She left a note, clipped with a bobby pin to the collar of his shirt. "I'll pick you up for dinner next Saturday night at seven-thirty," it said.

He spent the day thinking about Clara. He missed her terribly and felt guilty about what he'd done, but when Janine showed up in her Healey promptly at seven-thirty the following week, he was waiting for her outside the *dojo*. She was there again the week after that, and every Saturday until she left Okinawa. She was small and thin and not particularly pretty, but she possessed a worldliness and recklessness that made her appealing. She was his guide, driving him to the various corners of the island, eating with him in obscure little back-street restaurants she'd found during her two-year stay, taking him to after-hours clubs that few Americans knew existed, making love to him in the sand beside the tepid East China Sea.

He never said anything to her about Clara, nor did he write to Clara about her, promising himself instead to tell Clara in person about Janine when he got home. In his mind, he wanted to keep them separate—the woman he still loved and planned to spend his life with, and the woman he needed, there in Okinawa, to fill a void.

Janine was very interested in karate and questioned him at length about the particulars of his training, the intensity of it, and about the orienteering and tracking he taught the other students. She knew a great deal about Oriental philosophy and history and gave him several books, one of which, *The Way of Zen* by Alan Watts, he read three times. He was particularly intrigued by the Zen concept of acting without reflection, of a mind free from equivocation, and by the possibility of obliterating self-consciousness. It seemed to him this was in keeping with his striving for *mushin*, for the *kata* that performed itself. On the wall of his room he taped a piece of paper on which he'd written a two-line poem from the Zenrin Kushu: "Entering the forest he moves not the grass; Entering the water he makes not a ripple."

When Janine left Okinawa in the late spring, after the school year was over, neither of them made any promises to write or look each other up in the States. It was, he thought years later, as though neither of them had existed before they came to Okinawa, and ceased to exist, at least for one another, when she departed. It wasn't until four years later, when he was back in the States, that he learned her last name.

She had been gone a month when Higa came to Troy's room to tell him Miyazato wished to speak with him at the small bar where Miyazato sometimes drank sake with his friends.

"There is a man, an American, who has heard about you," Higa said after Troy pulled a chair up to Miyazato's table, bowed respectfully, and sat down. "This man has heard about the training we do with you in the jungle. He wishes to meet you. He has spoken to *Sensei* Miyazato about it. This shows he knows something about our traditions since he was told you are *Sensei*'s student and did not want to offend *Sensei* by coming to see you first. *Sensei* says this man has lived in Asia for many years, in several different countries. He works for your government, but *Sensei* is not sure exactly what he does. *Sensei* wonders about him."

"What does *Sensei* wonder?" Troy asked.

"*Sensei* thinks this man wants something from you. He wonders what it is."

And so Jack Ubinas came into Roland Troy's life. He was witty and urbane, a big man, always slightly unkempt, who looked like he belonged on a New England college campus trailing a host of adoring students. He reminded Troy of a sheepdog. He had found out about Troy from Janine.

"Our country could really use someone like you," he said. "You know, like Kennedy said, 'Ask not what your country can do for you; ask what you can do for your country.' I mean, you could wait around a year or so, get drafted, and do it that way, 'cause I'm going to level with you, there's big trouble coming over across the water there in Southeast Asia and you will get drafted, make no mistake about it. Personally, I don't think you'd like that, someone with your talent and independence. What I have in mind for you would be far more beneficial to America's interests and more interesting to you."

They were sitting in a club in Namina-ue, the section of Naha filled with bars, strip joints, and whorehouses. On a small stage in front of them, a nude Filipino dancer placed the filtered end of a lit cigarette in her vagina. As she rolled her hips, puffs of smoke came from between her legs. It was two in the morning and there were only a half-dozen people in the club. The Filipino smiled at them and licked her lips.

"She can do that to a cigarette, think what she could do to your dick," Ubinas said.

"What is it you have in mind for me, Mr. Ubinas?" Troy said.

"Jack. Forget the Mr. Ubinas shit. I'm Jack. Smiling Jack." He gave Troy a wide, toothy grin. "You said you wanted to be in the FBI, right? Well, this would be like working for the FBI, only in a foreign country. Information-gathering is what it mostly would be. That and surveillance. You work with two or three other guys. Operate from a base camp. You lead 'em through the jungle or up the river or over the mountain to where they have to go, they gather their information, do their surveilling, you lead 'em back again. The thing is, you wouldn't be attached to any military unit, at least not officially. You'd be a civilian, a freelance scout working for the United States government. You'd be working for me. Pay wouldn't be bad either. About three times what you'd make as a private in the army."

"Where would this work be?" Troy asked. "In Vietnam?"

"In Vietnam. Maybe other places. Wherever you were needed."

"Why me?" Troy asked. "Don't you have all kinds of guys trained to do that stuff already? Commandos. Whatever you call them."

"Oh yeah, we have 'em," Ubinas said. "Special Forces personnel. Very tough men. Highly trained in counterinsurgency, guerrilla tactics, linguistics, emergency medicine, you name it, those guys can do it. Actually you'd be working with some of them. You want to use up a year or two of your life, you could enlist and go through their training program. I'd recommend you without hesitation." Ubinas leaned across the table, put a beefy hand on Troy's arm, and looked him straight in the eye. "In your case, Roland, all that training is unnecessary, so why bother?" he said. "You're ready now. You think I go around over here prop- ositioning every American civilian I see on the street? You think I have time for that? I heard about you. Janine said you were special, so I checked you out. She was right."

"Can I think about it?" Troy asked.

"Sure you can," Ubinas said, "but you'll have to think fast. I'm leaving Okinawa for Southeast Asia in three days. If you want the job, I'll take you with me."

"I'd be a scout," Troy said.

"Look," said Ubinas. "I have nothing but respect for your *sensei*, Mr. Miyazato, so don't take this the wrong way, but what you're doing there, in his school, is practice. You were a football player. You know the difference be- tween practice—between a scrimmage—and the real game. What I'm offering you is a chance to play the real game, the ultimate real-life adventure. And while you're doing that you'd be helping your country stop the spread of com- munism. Who the hell you think killed Jack Kennedy?"

"How long would this job last?"

"Hey, like I said, you'd be a civilian. It lasts as long as you want it to last. You get sick of it, you quit and go home. You can't do that in the army. But see, I have this feeling about you. I have a feeling once you start playing the real game you won't want to quit so fast. I think you're the kind of man who'll enjoy the challenge."

"What about the army?" Troy asked. "What if it's like you say it's gonna be and I get drafted? What do I tell my draft board?"

"That's nothing but paperwork," Ubinas said. "Minor de- tails. I'll handle all of that. You come with me, you won't ever have to worry about any draft board. One thing you can count on, Roland. I take care of my people."

Before he left Okinawa, Roland Troy sent a letter to Clara. *Dear Clara,* he wrote.

I've been over here almost a year now and, as I've writ- ten, I feel much calmer now and not at all angry about life, and I thought I was about ready to come home, but I've been offered a chance to do something to help our country, so I'll be staying. I'm not sure how long it will

*be. I can't say much about what I'm going to do. I can
tell you that I'm going to Southeast Asia, where I'll be
sort of a scout, leading people through the jungle and in
the mountains. I guess it will be sort of dangerous but
don't worry, you know I'm more at home in the woods
than in a city anyway. I'll miss you very much—I think
about you all the time—but this is something that is very
important. When I come back we will be together always.
Take care of the land. Give my best to Halpatter, Waxe,
and your aunt and uncle. I love you and hope you'll understand why I have to do this. The rest has been practice. This is the real game. Love, Roland.*

For a while, it *was* a game. His base camp was in the
central highlands of Vietnam along the Laotian border,
where, according to official reports, there were no Americans. There were three men in his team. The other two,
men in their late twenties, were with U.S. intelligence. He
led them to the edge of the village, or the encampment, or
the mountain hideout designated on his map. They went in,
investigated, interrogated, did whatever else they had to do,
and he led them back.

On his first day in camp the Special Forces captain in
charge of the base took him inside a cave secured by heavy
wooden doors and said, "Take your pick, partner." Troy
looked around and saw racks filled with every kind of
handgun and rifle imaginable. He chose a .45 automatic
and, at the captain's suggestion, a Remington 1100 auto-
loading shotgun with a twenty-inch barrel and an extended
magazine that held eight shells. "It's a duckbill," the captain said. "Load it with number-four buckshot. Gives you a
nice wide spray."

When he went out with his team he kept the shotgun
slung tightly across his back and carried the .45 in a shoulder holster, but in three months he never had to fire a shot,
so he took to leaving the .45 in camp to save weight.
Ubinas had been right; he loved the work, loved picking his
way silently through the mist-shrouded mountain forests
and along the steaming jungle paths, guiding his team with
a series of hand signals he developed. The fact that he be-

lieved there was a noble purpose to what he was doing
made it even more exciting.

He knew there was a real enemy out there. On more than
one occasion when he was across the border in Laos he
saw what he assumed were enemy troops, although as they
squatted in primitive encampments or walked single-file
along a trail they appeared to be no more than ragged, un-
dernourished peasants. None of them ever saw him or his
team and he came to believe they never would. So silently
did he move through the landscape that he imagined he was
invisible. In his mind it was pure Zen: There was no space
between him and what he was doing, no room for reflection; he simply was there, totally in tune, the ultimate jungle animal, stealthy as a cat, but smarter.

Then one day he was returning from a mission with his
team when through the trees he saw smoke rising across the
river where the base camp was located. There were twelve
men living in the camp—four teams of three. Troy's team
had been the only one to go out the night before. The other
nine men had remained in camp, and Troy knew none of
them would ever build a fire to give away their position.
That rule had been explained to him on his first day in the
camp. He signaled, and the two other men in his team crept
to where he lay in tall grass on the riverbank.

"What the fuck's going on?" one of the men whispered
to him. He was nearly ten years older than Troy, a tough
little Irishman from San Diego named McNulty, but like the
other CIA operative on the team he deferred to Troy, who
had led both of them safely to and from their targets without ever making contact with the enemy.

"I don't know," Troy said, "but I'm goin' over there to
find out. You guys want to stay here and wait for me, that's
cool."

"We'll come with you," said McNulty. The other member of the team was a serious, taciturn man who wore rim-
less glasses and was incongruously called "Skipper." In
three months he had spoken no more than a dozen sentences to Troy, yet something in the way he moved made
him seem very familiar. Troy looked over at him now and
Skipper nodded in agreement with McNulty.

From the cover of a tree line they could see clearly what

had happened. The camp had been overrun; nothing remained but smoldering rubble. In the center, where the mess tent had stood, nine stakes, each about five feet high, had been driven into the ground in a circle twenty feet across. On each stake, the attackers had mounted the severed head of one of the nine men in the camp. As he stared at the hideous carnage, Roland Troy realized what a naive fool he had been. Shotgun or no shotgun, he had been playing hide-and-seek. Occasionally some of the men in the camp, returning from missions, made vague references to skirmishes they were in, but Troy, never having experienced an actual battle himself, never having been fired on, had crept through the jungle imagining the enemy to be something akin to an opposing football team or the other side in a game of capture the flag. In an instant he realized the game had been far more serious. In that same instant he realized he wasn't going to panic; his heart was pounding in his ears and for the first time in his life he was truly afraid, but he remained in control of himself. Wherever the men were who had killed his nine comrades, he was determined they would not find him and his team. The nine dead men had made a terrible mistake; they had overestimated the security of their position. He would learn from what he saw here and try never to commit the same error.

Troy looked from the circle of stakes to the two men with him. Skipper was on his knees, vomiting silently onto the ground. McNulty's eyes were wide with terror. "Get us out of here," he said to Troy. "There's nothing we can do for those poor bastards now. You've got to save us."

"We'll lay low right where we are until it's dark," Troy said. "We'll travel at night. Don't worry, we'll make it."

It took him three days to get them across a string of mountains to a small radar station just south of the DMZ.

"You can go home, or you can stay here and work with me," Ubinas said. He and Troy were sitting in a bar in a town that did not exist on maps but was there all the same, built in a valley in the mountains of Laos. The town, known only by a code name, was the operational center for the secret war being waged in Laos by American and Laotian forces against the North Vietnamese moving along the

Ho Chi Minh Trail. That morning Troy had flown from Pleiku in Vietnam to Udorn in Thailand, then ridden from Udorn in the back seat of a Cessna 0-1 spotter plane over jagged mountain peaks poking up through steep misty forests to a landing strip not far from the Chinese border. Ubinas had met him at the landing strip in a Jeep encrusted with mud.

"What is this place?" Troy asked. "What the hell's goin' on here?" The town, built amidst jagged outcroppings of limestone, was filled with native huts. Wires and cables were strung between many of them, and everywhere Troy looked he could see the telltale aerials of electronic communications equipment. Children and animals ran through the dirt streets, weaving among an assortment of military vehicles driven by men in civilian clothes. Outside the town, beyond the airstrip, lay a valley, lush with wild flowers, surrounded by rugged peaks rising into the clouds.

"Here?" said Ubinas. "Man, this is Dodge City with radar. Ancient history meets modern technology. The natives here believe in animism. Even the mountains have souls. It's your kind of town."

"I go home, I get drafted, right?" Troy said.

"Uh uh," said Ubinas. "I told you that was covered. You go home, you're home. I figure you for sticking around though. You're just getting warmed up. And then there's the element of revenge."

"Revenge, huh? You know what Shakespeare said: 'Heat not a furnace for your foe so hot that it do singe yourself.' I didn't sign on to kill people. I'm just a scout, remember? Lead 'em in, lead 'em out."

"It could've been your head on a pole, partner."

"Lucky me," said Troy.

"Lucky you is right. Here, have a cigar."

Troy, who at the time didn't smoke, took one from Ubinas and lit up. Immediately he felt light-headed but he liked the aroma. He stuck the cigar between his teeth, leaned back in his chair, and put his hands behind his head. "What all would I do, here in Dodge City?" he asked.

"Work the Ho Chi Minh Trail," Ubinas said. "We have these special forces teams—we call 'em Prairie Fire teams—being dropped onto the trail. You'd work with them. With the local tribesmen. Gritty little fuckers. The North Vietnamese have recently put together a special unit of their own—Group 565—supposed to secure the trail. We can't let that happen. We can bomb their asses 'til hell freezes over, but there ain't no substitute for some hit-and-run interdiction on the ground. It'd be right up your alley. Take my word for it. You've done very well for us, Roland. Now that I know I was right about you back in Okinawa, I'd like to keep you around. We got all kinds of Air America pilots coming in and out of here. You could learn to fly a helicopter in your spare time."

"If I don't wind up with my head on a pole," Troy said. "It ain't a game, Jack."

Ubinas smiled. "You're wrong," he said. "It's the ultimate game."

"Who wins?" Troy asked.

"It has to be us," Ubinas said. "I believe that and I think you do too. Give me six months, until the monsoons hit. Most of what you'll be doing will be recon, surveillance, positioning movement on the trail. Information-gathering. You'll still be the Phantom."

Troy puffed on his cigar. Two more Americans came into the bar. One of them wore cutoff jeans, cowboy boots, and a BSA motorcycle T-shirt. The other had a cartridge belt slung across his chest and a New York Yankees hat on his head. Their faces were flushed and they were singing an obscene version of "Goodnight Irene." Air America cowboys, Troy thought. Good thing they worked up in the sky. He was different. He was a samurai, an inconspicuous shadow, the Phantom. In the course of leading McNulty and Skipper to safety, his thoughts had been only about survival. In the days since, however, he had spent considerable time reflecting on his future course of action. The gruesome scene in the base camp had removed forever any romantic notions he harbored about combat, but even so, he didn't really want to go home. Perhaps adhering to *bushido*, perhaps assuming the role of a Zen warrior, *was* his destiny. Ubinas was right, he decided. He *was* necessary here. His country needed him. And anyway, slipping unseen through the jungle to track the enemy was far more to his liking than the notion of chasing bank robbers as a rookie FBI agent.

"Yeah," he said. "Why not. I'll stay with you 'til the monsoons. Who knows, maybe I'll like it so much I won't ever want to leave."

"Don't laugh," Ubinas said. "That happens. It happened to me. I came over for a year in fifty-four and I've been here ever since. But whether you stay on after the rains or not, there's one thing I want you to know, and this is personal, not official. You delivered for me, and as long as I'm alive you've got someone to come to." Ubinas stuck out his hand and Troy shook it. "You've got my word on that, Roland. I'm in your debt."

"What are you talking about?" Troy said.

"Skipper and McNulty told me you saved their asses. They said they wouldn't have made it without you." Ubinas paused and puffed on his cigar. "Skipper's my brother," he said.

XVII

♦

From his prone position in the brush and low-growing trees, Roland Troy watched the Cessna 180 Skywagon of Raimundo Villegas land on the hard-packed dirt and taxi toward him, raising a cloud of reddish dust. Long before the plane landed, Troy had reviewed the situation, anticipating what lay ahead exactly as though he were involved in a military operation: Villegas would have at least two men with him. They would be killers, men who had absolutely no respect for law or human life, men who, given the slightest opening, would waste him without a second thought. Troy had dealt with many men like this. In his heart, he knew he should handle them the same way he handled the traitorous Laotian pilot. *I should shoot the ones Villegas brings with him, get what I need from Villegas, and then shoot him too,* he thought. *That's the smart move, the only safe move with guys like this.* But when the plane rolled to a stop fifty feet from where he lay, he vacillated, unable to commit himself to killing someone without a better reason than the knowledge they were evil. *This is not the way to do it,* he thought. *This is not the way you fight a war. I must be getting old. Or soft. Or something.*

He peered through the scope of the Browning and watched three men get out of the plane. Two—a tall thin man in a long leather coat and a big guy with a belly—began walking in his direction. The tall thin one would be Villegas. The third man, a muscular blonde with a deep tan who'd flown the plane, stayed behind. He checked his watch, took a Granola bar out of his pocket, unwrapped it, and began to eat methodically, leaning against the fuselage. He had an automatic weapon, what looked like an old Swedish K, slung over his shoulder.

Troy waited until Villegas and Ernesto, the fat one, were ten feet from him. Then, with the Browning in one hand and his .45 in the other, he stepped from cover, keeping himself between the two men and the blonde beside the plane. "Don't move or you're dead," he said.

Villegas and Ernesto froze. The blonde hesitated for a second and ducked under the Cessna. Out of the corner of his eye, Troy could see him crouched on the far side of the plane. *Roland, you asshole,* he thought. *Now it's gonna get messy.*

"Whatever it is you are planning, Señor, keep in mind there are three of us and one of you," said Villegas. His voice was like thick oil being poured from one container to another. "Let us say you have made some error. You put away your guns, we work it out so no one is harmed." *He believes I won't shoot,* Troy thought. *He thinks if I was going to I would have already. He believes that by holding a gun on him I've already made a decision not to use it.*

As Villegas spoke, Ernesto's hand began moving toward his belt. Villegas began to say something in Spanish in the same mesmerizing, lullaby voice, but before he could finish his sentence Troy shot Ernesto three times in the chest with the .45. The fat man did a strange half-flip backwards, landing on his head, collapsed with a loud groan, and lay dead on the ground in a widening pool of blood.

"Get that other son of a bitch to drop his gun and come out from behind that plane or you're next," Troy said.

Villegas called to the blond man, who lay his weapon down and walked around the front of the plane. "This way," Troy said, motioning with his finger. "And keep your hands on top of your head."

The blonde had the mean face of someone who enjoyed hurting people. His skin was leathery and he walked with the side-to-side rolling gait of a body builder. Close up, Troy could see that his hair was bleached. Under his loose-fitting nylon workout jacket there was probably a handgun, but in any case Troy was through taking chances. When the blonde was ten feet away, Troy halted him with an upturned palm. "Right there's fine," he said. He pointed the .45 at the man and shot him twice through the heart.

Troy turned to Villegas. "Now you know I'm not fucking around," he said.

Villegas shrugged. "Señor, there is no doubt in my mind of that," he said. "But what I am wondering is what this is about. You want my plane? Go ahead. Is yours. If you intend to rob me, then you shed blood for nothing. I have no money with me. Or at least not enough for this." He gestured with his arm to take in the two men lying dead on the ground, then pointed toward Wayne Boudrie's Airstream. "You kill him too, that *comemierda*?"

"No, he's alive," Troy said. "But he ain't feelin' too good."

"*Ay, qué pendejo.*" Villegas shook his head. "Telling me there is a woman here who wants very much to see me. I should shoot *myself*, listening to someone like him." He sighed and looked down at the fat man beside him. "He was called *El Barriga*," he said. "The Belly. His appetite was never ending. He could eat more at one time than any man I ever saw. I know him a very long time. The other one . . . you did me a favor. He was a sewer rat. A turncoat. Once, before he decided to become rich, he was an agent for your DEA. He worked with that one who was killed in Mexico. You are aware of that, I think? Eventually I would have had to kill him anyway." He sighed. "So, Señor. What now? Now you shoot me, fly away in my plane, and the vendetta is complete? Those *puercos* from Matamoros, they sent you, no?"

"Nobody sent me," Troy said. "This ain't about no vendetta. This is about information. Now you and I talk."

"We talk?" said Villegas. "All this for a conversation?" In spite of the cold Villegas was sweating, but Troy could see that his hands were steady. This Villegas was no stranger to bloodshed.

"That's right," said Troy. "You know how to fly that plane?"

"Sure, I can fly it. Better than Señor *Músculos*, my former pilot." Villegas smiled at Troy, looking for an opening, a weakness. What he saw was a different sort of gringo than he was used to. He had met plenty of them who were hunters, who knew how to kill, but all of those were stone-cold. This one could kill too, but he appeared to have a soul. Villegas could see it in his eyes. Perhaps he could walk away from this place after all, and if he did, then this gringo with the beard and the baseball cap would be sorry he ever laid eyes on Raimundo Villegas. "Where you want to go?" he said.

"I ain't goin' anywhere," Troy said. "At least not with you. Take off your coat, put your hands on top of your head, and turn around." The only gun he found on Villegas was a .380 Walther strapped to his leg. He threw it into the bushes behind him, along with a pistol from the dead Ernesto's belt and another holstered to the pilot's hip. "Now then," he said. "Put your coat back on and sit yourself down on your friend, Mr. Belly. Go on, sit on him or I'll blow your fuckin' balls off right now, and keep your hands on top of your head." He fired a round into the dirt between Villegas's legs. "There's two left, in case you're counting. Plus a full clip in the Browning."

"*Coño,*" Villegas said. He sat gingerly on the dead body, trying in vain to avoid the blood.

"You tell me what I want to know and you can fly your ass out of here back to Chihuahua or wherever," Troy said. "Leave the mess for your friend the *comemierda* to clean up."

"And what about you? You disappear? What you do is forgotten?"

"Me?" said Troy. "I'm a specially empowered agent of the United States government had to shoot his way out of a den of thieves, murderers, and dope dealers. Ain't nothin' at all gonna happen to me. If anyone ever asks, that is."

"Oh," said Villegas. "I see. What is it you want to know?"

"Let's start with Myron McBride. And don't tell me you don't know who the hell I'm talkin' about or I won't shoot you, I'll cut your balls off and stuff 'em in your mouth. I imagine you've seen people die that way, businessman such as yourself."

"Myron McBride. A goldfish thinking he could swim in a pool of sharks."

"That why you killed him?"

"Ah," said Villegas, nodding his head. "The other gringo. The one with long dark hair . . ."

"The one who got away," said Troy.

"It was an accident, Señor. A badly aimed warning shot across the prow, intended simply to stop the truck. And besides, it was not me who did the shooting. I did not kill Myron McBride."

"Of course not," said Troy. "It wouldn't be you. All you did was rip him off. You guys are all the same. Sittin' there worryin' about the blood on your two-thousand-dollar coat, thinkin' about how maybe you can get your hands on my Browning, blow my brains out. It ain't gonna happen, Chico. Not at this party."

"No, I do not imagine so," Villegas said. Hunched in his coat, sitting on his dead friend's body, he looked like a buzzard.

"Who was McBride working with?" Troy asked.

"Not with," Villegas said. "*For.* He was working for a woman who procured the horses. It was she who made the deal. McBride was a delivery boy with ideas."

"Who's the woman?"

"Her name is Nikki Waters," Villegas said.

"Nikki Waters," Troy said. "I'll be a son of a bitch. You thought she was gonna be here, didn't you, instead of me? She's the one ole Wayne used to get your ass up here in such a hurry. She must've been some hell of a piece of ass, but not anymore. She's dead too."

"She's dead?" said Villegas. "*Qué lástima.* She was so beautiful." He shook his head.

"But you ripped her off anyway."

"Beauty is one thing. Horse trading is something else altogether."

"Horse trading? What about drug-running? What about murder? Amigo, you better start tellin' me what the fuck went on here and you better do it now. Where'd Nikki Waters get these horses? What the hell was she into?"

"Señor, you tell me you are some special agent of your government. Maybe you are, maybe you are not. Who am I to know this? I do know you managed to find this place. You got me to come here and gained the upper hand. I watch you kill two men, boom, boom, like that. Obviously you are somebody. Now you have me sit on one of them who was my friend. You do all these things so you can ask me questions? This is not the way things are usually done. So I say to myself, who is this man working for? What is it he really wants? I think perhaps if I tell you things, you kill me anyway. No?"

"I ain't workin' for anybody," Troy said. "My business with you has nothing to do with the government. It's strictly personal, and one way or the other you're gonna tell me what I came to find out. I know how it's accomplished, Villegas. Getting someone to talk. I think you understand that. I was taught the same tricks as all the guys in your country, the *Federales*, the bad guys, the ones who ran those torture chambers they found in Mexico City under the attorney general's office after the eighty-five earthquake. If the shoe were on the other foot, I wouldn't doubt your ability to pry something out of me."

Villegas raised his eyebrows. The corners of his lower lip curled slightly downward and he grunted. "You surprised I know about that?" Troy said. "I know about your sister and the Mexican minister of finance too. And the money you skimmed off the Ixtoc oil rig in the Gulf back in 1980, before you got rich running smack. The way I hear it, there's any number of people who'd love a piece of you, partner. So ... we do it the easy way, you fly away. We do it the hard way, you wind up like Mr. Belly and Mr. Muscles, only for you it won't be so quick. It could take weeks. Now, you tell me the story of Nikki Waters and the horse-trading business. Pronto."

Villegas looked at Troy and wet his lips. He no longer harbored any thoughts of overcoming this bearded gringo who was watching him with the unflinching, hypnotic gaze of an owl. Still, his instincts told him the man was truthful and might indeed let him live. "My hands are very cold, Señor," he said. "Can I put them in my pockets?"

"Sure. Go ahead," said Troy. He himself sat down on the cold hard ground, his back against a small tree, the Browning next to his left leg. He propped his right forearm on a raised knee, keeping the .45 aimed squarely at Villegas's chest. The two of them were no more than five feet apart, eyeing each other, their breath coming in short puffs of condensation. Villegas could see no hint of trembling in Troy's gun hand, nor did the gringo seem bothered by the weather. He appeared to be one of those who did not mind discomfort; perhaps he even enjoyed it. No doubt he was capable of sitting this way all day if necessary.

Villegas took a deep breath. "Nikki Waters was involved with a man named John Varney," he said. "He is from Orlando, Florida. He owns a bank. Maybe more than one, I don't know. He is very rich with powerful friends. He is like the Colombians. He would slit the throat of his own brother and drink the blood if it served his purpose. Even I worry about him, and I do not worry about very many men."

"John Varney, huh?"

"I suspect you know him."

"I know who he is. Nikki Waters made a cocaine deal with John Varney? Is that what you're tellin' me?"

"No. The cocaine had nothing to do with her. That was McBride. Nikki Waters made a deal separate from McBride. He was being paid only for delivering. His fee was some cocaine which, as you probably have already found out, stayed in Mexico, and some cash which I believe left Mexico with McBride's companion, the one with the long dark hair."

Villegas paused and cleared his throat. He had been trying to place the tall man with the long dark hair since the night the horses were brought across the river. Suddenly he remembered having seen him at the track in Orlando. This other gringo who held his pistol without a tremor must be connected to him. Either that or he had been sent by Varney. But if Varney sent him, why then was he asking about Nikki Waters? That made no sense. Villegas was wondering about this and contemplating what to say next when Roland Troy cracked him across the face with the barrel of his .45. Villegas let out a howl and brought his hand up to his cheek, which was cut and already starting to swell. He had barely seen the gringo move.

"No coffee breaks," Troy said.

Villegas took his hand from his cheek, glanced at the blood on his palm, and swallowed. "I met Nikki Waters in Florida," he said. "At a place where they train horses. Harness horses. The standardbreds, as you call them. I was there on business."

"At the Ben White Raceway?"

"*Sí.* I went there from time to time to see John Varney. It was on one of those visits that I met Nikki Waters. I took her to dinner. We were together. She was very lovely. Very ... imaginative. With a voice like nothing I had ever heard before in my life. We talked. She had been promised a lucrative horse deal of some sort by John Varney as payment for something she did for him. What that was I do not know. Varney kept stalling her. Finally he told her there was no deal for her. She was furious. She believed she had been cheated. I was a little angry myself at some things John Varney had done, and I was a little drunk as well, so I told her this and that ..."

"What's the 'this and that'?" Troy asked.

"Varney had six horses," Villegas said. "Good ones. Jumpers. All well insured. Supposedly they died in a fire in Kentucky. Only they didn't die. They were removed from the barn before the fire and hidden in a barn in Florida where no one would ever find them. At least no one from the insurance company. The horses that were burned beyond recognition were worthless. The six good ones were coming to me in trade."

"What do you know," said Troy. "John Varney, the banking wizard, dealing horses for drugs."

"I didn't say that," said Villegas.

"You didn't have to," said Troy. "Keep talkin'."

"I told Nikki where Varney's horses were hidden. If she wanted to take them, I told her I would make the deal with her instead of Varney."

"So she was supposed to get a load of dope," Troy said. "And then what? Ole Nikki was gonna become a dealer?"

"No, señor. Nikki Waters wanted nothing to do with drugs. She only wanted money."

"Which you never intended to pay."

"Not to her," Villegas said.

"Oh, I see," Troy said. "You got sober and a little less angry at John Varney—or a little more scared—so you blew the whistle on Nikki. What the fuck did Varney care, right? Now he didn't have to worry about transporting the horses. Nikki and her friends would do it for him."

"Nikki Waters was very clever," Villegas said, "but she

was . . . how you say? In over her head. Now you tell me she's dead. I had nothing to do with that. I am truly sorry to hear about it. Frankly, I would much rather it had been her waiting here for me than you."

"You'd have killed her yourself," Troy said. "You or one of your buddies here."

"I've done many bad things," Villegas said, "but I would not have killed Nikki Waters. I would have worked something out with her, in spite of John Varney. Not here. Not in your country. I would have taken her back to Mexico with me. To my *rancho*."

"To your *rancho*." Troy laughed. "That's wonderful. Your lovely *rancho*. That where you buried McBride's body?"

"There is no McBride's body," Villegas said. "It is gone. I do not know any details, only that there is nothing left. You could ask the one in the trailer. He took care of that."

"The *comemierda*? He makes bodies disappear?"

"Among other things. He is very resourceful when he is not stoned. You see how he managed to trick me into coming here, that *hijo de puta*."

"Right," said Troy, standing up. "Well, now you can go."

"I can leave?" Villegas said. "Just like that?"

Troy looked down at him. Faint sunlight had broken through the dull, heavy sky, bringing into sharp focus the deep creases on Villegas's face. The welt below his left eye had turned deep red and dried blood caked his cheek. He appeared very weary, as though he wanted to lie down next to his fat dead friend and go to sleep, but Troy was cautious. He picked up the Browning and took a step backwards. This man was as venomous as a bushmaster. In view of the carnage Troy had wreaked and the information Villegas had divulged, the sensible move would be to kill him. "Yeah," Troy said. "Just like that."

"There is one thing I would like to know," Villegas said, rising from his perch on the late Mr. Belly.

"There's only one thing you need to know," Troy said. "Don't come after me."

Villegas began to say something but Troy stilled him with an upraised finger. "No, no. Don't say a thing, Villegas," he said. "You've already begun thinking about it.

How to make the gringo pay for this morning's adventure. My advice to you is to go home and forget it, because right after I leave here I'm gonna be makin' a phone call to a friend of mine in Virginia, and after I do that if anything happens to me or my friend with the long dark hair . . ." Troy shrugged and smiled at Villegas. "You get the picture. You won't last a week. Believe me."

"So the dark-haired one *is* your friend," Villegas said. "He is why you are here."

"You figured that out," Troy said.

"You know, I saw him once before he brought the horses," Villegas said. "It was at the track in Orlando. He was drinking coffee with Nikki Waters. What is his name?"

"Billy," Troy said. "Billy Roseman."

"Billy Roseman," Villegas repeated. "I wonder then, why he came here with McBride."

"He needed money," Troy said. "He didn't know a thing about where those horses were from. His buddy McBride neglected to tell him that part of the story."

"McBride was his buddy?" Villegas said. "That is strange."

"What's strange about it?" Troy asked.

"What is strange is that Nikki Waters told McBride specifically not to bring him. I heard her. She said, 'Don't take Billy. Get someone else to help you. I don't want Billy involved.' "

They walked slowly to Villegas's plane. When they reached it, Troy slung the Browning over his shoulder, knelt down, and picked up the automatic rifle left on the ground by the blond man. "A Swedish K," he said. "I haven't seen one of these for twenty years. A lot of the spooks used to carry them."

"You are an unusual man," Villegas said. "I would like to know more about you."

"Hit the road," Troy said. "Before I change my mind."

Roland Troy lit a cigar and leaned back against the fender of the rented Cadillac he'd hidden before dawn in the woods behind the garage. Through the trees he could see Villegas's Cessna rise in a swirl of dust, bank steeply in the shadow of the mountains to the north, then head south back across the border. Now he had to decide what to do with Wayne Boudrie, who lay trussed in his trailer. Originally he was going to leave Boudrie tied up, but considering what had transpired, Troy decided it was better to have him running around loose, trying to cover his ass before Villegas sent someone to get him. Better that than to have him hog-tied on a mattress babbling about a bearded guy with a baseball hat in case the authorities showed up first.

Troy drove out of the woods and parked next to the garage. He popped the hood on Boudrie's Chevy Nova, took off the air cleaner, and dumped a couple of handfuls of dirt into the carburetor. There was a water hose coiled around a hook on the garage wall. The hose was attached to a spigot below the hook. Troy stuck the free end of the hose into the Nova's gas tank and turned the spigot on. Hours earlier, in the predawn darkness, he had slashed all the tires on the pickup trucks belonging to Boudrie's two friends—Calder and Butch, Boudrie had called them. Other than Troy's car, the only way out of the place now was on foot.

"You gonna kill me?" Boudrie asked when Troy climbed up into the Airstream. No doubt he had heard the shots Troy fired earlier. Beads of perspiration stood out on his forehead and his dark, furtive eyes darted from Troy to the window above the trailer's sink, as though he expected someone or something to appear there and add to the misery. He saw Troy's gaze lower from his face to the dark stain on the mattress where he lay. "I pissed my pants," he said. "What the fuck else could I do when you got me tied like this?"

"I'm gonna let you go," Troy said. "I never shot your buddies. You can go on across the way and cut 'em loose so you'll have some help deciding what all to do. It's a little messy up there on the landing strip, but from what I hear you're a pretty resourceful dude when it comes to tidying up. I wouldn't waste a lot of time though. Villegas'll be back and he won't be in a particularly good mood. Unless, of course, the law gets here first. And forget about drivin' off. Your car ain't up to no trip at the moment."

* * *

"It had to be pussy," Jack Ubinas said.

"I can't hear you, Jack," Roland Troy said. "You're gonna have to talk louder." Troy was standing in a phone booth at a truck stop on the interstate east of Pecos in the midst of a cacophony of cattle rigs firing up for the run to Fort Worth. He was dead tired, having driven from the outpost on the Rio Grande to the McCrossons' Monte Zorro Lodge in Shafter to assure Brenda McCrosson and her father she had nothing to fear, at least as far as Villegas was concerned. He had showered and changed clothes at the lodge, but declined Brett McCrosson's offer to spend the night. He wanted to return to Florida as quickly as possible, but promised to come back some day to fish the Cibolo with him.

"That Wayne Boudrie comes around here, he's dead meat," McCrosson told Troy as he climbed into the Cadillac which was caked with mud. "I been lookin' for an excuse to shoot that little bastard, now you come along and give me one. You drive safely now. And I hope you save your friend's ass that's sittin' in jail."

From Shafter, Troy drove 160 miles straight before pulling into the truck stop for gas, a cup of coffee, and the phone call to Jack Ubinas.

"What I said was, it had to be pussy," Ubinas repeated. "That's the only thing that would get a son of a bitch like Villegas up there to some godforsaken river crossing at that hour of the morning. I'm right, aren't I? It was pussy, wasn't it?"

"Yeah, Jack, you're right," said Troy. "It was pussy."

Ubinas would never change. Sitting up there on his farm in Virginia, in his study filled with files and notebooks, everything by now cross-referenced in his computer, he devoted himself fulltime to his passion for sizing people up, finding their weaknesses, assessing their strengths, figuring out how to pull their strings. After thirty-five years devoted to honing these skills, he had become the government's secret expert on human motivation. Though he had no degree in psychology, had published nothing in any clinical journal, or ever appeared as an expert witness at any congressional hearing, Jack Ubinas was the man called upon by all manner of government agencies desirous of a quick thumbnail analysis of someone in power—heads of state, leaders of industry, politicians, entertainers, criminals. It was Roland Troy's understanding that Jack Ubinas's opinion was held in such high regard at the state department because, unlike the late J. Edgar Hoover, Ubinas had no sexual hangups, no paranoid delusions, absolutely no hidden agenda at all. Having a folder full of dirt on someone was not what Ubinas cared about. His interest was the game, and for him the game was not so much getting the goods on someone as having the person's number.

Roland Troy took a deep breath and waited for Ubinas to ask him if it was pussy that had him chasing around the wilderness of west Texas too, but Ubinas left that one alone.

"The blond guy who flew the plane used to be on our side," he said instead. "His name was Terry Graves. A truly horrible person. Got immunity for testifying against a couple of Colombians down in your neck of the woods. Tampa, I think it was. Sooner or later we'd have popped him anyway. The fat one was Ernesto Echeverria. Villegas's bodyguard. Another bad one, but stupid. And here I thought all you were up to was building models and watching your real estate appreciate. I should put you back on the payroll. I could mail you a list. You should've taken care of Villegas too. Big mistake."

"There was no need to," Troy said.

"You could have looked at it as a service for mankind."

"Jack, if I were in this for the good of mankind, shooting guys like Villegas would be all I'd ever do," Troy said. "I'm just trying to save one innocent person's life."

"That isn't like you, Roland, leaving loose ends. That isn't like you at all, man. You're getting too old for this shit. Believe me, I've seen it before. The signs. Although, I tell you what, you don't know the difference you won't be around very much longer. Villegas would've drilled you in a second. You realize that, don't you? Do you have any idea who that man is? I bet he had a couple of machine guns mounted on that Cessna. Probably would've stitched your ass to the ground if you weren't hiding in the trees."

"Oh, yeah," Troy said. "I know exactly who he is. You think I went in there naked? Gimme a break, Jack. I know about his dope operation. I know about his ties to the Mexican government. I know about the customs agents on his payroll. I even know about the weapons he has stashed. The ones from that armory that got hit in San Angelo. You know about those? Ask me about that one sometime. I'll tell you who helped him get 'em. Meanwhile, he didn't get me and he ain't gonna get me. And besides, I don't plan on makin' this a habit."

"It isn't your habits I'm worried about, Roland," Ubinas said. "It's his. To Raimundo Villegas, revenge is an art form. You should 'a shot him."

Troy pictured Ubinas in a pair of old corduroys and a ragged crew-neck sweater, wearing a headset so both hands would be free to work his computer. As they talked, Ubinas would already be following the electronic trail of Raimundo Villegas, looking to see where it intersected the path of John Varney, searching for anything on Nikki Waters, the erstwhile radio personality, the ex-model, the would-be horse thief. "I didn't call you to discuss my encroaching senility, Jack," he said. "I called you for help."

"I know that, Roland. I know that," Ubinas said. "Anybody asks, that little episode down by the river was a shoot-'em-up between rival desperado factions involved in drug trafficking. The scum that's left on the pond will be dispersed. Couple of weeks from now you can tell that girl and her father, the guy who runs the hunting lodge, you know where they can get an Airstream real cheap. Throw in a bunch of tools from that garage they were running. A little thank-you present. Why don't you go catch yourself a plane back home and let me make some calls? Do a little digging. Give me a ring tomorrow night."

"Yeah. That's what I'll do," Troy said. "One last thing, Jack."

"What's that?"

"You wearing old corduroys and a sweater?"

For a moment there was silence on the line. Ubinas, plumber of the human psyche, was no doubt sounding the depth of Troy's question. Troy smiled. For the past twenty years, whenever he talked to Ubinas, he was reminded of the joke about the psychiatrist who passes a friend on the street. "Good morning," says the friend. "I wonder what he meant by that?" thinks the psychiatrist.

"It so happens I am," Ubinas finally said. "Why do you ask?"

"It's been a long time since I've seen you," Troy said. "I draw comfort from the fact that some things remain constant. That's the only reason. It's like being out on the water on a clear windless night. The stars are where they are. Insect noises. Night birds. The rhythm of it never changes. The sound of it. The feel of it. Keeps me from going crazy. You in your study, in your old clothes, same-same. The amber color of the Coacoochee River at noon. My friend Halpatter without any shoes. Things you can count on. I come up to Halpatter's house in my canoe, I know he ain't gonna have on any shoes. His feet look like a couple of baby hogs covered in dried mud. You never met my friend Halpatter. You should someday. He still hunts alligators with a sharpened pole, the old way. The Indian way. You know the word 'Seminole' means 'broken away.' Or maybe it means 'cut off from.' That's how I feel, Jack. Every day of my life. Every time I see his alligator pole, I think about those men. I never told Halpatter the story though. Never in all these years. Never told anybody. Every time I hear your voice, I see 'em. Those nine men in the jungle with their heads stuck on sharpened poles. You think a person ever recovers from seeing something like that? Even someone like me?"

"Get some rest, Roland," Ubinas said.

Two more cattle trucks fired up their engines, and in the din Troy thought Ubinas said "give it a rest." "I try, but it keeps coming around on the guitar," he said.

Ubinas had always marveled at Roland Troy's steadiness. Of all the men who had worked for him during both his military and civilian careers—the cold-blooded mercenaries, the undercover operatives and long-range recondos who thrived on sleep deprivation, the swashbuckling pilots, the counterintelligence computer freaks with data banks instead of emotions—among all of them, Roland Troy was without equal under pressure. The Hmong tribesmen in Laos, the ones Troy led through the jungle, called him "the man with no nerves." Given the life Troy had led, his levelheadedness and stability had always confirmed Ubinas's faith in human resilience. Furthermore, it confirmed his faith in his own judgment. After all, it was he who had identified Troy as *bushi,* one of the true samurai warriors, those fit to engage in, as he had always called it, the ultimate game.

Over the years they had stayed in touch, mostly by telephone, exchanging theories about human behavior, occasionally helping each other out with information, acting as sounding boards for one another, calling to recommend a book or record. On a number of occasions Troy had done investigative work for Ubinas. The jobs involved locating individuals who were hiding at various places in the United States. Troy had done the work calmly, efficiently, without any fuss, without in any way being detected. Smooth and unobtrusive. Those were the words that came to Ubinas's mind when he thought of Roland Troy.

Of course there was the incident at the courthouse. Ubinas had considered that outburst very carefully. Purely as a matter of pride it was important to him that he not misjudge Troy's behavior. Never did he worry about Troy cracking under stress and spilling the volumes of highly classified information he carried around in his head. Ubinas had come to the conclusion that Troy had been in total control of himself and the situation when he stuck his .38 in Timmy Hammond's ear. Once Ubinas made that determination, he allowed himself to be impressed. Nothing wrong with an occasional public demonstration of outrage, and besides, Troy had been chasing bad guys long enough. The odds were building against him. It was time for him to retire from active police work. Neither was Ubinas surprised when Troy devoted himself afterwards to building those exquisite models of crime scenes. That fit too. An eccentric expression of the man's creativity. A quiet commitment to perfection in a mundane arena. There was a certain sense of Zen righteousness to it. It was an appropriate way to ride into the sunset.

Even the nature of this phone call, at least the majority of it, was not out of synch with the Roland Troy Ubinas had known for more than a quarter of a century. In fact, Troy's journey to Texas, his solitary confrontation of

Raimundo Villegas for the sake of his old love's son, made perfect sense. It was a course of action befitting a samurai. And a romantic. If nothing else, Jack Ubinas told himself, Roland Troy was a romantic, as was every single true adventurer Ubinas had ever known. It was that romantic view of life, the conviction that they were upholding a set of noble ideals, that made men like Roland Troy far more durable than self-serving mercenaries like Terry Graves, who believed in nothing but the next payoff.

But Troy's rambling monologue, the reference to the long-dead men in the special forces encampment, took Ubinas aback. Ubinas had survived in his profession through cold-blooded manipulation and unsentimental detachment from the men he recruited and worked with through the years, but unlike all the others, Troy was one for whom he felt genuine affection. Roland Troy, after all, had saved his brother's life. For this reason it troubled him that he had not realized how much Troy had suffered. It troubled him even more that he had obviously missed something, for Jack Ubinas prided himself, above all else, on his ability to miss as little as possible.

"Don't worry, Jack," Troy said, reading Ubinas's mind. "The chain hasn't slipped off my gears. I'm just tired."

"Drive carefully, Roland," Ubinas said. He hung up and turned his full attention to his computer.

Troy bought a first-class ticket on the 8:20 American flight from Dallas to Orlando, guessing correctly that the coach section of the plane would be filled to capacity but that first-class would be nearly empty. He had been kept awake on the flight from Midland to Dallas by a screaming baby and was willing to pay almost anything for some peace and quiet. There were only two other people in first class—a very thin old man wearing a copper-colored, Western-style suit, and a stylish woman in her thirties dressed in a silk blouse, short skirt, and knee-high leather boots. Exhibiting typical first-class disdain for human contact, neither of them paid any attention as Troy took his seat. He told the flight attendant he wasn't hungry or thirsty and fell asleep before the plane left the gate.

Shortly before reaching Orlando, Roland Troy had a

dream. In the dream, Raimundo Villegas's plane was circling over his daughter Katherine's house in Massachusetts. The plane dropped lower and lower until finally it was heading straight for the upstairs window of the bedroom where Katherine slept. Just before the plane crashed into the house, Troy awoke with a start. In his head he heard the voice of Jack Ubinas warning him about Villegas. Ubinas's voice was so clear Troy glanced around, but other than the woman, who was reading, and the old man, who was staring out the window, the cabin was empty.

At the baggage claim Troy had to wait fifteen minutes for the aluminum suitcase that held his guns. He grabbed the case from the carousel and took the escalator down to the terminal parking level. As he descended, he checked his watch. It was twenty after twelve. Katherine would no doubt already be asleep in the tiny cottage she shared with her boyfriend down the road from the Woods Hole ferry dock, but Troy wanted to speak to her. He told the operator to charge the call to his home phone and had her dial Katherine's number.

"Daddy?" Katherine said. "Where are you? Are you all right?"

"I'm at the airport in Orlando," Troy said. "I'm fine. I just wanted to hear your voice. I woke you up, huh?"

"No, actually you didn't. I was reading. We're having a helluva storm up here. Power's out. I'm reading by kerosene lamp. Turner's out plowing. I'm glad you called me, Daddy, though I'm surprised you got through. I was actually going to call you tomorrow or the next day, assuming the phones are still working."

Typically, Troy called his daughter every couple of weeks. She was the most cheerful, optimistic human being he knew, full of joy, full of the possibilities life held, convinced the planet could be saved through good works. He loved talking to her and would have called more often were he not committed to letting her live life without a bothersome old man looking over her shoulder.

Their conversations were always the same. He'd ask about her work and listen eagerly as she told him about the progress her research team had made. She'd ask him about the land and his friends among whom she'd grown up—

Sheridan Halpatter and his wife, Tom Waxe, Teddy Chambers, and Thelma Tate, the old black woman who ran a bait shop at the confluence of the Coacoochee and St. Johns rivers and who had always brought catfish stew to Katherine when she was sick.

He'd ask if she needed any money. He knew before asking she'd tell him no, she was doing fine, even when she was too broke to get the heater fixed in the '67 fastback Mustang she drove until he insisted on buying her a new car. He sent her money anyway, never asking what she did with it, though he wasn't surprised when she told him she'd saved up enough to buy a twenty-six-foot sailboat, used, of course, for cash.

"Something's wrong, Daddy," Katherine said now. "I can feel it. You're involved in something dangerous, aren't you?"

"Sort of," Troy said. "But not that dangerous. Nothing's gonna happen to me." He had never lied to her about anything except her mother. As far as he knew, she had never lied to him either. From the time she was a little girl, he had encouraged her not to keep anything that bothered her inside, and she had taken his advice. If she had a problem, she came right out with it. Once she was old enough to understand, he told her things about his work. Now he filled her in on the murder of Nikki Waters, although he left out the part about Jack Ubinas's warning or about his dream. Even if Ubinas were right, Villegas wouldn't spend time tracking down his daughter in New England. The Mexican would come straight for him.

"Well, I'm glad you're helping Billy Roseman," Katherine said when he had finished. "I know him. He'd never kill anybody. But if you don't mind me saying so, you're getting a little bit old to be chasing criminals through the underbrush."

"That's what everybody keeps tellin' me, Katherine, but Jesus Christ, I'm only forty-seven."

"Daddy, you're impossible. I bet your leg's killing you from lying out in the cold. I bet you can barely walk."

"My leg's fine," he said. "I was just—I don't know . . ."

"What did you leave out?" she asked. "What didn't you tell me?"

"The Mexican," he said. "The drug dealer I let go. My friend Ubinas thinks he might come lookin' for a payback."

"And you're worried about me."

"And I'm worried about you."

"All the bad guys you've dealt with," she said, "and not a one of 'em's bothered me yet. It's me who should be worried about you, Daddy. You're stressed out. It has to do with Clara coming to you for help just when your life was finally running on rails. All those old memories dredged up. All the old feelings. All the violence. You have to be careful. Don't try to fix this one all by yourself. You're not the Lone Ranger anymore."

That was Katherine for you, getting right to the heart of things. Troy sighed and didn't say a word. Katherine didn't press it any further. Neither of them ever lectured the other. They would voice their concern for each other, point out the cause of a dilemma, but never pass judgment. Nor did they ever make one another pay for their shortcomings—the ultimate sign, Troy always believed, of true love.

"What you need is some good news for a change," she said, "which brings me to the reason I was going to call you. Turner and I have decided to get married. We'd like to have the wedding on the land . . . outside the house on the knoll leading down to the pond. We were thinking about April, before it got too hot. How's that sound to you?"

"Well," Troy said. "Well. I mean, Katherine, that sounds wonderful. Sure. You and Turner. Well, yeah. I'd be honored to have the wedding at the house. And . . . April's fine. Anything you want. Just tell me. I'll fix the porch and get the place painted."

"Daddy, that porch is you. I don't want you to fix it, or paint the house either. I don't want to change a thing. You go on and get some sleep and we'll talk later. I wouldn't even have mentioned it to you tonight except that we haven't told anyone else and I wanted you to be the first to know."

"You get some sleep too, and be sure to congratulate Turner for me, and, uh . . . I'll call him up myself of course, but in the meantime you tell him for me. Tell him I'm real happy."

"I will, Daddy. I love you."

"I love you too, baby."

He hung up the phone, shouldered his rucksack, picked up his gun case, and walked across the road to the parking garage where he'd left his El Camino. He half-expected someone to be sitting in the bed, waiting for him with information, with an outrageous story, with a loaded weapon pointed at his heart, but the El Camino was just as he'd left it. He fumbled around in the shoe box full of tapes behind the passenger seat and found one he'd made from an old Red Garland album featuring Coltrane on sax and Donald Byrd on trumpet. It was a two-record set, plenty of music to get him down the road and home. Once there he refrained from going directly into the house, but sat instead on his porch, smoking a cigar, watching the moon emerge from behind a series of thick, puffy clouds, listening for night birds in the trees along the shore of his pond. Before he went inside, unplugged his telephone, and went to sleep, he imagined the spot, on the sloping ground between the porch and the smooth, dark water, where his daughter would stand when she was married in the spring.

XVIII

✦

"Tom Waxe doesn't see that well these days," Sheridan Halpatter said to Clara Roseman. He was leaning over the porch railing of Tom Waxe's house, his huge, rust-colored arms bulging from the sleeves of a black Harley-Davidson T-shirt. Halpatter's large, seamed face peered down at her benevolently. In the open space below the railing, Clara could see his enormous bare feet, which appeared to be looking down at her as well.

"Tom made a very savory fish stew when he heard you were coming, but it was a strain on his eyes and he is taking a rest," Halpatter said. "Since his wife died he hasn't been the same. He was very excited about helping when he heard about your son's predicament though. He insisted on going out into the swamp with me again last night. We know some people there who have occasional dealings at the horse track—people we missed when we went out with Roland. I would have preferred to go alone, but you know Tom Waxe. As obstinate a man as ever walked this earth. Come up and sit here on the porch and join me in a glass of wine. Let me tell you what we learned."

Clara climbed the flight of sturdy wooden stairs leading up to the porch. Several years after Shima disappeared and Roland Troy gave the cabin to Tom Waxe, Waxe had jacked the cabin up and mounted it on poles, seven feet off the ground. A house so constructed, in the coastal Indian style, would be impervious to flooding during a hurricane, and also less likely to be damaged by high winds that could pass through the space beneath the structure. How Tom Waxe managed to raise the cabin by himself had always remained a mystery. When it was pointed out to him that he was on sheltered high ground to begin with, not on the edge of the ocean or the Gulf, he had merely laughed his throaty, resonant laugh and said, "You weren't here in twenty-six. Wait 'til the big wind blows again."

In any case, the cabin's new perch afforded Tom Waxe a much more imperial view from his front porch, to which he had affixed a wooden sign, two feet high by three feet long, with the word TIMPANA elaborately carved on it. "Timpana" was the Indian word for council-house, a fitting appellation for the dwelling where for many years those living in and around the swamp gathered to discuss problems and settle differences without the intrusion of the law.

Sheridan Halpatter poured some red wine into a glass that had been sitting on the porch railing and handed it to Clara, who had taken a seat beside him in a wicker barrel chair. Halpatter's waist-length hair, combed free of its usual braid, swung toward her and brushed her arm as she took the glass. The hair felt soft and smooth, in sharp contrast to Halpatter's skin that was thick and coarse as the hide of a rhinoceros. "It's a California merlot," he said. "What do you think? And be honest. If you don't like it, I'll open something else. We're having fish, after all."

"It's good," Clara said. "Really. This is good wine."

"I thought so too, but I wanted your opinion."

For a few moments they sipped in silence, then Halpatter cleared his throat. "How is Billy holding up?" he asked.

"He's doing better," she said. "I think having people like you and Roland believing in him has rubbed off."

"Good," Halpatter said. "When you visit him tomorrow, bring him some of Tom Waxe's fish stew. I'll visit him as well. He needs to *see* the people who believe he is innocent. That will make him even stronger."

Halpatter poured more wine for both of them. "Now then," he said. "Let me tell you why I called. I may have some encouraging news. Nothing conclusive, you understand, but maybe something of importance. I was going to wait until Roland returned, but I figure you would want to know at once." Clara, her glass at her lips, raised her eyebrows but was silent. Halpatter took two large sips of wine, scratched one of his feet with the heel of the other, and continued.

"Tom Waxe and I learned nothing from our friends in the

swamp, but as we were returning in my boat we noticed a campfire on the riverbank up near June's Prairie," he said. "We stopped to check it out and found the bikers who had been camping on Roland's island where the Indian burial ground is located. Did Roland tell you about these people?" Clara shook her head.

"Two men and a woman. Disheveled woman. One man fat, the other skinny. Escaping the northern winter. Getting a long head start on bike week. Roland was very nice to them, considering they were trespassing on sacred ground and had been quite rude to me when I initially discovered them. When they saw me for the third time last night, they acted like I was their long-lost cousin. Offered Tom and me some coffee, which we accepted. Even gave me this Harley T-shirt as a present.

"When Roland told them they'd have to leave his island, they asked whether they could stay in a cabin they'd found up a creek that runs into the river. Deet's Creek, but of course they didn't know the name of it. I'm sure you know the place. A long time ago it belonged to Johnny Wallace, the lawyer. He lost it in a poker game, along with twenty acres of land, to Lucky Painter. A while later, Lucky got into some financial difficulty and the cabin and land wound up belonging to John Varney's bank. The story I heard was that Varney got all of it for a hundred and fifty dollars at an auction that was not very well attended. In any event, Roland told the bikers they would be making a big mistake if they set up house in that cabin.

"So there we were, Tom Waxe and I, squatting next to their campfire, drinking a cup of coffee, when the fat man said to me, 'Hey, you remember that hot Porsche me and Kirby told you we saw next to that cabin on that creek?' I told him I recollected it vaguely. 'You remember I said there was a woman in it?' he said. 'Well take a look at this.'

"He reached around into the back pocket of his jeans and took out a folded piece of newspaper. He unfolded it and held it close to the campfire so I could see it more clearly. What he had was a picture of Nikki Waters. The one they printed on the front page of the *Journal-Express* the day after she was killed. 'This here's the woman that was drivin' that Porsche,' he said. I asked him if he was sure. 'Mr. Halpatter,' he said. I was impressed that he'd remembered my name. 'Mr. Halpatter, you can bet your ass I'd never forget a face like hers. Or that hair either, no offense, Lisanne.' He said the last part to the woman who was with them."

"He was sure it was Nikki Waters?" Clara asked.

"He said he was positive, Clara. Furthermore, those two saw her in the Porsche by that cabin the night she was murdered. While Tom Waxe was making his stew, I took a ride over to the cabin in my boat. I was in luck, because, as you know, it hasn't rained since that night. Tire tracks were still clearly visible in the dirt down near the dock. I took a snapshot of the tread with my Polaroid. Then I drove down to the lot where the police store impounded vehicles. I assumed that since drugs were involved the Porsche had been confiscated. The officer who guards the lot played high school football with my son. He was happy to let me browse around.

"Sure enough, I found the Porsche. Very fancy model. Black. Covered with dirt, and equipped with Pirelli P-Zero tires. These are extremely expensive tires with a highly distinctive tread design that precisely matched the tread in my Polaroid."

"What does it mean?" she asked him.

"I'm not sure," Halpatter said. "Perhaps Roland will be able to make something of it. But I'll tell you this much. Very few people know about that cabin. Assuming Nikki Waters was there, she surely knew where she was going, because the road to it off the highway is invisible unless one is aware of its existence. It isn't the sort of path a person would be likely to take if they were out for a leisurely night-time ride in an expensive sports car."

"Come inside and have some stew," Tom Waxe said. He had been standing in the doorway, listening to Halpatter and, as was his way, had waited for an appropriate time to interject. His deep voice was so mellifluous neither Clara nor Halpatter was startled when Tom Waxe spoke. It seemed, instead, as though his voice had been part of the background all along, like a cello playing for the entertain-

ment of diners at an outdoor restaurant that had suddenly
become more apparent during a lull in conversation.

Waxe the taxi, Clara thought. Strange, how a meaningless
childhood rhyme like that stayed with you forever, bringing
with it the memory of a decrepit, ancient pickup truck with
a lawn chair for a driver's seat. In her mind she could still
hear the whining sound the truck made in the granny gear
Tom Waxe used as he drove ever so slowly down the tracks
of thick sand threading through the forest, looking for signs
of wild hog and bear. He was old and stooped now and
drove a sleek white El Camino with an automatic transmission, leather bucket seats, and a Kenwood stereo system
given to him five years earlier by Roland Troy as a
seventy-fifth birthday present.

"I am glad to see you, Clara," Tom Waxe said. "Come
on. Let's eat. It's just the three of us. I had expected
Halpatter's wife too, but evidently she's off visiting one of
her many relatives. Where the hell did she go, Sheridan?
Naples? Fort Myers? Watch. He probably doesn't even
know."

"Marco Island," said Halpatter. "Visiting her sister."

"The one who's married to the bingo king," said Tom
Waxe.

"Right," said Halpatter. "Among other things."

"The bingo king with seven Cadillacs, one for each day
of the week," said Tom Waxe. "Each one a different year
and color. I've always wanted to meet him."

"Once you get past the car thing, he isn't that interesting," said Halpatter. "He has the personality of a toad. Even
you would have a hard time warming up to him, Tom. But
his wife is Zena's sister, so she goes over there every year
after Christmas to visit. I don't make no big thing of it.
Zena goes and she comes back and that's all there is to it."

Halpatter glanced from Tom Waxe to Clara and back
again to Tom Waxe, who, aware that his friend was sorry
his wife was not there with them to lend her support, tact-
fully dropped the subject.

During dinner, Clara had time to consider whether or not
to tell Halpatter and Waxe about Ethan Peoples. She had
yet to meet Peoples, and had missed his telephone calls, but
heard about him and what he had learned about Nikki Wa-

ters when she visited her son in jail. When Halpatter told her about his encounter with the bikers, Clara immediately made the connection between John Varney and Drew Parabrise. She was not dissembling, however, when she asked Halpatter what his discovery meant, but rather thinking out loud. Neither did her vacillation now indicate mistrust of Halpatter or Waxe. On the contrary, she had complete faith in both of them, but she felt uncharacteristically out of focus. It was as though she had been sitting too long in the sun and was looking at objects she knew were familiar but that somehow had become misshapen and distorted. In this state, when she could make no sense out of what she knew and could come to no logical conclusions, she did not want to talk about anything until she first revealed what she had been told to Roland Troy.

Clara only picked at her food, but both Halpatter and Tom Waxe were too polite to remark about that. It was she who said something, apologizing to Tom Waxe, who smiled and told her he understood. They made small talk that deteriorated into everlengthening periods of silence. Clara felt guilty. Perhaps she should show elation about the story of the cabin on Deet's Creek and Nikki Waters's Porsche, but all she could think about was her son sitting in jail.

Billy had not deviated in the slightest from his original account of events the night Nikki Waters was murdered, and he had told Stanton Feinberg, his attorney, he would not, under any circumstances change his plea to guilty. Feinberg maintained a relatively cheerful façade but Clara could tell that, having nothing upon which to build a defense, he was inwardly without hope.

"Tomorrow, when you bring Billy the stew, be sure to tell him that I also believe he is innocent," Tom Waxe said. "And don't despair, Clara. We will help you." She quickly looked over at him and smiled. Had he known she was just then thinking about her son? Of course he had. It would make perfect sense. Why else would she sit there staring off into space?

"I know," he continued. "You look at me and see an old man, slow as a box turtle, hunched over like a starving buzzard. How could such a creature help himself, much less someone else? The truth of it is, I was about ready to die.

My wife is gone. My children too, before either of them
could have children of their own. It's a bitch to outlive your
offspring, that's for sure. To the best of my knowledge I'm
the only Waxe left on earth. Time to go join my ancestors
under the burial mound, I figured. But not yet. Not now.
Not as long as your son is in such jeopardy. You are far too
young to be left alone. And far too nice, I might add.
Sheridan Halpatter and I and Roland Troy will not rest until
your son is cleared, and he will be cleared, of that I am certain, though it may take some time." Tom Waxe took a
drink of wine and licked his lips. He set the wine glass
back on the table, rested his chin on his folded hands, and
stared straight into Clara's eyes.

"Both Halpatter and I sense something hovering in the
area around the cabin at Deet's Creek," he said. "Something happened there connected to the death of Nikki Waters. The way the earth was torn up by the tires of her
Porsche. The lateness of the hour. Something transpired
there. Something lurking in the darkness, in the woods, in
the cabin itself, scared that woman out of her wits. Even
now the air around the place is still electric with her terror.
You think I'm blathering. It's all right. I understand. An old
worn-out Indian full of hocus-pocus. Full of shit. But trust
me, Clara. Disharmony is not a product of the imagination.
We'll figure it out. We'll get to the bottom of it. Don't for
a moment think we won't."

XIX

✦

In the early hours of Wednesday morning the cold spell that had lasted longer than usual for central Florida came to an end. The wind, slowly shifting from north to northeast to due east the previous day, swung around some more and began to blow from the southeast, bringing with it warm, moist air from the Atlantic Ocean. By mid-morning the temperature was in the high seventies heading for the low eighties, scattered clouds were moving in, and it seemed likely that by late afternoon it would rain. The wind would continue shifting, southerly and southwesterly during the period of precipitation, westerly as the rain moved off sometime late Wednesday night, then coming full circle to blow again from the north, ushering in more cool air. That was the cycle in winter. The wind, and its attendant weather, might hang up in one or another quadrant for a few days, prolonging a northern chill or some unseasonable warmth and humidity, but the cycle itself was as immutable as the daily thunderstorms and intense heat of summer.

In the huge bedroom on the second floor of his house—a room with large windows that were rarely closed, and a skylight cut into the eastern slope of the roof—the changing weather had no effect at all on Roland Troy, who slept the uncluttered sleep of a small child. While Troy slept, the following took place.

Tom Waxe paddled a canoe up Deet's Creek and secured it at the dock next to the cabin owned by John Varney. Before climbing from the canoe, he recited an ancient Seminole prayer asking that his mind be freed from extraneous thoughts and stimuli so that he might concentrate completely on the task at hand. He then climbed out and began

a painstaking survey of the spit of land on his hands and
knees, his head as close to the ground as that of a hound
dog following the trail of a rabbit. While he crawled, Tom
Waxe sang songs from *South Pacific*—"There Ain't
Nothin' Like a Dame," "Some Enchanted Evening," "Bali
Hai"—in a low voice, but loud enough so that he could be
heard from fifty feet away. In the unlikely event someone
discovered him near the cabin, they would assume he was
just a crazy old Indian and leave him alone.

Clara Roseman, attempting to deliver a bowl of fish stew
to her son, was prevented from doing so by two guards at
the county jail. During the night an inmate had apparently
hanged himself with a noose fashioned from the cloth of
his coverall and no visitors were being allowed in until the
matter was resolved. The guards assured Clara they would
give the stew to Billy Roseman along with a note Clara
scribbled on the paper bag in which she'd carried the
Tupperware bowl. Shortly after Clara left, the two guards
devoured the stew and threw the bowl and the note in the
trash.

"No stew for the Jew," one of the guards said, holding
up his hand for a high-five from his colleague.

Peanut Butter, tutelary of Billy Roseman, purveyor of
high-grade cocaine for *Journal-Express* editor Byron
O'Reilly and various other local celebrities, and witness to
the jailhouse hanging (which was by no stretch of the imagination a suicide), attempted unsuccessfully to place a call
to Roland Troy. Peanut Butter's intention was to provide
Troy with information in exchange for protection. The man
who was hanged worked for Peanut Butter, who had good
reason to believe he was next.

Ethan Peoples arrived ten minutes early for the
Wednesday-morning editorial meeting at the *Journal-
Express*. Peoples had come to work Monday with considerable trepidation, but Byron O'Reilly had acted perfectly
normal, which is to say he stormed around the newsroom
ranting and raving for about half an hour before retreating
to his office for the rest of the day. O'Reilly never mentioned the incident at the restaurant; in fact he didn't say a

word to Peoples at all. Because of O'Reilly's indifference, Peoples began to wonder whether the incident with the truck had been a coincidence with no connection to the Nikki Waters case at all. Maybe he'd just been the unlucky target of a couple of redneck assholes, still drunk from Saturday night, out to shake up an early-morning jogger they saw as a yuppie faggot.

Late Tuesday night Peoples finally reached Clara Roseman on the phone. When she answered he was taken by surprise. He expected a high-pitched, nasal voice like the ones belonging to the middle-aged Jewish women he'd heard as a child, women from West Newton and Brookline who ended every strident sentence with a question mark. This woman sounded like a country-western singer, her voice redolent of tumblin' tumbleweed, old cowboy boots, and roadhouses on the outskirts of town. Listening to her made him feel better, even though the only thing she told him was to meet her at her house in an hour. She gave him directions and hung up.

By Wednesday, when nothing further happened to him, Peoples had calmed down even more, but was still in a state of heightened awareness brought on by his initial terror. As he sat in the conference room, waiting for the meeting to begin, he noticed certain things about his colleagues that had never before been apparent. He saw, for example, that Dick Broome, the managing editor, had two yellowish perspiration stains that formed perfect circles under the arms of his starched white shirt. The large, horsy teeth of Becka Vosburg, the award-winning editorial writer, were almost the same color as the yellowish circles. And there was something he'd previously missed about Wanda Donnerstag as well, or something different about her, he wasn't sure which.

Peoples studied Wanda intently for nearly a minute, trying to figure out what it was. She was still dressed quite conservatively in a light gray suit over a white silk blouse, but her makeup was quite pronounced, not garish actually, but definitely apparent, definitely not the way Peoples recalled having seen her before. Her cheeks were a deep ocher, her eyes darkly shadowed, and her mouth the color of strawberry jam. Her fingernails were deep red too, and longer than Peoples remembered them being—when? Last week? Last month?

Wanda looked across the long table, caught Peoples staring at her and quickly turned away, but not before he saw her eyes, which seemed to burn with the kind of intensity he usually associated with absolute insanity. He leaned over and was about to ask Foley Frazier whether it was just him or whether Foley had noticed something even stranger than usual about Wanda when Byron O'Reilly walked into the room trailing a cloud of cigarette smoke and began to speak before he even sat down.

"Baseball," O'Reilly bellowed. He sat down and pounded a fist on the table so hard that Foley Frazier's Mickey Mouse coffee mug fell over, its contents spilling like a tan waterfall over the edge of the table onto the thick carpet. Frazier righted the mug and felt his pants for wetness, never taking his eyes off O'Reilly's jowly red face.

"Baseball!" O'Reilly shrieked. He took a drag on his cigarette and expelled smoke with an audible exhalation punctuated by three rapid juts of his tongue between his lips as he spat out pieces of tobacco. "I want every fucking one of you to stop what you're doing and think baseball. Think about what you, in your area of responsibility, can do to promote baseball in Orlando. This city's going to have itself a major-league baseball team and we're going to help it get one."

O'Reilly was wearing his three-piece, dark blue pinstripe suit. *Old Bombast Blue,* Ethan Peoples thought. Batten down the hatches. Forget about the fact that the local minor-league team routinely draws about three hundred people to a game. Forget about the fact that a whole community of poor black folks will have to be bulldozed to build a stadium. It's baseball *über alles.*

O'Reilly was ranting and raving, really getting into the national pastime from every conceivable angle, even down to all the great jobs it would provide selling beer and popcorn, but Peoples had stopped listening. Instead he was watching Wanda Donnerstag, who was staring off somewhere into the middle distance. He wasn't hallucinating; there was absolutely something different about her. Where formerly her brutal intensity had thrown a quick chill into

any room she entered, she now was broadcasting a con-
verse signal. Was he the only one who noticed it, or could
the others detect the change as well? Her lips, darkly wet,
were parted slightly, and her eyes still burned with fevered
madness. She had one arm across her chest with her hand
wedged under the other arm. It seemed a businesslike
enough, no-nonsense pose, unless, as Peoples now suspected, the hand was cupping one of her breasts. Her other
hand was under the table. Peoples had a strong desire to
stick his head down under there to see if Wanda was finger-
ing herself. What if she was, right in the middle of Byron
O'Reilly's tirade?

Peoples shook his head quickly to clear his mind. What
was wrong with him? Throughout his methodical professional life he had remained focused, always on task, as
schoolteachers called it. Shit, when he was in New York he
was so intent on his mission he hadn't even made a play
for the gorgeous Melissa, who, now that he thought about
it, was certainly available. And now here he was, in the
middle of a Byron O'Reilly scream-a-thon, wondering
whether Wanda Donnerstag was playing with herself. But
then, his involvement in the Nikki Waters case had changed
things. He was a participant now, at least on some level, not
an observer. He felt more alive, more aware. Maybe this
heightened awareness had zeroed in on a side of Wanda
Donnerstag all of them had previously missed. He was rea-
sonably certain no one at the paper had ever dated her. She
was one of those women that men speculate about but ultimately regard as unapproachable, as some sort of female
predator bent on devouring them, at least the kind of men
employed by the *Journal-Express*. She approached her job
like a table saw cutting through an endless stack of plywood. She was brutal to her subordinates. Here in Florida
she drove a Saab, a sexless machine good for attacking
snowbanks. Peoples had always thought of her as a cold,
dead planet orbiting in a solar system all her own. Now he
wasn't so sure.

Wanda Donnerstag sat at the Wednesday editorial
meeting working on three hours of sleep. The night before,
she stayed at her desk until seven-thirty, then drove to the
Tri-County Mall, where she had chicken salad on a crois-

sant and a glass of red wine at Sandwiches-and-Spirits. They had little round tables with umbrellas over them, set out in front in a mock courtyard, where you could sit and watch the steady flow of shoppers almost as though you were at a sidewalk café.

After dinner she wandered into Victoria's Secret and purchased a pale blue stretch lace bodysuit she put on under the long brown skirt and tan sweater she was wearing. She stopped at Burdines and bought a new lipstick—Chanel's "Dusky Claret"—and from there went into the Super Snip Hair Salon and had her nails done for the first time in her life. The manicurist was a tall black woman named Gretchen, with hair straightened into a pageboy, who told Wanda she had lovely hands and invited her to a party all the way up in Timicuan. Wanda drove. On the way Gretchen fired up a joint of some very potent Jamaican weed. The rest of the night was a blur of flesh and pulsing rap music, which ordinarily Wanda didn't consider music at all but on this night, with the grass behind it, sounded like the essence of all rhythm, entering her body at the crotch and working its way up until the tips of her breasts tingled. She left the party at four, not with Gretchen, who had disappeared, but with a woman named Ro who needed a ride and who sucked and fondled Wanda's nipples all the way back to Orlando. But as Wanda sat through Byron O'Reilly's harangue, under reasonable control considering she was still stoned out of her mind, it was not Ro, nor Gretchen, nor any of the other women at the party about whom she fantasized (it was no figment of Ethan Peoples's imagination; she was indeed fondling herself), but Nikki Waters, the woman she had fixed on as her one true love.

Byron O'Reilly closed the Wednesday meeting by telling all those present to get their asses in gear. He walked into his office and placed a call to the man he had been told was temporarily replacing his usual source of cocaine, Premont "Peanut Butter" Blasingame, during Peanut Butter's stay in jail. The number O'Reilly dialed was that of the reggae disc jockey, Cool Babba Wisdom, who, though sound asleep when his phone rang, understood at once what was going on.

"I need an oil change, filter, and lube," O'Reilly said.

"Have to be tomorrow, chief," Wisdom answered. "Garage be busy bumper to bumper all this day and all tonight. Bring the car in around nine in the morning we get you straightened away in proper fashion."

"I need it changed now," O'Reilly said.

"Like I tell you, not a chance until then," said Wisdom. "You could try another location, maybe Palmgate, but the boys there been known for disreliability, you catch my meaning."

"I'll see you tomorrow," O'Reilly said.

"At nine," Wisdom said, and hung up.

Beverly Roseman, Billy Roseman's soon-to-be ex-wife, showed up at the front door of his house at eight in the morning with John Chadwick's slovenly, hulking groom at her side. Beverly had made no attempt to visit Billy, but had heard through the grapevine that Clara was living in the house and came looking for the Corvette. Clara told Beverly she had no idea where the car was and slammed the door in her face.

Strictly speaking, Clara was not lying, since she had given the car to her friend, Connie Alderman, and told her to hide it somewhere. Clara knew full well the avaricious but stupid Beverly would sooner or later show up trying to pry loose the car or anything else she thought she could carry away. Eventually the court would probably award the car to Beverly, but, unlike her son, Clara Roseman was going to make Beverly work for it.

"It'll be her lawyer driving Billy's 'Vette, not that miserable gold-digging bitch, you mark my words," she had said to Connie Alderman.

Jack Ubinas rose before dawn, made himself a pot of strong coffee, and took it from the kitchen of his farmhouse to the room that housed his computer and several fireproof steel cabinets filled with carefully catalogued folders. He already knew about Nikki Waters and Drew Parabrise. He knew all about John Varney and Raimundo Villegas too, and was probably the only man connected with the government who had a file on Chotoku Nakama. What he didn't know was who had put a bullet in Nikki Waters's head. He turned on the computer and began reading through dozens of files, cross-referencing names of people and places, looking for a significant connection, searching for the whereabouts of anyone who might have been involved in Waters's death.

The electronic trove of information Ubinas had before him was vast, occupying a sizable chunk of a 210-meg hard drive, and delving into it Ubinas felt like an undersea explorer twisting his way through a labyrinth of murky, uncharted caverns. Some of the information was catalogued "situation/actual," or SIAC, and included clandestine gatherings of known terrorists, secret conferences held by international arms and drug traffickers, planning sessions that had resulted in armed insurrection often in parts of the world far removed from the recorded encounter.

Events in SIAC were known by Ubinas to have occurred. In SIAC, for example, was a detailed account of a meeting among a Saudi Arabian arms dealer, two Hong Kong bankers, a Turkish drug transporter, and the field representative of a major multinational oil company. The meeting was held inside the bankers' 707, which was parked on a remote airstrip the oil company owned in eastern Algeria, not far from Hassi Messaoud. It was convened not to arrange a specific arms or drug deal, but to discuss the financing of a coup in Indonesia and the ramifications of this coup for that nation's prodigious oil supply. The pilot of the 707 was an undercover agent who reported directly to Jack Ubinas.

Other of Ubinas's information was catalogued "situation/speculative," or SISPEC. In SISPEC were juxtapositions that may or may not have been related but were of enough significance to warrant Ubinas's attention. Here, for instance, was the file of a mysterious Argentine assassin known as *El Papagayo*—the Parrot—because of the shape of his nose. An operative who worked for an airplane-customizing company located at Miami International Airport claimed to have seen *El Papagayo* in a bar frequented by nonskeds—pilots who flew non-scheduled flights, anywhere, anytime, no questions asked. The date of the operative's report was three days before a helicopter carrying a United States Senator and two influential businessmen crashed and burned in the Smoky Mountains. All three men plus the pilot died. Ubinas paused at *El Papagayo*'s file, sipped from his mug of thick black coffee, and ruminated for several minutes. Then he moved on. To the best of his knowledge, *El Papagayo* had not been in the United States since the crash.

At nine in the morning on Wednesday, Ubinas finally found a connection that bore further investigation. He picked up the phone, automatically checking to make sure the light on his Safeline tap-detector was green, and dialed a number in Del Mar, California. The man who answered was a real estate investor who had worked for Ubinas in much the same capacity as Roland Troy.

"How's the weather?" Ubinas asked.

"Surf's up," the man said. In spite of the hour, he knew at once who was on the other end of the line.

"I need a favor."

"I figured," the man said.

"I need you to take a ride across the border. See a Chinese guy who lives on the beach south of Ensenada. I got directions here I'll fax you in a minute. I'd like you to see that this guy gives me a call in a hurry."

"Shouldn't be a problem," the man said. "But why don't you give him a call yourself, if you don't mind me asking?"

"He doesn't have a phone," Ubinas said.

"That explains it," said the man. "I'll leave in an hour. Happy New Year."

"We'll see," said Ubinas.

"I have an important meeting in my office," Drew Parabrise said to his wife that Wednesday morning. Dorothy Parabrise lowered the section of the *Washington Post* she was reading, smiled at him, ran a hand through her shoulder-length brown hair, and said nothing. She may or may not have believed him, there was no way of telling, and in any case, whether she did or didn't made no difference to Parabrise.

Parabrise had never loved his wife. She was the daughter of Ellington Chadwick, land baron, attorney of choice for the Florida sugar industry, former lieutenant governor, and, when Parabrise met his daughter, state chairman of the Republican party. Parabrise, who was in his first year of law

school at the time, took one look at Dorothy Chadwick's
compliant face and knew instinctively that marrying her
was the right move.

Drew Parabrise loved being a senator. The Senate's free-
wheeling, clubby atmosphere, its sense of informal
exclusivity—like a custom-made shirt slightly frayed
around the cuffs and collar—fit him perfectly. He also rev-
eled in the power. Parabrise never forgot something he was
told when he was first elected in 1976. A colleague from a
Midwestern state had come over to him at a cocktail party
honoring the Senate's new members. "You'll like it here,"
the man said. "Nobody ever refuses a telephone call from
a United States Senator."

His more noble colleagues used this environment to promote legislation beneficial, at least in some respect, to their
country. Parabrise used it solely to promote himself. His
role model was the late Lyndon Johnson, master of the political full-court press. As with Johnson, even those who despised Drew Parabrise were in awe of his manipulative
skills, his ability to flatter, wheedle, bargain, and persuade.
The only skill Parabrise lacked was Johnson's ability to
threaten. For that he was too weak, but then there were
those in his camp, visible and unseen, who took care of any
threatening that was deemed appropriate.

Parabrise did in fact have a meeting that morning in his
office. It was with the senior senator from Connecticut and
was quite brief, taking place over a hurried breakfast of
coffee and doughnuts. During that time the two men basically agreed to support legislation beneficial to each of
them. After the other senator left, Parabrise walked from
his large, airy office to a much smaller one belonging to
one of his aides, a twenty-five-year-old woman named
Shannon Kinney. She was a short, thin, intense woman with
stick-straight dark red hair and freckles, who groaned
loudly the entire time she made love. But this was a quies-
cent time in Washington, and she was the only member of
his staff who was in the building, so, noisy though she was,
there was little chance the two of them would be discovered, half-undressed, writhing together on the wine-colored
carpet beside her desk. That was where the two of them

were when Parabrise's private phone line rang twenty times shortly before noon.

Billy Roseman lay on the cot in his cell, eyes closed, re-creating, for the hundredth time, his Breeders' Crown victory with Steakhouse Papa.

"Rosy, whatchu be thinkin' about, man?" Peanut Butter said to him.

Billy opened his eyes and turned his head in Peanut Butter's direction. "I should 'a died with my horse," Billy told him.

"Even Roy Rogers isn't that crazy," Peanut Butter said, "and he had his fuckin' horse stuffed."

"Nobody ever accused Roy Rogers of rape and murder," Billy said.

"I can't argue with you there, my man. But since you didn't die with the horse, don't you be tryin' to die now. Least not 'til Rolan' Troy come back aroun' and I have a few words with him."

"Don't worry, P.B.," Billy said. "I was kidding. I don't wanna die any more than you do."

"Good. Good. That's what I like to hear," Peanut Butter said. " 'Cause Rosy, you may be a strange muthafucka, but I'm gettin' to like you. I'm gonna see maybe somebody I know can dig up some shit on that dead woman. See maybe we can put Rolan' Troy on the right track."

" 'Cause you like me," Billy said.

" 'Cause I want to get my ass outa this place," Peanut Butter said. "Ain't nothin' wrong with that now, is there? Maybe get both our asses the hell out of here."

"Hey," Billy said. "Dig away, man. You ain't gonna get no argument from me."

"So Rosy, tell me," Peanut Butter said. "Say you do get outa here, and you can go anywhere you want in the whole world, where would you go?"

Billy sat up, stretched his long arms over his head, and stared across at Peanut Butter, who was pacing back and forth in his cell. "I'd go to the track," he said. "To train my horses."

Peanut Butter stopped pacing and faced Roseman. "You ain't serious?" he said.

"Yeah, I'm serious," Billy said. "Where the fuck else would I go? That's what I do. That's who I am. Why, where would you go?"

"I don't know for sure," Peanut Butter said. "But I wouldn't go lookin' for no horse. I'd find me some booty."

"Booty's exactly what I *wouldn't* go lookin' for," Billy said.

"Yeah, I hear you," Peanut Butter said. "I was you I probably wouldn't either."

John Varney was in a good mood. He and his wife were driving south on I-75, heading toward Orlando from their retreat. Even the endless succession of country-and-western tapes Kirsten had played since they left North Carolina couldn't dampen his spirits, though he had finally suggested she listen through her headphones so he could think.

Varney was constantly amazed at the endless advantages of owning a bank. Recently, for example, he had bought a golf course, or, more accurately, his bank loaned him the money to buy a golf course. Within two weeks, he would sell the golf course and pocket two million dollars. The deal worked liked this:

Faced with the task of salvaging at least something tangible from the failure of an overwhelming number of savings-and-loan institutions, the federal government created an organization known as the Resolution Trust Corporation. The RTC's mission was to auction off the holdings of these defunct S&Ls. The majority of these holdings were thousands of pieces of real estate—office buildings, churches, shopping centers, entire industrial parks, outrageously expensive personal homes—all backed by the S&Ls with money they were now unable to collect.

As luck would have it, Drew Parabrise had overseen the passage of some legislation involving access to deep-water ports that was highly favorable to certain constituents of a senator on the Senate Finance Committee. In turn, this senator made sure one of Parabrise's close friends was appointed to the RTC. It was this close friend who engineered John Varney's purchase of the golf course, located outside New Orleans, for five million dollars, even though a group of investors had already offered seven million.

Who would ever know, given the vast amount of real estate to be auctioned, that the United States government sold the golf course to John Varney for two million dollars less than the other investors offered? Who cared? If anyone asked, it would no doubt be pointed out that Varney had much better credit than the others, that his affairs were more in order. Who knows whether their bid, submitted to a faceless committee somewhere in Washington, could even be found? Surely the other investors would never object. They were getting what they wanted, seven million bucks for a nine-million-dollar piece of property. Everybody was making out. Everybody was happy.

Furthermore, the woman who had killed Roseman's horse, the woman who had thought she could go head to head with him, the woman who had spit in his eye and called him a redneck in a fifteen-hundred-dollar suit, was dead, closing the final chapter of the harness-racing episode he had so smoothly carried off. Twenty million dollars, that deal had been worth to him. He smacked the steering wheel and laughed so loud, Kirsten leaped up from her reclining position in the back seat and yanked her headphones off.

"What is it, honey?" she asked. "What's so funny?"

"Nothing important," Varney said. "I was just thinking how easy it is to make money."

"Oh, that's 'cause it's you that's makin' it, baby," she said, giving him a kiss on the neck. "Other folks don't find it that simple. It's easy for you 'cause you're so smart."

"You got that right," he said, but she had already flung herself back onto the deeply cushioned leather seat and put the headphones on, so she didn't hear him.

There had never been a syndicate, at least not in the sense that there was ever a group of individuals who invested their own money in the horse. The fifteen million dollars they supposedly put up had come from John Varney's bank, loaned, against the current and future value of Steakhouse Papa, to the members of the Orange Blossom Syndicate at no interest for the first eighteen months. In eighteen months, so the syndication prospectus declared, the Orange Blossom Syndicate would be well on its way to reaping the benefits of Steakhouse Papa's breedings. The bank and everybody else would make money. If not, if something untoward happened—if Steakhouse Papa became sterile, for instance, or if he died—an insurance policy written by Lloyd's of London, with a premium of three hundred thousand dollars, would cover the fifteen-million-dollar loan.

There were a number of people listed as members of this syndicate, but none invested a dime, nor did they ever lay a hand on any of the money from the loan. It may have appeared that each of them received funds which they in turn invested with John Varney, but in actuality the fifteen million dollars went straight from the bank into Varney's pocket. Varney paid the insurance premium and put the rest of the money to work, doubling it almost at once as the middleman in a giant cocaine deal between a California-based Chinese underworld clan and a group of Mexicans. He kept twenty of the thirty million dollars and gave ten to Chotoku Nakama, the man who arranged his meeting with the Chinese gangsters.

The rest had been simple. The synthetic adrenaline Nikki Waters injected into Steakhouse Papa would have been detectable only if a test had been run immediately after the horse's death, but in the aftermath of Steakhouse Papa's collapse and the multihorse pileup that ensued, there had been far too much tumult and confusion on the track for anyone to think of testing the horse right away. Two other horses had been destroyed and three drivers seriously injured. One of them, the famed Lambert D'Artigue, was paralyzed from the waist down and never drove again. It was hours, therefore, before an autopsy was performed on Steakhouse Papa, by which time all tests for the presence of drugs proved to be negative.

It had taken nearly a year, but Lloyd's paid off on the policy and John Varney promptly repaid his bank the fifteen million dollars it loaned the syndicate. Since none of the members of the syndicate actually invested any money, they were not, according to the terms of the syndication agreement, entitled to any of the insurance payoff. Only those individuals or institutions actually providing funds were legal beneficiaries of the Lloyd's policy. That meant Varney's bank was reimbursed, but Billy Roseman, who traded his horse to John Varney for shares in the syndication, got nothing. Roseman protested, claiming that using his horse to obtain shares was the same as using money.

"Go ahead and sue me," Varney told him. "I'll tie you up in court for ten years. You'll spend three times as much in legal fees as you'll ever get out of me, if you do wind up getting anything. You want some free advice? Next time you make a deal for one of your horses, get cash."

"You told me my shares were better than cash," Roseman said.

"I lied," said Varney. "Nothing's better than cash."

Nikki Waters had not been as easy to brush off. In addition to the job at the radio station, she wanted a share in the syndication of one of Varney's other horses. Varney, who wanted no evidence of any connection to Nikki Waters, refused, instead offering her twenty-five thousand dollars.

"I could have a person killed for less than that," he told her. "All you're going to do is kill a horse."

"I don't want your twenty-five grand," she told him. "You don't like my terms, kill the motherfucking horse yourself."

In the end, he agreed to include her in the syndication of Blue Monday, the horse that Steakhouse Papa beat, but there was nothing in writing, and he never delivered. It was only later—when Nikki Waters went to bed with Raimundo Villegas, got the Mexican drug dealer to tell her about his transactions with the gringos across the border, and went into business for herself—that Varney realized he had underestimated her.

But now she was dead, her secret undiscovered, her liaison with Drew Parabrise unrecorded—and Billy Roseman, the hapless, romantic fool, was going to burn for her murder. Her friendship with Roseman, the role she assumed at his stable, which at first worried Varney to some degree, had proven in the end to be a stroke of good luck. He had to admit Nakama had been right. When he protested that giving her a radio job in Orlando was a mistake, Nakama disagreed.

"No matter how much you try, there is no way you can go against human nature," he said. "She and Drew-san need one another and will find ways to be together no matter what you or I might desire. Orlando is his hometown, after all. Better to have her in a place that is natural for him to visit than in a place where his presence might draw unnecessary attention."

At least Parabrise had had the sense to cover his tracks, or, more accurately, Nakama had seen to it that he did. Rumors might surface about the senator and the dead ex-model; you could never be absolutely sure they wouldn't. But no trail of motel receipts, phone calls, or expensive dinners on Parabrise's personal credit card would ever be uncovered. Nakama even had Parabrise drive his own car to a garage near Washington and switch to one registered to someone who worked for Nakama's organization when Parabrise was meeting Nikki Waters. You never knew when a private investigator, looking for who knows what, might be prowling around a motel parking lot checking license-plate numbers.

"A Kennedy in Massachusetts could stick his *chimpo* out the window, wave it at a group of passing nuns, and still be reelected," Nakama said. "But Drew-san is not a Kennedy, and Florida is not Massachusetts. If he wants to continue seeing her, okay, but there is no point in his being flagrant about it."

Varney had thought these precautions were overkill, but then look what happened to Gary Hart. Only recently, newspaper headlines all across Florida identified the president of a major Florida university as someone being questioned in a statewide probe of prostitution rings. The fool had called several escort services from his hotel room when he was in Tallahassee on school business. The phone calls showed up on his bill, and now he was trying to cover his ass by claiming he was only looking for a massage for his bad back.

John Varney himself was perfectly happy being the power behind the throne with no desire whatsoever to be the man sitting on it. Not in times like these. He could fuck anyone he wanted to, with as much flagrance as he liked, and all he had to worry about was an irate wife. The one he had now was beautiful enough, but as easily replaceable as the car he was driving.

Varney sighed contentedly. The goal he had set for himself—a position of great influence next to the ultimate seat of power in the United States—was now clearly in view. The drug deal solidified his financial situation; it was one of two he had engineered with total net profits of thirty-eight million dollars. He had no intention of becoming involved in another. The real estate windfalls made possible by the RTC auctions were merely icing on the cake, a few extra million added to a fortune that by his reckoning now made him the third richest man in Florida, a good twenty years younger than the two men ahead of him in wealth. In three years he would pull back from his wheeling and dealing, assume a high-profile post for a nominal salary in either an environmental or transportation agency—he and Drew Parabrise would decide on the appropriate spot for him when the time came—and devote himself to getting Parabrise elected president. That might take a while, but Parabrise was only in his late forties, and with the vast media holdings controlled quietly by Chotoku Nakama it was distinctly possible. By the time it came to pass, Varney's own public image would be sufficiently polished to warrant a cabinet appointment. And why not? He had known one cabinet member personally who early in his career had run a ring of highly skilled hit men, who had been, in effect, a coordinator of international assassinations.

The only thing that bothered Varney, to the point where it had become an obsession, was the presence of the omnipotent Nakama. Varney was deeply disturbed by the power Nakama wielded, not only in the shadowy arena of multinational influence, but in the personal control he had over Drew Parabrise—and, if Varney were honest, over him as well.

There was another thing, too. John Varney was far too cynical to privately espouse anything resembling patriotism. Without the slightest compunction he was capable of waving a flag in one hand and selling inferior weapons systems to the army that defended it with the other. He was, however, an unmitigated racist, and the notion that a Chinese, or Burmese, or Okinawan, or whatever Nakama was— Varney never had been able to determine—the notion that he might be the one jerking the strings of the President of the United States, like some slant-eyed puppeteer, filled

Varney with absolute loathing. He would bide his time on
that one, but it wasn't easy for him, especially when
Nakama told him what to do.

They were almost home, and Kirsten climbed into the
front seat next to him. She waved and said hi to the guard
at the gate and began babbling for at least the tenth time
about the havoc the frost must have wrought to all their
beautiful plants, even though he had told her repeatedly the
gardeners would put in all new ones as soon as it warmed
up a bit. They turned into the long circular driveway leading to their house and, sure enough, there was the landscap-
er's pickup truck parked in front of the garage. Two men
were digging around in the bushes at the side of the house.
Obviously the company had sent someone out to check on
how much damage had been done.

"See, what did I tell you," Varney said. "They'll pull the
dead stuff out today and have new bushes in by next
week."

"I don't recognize those guys," Kirsten said. "It's like
every time you turn around they've got someone else doing
the work. And none of 'em speak English. How can I tell
them what to do?"

Loath as he was to getting his own hands dirty, Raimundo
Villegas realized that the current situation left him no choice.
He had spilled the beans about John Varney to the gringo
with the beard. Varney had to be killed before he found this
out, and Villegas had no time to find someone else reliable
enough to do the job for him. While flying home from his
border encounter with Roland Troy, he radioed ahead to an
assistant in Chihuahua, explaining in code what he needed.
Shortly after he landed the Cessna, a Gulfstream registered
to a company in Honduras, carrying him, his pilot, and a
small, wiry man known as *El Chivo*—the goat—took off,
heading due east to Florida.

John Varney and his wife had climbed from their car and
were removing their luggage from the trunk when Raimundo
Villegas, wearing dirty work clothes and an old straw hat,
emerged from the bushes at the side of their house and
walked quickly across the driveway. Hearing him, Varney

turned, a leather suitcase in one hand, a nylon gym bag in the other.

"Villegas?" he said, and was about to say more when the Mexican shot him three times in the chest with a silenced 9-millimeter Browning. Varney's wife began to scream, but Villegas fired twice more into her open mouth, killing her before she could make more than a faint sound. *El Chivo*, who had come up behind Villegas, put a round between the eyes of Varney and his wife just to make sure, then got into the truck, behind the wheel. Villegas pulled the straw hat low over his eyes and climbed into the passenger seat beside him.

"Ahora el otro con la barba," Villegas said. "Now for the other one, the one with the beard. He will be considerably more difficult."

After four hours on his hands and knees, Tom Waxe, who had discovered nothing, climbed into his canoe and paddled home. Convinced some link to Nikki Waters's murder lay in the vicinity of the Deet's Creek cabin, he vowed to return there until he found it.

XX

♦

It was early afternoon when Roland Troy awoke. He rose from his bed and walked across his bedroom to the wooden enclosure at the far side of the room that housed a shower and large soaking tub. He filled the tub with hot water and sat in it for ten minutes, tensing and relaxing his muscles, trying to rid his joints of stiffness, but when he emerged and crossed the room again his limp was still more pronounced than usual. Dressed only in a pair of old denim cutoffs, he stood in front of the open French doors near his bed and did a series of stretching exercises.

Troy's bedroom was an enormous open space that occupied the entire second story of his house. At one end, where an oriental rug covered the floor, was the bed, an old easy chair with a low wooden table in front of it, a clothes closet with built-in shelves, and a floor-to-ceiling bookcase filled with books and stacks of magazines and old newspapers. Above the bed was a gun rack that held a high-powered, scoped rifle, a semiautomatic shotgun, and a Smith & Wesson Model 29 .44-Magnum revolver. The rest of the room, with the exception of the bath and shower enclosure, was an open, empty space bathed in light during the day from pairs of large, outward-opening windows on three walls. Here, on the polished hardwood floor, Troy practiced his *kata* and meditated below the two-hundred-year-old samurai sword stuck in its scabbard that once belonged to Ansai Shima and that he, like Shima, had mounted on the wall.

A door in one corner of the room led to a staircase that went down to the first floor, and also up to a turret-like room above. This large third-floor room was hexagonally shaped, with a broad, cushioned window seat all the way around, and windows on all the walls. It was formerly the bedroom of Troy's daughter, but was now empty, save for Katherine's old four-poster bed and several cartons filled with her childhood toys. Sometimes, on stormy nights, Troy would climb the stairs to Katherine's old room, throw open the windows, and let the warm wet wind swirl around him. In the darkness, he would poke his head out of one window after the other. Feeling like the keeper of a lonely lighthouse, he would sing into the blackness, bellowing old sea chanteys or fifties rock and roll songs like "Angel Baby" or "In the Still of the Night" at the top of his voice. This made him feel close to his daughter since they had done this together when she was a young girl.

Now, Troy finished stretching, did a hundred push-ups, two sets of twenty pull-ups, and fifty sit-ups. He moved to the center of the polished wooden floor and did a single *kata*, called *ro-hai*, twice in slow motion, once at medium speed, and twice more with full power. Then he took a quick shower and got dressed in a pair of faded gray Levi's corduroys, an old blue chambray work shirt, and desert boots. He went downstairs into the kitchen, put a kettle of water on the stove for tea, and plugged in his phone. Before the water came to a boil the phone rang. It was Clara, calling from a phone booth outside a Handi-Way on Lee Road.

Like Jack Ubinas, Troy had a monitoring device on his telephone that indicated whether the phone was being tapped. Clara knew this and said nothing of any consequence until Troy told her it was okay to talk. She asked about his trip; Troy said it was productive but didn't elaborate. Then she told him what she had learned from Ethan Peoples, Sheridan Halpatter, and Tom Waxe.

"So what happens now?" she asked him when she had finished.

"Call Peoples and tell him to carry on business as usual," Troy said. "They were just trying to scare him. If they'd wanted him gone he'd already be gone. Tell Billy to keep his chin up. I'll go see him tomorrow. I got some other stuff to do today. Couple of people to see. How about you come up here tonight and we'll talk."

"Okay," she said. "What time?"

"Eight," he said.

He was halfway out the door when his phone rang again. This time it was Peanut Butter. "I got a deal for you," Peanut Butter said.

"I'm listening," said Troy.

"Twice in the same month you're up here," Teddy Chambers said. "Shit, Roland, maybe I ought to get you a desk." Chambers was wearing brown suit pants, a pink shirt, and a maroon silk jacquard tie with a flowered print. His custom-made snakeskin cowboy boots propped up on his desk were immaculate.

"I see you got rid of the suspenders," Roland Troy said.

"My daughter's skiing in Breckendridge," Chambers said, "so I thought I'd take a break. They were cutting into my shoulders. I don't know how these fuckin' Wall Street guys do it, wearin' those things week in and week out. Maybe they got no nerve endings below the neck. You have any idea what a week skiing out there costs?"

"I don't know," Troy said. "A thousand, twelve hundred? Somethin' like that."

"That's right," Chambers said. "You got it right on the nose. How the fuck you know that? You don't even ski."

"I keep abreast of things," Troy said.

"Like the murder of Nikki Waters," Chambers said. He took two cigars from the box on his desk and handed one across to Troy. Both of them lit up and puffed for several seconds.

"She wasn't just some sexy disc jockey," Troy said. "She was fucking Drew Parabrise, our esteemed senator, and doing business with his buddy John Varney. Or trying to do business with him. She was up to her neck with the big boys, this Nikki Waters."

Teddy Chambers puffed on his cigar, blew smoke at the ceiling, and shook his head back and forth. "I understand what you're doing, Roland. I mean, as your friend I understand it and I admire it. But you're banging your head against the wall. I don't doubt for a minute that your information's good. It always has been and it probably always will be. But, Bubba, it doesn't matter who she was fucking. She could have been fucking the pope for all the good it's gonna do you. What matters was who was in that barn with her. Who wrapped his hands around that Colt and blew her brains out and then cut her tit off. It sure as shit wasn't Drew Parabrise. He was in New Hampshire. There was a picture of him the next morning in the paper, all jolly and bundled up in the snow."

"She could've been hit," Troy said. "She was tangled up worse'n a week-old bowl of spaghetti with Varney and some other slime. Billy Roseman could've been set up. I think it's worth looking into, Teddy."

"You want to look into it, Roland, you go ahead. You have my blessing. But forget about squeezing information out of John Varney. Somebody took him out late this morning. His wife too. Right in their driveway. Nobody heard a sound. All the guard at the gate remembers were two Hispanic-looking guys driving a truck that appeared to be from the company that takes care of Varney's property. One of 'em was wearing a straw hat. Somebody—they assumed it was Varney's wife—called the gate last night to tell them the truck was coming, but Varney and his wife were in a motel in Valdosta, Georgia, last night and they didn't make any phone calls. And the landscaping company says they didn't send anyone to the Varneys' house today. Now, if we're going to talk about a hit, pardner, that was a hit."

Troy set his cigar down in a large glass ashtray at the edge of Chambers's desk. He rubbed his eyes and the bridge of his nose with the thumb and index finger of his right hand, took a deep breath, and stuck the cigar back in his mouth.

"How about delaying the prosecution a little," he said. "Buy me some time. I got an idea about the missing tit. Let me run with it."

Teddy Chambers stood up and walked back and forth in front of the row of windows behind his desk. His compact little body seemed to bounce slightly each time he took a step. Suddenly he turned, put his hands on the edge of the desk, and leaned toward Troy. Small beads of perspiration were visible high on his forehead.

"You don't seem to understand," he said. "First I get a local cult figure fucked, murdered, and mutilated. Now I got a pillar of the community—the owner of a prestigious bank, no less—gunned down, along with his beautiful wife, in their driveway in what is considered to be a secure neighborhood. I mean, *you* know he was a scumbag, and *I* know he was a scumbag, but to the unschooled public out there John Varney was a man of substance. And I got that hanging at the jail. Third one in the last six weeks. And I got that guy they found in a culvert on the grounds at Disney. Foul play cannot be ruled out, the sheriff's department says. Jesus Christ, man, the motherfucker had six bullet holes in him. Nine millimeter. Same caliber that wasted the Varneys. That's what they're using these days, the cowboys. And I got Conrad the Climber. The one who went in hotel-room windows after old ladies. All right here in America's mecca of family fun. And you want time because you got an idea about the missing tit. Hey, take all the time you want, that boy is going to trial. And he's gonna be convicted. You got plenty of time, Roland. You know how the system works. It'll be years before they fry his ass."

"You gotta calm down, Teddy," Troy said. "The pressure's gettin' to you."

"The pressure's getting to me? The pressure's getting to me? Well I guess maybe so, but then I'm living in the pressure *cooker*. How about you? You don't feel any, huh?"

"Every day of my life," Troy said. "You should'a been with me yesterday. Or was it the day before. Tell you the truth, I've lost track."

Chambers sat down, picked his cigar off his desk, and relit it. "I'm sorry," he said. "I got no right to judge you. You been there."

"Katherine's getting married," Troy said.

"Katherine? Katherine your daughter? She was just a little girl."

"She's bigger 'n you, Teddy."

"Bigger 'n me. Well, that ain't sayin' a whole lot. When's this gonna be?"

"April. At my place. Outside by the pond is where she wants to have it."

"I sure would like to be there," Chambers said. "Now you're probably so pissed off you ain't gonna invite me."

"Don't be ridiculous. You're invited. Your whole family's invited. You're just doin' what you gotta do. You got a hard job. I understand."

"Don't think I don't feel shitty about it. I went to call Clara a couple of times, but you know I can't do that." Chambers unbuttoned the top button of his shirt and loosened his tie. "I can't believe Katherine's getting married. You know, I was just getting used to the eighties and now they're gone. A whole decade and I don't know where it went. I'm trying cases, building this here career of mine, helping to raise three kids, bunch of bankers and motherfucking corporate raiders out there stealing everything in sight. Did you see 'em? Did you feel anything when the whole fuckin' load fell off the truck? I didn't. Now everybody's going broke. Skeets Lanier's going out of business. Can you imagine that? A Chevy dealer? The heartbeat of America, Bubba. Couple of Mafia guys from New Jersey bought his place, twenty cents on the dollar. And Katherine's getting married. I feel unprepared. Roland, I feel old."

"Yeah," Troy said. "Me too. I creak when I walk."

"That bullet's still in your hip, ain't it?"

"A piece of it's in there somewhere."

"Tell me about the missing tit," Chambers said.

Troy puffed on his cigar and blew smoke toward the ceiling. "It's just an idea," he said. "There's some people I know about who would do that after killing a person. Certain Asians. Cut something off the victim's body so they wouldn't make the journey to the next life in one piece. To some Buddhists that would demonstrate the ultimate disrespect. A sign of complete contempt."

"You think Nikki Waters was whacked by people like that?"

"Teddy, I don't know. I'm gonna talk to a guy tonight who may be able to help me. If I find out anything, I'll tell you."

"Right," Chambers said. "You tell me. You know, Vanderbilt University Law School's been after me to teach there. Did I mention that to you? Them and two others, but they're the best of the bunch. The president himself called me up the other day. Said he read my criminal prosecution book and wanted to personally ask me to join their faculty.

He told me all three of my kids get a free ride if I sign on. A free ride, Roland. You know what that's worth these days? And at a good school like that, too. It's awful tempting. Work this job 'til the middle of June, go camping in Colorado for two or three weeks with my boy, then move on up there to Nashville and spend the rest of my working days lecturing to eager law students. No more rest-stop rapist. No more South American hit men. No more child-molesting Sunday school teachers. No more Nikki Waters. I ain't gonna keep doin' this shit the rest of my life, no, sir. You're the only person I've told, so don't say anything."

"Not a word," Troy said.

"And then I have to sit still for assholes like Mayor Widgy Hornbuckle. He called me up, that pampered, publicity-seeking son of a bitch, wants me to ride on some fucking float in a parade down at Disney. The Wheels of Justice, the float is called. Can you fuckin' believe it?"

"Maybe you could get a straw hat to go with your suspenders," Troy said.

"It isn't funny," Chambers said. "Because him and his buddies are who's running this town now, and underneath all those big smiles and slaps on the back and come on up and party with us in my skybox at the Magic game, underneath all that, my friend, those dudes got no sense of humor at all. They ain't like the old-timers. They ride exercise bikes and hump stair-climbing machines. They all have personal trainers who measure their percentage of body fat and wipe the Nautilus machines off with disinfectant so they won't have to touch anybody else's sweat. Those are the boys who want Billy Roseman dispensed with forthwith. People like that, they got no time for theories about the Buddhist hereafter. They want their nirvana right here and now. So you go find your slice-'em-and-dice-'em Asians, but do it quick. Do it real quick, Roland."

"I think that teaching job's a good idea," Troy said.

"Like building models of crime scenes," Chambers said.

"Only in front of an audience," Troy said. "And with a better retirement plan."

Roland Troy was about to ease his El Camino out of the courthouse driveway when he saw the woman out

of the corner of his eye. He was going to stop at the phone
booth at the ABC Liquor Store down the street and call
Clara to tell her not to come out to his house that night for
dinner. Something had come up that he had to deal with, he
was going to say, and he'd meet her later that night, either
at Billy's house or at the jail, he wasn't sure which. He'd
explain everything then.

Troy had said nothing to Teddy Chambers, but there was
no doubt in his mind that Raimundo Villegas had murdered
John Varney and was now going to try to kill him. Ubinas
had been right. It had been pure folly to let Villegas go, and
now he was going to have to deal with him again, only this
time Villegas was the hunter. He didn't want Clara in the
middle if things got nasty. Troy cursed softly. He should
have made the call before he left the building. Now it was
too late. No way was he getting out of his car in the middle
of a parking lot.

The woman was sitting in a tan Nissan pickup parked
across the street from the courthouse, reading a magazine.
She had short dark hair and was wearing a denim jacket
and a pair of Oakley's. She never looked up as he pulled
into traffic, but he knew she'd been waiting for him. He
could feel it. Interesting, he thought, that Villegas would
send a woman to track him, but clever. She was young, too.
No more than twenty-five. There'd be a phone in her truck.
One you could operate without holding. And some sort of
lightweight weapon. A Tech-9, maybe. Or one of those new
thirty-shot Grendels. Without looking down, he took his .45
out of the console and placed it on the seat next to him.

The man with Villegas—the other guy the guard at the
gate had seen—would be a Mexican, someone Villegas had
worked with before. The woman was probably the one
who'd called the landscape company pretending to be
Varney's wife. Troy was willing to lay odds Villegas had
picked her up in Miami, where he'd probably switched
planes so he couldn't be traced. Maybe she was Hispanic,
maybe not, but in any case she had to know the Orlando
area. She was slick too. She'd tailed him to the courthouse
and he hadn't seen her.

The way they'd work it, Troy figured, was that she'd follow him. If the opportunity presented itself, she'd shoot

him. Otherwise she'd let Villegas and his buddy know where he was and the three of them would close in and take him. He better not get sloppy, he told himself, or they'd nail his ass right here in his own backyard. He checked the woman out once more in his rearview mirror and gunned the El Camino. "We'll take the scenic route home," he said out loud. "I hope you like snakes."

After less than three minutes on the well-traveled four-lane highway, Troy turned onto a paved secondary road and drove west at a steady seventy miles an hour. The woman was smart; she'd fallen in behind some other fast-moving traffic, but once or twice Troy caught sight of her a half-mile or so behind him.

In a while the road narrowed, dropping down to a concrete bridge across the Coacoochee. Just beyond this bridge, in the middle of a short incline, Troy braked hard and swung the El Camino onto a dirt path that wound through a forest of oak and pine. The path ran for a mile and a half, ending abruptly before a brick chimney and a crumbling cistern—the last visible remnants of a ghost town called Minerva. Troy shut off his engine, grabbed his .45, and climbed out of the El Camino. For a moment he stood still, listening to the woman's truck work its way through the woods. Then, holding the pistol in his hand, he disappeared into the trees.

He was two miles north of his house. The firm terrain where the hamlet of Minerva once stood quickly gave way to acres of dark, shallow water obscured by vine-hung cypress trees and thick brush. Through this morass, trailing off from the ghost town like the tail of a kite, ran a serpentine strip of high ground, left by the receding ice age, that stretched all the way to the slope behind Roland Troy's house. Like the water around it, this low, meandering ribbon was covered with leaves and branches making the boundary between dry land and swamp nearly impossible to distinguish, but Roland Troy knew this trail so well he could walk it in the dark. As a boy he had traversed it more than a hundred times. He and his friends had called it "the gauntlet," for on either side lurked water moccasins and gators. Occasionally, on a dare, they had run it barefoot.

In spite of his sore hip, Troy moved quickly along the

natural levee. As soon as the woman in the pickup got to
the ghost town and saw he had taken off into the woods,
she'd know he had made her. She would then either try to
follow him or double back to wherever Villegas was waiting. He could have stayed hidden at the edge of the ghost
town and tried to take the woman when she pulled up in
her truck, but if he missed, or she bolted, he would lose
valuable time. More than anything, he wanted to get home
as soon as possible and call Clara to keep her away from
his house. After that, he would take his other vehicle—a
four-wheel-drive Ford Bronco that was sitting in his barn—
circle around, and cut the woman off. If she did try to follow him, Troy was certain she'd either get lost in the
woods or give up after a few minutes and return to her
truck. If she left the ghost town right away, he'd catch
her as she retraced her route and run her off the road. In either case, he wanted the woman alive. Then he could use
her as bait for Villegas, the same way he'd used Wayne
Boudrie out in Texas.

Twice, when Troy paused along the trail, he could hear
the sounds of someone far behind him thrashing through
the brush, but when he reached the end of the levee and
stopped he heard nothing except for the rustle of small animals and birds. As he suspected, the woman had given up
and returned to her truck. Still, Troy took no chances, staying inside the tree line and approaching his house from the
far side of the barn, out of sight of anyone in the swamp.
Avoiding the exposure of his porch, he entered the house
through the side door to the kitchen, transferred the .45 to
his left hand, and opened the refrigerator to get a drink of
ice water. At that instant, as his hand closed around the
neck of the water jug, he heard the creak of a wooden
floorboard followed by the roar of a shotgun that blew the
refrigerator door hard into his right arm. He whirled
around, as something crashed into his other hand, knocking
the .45 to the floor. Two feet from his chest was a short-
barreled Remington held by a small man with a goatee.
Raimundo Villegas stood beside the man, holding an automatic pistol fitted with a silencer. He had discarded his gar-
dener's clothes and was dressed in gray slacks and a white
turtleneck over which he wore his long leather coat.

"*Buenas tardes*, Señor Troy," Villegas said. "The shoe is now on the other foot, no?"

Troy eyed the two men, waiting for the pain in his arm and hand to subside. The blast of the shotgun still rang in his ears and he could feel sweat trickling down his back. So the woman had run him straight into their arms, he thought, just like herding cattle. After all he'd been through, after all the traps he'd dodged, he'd fallen for one of the oldest known to man and now he was going to die right in his own kitchen. He shook his head and took a deep breath. The smart thing would have been to shoot him in the back, but Villegas was too vain for that. He wanted to make a show of it. He wanted to make him pay for the humiliation out in Texas, and that had bought Troy a little bit of time— maybe enough to get his hands on the bearded guy's shotgun. Villegas would launch into some sort of speech. That's when he'd make his move. Troy focused on the shotgun barrel and got ready to spring.

"There was a message for you, tacked to your door," Villegas said. "Someone named Clara, who says she will return for dinner at six-thirty. I have an idea she is someone special. At first I had thought of waiting here for her so that I could make you sit on her dead body before I shot you, but I don't think that would be wise. Instead, my friend *El Chivo* and I will leave a gift for her. A surprise."

Villegas, his mouth open, was about to say more, but instead he let out a loud groan and toppled forward onto the floor. A hunting knife buried to the hilt protruded from the left side of his back. Startled, *El Chivo* turned slightly. As he did Troy grabbed the barrel of the shotgun and snap-kicked him in the groin, but before he could wrench the gun from *El Chivo*'s hands a burst of automatic fire stitched the Mexican from his neck to the top of his head. Instinctively, Troy recoiled from the noise, pivoting at the same time, so that he was looking straight into the face of the woman he'd seen once before, sitting in the tan pickup truck. She was standing behind the two men who lay dead on the kitchen floor, an Uzi cradled against her right shoulder. From head to toe, she was covered with mud.

"I have to tell you, Troy, you are one difficult son of a

bitch to follow," she said. "I lost a brand-new hundred-and-
thirty-dollar pair of sunglasses in the swamp back there."

"Who in the hell *are* you?" Troy asked.

"My name's Amber," the woman said. "I'm a friend of
Jack Ubinas."

Roland Troy sat on his porch with the portable phone in
his hand, watching the sky turn orange behind the trees on
the far side of his pond. The rain had come and gone in a
hurry; the wind was once again out of the northwest, bringing cold, clear air. After the guys from the morgue had
carted the bodies away, he had cleaned up the kitchen, put
up a pot of lentil soup for him and Clara, and gotten a fire
going in the living-room fireplace. Jack Ubinas had called
just as he finished patching the gaping hole in his refrigerator with a piece of Styrofoam and duct tape.

"I heard about Villegas," Ubinas said.

"From Amber," Roland Troy said.

"From Amber," Ubinas said.

"She's damn good," Troy said. "Where'd you find her?"

"She didn't tell you?"

"She didn't tell me shit. She wouldn't even let me walk
her back to her truck. She said she could find her own way.
I had enough to do with the mess in my kitchen, she said."

"She's a government employee," Ubinas said. "She
moonlights now and then, same as you."

"I left her out of the statement I gave," Troy said. "Although they'd probably give her a medal. Solved the
Varney murder in less than a day and saved the state the
cost of a trial."

"Saved your life too, the way I heard it," Ubinas said.

"Yeah," Troy said. "I guess she did."

"She said you didn't seem all that grateful."

"You should've told me you were sending her, Jack. I
thought she was with them. She got me off on the wrong
track. She threw me off stride."

"I have some information that'll get your rhythm back,"
Ubinas said. "Chotoku Nakama gave Nikki Waters her
disc-jockey job in Orlando."

"Nakama? Jesus Christ, I don't believe it. C'mon, Jack.

You're shittin' me. Why would he mess with someone like her?"

"Any number of reasons. He owed her. Or someone in his organization did. I'm just telling you what I heard. And from an impeccable source. Chinese fella, lives out in Baja. Almost as good as you. She never met Nakama, mind you. She probably didn't even know he existed. But he knew about her. With all the subjects in that man's kingdom, he knew about her. When the station manager tried to fire her it went through more layers than a Cosa Nostra wedding cake, all the way up to Bassai himself, and he said no way, José. Station manager's pulling cable for a religious television channel in Tampa these days."

"She was sleeping with Drew Parabrise," Troy said.

"That's life for you," Ubinas said. "One big jolly circle. When I was a kid I hitchhiked all over England and Scotland. I got picked up outside a town called Tongue, way up in the middle of nowhere, by my father's accountant and his wife touring the isles in a Humber. She must have said 'What a coincidence' four hundred times before I got out in Aberdeen. It was depressing."

"So now I go talk to Bassai Nakama," Troy said.

"Maybe you'll learn something," Ubinas said. "But you better be careful. Maybe he'll shoot you. He's been known to do that, even to old acquaintances."

"Where's he hangin' his hat these days?"

"Costa Rica. Where the sea turtles come up on the beach to lay their eggs. Apparently they've been laying them there for a few million years. Nakama would like a place like that. The continuity of it all. I got a guy in San Jose who'll fly you in. He brings groceries to the people from the New York Zoological Society who count the turtle eggs. He can get you a boat, too, and point you up the river in the right direction. After that, you're on your own."

"How do I find this guy in San Jose?"

"He has breakfast every morning at the Bougainvillea Hotel. You can't miss him. He's a short, wiry guy, about five-seven. Wears a Cincinnati Bengals hat. Has a tattoo of an eagle on his right forearm. Runs a tropical fish business. His name is Lester. Damn good pilot."

"Bengals hat. Eagle tattoo. Bougainvillea Hotel. Okeydoke. I appreciate it, Jack. By the way, who the hell flies to Costa Rica now that Eastern's gone under?"

"American," Ubinas said. "Every day. Miami to San Jose and back."

"I'm an optimist," Troy said. "I'll buy a round-trip ticket."

"You watch yourself, Roland," Ubinas said. "I don't need to tell you about Chotoku Nakama. Call me when you get back."

"Will do," said Troy. "And Jack . . ."

"Yeah, Roland."

"Thanks."

"Anytime," Ubinas said.

XXI

◆

The barred owl was back, its bark-like hoot—howwho-haWHOO ... howWHO-haWHOOAahh—echoing across the pond.

"Who-cooks-for-you? Who-cooks-for-you-all?" Troy said. He was stretched out on the floor in front of the fireplace, poking with an old tire iron at the blazing logs.

"That's what your grandfather claimed they were saying," Clara said. "Your grandmother said they were the most elegant of all owls, but Tom Waxe told me that Indians believed barred owls were inhabited by the souls of crazy people. He said you could tell by that insane laughing sound they make."

"Have you ever seen one up close?" Troy asked.

"Uh uh," Clara said. She was sitting in Troy's old overstuffed armchair. Her long hair was loose and spread in dark profusion over the goose-down comforter she had wrapped around herself. Her feet, clad in a pair of thick orange socks, stuck out of the bottom of the comforter and rested on a hand-tooled leather hassock.

"They're very beautiful, barred owls," Troy said, turning his head to face her. "Like you."

She smiled. "Who cooks for you all?" she said.

"It should have been you," he replied. The episode with Villegas had left him drained. His guard was down. "Is it too late?" he asked. He turned back to the fire as he spoke the words and jabbed at a log. The fire crackled and a shower of sparks flew up the chimney.

"Tell me what happened to you over there, Roland," she said. "I think I have a right to know. Even after all this time, I think I do."

He got up, went over to the couch, grabbed two small

pillows, and returned to his place in front of the fire. He lay on his back with the pillows under his head and began to talk. He told her first about the *dojo* of Gishin Miyazato, about his life in Okinawa, and how he came to work for Jack Ubinas. His voice was even deeper than usual and she had to strain to hear him over the hiss and crackle of the flames. Occasionally he stopped to stoke the fire. Then he resumed, precisely where he left off, as though someone had lifted the needle from a phonograph record and replaced it in exactly the same groove.

When he rose to get himself a drink from the kitchen Clara didn't move. He returned with two glasses of apple juice and when she extended an arm from the comforter to take her glass, she placed her fingers over his for just a moment. She was surprised at how cold his hand felt.

"By the fall of sixty-five I knew goddamn well the war was gonna go on for a long time," he said. "No matter what they were writing in the press. I told Ubinas I wanted to pack it in. He asked me to do one more job before I left, with a team of Navy SEALs down in the Mekong Delta. Ubinas wanted me to scout for 'em. Get 'em in and out on three or four enemy installations. The CIA had some South Vietnamese working with these guys too. The Vietnamese were nothing but a bunch of thugs, so I think part of what Ubinas wanted was for me to ride herd on them. They wound up killing a few of their own people but they didn't mess with us.

"The operation took about two weeks in all, counting planning and interrogation of prisoners. At the end I was dead tired. More tired than I'd ever been in my life, because in my mind I'd already let go, and then when Ubinas asked me to do that last job I did it but it was like the spring inside me was already unwound.

"I could have taken a flight out right away, but I was so exhausted ... if I had, then things would have ... but I didn't. I decided to wait a couple of days. I think I slept the entire first day. Then I went out and just walked around in sort of a daze. A guy I met up in Laos told me about this CIA bar in Saigon where there was supposedly some half-way decent music, so I decided to check it out. There was a jazz trio in there from Singapore and they weren't half bad. I was sitting there by myself, drinking ice-cold beer, listening to the music, thinking about you, trying to imagine how you'd look when I got off the plane, and all of a sudden I heard somebody call my name. I turned around and standing there not six feet away was Drew Parabrise, grinning at me like I'm his long-lost rich uncle.

"The thing of it was, as much as I'd always thought he was nothing more than a country-club punk, I was glad to see him. He was from my home town. A *paisano*. A homeboy, there in the middle of all that death and destruction. I stood up to shake his hand and he actually gave me a hug. He was with a couple of other guys but he brushed 'em off. Said he wanted to have a beer with his old high school football rival. He sat down at my table. Said he'd graduated from Virginia and joined the navy and gotten his commission, just like Kennedy, although he'd gone to Harvard, and now there he was, running a patrol boat in the delta. They'd given him a prototype for the thirty-one-foot PBRs, the river patrol boats they were having built, and he was all puffed up because it was like he was a test pilot. He was wearing his officer's uniform, and I'll tell you what, he looked good, all full of himself and weathered from a couple of months of wind in the face. He asked me who I was with. I told him I'd been a scout for a couple of recon units and he left it alone. He could tell where I'd been just by looking at me. He'd been there long enough himself by that time to know.

"We drank a couple of beers, listened to the music, bullshitted about home, about sports, who'd enlisted, who got drafted, who'd gone to what college, who got married, that kind of stuff. Then all of a sudden he got serious. He told me he'd come across something while he was out patrolling that he wanted to deal with on his own, with one or maybe two other guys he could trust. He said he'd found out where some major drug deals were going down—a drop where shipments of heroin from up north were exchanged for cash and gold. He said he'd only just discovered this. He was going to take a couple of UDT guys—frogmen—with him, but that was before he ran into me.

"At first I told him no. No more night crawling. I'd had enough. I was going home. But he wouldn't let up. He

knew he could trust me. He'd seen me on the football field
and knew I was tough under pressure. All that kind of stuff.
I kept telling him no. Finally he leaned across the table and
got that big, sincere, all-American face of his about a foot
away from mine and said something I'll remember for as
long as I live. 'You know where all that dope is headed?'
he said. 'It's headed for the United States of America. We'll
throw that crap in the river and save a few American lives.
You can fly out of here knowing that on your last job you
did an honest-to-God service for the folks back home. And
you'll have a shitload of money in your pocket to boot.'
That's what he said, and finally I told him yeah, okay, I'll
help you bust it up. To this day I don't know why I went
along with him. Maybe it was because I was so damn tired,
or maybe because I was drunk, or maybe because deep
down I still wanted to show that son of a bitch what a hard-
ass I was. I don't know. I was half fuckin' crazy by then
anyway.

"We did it two nights later. He told me he had the whole
thing cased and that was when they made their weekly connection. The plan was simple. We'd go in, get the drop on
whoever was there and tie 'em up, take their money, throw
the heroin in the river, and boogie. Once I made up my
mind to do it, I really got into it. That was the way I operated over there. If I did something I went all the way.
That's how I stayed alive. Judging by how much dope
Parabrise claimed he saw them unload, we figured to walk
out of there with around a hundred grand apiece. I'd gotten
into the idea of that too. Stacks of hundreds danced in my
head.

"Except for the dope and the fact that we weren't gonna
take any prisoners, the deal didn't sound much different
than a lot of the stuff I'd been doing. We went up the river
with his boat—it was basically a souped-up offshore oil rig
workboat with some armor-plating and a fifty-caliber machine gun—and he was damn good with it, I'll say that for
him. It was like his personal toy. He told me he and his
crew used to take Vietnamese women out on it at night and
party. In 1965, it was that kind of war. We could have
looked around for something smaller, but we figured if they

had people on their boats who tried to come after us then I'd tear into 'em with the fifty-caliber.

"We were coming downstream, so a quarter-mile or so from where we were going he idled it way down and we drifted along the shore, up under some overhanging branches where we tied up about a hundred yards from this old wooden dock where we could see a couple of boats were moored. You'd have to have been looking for us to find us, and there was no moon. We were camouflaged. Had our faces painted black. There was a shack in the trees up from the dock and we could see lights there. We came up on it by land, through some pretty thick jungle, thicker than anything Parabrise was used to. He was lucky he had me with him.

"Surprise was the key element in an operation like that, and I had become an expert at surprise. If I was going in to take a prisoner, it got so I'd have the guy out his door and down the trail before anyone else in his house would realize what was going on. But in this deal with Parabrise we weren't after prisoners. It was knock down the door, overpower everyone inside, take the goods, and run. I had a sawed-off shotgun, he had an M-Fourteen, and we both had forty-fives.

"I went in first. Parabrise was right behind me. All I remember is incredible noise and this searing heat going through me, like bolts of electricity, and something hurling me through the air. Everything else that happened that night I learned about later."

Troy got up, put another log on the fire, and poked around with the tire iron until the fire was blazing. "You want some more juice?" he asked.

"Just a little," Clara said.

He went into the kitchen and came back with the apple juice container. She held out her glass. He poured her some and finished off what was left in two long swallows straight from the bottle. Then he lay back down on the floor. The fresh log hissed and crackled. Clara waited, saying nothing. He lay on his back, breathing deeply. His eyes were closed and she thought he might have fallen asleep, but in a few seconds his eyes opened and he began to talk again.

"When I came to I was in a room with a long window

that was propped open. It looked out on a garden where a little girl about seven or eight years old was picking flowers. She was the most beautiful child I'd ever seen. She was the daughter of Chotoku Nakama, a warlord, a man of such power he had his own army. Stockpiled weapons like you wouldn't believe. He had his own schools. The children of his soldiers and the farmers who grew his opium and the men who smuggled his drugs and diamonds and gold and guns went there. Nobody fucked with him. Not the CIA. Not the Viet Cong. Not the Pathet Lao. Not the Russians. Nobody. He dealt with all of them. A little for you, a little for you, this for you, that for you. And everyone had something for him. He was the ultimate manipulator, the ultimate coordinator, the ultimate enforcer, a couple of thousand years of empire-building skills distilled into one man. The only thing he didn't have was his own country to rule, but he told me he didn't need or want one. In the future, he told me, power will transcend the whims of any single country. The king of the future will exist in the shadows, Nakama said, doing business despite the ebb and flow of revolutions and international disputes. He will be anonymous. That was in 1966. I'm still waiting to see whether he was right.

"I was in his stronghold, in northern Burma, not far from the Chinese border. He had his own field hospital there with two fulltime doctors and three or four nurses. He saved my life. The men Drew Parabrise decided to rip off worked for Chotoku Nakama. The instant I walked through that door Parabrise opened up on 'em. Opened up on me too. At least that's what Nakama told me. He said only one of the men in that hootch returned fire and the holes in me were back-to-front.

"There was almost three hundred grand in that room and Parabrise wanted all of it. With me dead there'd be no one around to tell any stories. If they found me, hell, it would just be a renegade mercenary who got caught in the cross fire of a drug deal. No loss. Whether he shot me or not, he sure as hell left me layin' there. He scooped the money and ran, but he didn't get thirty yards from that shack before Nakama's men who were waiting in the boats grabbed him. All the stuff they printed about him when he ran for

office—that he'd been held captive by the Viet Cong somewhere in the mountains and made this daring escape—was
all bullshit. Drew Parabrise was captured by Chotoku
Nakama, who decided to let him go. There was no Cong in
it at all. Parabrise was Nakama's prisoner, and he still is to
this very day."

Clara wrapped herself more tightly in the comforter and
cleared her throat but said nothing. She was afraid that if
she spoke, if she interrupted him at all, he would stop, dried
up forever like the bed of a diverted stream.

Troy could not see her. He was still staring straight up at
the ceiling, awash in a flood of memories whose clarity, after so many years of silence, astounded him. The little girl
in the garden had somehow sensed he was watching her,
for she had turned from the flower bed and stared at the
open window of his room. He could picture her face in
vivid detail—its Oriental, almond-shaped eyes, the narrow,
European nose and prominent cheekbones, the sun-
drenched flawless skin, the lustrous dark hair that hung
about her shoulders much like the hair of Clara Roseman.
The little girl had smiled at him and run away. He fell
asleep, and when he awoke there was a vase filled with
flowers sitting on the table next to his bed.

An Oriental man who looked to be in his mid-thirties sat
in a straight-backed wooden chair in the far corner of the
room. He wore pilot's brown leather jodhpur boots, perfectly pressed khaki pants, and a white dress shirt with
rolled sleeves. He was not tall, but every part of him exuded strength. His forearms, resting on the arms of the
chair, were thick and laced with prominent veins, and his
huge, misshapen hands bore the unmistakable calluses of a
karate-ka, a martial artist. His broad, smooth face, with
dark, penetrating eyes shaped just like the little girl's, was
implacable.

"So, thanks to me, you will live, Roland Troy," he said.

The man rose from the chair, and as Troy watched, he removed his shirt. High on his right arm, just below the
shoulder, was a tattoo of an open-mouthed tiger standing on
its hind legs. Below the tiger was the same Chinese ideograph inked beneath the prancing tiger on Troy's own arm,
the ideograph that symbolized both danger and opportunity.

"I am Chotoku Nakama," the man said. "I have another name as well. It is Bassai. It means 'to penetrate a fortification.' It was given to me many years ago by my cousin, Ansai Shima."

Nakama buttoned his shirt and tucked it back into his pants. "Now you rest, Roland Troy," he said. "Later, you and I will have plenty of time to talk." He smiled, bowed ever so slightly, and left the room.

"When his men came into that hootch I was the only one there who was still alive, and I wasn't alive by much," Troy said to Clara. "They were just about to throw me in the river with the others when one of them saw my tattoo. Lucky for me he recognized it. They took me to an underground Viet Cong hospital and kept me there for a week until I had stabilized. I'd been hit four times with automatic fire in my back. Three of the rounds went straight through. The fourth one lodged in my hip. They took a piece of it out, but part of it's still there. I lost an enormous amount of blood, my hip bone was shattered, two ribs were split, and I had a lot of soft-tissue damage, but the bullets missed my vital organs and my spine. Pure luck. A quarter of an inch one way or the other and I'd've been dead before they even found me.

"I was still unconscious when they moved me from the hospital. They took me by boat north into Cambodia, where Nakama came and picked me up in one of his planes. He flew it from Burma himself, almost a thousand miles each way. That's why he had me moved into Cambodia first. He didn't want to chance flying into Vietnamese airspace."

"Why?" Clara asked. She hadn't spoken for so long her voice cracked at first and she had to repeat herself. "Why did he do that?"

"I was a member of Prancing Tiger. He was bound by its code of honor to try to save me. And, I was the only American Prancing Tiger. I was of considerable interest to him. Of course, if he later determined I had knowingly plotted against him he would have killed me without a second thought, but only he would decide that, and he had to get me talking first.

"Then there was the coincidence of my busting in on that drug deal. See, Nakama already knew about me. He had heard about me from Shima, who by the way was dead before I ever got to Okinawa. Nakama and I would have met sooner or later. He had decided that long before I ever went stomping around the jungle for Jack Ubinas. But the way in which our paths crossed fascinated him. Nakama could have shown up at Miyazato's *dojo* in Naha. He could have hopped over to Laos—he and Ubinas knew all about each other. Or he could have had me delivered to him any old time. But he wasn't ready. He wanted to see what course the life of this American Prancing Tiger would take all on its own. And then there I was, shot to shit, bleeding to death, cast by the hand of fate into the cabin of this high-powered speedboat in the Mekong Delta.

"Fate intrigued Nakama. Chance. The vagaries of fortune. That and human behavior were the two things that interested him most. Why people did what they did. What certain people would do if they were thrown into one situation or another. How they'd react. He'd experiment. Throw people together to see what happened. Send someone off on an assignment for no other reason than to watch what he'd do. He understood human nature better than anyone else I've ever met. He understood it, and he was willing to act without hesitation on his instincts. That's what got him where he was."

"What happened to Shima?" Clara asked.

"Ah, Shima," Troy said. "*Sensei* Shima. What a twisted path his life must have been. Shima worked for Nakama. He was part of Nakama's inner circle. And he was family to boot. That's another reason Nakama felt it was his obligation to save my ass. Because it was Shima, a relative and a man he trusted, who inducted me into Prancing Tiger. That counted for a lot with Nakama."

Troy stretched, tensing his muscles, relaxed, and took a couple of deep breaths. He glanced at the dwindling fire but left it alone.

"Shima was a very complex man," he said. "I've thought about this a lot over the years, and the best I can come up with is that he was torn between good and evil. Or between peacefulness and violence. Probably that's a better way of putting it. You and I, all those years ago, we saw one side of him, I mean forgetting about the karate for a minute and just thinking about the way the man lived. But there was another side. Among other things, he killed people for Bassai Nakama. I know that's hard for you to believe—it was for me, too—but it's a fact. Ansai Shima was an assassin. One of the best in the world, according to Nakama, who ought to know.

"A little while before Shima came to Florida, while he was still based in Hawaii, he killed a man in Singapore. This guy smuggled jewels for Nakama and Nakama found that he'd been skimming, big-time, almost a million bucks in less than a year.

"But Shima, good as he was, made a mistake on this job and was identified. The man he killed had two sons, who vowed revenge. Nakama sent Shima into hiding where he figured no one would think to look while he settled things with the sons. Around that time Nakama decided to establish himself in America—to start investing in American real estate and various businesses, mainly shipping and communications—and Florida was one of the places where he wanted a foothold. All the time Shima was living in my grandfather's cabin he was buying up Florida real estate in the name of a corporation owned by Nakama. Every single buy was with cash. Meanwhile, Nakama tried to straighten it out with the two sons. When he couldn't get anywhere with 'em, he decided to kill them. He got one but the other got away, vowing revenge on Shima and Nakama. Years went by and Shima, figuring he was safe, decided to go home, but the surviving son had finally caught up with him. The guy followed Shima from here to Miami and shot him in the airport parking lot. Two months after Shima's death one of Nakama's men cut the son's throat in the kitchen of a restaurant in Chinatown in New York.

"And there you have the Shima story," Troy said. He rolled onto his side and stared at what remained of the fire.

"Don't let it die out," said Clara.

He turned and smiled at her. "Oh, I won't," he said. "You got me started. I ain't gonna stop." He got up onto his knees and put two pieces of split oak on the fire. The wood was dry and caught almost immediately. Troy closed the fireplace screen and stretched out again on his back.

"Nakama had a French surgeon working in his hospital

who put me back together. He told me I'd always have a limp and I'd never run a marathon but I'd be able to walk just fine. He told me whatever else I did depended on how hard I was willing to push myself. Nakama had a gym there and he and I worked out together. He was tougher on me than either Shima or Miyazato. A couple of times I was in so much pain I passed out, but he got my ass back into shape. Before I left I was climbing up and down the mountains with him and his kids.

"He decided right off the bat that I was on the level—that I had no idea what I was walking into down in the delta in spite of what Parabrise told him—and he made me part of his family. I think he really liked me, and then, too, I think he felt real bad about Shima's death. Taking me in was partly to atone for that. And, like I told you before, there was his curiosity—what is this guy like, this American who his trusted cousin met on a lonely little river in the Florida woods when he was just a kid?

"Nakama's house was huge. The living room had a fireplace so big you could put almost a whole tree in it. Everything was in good taste though. The proportions were all right.

"The house was made of stone, like a French manor house, with lots of windows, and it was full of Oriental and French antique furniture. Nakama's wife was French. She was very beautiful. Tall and thin. Taller than Nakama. She had been a model. He met her when she was on an assignment in Mandalay. She ran Nakama's school. She could have done anything she wanted, traveled anywhere, bought anything. But that's what she did. She absolutely loved the kids. I have no idea what she thought about Nakama's business, the violence, the constant threat of violence. I wouldn't have asked her and she never said.

"He was from Okinawa, like Shima, from the same seafaring stock that went all the way back to a group of Chinese pirates. He talked to me quite a bit about his ancestors. He was very proud of them, especially the pirates. He felt he was following in their footsteps—the footsteps of the first Prancing Tigers—doing nothing different than any ruthless captain of industry or political leader would do.

"Family meant a lot to Nakama. He had two children,

the little girl who was eight and a boy who was ten. He judged a man to a large degree by how devoted he was to his family. How does that compute with all the shit he was smuggling and the people he had killed and the terror he brought down on a whole lot of others? I have no idea. I truly have no fucking idea. But then, I have no idea how a lot of respected people manage to sleep at night. Which brings us back around to Drew Parabrise, the esteemed United States Senator.

"Parabrise was dealt with and gone by the time I was flown to Burma. The reason they didn't shoot him right there on the river was because they wanted that PBR and they needed him to run it. They took all the money from him, marched him through the jungle to where we'd tied up, put a gun to his head, and pointed up the river. I don't know what that prototype was worth, but the U.S. Navy never got it back.

"Nakama wanted to talk to Parabrise in person. Why? I don't know the answer to that one either. Instinct. Whim. It'd been a boring week in Burma. He got Parabrise up there at his place, sat him down, and let him waffle. Parabrise handed him all manner of crap, not the least of which was that the score had been my idea. None of it mattered to Nakama. He knew Parabrise was a complete bullshitter thirty seconds after he opened his mouth. What Nakama paid attention to was the delivery. It hypnotized him, and he figured if it could hypnotize *him*, Bassai Nakama, he had discovered a jewel as rare as the rubies and sapphires he was trading for hotels in Hawaii.

"Nakama asked Parabrise what he would do if he let him go—what he intended to do with his life if he made it back to the States in one piece. Parabrise told him he wanted to go to law school and eventually get into politics, which was precisely what Nakama imagined he'd say—precisely what Nakama *wanted* him to say. So then Nakama says 'Okay, I'll let you go, and when you get home that's what you will do. You will become a lawyer, and then a congressman, and then a senator, and one day you will become President of the United States. Only one thing. I own you. You will be *my* congressman, *my* senator, and *my* president of the United States. That is the price you pay for me not killing you.'

"I know. You don't have to say anything. You're thinking this is some kind of fairy tale—this Nakama guy is some kind of egomaniac nutball. Sitting there in his mountain hideaway telling a jive-talking twenty-three-year-old navy lieutenant with a shit-eating grin he's gonna be president. I thought the same thing. But Nakama's no nutball. He just operates on a different frequency than most people. You know, the average man meets a woman, he thinks maybe she's the one. Next week he thinks maybe she isn't. Next month it's another one. He winds up married to a third one, who turns out to be the wrong one. Happens every day, right? Nakama sees a young model on the street in Mandalay and he says she's it, she's the one I will marry. Not just because she's beautiful—guys like Nakama can have a different beautiful woman every night of the year if they want—but because he sees something reflected in her face. Some inner quality that goes beyond that gorgeous face and those long legs. He doesn't wonder, am I right? Am I wrong? Is she too tall for me? Will my mother like her? All that crap that keeps shrinks in business doesn't exist for him.

"He read all the time at night. Had this enormous library in his house and he'd sit in there 'til two or three in the morning reading. History mostly. He was an expert on American history. When he told me about Parabrise, I almost shit. I said, 'That son of a bitch shot his own man in the back, and that own man was me. And you're telling me he's gonna be a senator? Maybe the President of the United States? He ain't gonna be no senator after I get through with him, I'll tell you that.' I'd never talked like that to Nakama. I mean I walked around that place just feeling lucky to be alive, but I was hot. Royally pissed. It was my firm intention as soon as I left there to find Drew Parabrise and kill him.

"You know what Nakama said to me? He said, 'Roland-san, you are a romantic person. You will spend your life searching for justice. That's good. Idealism is a fine thing. But you are naive. You think your country has never been led by men who one way or the other shot their comrades in the back?'

"After Nakama gave his little speech to Parabrise, he put

on a demonstration for him. He had this guy who'd fucked him over one way or the other. South African, I think he was, because as I recall the fucking over had to do with diamonds. Nakama took Parabrise with him in a plane to where they were holding the man down in the jungle in Thailand, and he made Parabrise watch while they skinned the guy alive and tied him to a tree, where the animals could get him. Nakama made it clear to Parabrise that the same fate would be his if he ever, ever did anything to cross him. Parabrise could live and prosper but he was bought and paid for, part of Chotoku Nakama's grand experiment in human engineering. Part of Nakama's game.

"The price for my life was a little different. Nakama knew damn well what I'd been doing for Jack Ubinas. He knew as soon as I was able I'd go after Parabrise and kill him, which wasn't at all what he had in mind. My deal with Nakama was that I had to leave Drew Parabrise alone. If I didn't, it'd be my ass tied to the tree. So I was part of Nakama's game too. Send the romantic back to Florida where he could sit and watch Parabrise climb the political ladder. I always wondered whether Nakama thought I'd try to figure out a way to get Parabrise anyway, to try to outfox him. I would have if it had been just me, but then when Katherine was born I changed my mind.

"I stayed up there in the mountains of Burma for about eight months, until the fall of sixty-six. Then one day I decided it was time to leave. When I told Nakama he was genuinely sad. He liked having me around. I probably could have stayed there forever, working for him, traveling with him, but I knew that wasn't the kind of life I wanted to live. He knew it too. When I told him I was going he said I was doing the right thing. 'Roland-san,' he said, 'you are not the kind of man who will ever be king, but you are also not the kind of man who will follow the king around.' That's the last thing he said to me. We talked for hours and hours while I was there, but I've never seen him or spoken a word to him since. Before I left, he came to my little cottage and handed me an envelope. Inside was my passport and twenty-five thousand dollars in hundred-dollar bills.

"Nakama had an Air America pilot working for him who flew me to Udorn, in Thailand. This guy's still with

Nakama, from what I hear. His name was Brownie, and he was a well-connected booger. He knew everything and everybody. We get to Udorn and he says to me, 'Well, son, where to? You name it, I'll get ya' there.' I remember sitting there with him in this little sort of restaurant, nothing more than a tin-roofed hut actually, drinking black coffee and eating these greasy rice rolls, and I'm thinking, 'Where the hell *do* I want to go?' I wasn't ready to go home. As much as I missed you, I wasn't ready to go back and live in the same place as the man who tried to set me up—to kill me. I sat and thought and finally I asked this guy Brownie if he could get me to Okinawa. 'Piece of cake,' he said. 'I thought you were gonna try for someplace hard, like Moscow or Havana.'

"He talked to a couple of people there at the airstrip and next thing I knew I was on an Air America C-123 on my way to Naha. Caught a cab and had the driver take me straight to Miyazato's *dojo*. I walked in and *Sensei* Miyazato was sitting behind his desk in his tiny little office, same as always. He looked up at me, gave me a great big smile, and said, 'Ah, Roland-san, you want work out?' It was as though I had never left.

"I rented a tiny apartment up the hill from the *dojo* for fifty-six dollars a month. The first night I was there I remember I looked at my passport and it had the entry stamp from when I came to Okinawa from the States. That's all it had in it. There was no record of the other places I had been, and I thought, 'Here I am, still a young man, and a portion of my past is untraceable. On paper it doesn't exist.'

"I stayed in Naha a year. I trained in the *dojo*. I read a lot. This pilot who trained with Miyazato had a comparative literature reading list his girl friend sent him. I read all the books on the list. Dostoyevsky, Dickens, Melville, James Joyce. I read *Ulysses* twice. It was like taking a voyage inside the main characters' heads. All of 'em were trying to connect with humanity, trying to deal with their isolation. Boy, did I relate to that."

"Why didn't you ever write?" Clara said. "Why didn't you try to connect with me?"

"I tried to," Troy said. "I must have started fifty letters

to you but I never finished them. See, outwardly I was calm and cool, but inside I was a bomb with a lit fuse. When I started to write you my head would be filled with nothing but images of what I'd seen over there mixed up with images of Drew Parabrise and his big grinning face. It would make me nuts. I'd crumple the letter up and throw it away and tell myself, another few days, another week, and I'll get my mind right, but months went by and it didn't happen.

"I had an old VW Bug I'd bought from an Air Force doctor who was shipping out. On Saturday nights I drove up to another *dojo* run by a man named Uesu. In *Sensei* Miyazato's *dojo* there was no free-style fighting, but in *Sensei* Uesu's *dojo* they fought. I went up there every Saturday for four months and never lost a match. Then one night I almost killed a guy and on my way back to Naha I broke down. I was crying so hard I had to pull off the road. I realized what I was turning into. I realized the only way I'd ever come to terms with what I'd been through—the only chance I had to heal myself—was to go back to Florida and deal with my anger there. So I came home. So much time had passed ... I didn't know if you'd still be here, but you were, and as soon as I saw you I thought, 'Now it'll be all right. As long as I have her it'll be all right.' Then you told me about you and Parabrise."

"And the bomb went off," Clara said.

"It wasn't your fault," Troy said. "I knew that even while I was watching your car drive off. I had no claim on you. You thought I was dead. Parabrise thought I was dead too. Nakama never told him he'd saved me. He wanted it to be a surprise. Throw the fear of God into him. The war hero. Kills his old rival and then goes home and fucks his girl. When he heard I wasn't dead, he pissed in his pants. Called the contact Nakama had given him, some fuckin' ex-spook living out in Oregon. 'What should I do? What should I do?' One night a couple of weeks later Nakama calls him, tells him you don't do nothin' but study them law books and keep practicing your smile, Troy won't hurt you. Just don't forget about that guy tied to the tree."

"And then we lived our lives," Clara said.

"And then we lived our lives," said Troy.

She unfolded herself from the comforter, came over, and stretched out next to him in front of the fire. He put his hand behind her head, drew her close, and kissed her, softly at first, then hard. He could feel wetness on her cheeks, and a lump grew in his own throat.

"I'm sorry, Clara," he told her.

"I know you are," she said.

For a time they lay there in silence, neither of them moving. Then finally Clara spoke. "Oh Roland," she said. "I'm trying my best to keep it together. I truly am. But this whole thing is like a bad dream that just won't end. I mean, two men were killed in this house today. The truth is I can't believe it. It's beyond . . . Roland, what is going to happen next? Where will it stop? What's going to happen to my son?"

"Billy's gonna be okay. We'll get him out of this mess. I told him that when I talked to him on the phone earlier today."

"Did you tell him Varney and Parabrise had Nikki Waters murdered?"

"I told him I was making progress and to hang tough," Troy said.

"But that's what you think, isn't it?"

"I don't know. Varney was up to it. But John Varney's dead."

"And you can't touch Drew Parabrise? Not even after all this time?"

"Nakama ain't done with him. He ain't president yet."

"You mean to tell me you can't *talk* to the man?"

"And say what? 'Hey Senator, did you order a hit on that chick you were screwing? You remember. The one who your late buddy, your late chief fund-raiser, ripped off?' It don't work that way, Clara. You know that. Parabrise'll be insulated from any direct involvement anyway. What I have to do is go talk to Chotoku Nakama. Ole Bassai himself. See whether he'll tell me anything. See whether he's willing to change the rules of the game."

"So now you go to Burma?" she said.

"Nakama doesn't live in Burma anymore," Troy said. "He has houses all over the world, but the one in Burma is gone. Right now he's in Costa Rica. I'm gonna go down there and see him."

"You aren't leaving tonight, are you?"

"Uh uh. Tomorrow."

"That's good," she said, "because right now I'm thinking about something else."

Wordlessly, she led him up the stairs to his bedroom, where they made love under two thick blankets, gently at first, tentatively, as if any suddenness in one would cause the other to withdraw. Carefully, slowly, he ran his hands over her body, remembering her, aware that she was not the same. She was softer, her breasts heavier, her nipples more pronounced, and as he felt these changes and inhaled her aroma he was inflamed. His fingers moved faster between her legs. He felt her wetness, felt her open wider and draw him in, felt her mouth moving along his neck and shoulders. She felt him thicken and grow inside her and quickened the movement of her hips as they sought each other in the darkness, urgently. But for their hoarse, audible breath they were silent still until she came and cried out, and with a groan he followed her. They lay then clutching each other, their legs entwined, her breasts close against his chest, and as their breathing slowed, they listened to the wind and the creaking of the old house. They were spent, emptied, once more together.

Afterwards, her fingers traced the scars along the length of his back and the slight protuberance of bone beneath the skin of his right hip. "Do you think Parabrise meant to kill you all along?" she asked.

"No," he said. "I think he went for the money and decided to shoot me at the last minute, when he got the idea he could get out of there by himself. It looked so simple to him going in."

"It's so strange," she said. "You coming home after all that and becoming a cop."

"Not really," he said. "Nakama was right. I was a romantic. The white hats against the black hats. And I knew catching bad guys was something I'd be good at. I told Teddy Chambers some of what I'd been doing over there. Teddy was an assistant to Orin Whitman back then. He talked to Orin and they put me in homicide right away. It was a whole lot different in those days. They gave me a badge and they gave me a gun and they said, Go solve this murder. They were real surprised how quick I got into it, but I was out for blood. I wanted justice. If not for me, then for somebody else. Revenge, any way I could get it."

Her fingers still lay against his back. "He came here to comfort me," Clara said. Troy knew she meant Parabrise. "To make sure I was doing all right. I wasn't doing very well at all. I was an easy target."

"That's another thing we have in common," Troy said.

XXII

✦

"Make it quick and make it good," Troy said. "I got a plane to catch."

"Hey, it be as quick as possible," Cool Babba Wisdom said. "Dis be an early time for I."

Troy set his Styrofoam cup of coffee on the top rail of the fence and turned away from the track where the first horses of the morning were barely visible, circling slowly with their trainers in the mist. He looked at Wisdom, who towered over him, and spat in the dirt. "And you can cut the rasta shit out too," he said. "Talk fucking English or I'm outa here."

"I mean no offense," Wisdom said. "Dis de way I know. I try to help my friend, Mr. Peanut Butter, dat's all."

"Mr. Peanut Butter's gonna have all the help he needs, just as long as he keeps doing what I told him to do," Troy said.

"Dis is extra," Wisdom said. "To demonstrate dat his intentions are sincere." He took a Polaroid snapshot out of his jacket pocket. "Dis be a bonus. A respected individual here, Mr. Byron O'Reilly of the *Journal-Express*, purchasing drugs. Cocaine, to be precise."

"Yeah, well I appreciate the effort," Troy said, "but it's about a day late. I don't need O'Reilly anymore. Tell your friend Mr. Peanut Butter he's gonna have to avoid a necktie party on his own."

"Why you so belligerent, Mr. Troy?" asked Wisdom. "You never know from what direction help may come. Could be I who help you. Could be I wit information for your purpose."

"My purpose, huh?" said Troy. "And what might that purpose be?"

291

"De boy in jail. De one Mr. Peanut Butter watching over. To save dat boy be your purpose."

"And you're gonna help me. From what I hear, your radio station's going to a talk-show format twenty-four hours a day. Goodbye, reggae. Adìos Cool Babba Wisdom Show. You're gonna be lookin' for work is what you're gonna be doin'. Maybe your new job's gonna be fronting for Mr. Peanut Butter while he's indisposed and his other employees are turning up dead. See where I'm headed, Mr. Babba? I get belligerent standing around wasting my time with coke dealers."

"T'ink of dis den," Wisdom said. "T'ink of I talkin' wit Miss Nikki Waters on de station roof de night she was killed."

"I already thought of it," Troy said. "So did the MBI and the state attorney's investigators."

"All I told dem boys is what she say and what I say and what de time was when she left," said Wisdom. "Dat's all dey want to know. Dey have no need for I, who was on de air at de fateful hour."

"What the fuck are you driving at?" Troy asked. He took a sip of coffee and looked at his watch. He and Clara had talked until two in the morning; it was now only quarter after seven and Wisdom's sing-song voice was making him dizzy.

"Catch your plane, Mr. Troy," Wisdom said. "Call me up when you return. Meantime lemme t'ink about a few more t'ings relating to de Raven so I be certain not to waste your time." He took out his wallet, removed one of his business cards with the logo of the radio station on it, and gave the card to Troy. "De number of my home is on de back side," he said. "I be grateful you don't hand dat one aroun'." He smiled, nodded ceremoniously, and strolled ever so slowly to his black IROC Camaro parked thirty yards away beneath a tree.

Troy saw the Bengals hat facing the door in the far corner of the Bougainvillea Hotel dining room and worked his way toward it. When he was three quarters of the way across the room, the man Ubinas had identified as Lester looked up from the newspaper he was reading and watched impassively as Troy approached. Troy reached the corner table, swung an empty chair around against the wall so that he too would be at least partially facing the entrance, and sat down.

"You get a good night's sleep?" Lester asked.

"Just fine," said Troy. "It's a nice hotel."

The waiter came over and Troy ordered orange juice, whole-wheat toast, scrambled eggs, and coffee. "You're in luck," Lester said when the waiter left. "Winter storm blew out to sea yesterday. Should be good flying weather for the next week."

"All I need is today and tomorrow," Troy said. "After that it can rain dog piss and raw potatoes."

"You never know," Lester said.

"Oh, I know," said Troy. "I ain't out 'a there by tomorrow, the weather won't ever be a problem for me again."

The waiter brought the food and Lester went back to his paper while Troy ate. When Troy was finished he sat back and lit a cigar.

"Back in the States they won't let you do that no more," Lester said. "Even in the smoking section, they tell me."

"Depends," Troy said. "Some places will, some won't. I rarely go out to eat anyway, so for me it ain't a problem."

"I always go out to eat," Lester said. "Not so much for the food. I like to watch the people come and go. What kind of weapon you think you'll need?"

"No weapon," Troy said. "It ain't that sort of visit. I'm just going to talk to the man is all."

"You might at least want a thirty-eight," Lester said. "For the snakes. Dude got bit by a fer-de-lance back in there a month ago. Would 'a died if I hadn't flown him out. I never would've found him if he hadn't fired off a couple of rounds, but suit yourself."

"I'll take my chances," said Troy.

Under a cloudless sky they flew in Lester's single-engine Cessna due east from San Jose up over the 11,000-foot Irazu volcano, then angled northeast toward the Atlantic coast. They passed over logged-out forests that now were ranches encroaching on the jungle, and over stretches of the jungle itself—the fecund coastal rain forest—filled with

tightly packed trees that from the air resembled thousands
of upturned broccoli spears. When they were above the
ocean, Lester banked the plane hard to the left and headed
due north, dropping down to swoop no more than two hundred feet above the waves that broke along a twenty-mile
stretch of black sand.

"We put her down there," he said, pointing to a strip of
land no wider than a football field that ran between the
ocean and a broad river. "They still clear that strip with
nothing but machetes so we might bounce a bit, but don't
sweat it. I've done it before. Couple of hundred times to be
exact."

"I've seen worse," said Troy.

"I bet you have, my man," Lester said as he dove in tight
over a line of trees, rammed the small plane hard onto the
calf-high grass, and taxied up next to a couple of rough-
hewn wooden buildings that were boarded up. A large
wooden sign in both Spanish and English mounted on three
posts read GREEN TURTLE RESEARCH STATION.

Lester shut the engine off, hopped from the cockpit,
unzipped his pants, and urinated in the high grass. "Flying
always does that to me," he said. "In the summertime this
stretch of beach is where they tag the female turtles and
count their eggs. The joint's jumping then. People from all
over the world come to help. Nobody here now except
Fritz, the German dude who runs the fishing lodge over
across the river. He's a piece of work. Got caught making
bombs for the Red Orion terrorist organization. Remember
them? His old man's a millionaire industrialist with plenty
of political influence. Cut a deal to keep young Fritz out of
jail. Basically they said okay, your kid can walk, but we
don't ever want to see him inside Germany again. The father bought this place for him. Come here. Just take a look
at it."

Troy shouldered his knapsack and followed Lester down
a path away from the ocean and toward the river. They
walked down a slope covered with sea grapes and came out
on the riverbank, where a dinghy with a small outboard motor was tied to an old wooden dock. Alongside it was a
square-ended cayuca—a native dugout canoe—also equipped
with an outboard. The river was about fifty yards wide and

on the other side, Troy could see a beautifully manicured lawn extending up from the shore to a large, two-story log building. Colorful beds of tropical flowers grew along a split-rail fence enclosing the entire spread. Everything was absolutely immaculate, an oasis of Teutonic order carved into the tangled profusion of the jungle.

"Very exclusive place," Lester said. "The finest wine. Venezuelan chef cooks four-star meals. Rotating cast of beautiful hostesses. Oil millionaires, Arabian sheiks, movie stars, professional athletes, gangsters. All come to fish for tarpon with Fritzy the ex–bomb maker. There he is now."

A red-haired man of medium height with a carefully trimmed beard stood in the log gazebo on the far shore. A large German shepherd sat at his side. "You want to meet him?" Lester asked. "He's a very entertaining guy. Once had the CIA here one week, Fidel Castro here the next. Everybody loves him. Tells great stories."

"I think I'll pass," Troy said. "I've heard enough stories."

"Suit yourself," Lester said. "I'll play gin with him while you're gone. See if I can win us both some Cuban cigars." He took a sheet of paper out of his jeans and unfolded it. "Here's a map," he said. "There's plenty of gas in the cayuca to get you where you're going and back, but if you do run out or the motor quits on you, there's a paddle. Coming back is all downstream, so you shouldn't have any trouble. It's a pretty direct trip. What you want to do is follow this river upstream about four miles until it splits. Then you bear to the right, here, just south of Tortuguero." He pointed to a spot on the map where the thick blue line split in two. "If you go straight you'll wind up in Parismina, or worse, in Puerto Limón. After you make that right, you go about another two miles until you hit your very first tributary, again on the right. That's Arroyo Mono. Monkey Creek. Take that. It runs north, bends to the northeast, then, see here, it snakes around a little and ends at the base of Monkey Mountain, Monte Mono. Got its name from a tribe of howler monkeys who live up there. Your boy's up there too. Got him a place overlooking the ocean. Hell of a view, from what I hear. I ain't ever seen it, except once from the air when I was flying down from Nicaragua. Mountain's

only about eight miles from the border, but none of 'em—
the Sandinistas, the Contras, the Indians—not a fuckin' one
of 'em would go near it. You want company, say so now."

"I appreciate the offer," Troy said, "but I gotta make this
trip by myself. I'll be all right."

"I heard that before," Lester said. "If you ain't back in
two days, I'll get help and come after you."

"If I ain't back in two days, it won't matter," said Troy.

When he had gone about a mile or so up Arroyo Mono,
Troy cut the outboard and began paddling the cayuca. The
paddling wasn't bad; the flow of the creek, fed by drainage
from the swamp rather than mountain runoff, was gentle,
and anyway he had had enough of the motor's insistent
drone. Almost immediately, he was surrounded by sounds
of the jungle—the drone of millions of insects, the cackle
of laughing hawks in the branches high above him, the distant cry of a howler monkey, presumably from somewhere
on the same mountain as the one where Chotoku Nakama
had built a house.

The creek, black as onyx from decaying organic matter,
was lined with vine-covered trees and smooth as polished
steel. Here and there, lambent sunlight played on the water,
glancing off schools of needlefish that darted before the cayuca's bow. Troy rounded a sharp bend to the right and a
startled celery-green basilisk—the foot-long lizard called
"Jesucristo" by the Spanish settlers—leapt from the bank
and skittered across the water, its legs churning the surface
in a windmill blur. Troy paused to watch it streak away into
the underbrush and as he did he heard the unmistakable
rumble of an inboard V-8 approaching from upstream. He
resumed paddling, rhythmically but without any sign of un-
due haste. In a moment he saw the approaching craft, a
twenty-one-foot jet boat, with two men on board. The pilot
was a small, vicious-looking Oriental. His sleeveless cotton
work shirt was unbuttoned revealing a long scar that ran di-
agonally across his chest and a gold coin that hung from a
thin gold chain around his neck. The other man, cradling an
Uzi, was a tall, muscular black wearing a tank top that bore
a faded Navy SEAL insignia. The jet boat swung around
broadside, ten feet from the cayuca, blocking Troy's path.

"*Alto,*" the black man said. He had the Uzi pointed slightly to Troy's left, but not very far. "*No se puede pasar.*"

"Why's that?" Troy asked. "You own the river?"

The black man chuckled. "Where you from, Hoss?" he asked. "Alabama?"

"Florida," Troy said. The cayuca had drifted back several yards and come to ground against the soft sand near the shore of the creek.

"Well, Florida, turn yourself about and paddle your canoe up some other stream. Keep your problems to a minimum."

"I'm gonna take my shirt off," Troy said. "I ain't armed, so don't be gettin' in a hurry." He unbuttoned the long-sleeved cotton shirt he had worn against the mosquitoes and slowly removed it. The two men on the jet boat eyed him silently. Troy watched the man behind the wheel and saw him take note of his tattoo. The Oriental mouthed the Chinese word that Troy knew was represented by the ideogram inked into the skin of his arm below the prancing tiger. Now that he was close enough, Troy could see that the gold coin hanging just below the man's breastbone had a sharpened edge. Once, in Laos, Troy had seen a man throw a similarly sharpened coin through the wall of a bamboo hut with just the flick of his wrist.

"I want to talk to your boss," Troy said. "My name is Roland Troy. Mr. Nakama and I are old friends."

The black man looked at the Oriental who nodded and made a low growling noise deep in his throat. "Tie up to that tree over there," the black man said. "You'll ride with us. I hope for your sake you're telling the truth."

They followed the creek for several miles until they reached a low wooden bridge no more than four feet off the water. The black man kept the Uzi pointed at Troy while the Oriental made the jet boat fast to an iron ring hanging from one of the bridge's cross-members.

"You and I'll wait here, Hoss," the black man said. "He won't be long."

"Your buddy don't say much," Troy said when the Oriental had left.

"My buddy don't say nothin'," the black man said. "He

don't have a tongue. Had it cut out by the same guy who sliced his chest."

"Be a tough guy to interrogate," Troy said.

"Dude's a tough guy, period," the black man said. "Put that coin right through your eyeball into your brain from twenty feet, and that's no bullshit."

Troy stretched out across the back seat of the jet boat and pulled his baseball cap down over his eyes. He took a cigar out of his shirt pocket and lit it. The smoke drifted out over the stream and hung in a shaft of sunlight until a gust of wind carried it away. Two howler monkeys, much closer than the one he heard earlier, began calling to each other. Soon, they were joined by a third.

"It's only the males that howl," the black man said. "They been noisy last couple 'a days. There's jaguar tracks up near where they nest. They're spooked. How you know Nakama?"

"I met him in Southeast Asia a long time ago," Troy said.

"You were in Laos," the black man said.

"Why's that?" Troy asked.

"All his long-time-ago American friends were there," the black man said.

"At least all the ones you've met," said Troy.

The black man chuckled for the second time. His laugh was not unlike the rumble of the jet boat's engine. "You must know him," he said. "Come in here unarmed and smoke a cigar. Either that or you're nuts."

"Your friend's back," Troy said.

The black man turned his head slightly. Ten seconds later the Oriental emerged from the jungle. He walked onto the bridge and beckoned with his hand. The black man laughed for the third time. "I won't come crawlin' through your back window," he said.

With the Oriental leading and the black man bringing up the rear, the three of them climbed through the jungle along a steep trail of switchbacks densely overhung with vines. The trail ended at a helicopter pad on which sat a Bell Jetranger and a TV satellite dish. A lean, weathered man in his fifties, maybe older, stood at the edge of a path lined with breadfruit trees holding a large male Rottweiler on a leash. The man wore jeans, cowboy boots, and aviator sunglasses. He had a platinum Rolex with a Navajo watchband on his wrist and a ten-millimeter Automag in a shoulder holster.

The path led to a magnificent three-story house of rough wood, cantilevered into the side of the mountain. Chotoku Nakama stood on the second-story deck. When he saw Troy he raised his right hand in a relaxed salute. Troy walked toward the house and climbed the outside staircase to the deck, which looked out over the ocean. Nakama smiled at him, nodding his head. Other than his white hair and the creases in his face, Nakama looked the same as he had the last time Troy saw him twenty-four years earlier, in 1966. He was even wearing pressed khaki pants and a white dress shirt, although the flyer's boots had been replaced by a pair of brown tasseled loafers.

"Nice view, *ne*," Nakama said, shaking Troy's hand. "Here, sit, sit. You must be tired."

"I'm fine," said Troy, but he accepted the offer and sat down next to Nakama in one of the thickly-cushioned patio chairs. A woman, at least partly Oriental and almost as tall as Troy, came onto the deck through a sliding glass door. Troy started to get up but she stayed him with a hand on his shoulder.

"No need, Mr. Troy," she said. "I'm Dana. Would you care for some iced tea?" Her voice was very low and she spoke with an upper-class British accent.

"That'd be wonderful," Troy said.

"Bring some sandwiches too," Nakama said. "Paddling a cayuca can make a person very hungry. Would you like ham and cheese, egg salad, veal?"

"Just bread and cheese would be fine," Troy said. "I don't eat meat anymore."

"No?" Nakama said. "Well, from what I read that's probably better for your health. Myself, I haven't given it up. Do you think I should?"

"You look pretty good, Bassai," Troy said. "If I were you I'd keep on doing whatever you been doing." He smiled up at Dana, then looked back at Nakama. "Within reason, that is."

Nakama threw back his head and laughed loudly.

"Within reason," he said. "Ah, Roland-san, I like you. I liked you from the moment I met you, even though you were unconscious. Within reason indeed."

Dana went back into the house. Nakama sighed and stretched his legs out in front of him. "So many years, Roland-san," he said. "So much time. You should have visited me sooner, but I understand. You look well. Very fit. The vegetarian life-style appears to agree with you. How is your daughter?"

"She's doing real well, Bassai," Troy said. "She has her degree in marine biology. And she's getting married this spring, in April."

"April," Nakama said. "An excellent month. No matter what T. S. Eliot said. I must remember to send her a present."

"How's your family doing?" Troy said. "How's Dominique?"

"Dominique died four years ago," Nakama said. "Ovarian cancer. Nothing could be done. Things have not been the same for me since then."

"I'm sorry to hear that, Bassai. She was a remarkable person."

"She was very fond of you. Many times she asked me why you had never gone to work for me. I told her your path lay in another direction. A man must follow his path, *ne*? She died here. Of all our houses, she loved this one the most."

"It's a magnificent house."

"It's the place itself she loved," Nakama said. "This corner of the world that seems on the surface to be nothing much. Hot, humid, many insects, poisonous snakes. It rains eighteen feet a year on this coast. It did have its moment of fame a number of years ago when Ted Williams, the famous baseball player, discovered that the Parismina flats had the best tarpon fishing in the world and wrote about it in *Field and Stream* magazine. That naturally brought fishermen from all over the place. Dominique, though, was not interested in fishing. She was already sick when we built this house but still she spent hours walking the beach. She loved the black sand. She found this place mystical. Do you know about the green turtles?"

"They lay their eggs along this beach," Troy said.

"That they do, Roland-san. But what is mystical is that they have been coming here for more than ninety million years. The little hatchlings who don't get eaten by wild dogs or by the tepescuinte swim from the shore to the far corners of the earth. The males never come back. Never do the males touch land again. But the females return to Tortuguero, to the beach of the turtle, to the nesting place of their ancestors. They are obviously most remarkable navigators. Some come from several thousand miles away."

The sliding glass door opened and Dana came onto the deck with their food and a pitcher of iced tea. She sat with them while they ate, then went back inside the house. "So, Roland-san," Nakama said when she was gone, "now tell me the reason for your visit."

Troy took a fresh cigar out of his knapsack, offered one to Nakama, who shook his head, and lit his. He sat back in his chair and puffed silently for a couple of minutes, staring out at the ocean that lay calm below a bright sun. Nakama, his hands folded behind his head, waited. Troy was not sure how much Nakama knew, but decided to operate under the assumption that he knew everything. With a man like Nakama that approach was the safest, and in any case there was no reason for him to be cagey. He had nothing to hide.

"I'm trying to save an innocent man from the electric chair, which is where he'll go if he's convicted of murdering Nikki Waters," he finally said. "His name's Billy Roseman, but I think you already know that. John Varney is dead. I'm sure you know that too. I can't go after Drew Parabrise, not unless you tell me it's all right. So I thought I'd come talk to you. I came to ask you for help. I know Parabrise was sleeping with her and I know about her dealings with Varney and Raimundo Villegas. I also know that for some reason or other she was worth your time. You authorized the radio station in Orlando to hire her and you wouldn't let the station manager run her off. I have to conclude that you wanted her in Orlando. I'm not sure why. My guess would be you wanted to make it easier for Parabrise. Keep him from running off to Kalamazoo. But then, that's the obvious conclusion and you're not an obvious man. Could be she was there for an entirely different

purpose, an actor in a play the script of which exists only
in your head. I never met her—I heard her on the radio,
and I'll tell you this, she had one hell of a voice—but from
the way things look to me she was beginning to spin out of
control."

"And you think I had her killed," Nakama said.

"It crossed my mind. She could have been damn embar-
rassing, especially in an election year. Whoever did kill her
cut off one of her nipples. A hit with mutilation. Disgrace
for Nikki Waters instead of nirvana." Troy shrugged. "It
has a familiar ring to it, Bassai."

"You know, Roland-san," Nakama said, "when Ansai
Shima told me he had made an American a member of
Prancing Tiger—a non-Oriental American, and in addition a
very young one—I was quite surprised. I, in fact, was
shocked. I said 'Why? What made you do such a thing?
Who is this person?' Do you know what he said to me? He
said, 'Bassai, this man is young but already he understands
honor. He understands commitment and discipline. And
most of all, he has a noble soul. He is a warrior in the true
sense of the word. He will make an excellent Prancing Tiger.' Perhaps you find a certain irony in these words, considering the business Shima and I engaged in. Perhaps not.
Perhaps you understand enough about the way in which the
world works to know there are inconsistencies in everything. In everyone. No matter. The fact remains that about
you Ansai Shima was right. All those qualities he saw in
you are what brought you here. Unlike the recently dead.
John Varney, who was faithful to nothing but his greed.
Raimundo Villegas who was a traitor, a man with no sense
of honor. If the two of them had been brothers they would
have killed their father and gone to war over his wallet.
And Nikki Waters, blessed by the gods with a voice for the
ages, blessed with beauty too, but whose pride and lack of
restraint caused her downfall. Unlike Drew Parabrise, the
andaguchi, the oily mouth, the man with no convictions at
all."

"The future president," Troy said.

"Indeed," said Nakama. "A politician. One who would
circumvent God."

"I remember that line," Troy said. "It's from *Macbeth*."

"No, no, not from *Macbeth*," said Nakama. "From *Hamlet*, the play about a man who pretended to be crazy and—unlike you, who seems to have survived the madness of life—declined to act. It is from the scene in the graveyard, which is where you would like to send Drew-san, and where I would let you send him if I thought it would do you any good, even if it meant I would not have a president."

"I should have killed him," Troy said, "in spite of you and your threat. I should have come straight home from Burma and wasted that worthless motherfucker instead of pissing around in Miyazato's *dojo* doing *katas*, kicking and punching the air. Even when I finally did come back, a year later, I should have done it, instead of giving the boot to a woman I loved. I killed the wrong thing, is what I did."

"You proved yourself in battle," said Nakama. "What you did in the jungle was not kicking and punching the air. We made a deal, you and I. You gave me your word and I spared your life."

"The enemies I fought in the jungle were faceless," Troy said. "They meant nothing to me. I meant nothing to them. Other than the fact that we were trying to kill each other. The one enemy that counted slipped away. Why? Because we made a deal? *We* made a deal? *You* made the deal, Bassai. You saved me because I interested you. Just like Parabrise interests you. Wind him up and see how long he keeps on running. See how far he can get. And Nikki Waters. What did she do? What was she paying for? How did she wind up in Bassai's human zoo?"

Troy took a long pull on his cigar, inhaled, and blew the smoke out with an audible exhalation. "I never did shit to you intentionally," he said. "You knew that from the beginning. I walked in a door and got shot by my own man, and I fell into your trap because I was ashamed. I was humiliated, me and all my Prancing Tiger qualities. I went along with Parabrise because I was a vain, macho asshole and I believed for that I had to pay a price. And pay I did. Every day that cocksucker walks the earth I pay."

"And now it is his turn, *ne*?" Nakama said. "Now you believe the circle has been completed. You have waited and waited and finally circumstances have brought Drew-san within your grasp. After a quarter of a century, revenge will at last be yours. You will settle a score that has been gnawing at your soul for so long. At the same time you will solve the murder of Nikki Waters and once again be Mr. Tooth, but first you come to me."

"Not because of honor," Troy said. "Because of my daughter. Because of Katherine. I want to make sure she gets to enjoy her wedding presents, including the one you intend to send her."

"Your daughter is in no danger from me, Roland-san. I give you my word on that. Neither are you. But Drew Parabrise had nothing to do with the death of Nikki Waters. Nothing at all. Nor did Varney or Villegas. Nor did I.

"I was considering it. I will admit that to you. She was becoming far too dangerous. Stealing horses. Hopping into bed with this one and that one. She was out of control. She was not . . . what is the word they use? A bimbo. She was not a bimbo. She was very smart, very calculating, but, like many people, she was not as smart as she thought she was. She was driven by the kind of ambition that can never be satisfied. No matter how much money she accumulated, no matter what professional success she achieved, she would one day have sold the story about her and Drew-san to the highest bidder. Dead, she would sell no story. She might have been linked to him by some excavating journalist like the one in Orlando who was nearly run over by a truck, but that would not be quite the same thing. She would have made no appearances on Geraldo or the Phil Donahue show. Not if she were dead.

"So, I tell you again, strictly between you and me, between one Prancing Tiger and another, she was bad for my business, bad for my future plans. I would have killed her. I told Drew-san to stay away from her, to go spend time with his family where he belonged, and I was going to have her killed, but Roland-san, I did not have to do it. As with the deaths of John Varney and Raimundo Villegas, someone did me a favor. With Varney in particular. He was the most threatening to me personally. Every time I looked in his eyes I saw a plot brewing to do away with me. He would have been done away with himself before long, even without the assistance of the Mexican. Villegas too. He thought

I did not know about his dealings behind my back with the Chinese in California. He would have been gone within six months. They say things come in groups of three. Nikki Waters was the third, but like the other two, I had no hand in it. If I had, do you really think it would have been done as it was? A bloody mess perfectly orchestrated for the media? Surely, Roland-san, you know me better than that. Had it been me, she simply would have disappeared. Poof! Gone! No pictures. No story. No missing nipples. The murder of Nikki Waters was a crime of passion, not a well-planned hit."

"So who killed her?" Troy asked.

"I have no idea," said Nakama. "I have looked into it, as you might imagine I would given the circumstances, and I have absolutely no idea at all. None, Roland-san. There is nothing I can tell you that you don't already know. But I can tell you this. You are correct in assuming there was another reason for her presence in Orlando besides making things convenient for Drew Parabrise. Unfortunately, though, this reason will not help the case of your friend Billy Roseman, because it was Nikki Waters who killed his horse. The horse who was champion of the world."

"Nikki Waters killed Steakhouse Papa? Are you kidding me?" Troy felt as though a gust of wind had come up off the ocean and moved him and his chair slightly sideways. He took the cigar out of his mouth, sat up straight, and stared wide-eyed at Nakama.

"No, Roland-san, I am not kidding. I would not kid with you. I hope you understand that. From the beginning you were honest with me, therefore I have never been anything but honest with you. You may not always like what I say, but at least you can depend upon the fact that I am not kidding. Nikki Waters had worked with horses years before she met Drew-san by chance in New York City. She worked for a veterinarian in Mississippi, where she was born. She knew how to inject the horse so that its death would seem perfectly natural, a heart attack, as I remember. It was part of a plan concocted by John Varney. A complicated scheme involving drugs and insurance payoffs that made him lots of money. The details are no longer important, believe me, especially when you consider that to know this about Nikki Waters would only provide Billy Roseman with a motive for her murder.

"I must tell you, by the way, that I admired what he did with that horse. Together they conquered everything in their path, against formidable odds. But Roseman was another one who was not satisfied. Steakhouse Papa was his life-blood, yet he turned around and sold him, sold his lifeblood for some fantasy dangled by John Varney before his nose. Now he sits in jail, accused of murdering the woman who killed his horse. She broke his heart and he does not even know it."

"Nikki Waters could just as well have been put in Baltimore or Richmond or Philadelphia," Troy said. "All near enough to Parabrise so he could have carried on with her and not drawn any attention. You put her in Orlando so she could see what she had done. And so you could see what she would do when she found out. Is that what you imagine God does with the human race?"

"Roland-san, four years ago, just after Dominique died, I sat on this deck, in the very chair that you are sitting in now, and I watched cayucas filled with Mosquito Indians and all their earthly possessions flee south along the coast from Nicaragua to Puerto Limón. They were running from the Sandinistas. 'These are the Montagnards of Central America,' I thought. 'People with courage, but simple and trusting, being used by one group after the other.'

"The Spanish explorers used them to clear the land. The captains of the whaling ships used them to harpoon the whales. The Contras and the CIA used them. Then the Sandinistas came and raided their villages and, like the Viet Cong and the Pathet Lao and the Khmer Rouge, they put these Mosquitos in what they called 'resettlement villages' inland from where they had lived for hundreds and hundreds of years. They were kept from the sea so they could not fish. They were not allowed to have guns so they could not hunt or protect their farms from the wild dogs or the tepescuintes. As you would say, Roland-san, they were fucked.

"By the time I sat on this deck and watched those that dared flee down the coast in their overloaded canoes, they were starving and diseased. They were people who no

longer had a home. They were forgotten. I watched and I
asked myself the very question you just asked me. Is this
what God had in mind for the human race? It was not the
first time I asked myself that question. In spite of what you
think of me, I do not think I am God, Roland-san. If I were,
I would not have had to flee from my home when the
winds of fortune began to blow from an unfriendly direction.

"When my ancestors were forced to flee their homes
they fled like the Mosquitos, at night, in poorly equipped
ships. The best sailors among them survived. The most
ruthless of the survivors became Prancing Tigers, the
scourge of Formosa Strait and the East and South China
seas. I fled in my own jet plane, protected by loyal troops.
I own property on every continent on the face of this earth,
so I had my pick of places to go. I had millions of dollars
in banks all around the world, in addition to millions more
in cash and jewels. My empire was still intact. It still is,
but just the same I had to run. God, I do not think, has
to run.

"I manipulate people, Roland-san. That I do not deny.
When I was eight years old, living on the streets of Taipei,
before I learned to read books, before I made my way to
Okinawa and learned karate with my cousin Ansai Shima,
before I learned to make money, I learned that if I did not
manipulate people they would manipulate me. I learned I
would have to destroy certain people or I would be destroyed. I found the former of these two choices far more
appealing to me than the latter.

"I kept Nikki Waters in Orlando because when I was told
what she had done I found it monstrous. To kill an animal
like that, a horse with such a heart . . ." Nakama shook his
head, held both hands, palms up, in front of him, and
formed his mouth into a look of disgust.

"The man who put her up to it—who offered her a deal
she should have refused—the late John Varney, was beyond
redemption. He was a worthless piece of scum. I did business with him, but I had already decided I would have to
one day kill him before he tried to kill me. Nikki Waters,
on the other hand, intrigued me. Not as much as you intrigued me, or Drew-san, or various others who have

crossed my path over the years, but enough. You are right.
I kept her in Orlando to see what would happen, to see
what she would do when she discovered who the horse was
she had killed. I had no doubt she would be drawn to the
training track. She couldn't miss it, sitting as it does in the
middle of the city, less than a mile from the station where
she worked. She might travel past it once or twice or six
times, but horses were in her blood. Sooner or later her nature would compel her to drive through the gate to see what
was going on. Like you, I never met her but I heard her
voice. I do not know this Billy Roseman either. I wonder
whether he would have forgiven her if she had confessed to
him. Now it seems she will have killed him twice. I'm
sorry about that, Roland-san."

"I'm sorry too, Bassai," Troy said. "I appreciate your
openness with me. I don't imagine you have too many conversations like this."

"Very rarely, now that Dominique is dead," Nakama
said. "Sometimes I talk with Brownie, my pilot, who by the
way remembers you well. He is in San Jose, having my
plane serviced. He will be dismayed to learn he has missed
you. He has been with me now for twenty-six years, but
even with him there are things I don't discuss. He is a good
man, but you are a Prancing Tiger. There is a difference, although I wonder if you believe that. I wonder if now you
think that it is meaningless. A bunch of ancient baloney un-
fit for contemporary consumption."

"I believe it, Bassai, or I wouldn't have talked to you the
way I did. There are too many people with weapons around
here for me to take unnecessary risks."

"You think I would shoot you for speaking your mind?"
Nakama laughed loudly.

"No," said Troy. "I guess not. Only for interfering with
your plans for Drew Parabrise."

Nakama rose from his chair, crossed the deck, and
whirled around to face Troy. His arms were folded, his eyes
narrowed, and the veins bulged in his neck. When he
spoke, his voice was low and guttural, a feral snarl. "That
was a matter of honor," he said. "Drew Parabrise was mine,
not yours, in spite of what he did to you. He got the better
of you, but I captured him. I showed him who he really

was. A few years ago, he forgot and I was forced to show him again. Do not forget that."

Nakama turned his back on Troy. He leaned on the railing of the deck and looked out to sea. Troy said nothing. He listened to Nakama's breathing, waiting for the fury to subside. Slowly, the color of Nakama's neck returned from a deep red to its normal tan. A minute later he turned to face Troy again.

"I let him live as an experiment," he said. "Thus far, it has been a successful experiment, but if it is still so important to you, you can have him and I will look for someone else. Presidents are not what they were once cracked up to be. Your last one slept for eight years. Occasionally they woke him up to say something the people wanted to hear. The one you have now whines like an old woman. With him the handlers have more trouble. Unlike the actor who preceded him, it is harder for him to pretend he believes what he is saying."

Nakama was pacing up and down the deck now between Troy's chair and the front railing. His rage, which had appeared and vanished like the sound of a gunshot, was replaced by a kind of professorial enthusiasm. Listening to him and watching him gesture with his hands, Troy was transfixed. In spite of himself, he felt like a long-wandering pupil who had returned to the feet of his master. He scratched idly at his tattoo, realized what he was doing, and forced himself to stop. Naturally, the skin of his upper arm then began to itch furiously.

"Up there, on my mountain, there are howler monkeys," Nakama continued, pointing to the dense forest above his house. "In America, candidates for high office have become media monkeys, facsimiles of some design dreamed up by public-relations firms. Their ratings rise and fall like popular songs, for reasons that have nothing to do with truly important issues. Outside a very small circle, no one knows I exist. My name does not appear in magazines, on those lists of the world's richest men, though I have more money and power than many of those who do. I, Roland-san, have perfected the art of the low profile, while at the same time I control the means for keeping one of these monkeys at the top of the charts longer than the rest. I can arrange it so he is presented over and over again in a slick package with correct lighting and camera angles like an MTV video or a Pepsi commercial until he becomes number one. If there were a Teddy Roosevelt around, or even a Harry Truman, I could not do it, but in this time of mediocrity I can, and I will.

"That is a frightening thought to you, *ne*, Roland-san? I can see by the look on your face. It is frightening to you that a man such as I, a pirate, can even *say* these things, much less be capable of carrying them out. However, they are true. And before you become indignant, think for a moment about your country's recent past. Think hard about it and you will see that my own scenario is far from preposterous.

"Take Richard Nixon, for example, a man who surrounded himself with petty criminals who wouldn't have lasted a week in my own organization. Once ignominious, he is now regarded as an elder statesman, an expert on foreign relations. Between you and me, if Nixon ran again I would put my money on him to win. But he won't, so my money must ride with Drew Parabrise, whose perfect smile alone will carry twenty states. Unless, that is, you want to go to Virginia and blow him away."

"I'm not interested in Drew Parabrise anymore," Troy said. He was beginning to experience the same unsettling sensation of separation from his body that had overtaken him when he called Jack Ubinas from the interstate rest stop in Texas. In the distance, far below him, he could see another of Nakama's men, armed with an assault rifle, strolling along the beach. Above him, the cries of the howler monkeys were incessant. Howler monkeys. Media monkeys. What kind of monkey was he? Maybe a Prancing Tiger monkey, a samurai monkey pissing up a rope.

Troy studied Nakama, the man who said all sorts of things to cloud his mind but who, he ultimately believed, had saved his life as part of an experiment, the man who leaned now against the railing of the deck, smiling at him with parental tolerance. Murderous thoughts overtook him. From deep inside came an instinctive urge to do away with Chotoku Nakama and for a fleeting moment he thought about jumping out of his chair, rushing Nakama, and shov-

ing him over the railing. It was a straight drop of at least
forty feet to the rocks below. Catch him off balance and flip
him quick. Watch him fly and then sneak up on that griz-
zled cowboy guarding the chopper. The Jetranger was good
for nearly four hundred miles. If the tanks were full, and
knowing Nakama they were, it would take him on the short
hop to Tortuguero, then all the way to San Jose before dark.
Grab the night flight to Miami and he'd be home free. He'd
bet the ranch that with Nakama dead his whole empire
would fall apart within days. No one would even bother
looking for him. They'd all be too busy cutting up the pie,
the same way John Varney's pie was being sliced by a
bunch of lawyers in Orlando. That's how it always was
with one-man shows.

It was a nice fantasy, the murder of Bassai Nakama, a diversion that actually calmed him down, but pure folly.
What about the Oriental with the sharpened coin and the
big black guy and the dude walking the beach? He didn't
even have a jackknife in his pocket, and they were armed
to the teeth. The black guy had a K-bar strapped to his leg,
SEAL-style; he'd be a handful all by himself. And anyway,
what was the point? To prove he was nobody's monkey? So
he could tell Clara, 'Well, baby, I had the whole thing figured wrong, but I snuffed the old fucker and escaped, so it
wasn't a total loss. At least I accomplished something.' So
he could check out the Jetranger? He stuck his cigar into
his mouth and smiled at Nakama in what he intended as the
picture of bonhomie.

"Go ahead and make him president," he said. "Make him
the fucking pope for all I care. To tell you the truth, Bassai,
I don't really give a shit what you do with Drew Parabrise.
If he can't lead me to Nikki Waters's killer, he isn't worth
my time."

"He never was worth your time," Nakama said. "My
time, yes, your time, no. And in the end you've had your
revenge after all. You are a free man. But now I feel bad.
You have come a long way and have gotten nothing. Worse
than nothing, I'm afraid, since now you must start down a
new road to help your friend. Is there anything I can offer
you?"

"Yeah, there is," Troy said. "You can make sure they lay

off Ethan Peoples, the guy from the newspaper who found out about Waters and the senator. In fact, you ought to give the son of a bitch a raise. That was a good piece of investigative reporting."

"I like that," said Nakama. "Ha ha ha! Give him a raise. That is an excellent idea. Okay, I will do that. They will not bother him again and he will get a New Year's raise, as long as he understands that without concrete evidence, of which there is none, there will be no story about Drew-san and Nikki Waters. Anything else?"

"Not really," said Troy. "But while we're talking about the *Journal-Express*, you ought to know you got a problem there with your editor."

"You mean a problem with Byron O'Reilly and his cocaine habit?" Nakama said.

"You know about that? And you keep him around? That motherfucker's unstable. He ought to be shit-canned before he kills somebody."

"No, Roland-san, shit-canned is not the way. Byron-san is very useful. He is good at reorganizing. He only needs to get himself cleaned up, and for that purpose he is being reassigned. To Buffalo, New York, where some of his abrasive tactics are in order. A straight player deal, as they say in baseball. He goes to Buffalo, the Buffalo editor, a calm, peaceful man, goes to Orlando. Byron-san, however, will make a short detour through my version of a detoxification program, where he will be shown what awaits him if he doesn't change his life-style."

"Bassai, tell me something," Troy said. "Why do you bother with all this crap?"

"Oh, I don't bother with it, Roland-san," Nakama said. "On any given day there are ten Byron O'Reillys to deal with. Maybe more. One man could never handle that. Other people do the bothering. I only know about it in case the manner of bothering is inappropriate. Come here. Come inside with me. I want to show you something."

Nakama walked past Troy and opened the sliding glass door. Troy followed him into a large, thickly carpeted den furnished with leather couches and easy chairs. They crossed the den and Nakama opened a door in the far wall, motioning to Troy with his head as he did. The two of them entered another room, as big as the den but windowless, with equally thick carpeting and more leather furniture. At one end was a giant TV screen at least seven feet square. On the wall opposite the big screen was a bank of smaller screens—twenty of them, by Troy's count. On a long, L-shaped desk in front of the bank of screens were three computers, a half-dozen telephones, and a couple of fax machines. A copy machine stood in one corner next to an open wooden cabinet containing shortwave equipment, a radar scanner, a dozen VCRs, and several electronic devices Troy couldn't immediately identify.

"Upstairs are my living quarters," Nakama said. "Downstairs live my men. This level is my connection to the rest of the world. That satellite dish you no doubt saw when you arrived is the most advanced design available. It was built specially for me by a company in Yokohama. I have six more at my other homes. I have the same decoder as the CIA. If it is beamed up to a satellite, I can see it. If it is broadcast over the radio, I can hear it. Now, you and I will take a swim in the pool. Then we will have a nice dinner and afterwards we will come here and fool around. Russian rock and roll is most interesting to see. Like going back in time."

"It's kind of you to offer, Bassai, but I'm gonna head back to Tortuguero," Troy said. "I want to catch the early-morning flight to Miami tomorrow."

"You should not even think of returning to Tortuguero until tomorrow," Nakama said. "It will be dark in less than an hour and the river is too dangerous at night, even for you. Among other things, sharks swim upstream from the boca. An experienced fisherman was eaten by several of them one night last week. Apparently, his boat struck a log and he was thrown into the water. All they found was his shirt. If you stay here, you will get a night's sleep beyond compare. The air coming up the mountain from the ocean is hypnotic. When my children come here, they always say, 'How can you sleep in this place with those monkeys carrying on all night?' Then they pass out as though they had been drugged."

It occurred to Troy that in his own way Nakama was begging him to stay. *He's lonely,* Troy thought. *More pow-*

erful than some countries, but lonely. As secretive a man as ever lived, yet he needs an audience. How strange. He needs me to confirm who he is.

"How are your kids?" Troy said. "I forgot to ask you about them."

"You had more pressing matters on your mind," Nakama said. "My children are doing well. My daughter is a doctor. She lives in San Diego with her husband, who is also a doctor. They met in medical school, in Ohio. He is an anesthesiologist. She became an oncologist, no doubt because of what happened to her mother. My son is an architect in Paris, married to a television reporter. They have a child. My granddaughter. In fact, I am going there in a week to visit them, which is why Brownie is taking care of the plane. I have a new one that can fly across the Atlantic."

"I'm glad about your kids," Troy said. "They were beautiful little children. It's nice when they turn out well later on. I know the feeling. It beats winning the lottery."

"They did turn out well," Nakama said. "Thanks to Dominique, neither one followed in their father's footsteps. And thanks to her, neither of them hates me for who I am. In that way I am lucky." He clapped his hands and held them together. "So," he said, "shall I tell Dana you intend to have dinner with us?"

"I'll accept the offer of dinner," Troy said, "but then I'm gonna leave. My mind's made up."

"At least let me fly you to Tortuguero in the chopper," Nakama said. "My men will return the cayuca tomorrow."

"Uh uh," Troy said. "Don't you remember? I like paddling down rivers at night. Always have. Probably always will. Even ones with sharks in 'em."

They ate in a room with a wall of glass looking out over the ocean. Nakama tried once more to convince Troy to stay, but Troy was adamant. When they had finished dinner, Nakama put on a camouflage jacket and walked with him to the edge of the trail leading down to the river. The black man and the tongueless Oriental were waiting there for them. When Troy bid Nakama good-bye and thanked him, Nakama reached into the pocket of his jacket and handed Troy a nine-millimeter Glock 19.

"Take this," Nakama said. "There are other kinds of sharks on the river at night. At what hotel are you staying?"

"The Bougainvillea," Troy said.

"Just leave it at the desk," said Nakama. "Mention Brownie's name and there will be no problem."

When the jet boat's running lights picked up Troy's cayuca, the Oriental idled his engine down and pulled along-side so that Troy could board the canoe without getting wet. Troy untied the cayuca, picked up the paddle, and held it up in a salute to Nakama's two men.

"Say, Slim," the black man said to him, "I ain't ever seen Bassai hand a piece to someone who wasn't on the payroll. Who the hell are you anyway?"

"I'm Mr. Tooth," Troy told him.

"Mr. Tooth, the baddest dude in the jungle," the black man said.

"Believe it," Troy said.

As soon as they were gone and the thick, wet darkness enveloped him, Troy felt at ease, as comfortable and secure as if he had climbed into a bed and wrapped himself in a smooth, warm quilt after a long day's journey. He had long ago quit trying to explain the calming effect on him of the swamp at night, the combination of animal strength and tranquillity that flowed through him as he glided down a murky river, barely visible beneath him, or crept unseen through a pitch-black forest. Neither Jack Ubinas nor Nakama nor Clara Roseman, nor even his friend Sheridan Halpatter, the shoeless alligator hunter, had understood it. When he told Nakama's two men where he was going, they had looked at him with the kind of rapid, sidelong glance one gives to a freak. Troy was used to it. On two or three occasions he had gone up jungle rivers at night with teams of Navy SEALs. Tough as they were, they had considered him crazy when they discovered he enjoyed it.

On his way in he had made a mental picture of the route from Tortuguero to Monkey Mountain and now had no trouble retracing it. He had no encounters with sharks, but once, on the branch connecting Monkey Creek with the main river, two men in a small runabout passed him going in the opposite direction. *"Mierda,"* he heard one of them say. *"Que noche bruta. Me mata la cabeza"*—"Shit, what

a bitch of a night. My head is killing me." They had a spot-
light mounted on their boat and were scanning the river for
something. When the light swung around, Troy could see
that the one in the back of the boat was cradling a shotgun.
He slid beneath an overhanging branch and they did not see
him.

By the time he reached the dock of the German's fishing
lodge, his mind was clear, as though he had been in a deep,
cleansing sleep. On Nakama's deck he had been skeptical,
wondering, as he listened to Bassai hold forth, whether he
was being derailed. Nakama's slightly stilted English and
his didactic tone had taken Troy back a quarter-century. He
had felt childish, foolish even, like a supplicant bowing and
scraping at a shrine. This in turn had angered him and must
have been the reason his head had filled with murderous,
destructive thoughts. Now it seemed to him Nakama had
been telling the truth. Now it seemed logical that no one
sent by the warlord to kill Nikki Waters would have left
such a mess in Billy Roseman's barn. Whoever had done it
had followed Nikki Waters and been clever enough to cap-
italize on a scene that clearly implicated Billy, but Nikki
Waters was no Jimmy Hoffa. The killer was no anonymous
professional hit man, and he was Mr. Tooth. He couldn't let
himself forget that if he intended to prevail.

He moored the cayuca to the dock and walked up the
manicured lawn leading to the main building of the lodge.
Lester and Fritz, the bomb-building innkeeper, were sitting
out front under the overhang of the roof, sipping cognac
and smoking cigars in the amber light of a kerosene lantern
hanging from a wooden overhead support. Silently, Troy
circled around behind them and sat down in a wood and
leather chair. The German shepherd sleeping at Fritz's feet
stirred slightly but did not awake. For almost five minutes
Troy sat this way, listening to the two men talk. Then, without warning, he spoke.

"I wouldn't mind trying one of those cigars," Troy said.

At the sound of Troy's voice, the German shepherd rose
up with a yowl, bumping into the table on which both
glasses of cognac and the cognac bottle were resting. The
bottle crashed to the floor.

"Jesus Christ!" Lester shouted. "Where the fuck did *you* come from?" Both he and Fritz leaped from their chairs. Fritz yelled something at Troy in German, chased the dog off the porch, and disappeared inside the lodge, presumably to find someone to clean up the mess. The German shepherd remained behind, lapping noisily at the puddle of cognac.

"From Monkey Mountain," said Troy.

"Man, you shouldn't do things like that," Lester said. "You could get hurt. You could get killed, for Chrissake."

"Me?" said Troy. "I'm Mr. Tooth. I'm invincible. And invisible. It ain't me you should be worried about. C'mon, let's fly away."

"Right now?" Lester said. "I never even paid Fritz for my dinner."

Troy picked up the table, fished two twenties out of his wallet, and lay them under a heavy metal ashtray. "If you ate more than forty bucks' worth of food in this place you'd explode," he said. "Let's boogie. Unless you don't like flying in the dark."

"Dark ain't a problem," Lester said. "I got instruments. I've flown in and out of jungles in monsoon season. But what's your hurry? Fritz's chef cooks up a breakfast you wouldn't believe."

"No offense, but I'll pass on the breakfast," Troy said. "My mind's on other things. *La cotorra que chi, no canta.*"

"While the parrot pisses, it doesn't sing," Lester said. "I can dig it. I'll get you out of here. It's your show."

They didn't speak again until they were airborne, heading west toward the mountains and San Jose. "You weren't in there very long," Lester said. "I hope you got what you came for."

"I didn't get shit," Troy said, "except a bucketful of memories. Seems that's the hand I've been dealt lately."

"So you snuck up on me and Fritz to get something," Lester said.

"Maybe," Troy said. "I thought I was just fuckin' around, but maybe that was it. I wanted to get something. Don't take it so hard. I didn't mean any harm."

"No problem," Lester said, turning away from the controls and smiling at him. "But tell me one thing. How the hell come you didn't wake up Fritz's dog?"

"I moved like his dream," Troy said. "Like the shadow of a bone."

XXIII

✦

Troy drove as fast as possible from the airport to his house, afraid that when he got there Clara would once again be gone. When he nosed the El Camino through the pine grove into his yard and saw the big Buick parked alongside the toolshed, his spirits lifted momentarily. Then almost immediately they began to sink as he thought about his lack of success in Costa Rica.

From the kitchen window, Clara saw him climb out of the El Camino and walk toward the front porch. His limp was more pronounced than usual—it appeared as though he was almost dragging his right foot—and as he drew closer she could see that the lines around his eyes had deepened. Obviously he was in pain, and she sensed that it was more than just physical discomfort he was experiencing. He wasn't bringing good news. She knew that immediately; he didn't have to say a thing. Still, his face was impassive, his head erect, and his back as straight as a marble tombstone. It was the way Troy walked the day she met him outside the barn at the track, the way he would walk at eighty, she thought, if he lived that long.

He stopped and turned to look off across the pond at two sandhill cranes who were feeding in the marsh grass on the far shore. He stood absolutely still, watching them for several minutes, and when he turned back and continued up the path to the house, his eyes had brightened. Glancing up, he saw her in the window, smiled, and waved, and suddenly the inner turmoil and pain on his face was mixed with joy.

She ran out onto the porch to greet him. The afternoon was warm and all she was wearing were a pair of old cut-offs and a tank top. A gust of cool wind came up off the pond and he could see her nipples grow erect under the

shirt and goosebumps appear on her long, tanned legs.
The wind blew her hair across her face; she pulled it away
with one hand, tilting her head at the same time in a gesture
so unaffectedly sexy his breath caught in his throat.

"You look tired," she said. "I think you better come upstairs to bed."

"I didn't find . . ." he began to say, but she stopped him
with a kiss.

"Tell me later," she said.

They made love, then slept. When Troy awoke it was
dark and had begun to rain. He lay on his back, listening
to the hiss of raindrops on the leaves, to the rise and fall of
the wind. Already the wind was shifting; by morning the
weather would again be clear and cold. *The circle of the
winter wind,* Troy thought. *The pattern never changed.*

He turned his head to see whether Clara was awake. In
the darkness he couldn't tell for sure whether her eyes were
open. He reached over, gently put his hand on her head,
and stroked her hair. She sighed, squeezed his hand, and
ran her fingers up and down his arm.

"I'm sorry," he said. "I thought I had it solved, but I was
wrong."

"Could he have lied to you?" she asked.

"I don't think so. He wouldn't have done it that way.
Nikki Waters would have just disappeared. No fuss. No evidence. Nobody would have been implicated. I should have
seen that myself, but I wanted so badly to get it solved . . .
I should have known better."

"Roland, you're doing everything you can," she said. "I
know that. Billy knows that. Everybody knows that but
you. You have to let up on yourself a little bit or you'll collapse."

"I don't want to fail," he said. "I don't want to fail you.
Not this time. You deserve . . . You've been through
enough. You told me yourself Billy was all you had left.
Don't worry, I won't collapse. I'm tired and I'm upset but
I ain't gonna unravel."

"I'm not so sure," she said. "I mean, from the moment
I showed up here, hysterical, begging for you to help me,
you had to start reliving every painful event of your life.

All the stuff that happened between us, all the Drew
Parabrise stuff, things I never knew anything about, the
stuff with this guy Nakama and the other one, whatever his
name is up there in Virginia, and your grandparents and
parents and brother, all the dead Vietnamese and Laotians.
And Shima. I almost forgot about him. A whole world of
trouble. A stew of human emotions that you had all nicely
packaged in the deep-freeze and now it's bubbling on the
stove. I want to save my son, Roland, but he isn't all I have
left anymore."

"You know," Troy said, "I must've been doin' eighty on
the interstate comin' from the airport, and when I came up
the driveway I was goin' so damn fast the back end of that
El Camino was fishtailing off the dirt and into the weeds,
but when I got to the pine grove I slowed way down, so
slow that if I was goin' any slower I wouldn't have been
moving at all, because I was afraid I'd come out of the
trees and your car wouldn't be there. And there it was, and
I felt so damn good, and then just like that I felt awful because I knew what I had to tell you. I felt that I had let you
down."

"Letting me down's the last thing you've done, Roland,"
Clara said. "In fact, the whole time you were gone I was
thinking just the opposite—about how you've come
through for me no matter what the outcome of this is. I
thought about that, and about how I've been confronted
with the supreme irony of my life: My only child gets
charged with a rape and a murder he didn't commit, and
because of that I have a chance to get back together with
a man I love. Is that madness or what?

"You *know* it's true. You know if I hadn't come to you
for help we would have lived out our separate lives, you on
your land, building your models, paddling your canoe,
smoking your damn cigars, trading cynical observations
with Halpatter and his unspeakably horrifying bare feet, and
me up in Hilton Head, playing some tennis, playing some
golf, going to dinner. I was planning to travel too. I was
thinking I'd like to go back to Texas, back where my daddy
drilled for oil, just to look around. You know, check it out,
see how things have changed.

"I'm terrified of what may happen to Billy. I'm just

scared to death. I'm not going to pretend I'm not, but I don't want to leave you. And if, you know ... If after all our trying, if he doesn't get off, if that's what you're afraid of, I'd still ... I'm not ..."

He touched her cheek, felt the wetness, and kissed her there. "I think I know what we better do," he said. "To buy us all a little time. Let's you and me get dressed and go talk to Billy."

"I see your daughter's come back from skiing," Roland Troy said to Teddy Chambers.

"Because I'm wearing the suspenders. Good observation," Chambers said. "These are different ones, you know. She thinks I look so distinguished in suspenders she got me another pair. What about you? Katherine send you suspenders for Christmas? You could use a little distinguished."

"Uh uh," said Troy. "She got me a Randall knife. One of the last ones the old man made before he died. Sent it to me and had me send her a penny to pay for it 'cause a knife present is bad luck. Do you believe that?"

"Only if the giver sticks it between your ribs," Teddy Chambers said. He rocked back in his chair, put his boots up on his desk, and folded his hands across his flat stomach. "I don't mean to be inhospitable, Roland, but why are you here?"

"Busy day, huh," Troy said. "That's cool. I got a deal for you, Teddy."

"A deal? For me?"

"Billy Roseman pleads guilty, he gets life."

"That isn't like you, Roland, giving up so quickly."

"I ain't giving up. It's just gonna take me longer than I thought it would."

"And you don't want him cookin' while you're lookin'."

"Maybe they'll let you teach poetry at that college in addition to law," Troy said.

"Let me talk to some people," Chambers said. "Call me later. By the way, what's Billy think about this deal, which I'm assuming was your idea?"

"He doesn't like it much. You or I wouldn't either if we were innocent of some crime we were going away for. Clara and I talked to him a long time the other night. It took us a while, but now he understands that if he goes to trial pleading not guilty with what we've got, he doesn't stand a chance. He'll get the chair."

"Yes, he will," said Teddy Chambers. "No question about that."

"I don't want that hangin' over his head. Or mine either, truth be told. I'm gonna find the motherfucker who killed Nikki Waters, Teddy, but it won't do Billy no good, now, will it, if he's dead by then?"

"The wedding still on?"

"Hell, yeah. Clara wouldn't let Katherine cancel it. She told her, don't be ridiculous, it could be ten years before Billy's cleared. I personally do not think it will be that long, but Clara's got that number set in her head. So she won't be disappointed. She's like that. Once she has something fixed in her mind, she can deal with it. Twisting in the wind is what fucks her up."

"How's that going, you and Clara?" Chambers asked.

"Sort of like a gourmet picnic on a cloudy day," Troy said.

The sentencing of Billy Roseman took place in late January. By then, the first section of the *Journal-Express* was filled with news about Operation Desert Storm, America's war to drive Saddam Hussein's troops from Kuwait. The story about Billy Roseman's sentencing occupied less than half a column in the paper's state-and-local section. Under the conditions of the plea bargain worked out by Roland Troy and Stanton Feinberg, Billy was not required to submit to any further questioning by the state attorney's prosecutor, but that fact was not included in the story. Billy pleaded guilty to one count of rape and one count of second-degree murder and received a sentence of twenty-five years to life in prison. The plea bargain required that he serve at least fifteen years before being eligible for parole. He was immediately transferred from the county jail to the state penitentiary in Starke. Unless the actual killer was found, he would be forty-six years old when he got out.

Roland Troy rode in the car with Billy and two sheriff's deputies from Orlando to Starke, thirty miles north of

Gainesville. During the ride they said very little, but Troy could feel Billy's anger, which still smoldered from the night he and Clara went to the jail to explain to him the wisdom of changing his plea. In spite of being charged with a hideous crime he didn't commit, Billy had managed to control his fury, convincing himself he would shortly be cleared. But admitting guilt had absolutely enraged him. Billy had screamed and shouted and pounded his fist into the mattress in his cell. It had taken Troy close to two hours to calm Roseman down and get him to listen to reason. Then Troy told him about what Nikki Waters had done to Steakhouse Papa.

"She killed Steakhouse?" Billy had said. "That bitch fuckin' killed my horse?" He began to tremble and started to rise from his cot, but sat back down. He was spent by this time, his voice hoarse and barely audible, even in the tiny cell. "Why would she do something like that? Something so horrible? She loved animals. She was the best hand I ever had around horses."

"She did it to get the job at the radio station," Troy told him. "So she could be the Raven. She thought she was buying her freedom."

"So she sold her soul," Billy said. "And then she came looking for me? That's sick, Roland."

"She didn't know about your connection to Steakhouse Papa before she came to Orlando," Troy said. "You were out of the picture by the time she made her deal with Varney. You'd already dealt him the horse." Then he told Billy about Nakama and how Nikki had been sent to Orlando on purpose.

"So that was it," Billy said. "She was trying to set it right. That's why she helped me at the barn." He shook his head. "You think you know somebody. You think you understand them . . ."

"There's more," Troy said. "Those horses you and McBride took across the Rio Grande were hers. She stole 'em from Varney to sell to Villegas, but he double-crossed her. She told McBride not to take you with him. She didn't want you involved."

"Nikki Waters stole horses from John Varney," Billy said. "Why?"

"Varney fucked her over," Troy said. "She wanted revenge. And money."

"And she didn't want me involved," Billy said. "Holy shit. And I always thought it was me whose life was fucked up. I thought Nikki Waters had it made. The Raven. And you don't know which one of them killed her. Which one blew that woman's brains out in my office."

"No, I don't," Troy told him. "Not yet."

"Sentence won't last no fifteen years if I get AIDS," was what Billy said in the car.

"You ain't gettin' AIDS or anything else up there," Troy said. "You got any fuckin' sense, you'll start right in taking courses toward your college degree. Get a jump on things for when you get out."

Clara, of course, was worried sick that something terrible would happen to him at the prison, but Troy assured her he had already made careful arrangements for Billy's safety. Earlier that week, Troy had flown to the prison to meet with Trevor Blanding, the ex-enforcer of the Renegades motorcycle gang who was serving three consecutive life sentences with no chance of parole for his part in a triple murder.

Blanding controlled the white population in the wing of the prison where Billy would be housed, and in that capacity, had considerable influence with the leaders of the blacks and Hispanics. Troy's proposition to Blanding was simple. Complete protection of Billy Roseman in exchange for an eighteen-month sentence plus probation for Blanding's younger brother, who was on trial for armed robbery, auto theft, and assault with a deadly weapon on a police officer.

"It's a done deal," Blanding said.

"Be sure it's a done deal," said Troy. "Be sure not a hair on his head gets touched. Make it your life's work."

"Or what?" said Blanding.

"Well, for starters, they'll find enough crack on your daughter—Angelina, isn't that her name? Nineteen. Five-six. Brown hair, blue eyes. Drives a white eighty-seven Trans Am. Lives out there in Apopka with her boyfriend. See, I do my homework, bubba," Troy said. "They'll find enough dope on her to put her away 'til she reaches menopause. And then, after I'm through making her life a living hell, I'll pay one of the Puerto Ricans up here twenty-five grand to slit your throat. Either that or save my money and come up here and kill you myself."

"You think you could do that?" Blanding said.

"Ask around," Troy said.

XXIV

♦

In early February 1991, Senator Drew Parabrise received a phone call at his office from Wanda Donnerstag, who identified herself as an editor from the Orlando *Journal-Express*. A week earlier the *Journal-Express* had done an extensive interview with Parabrise, getting his views as a former navy man—a former war hero, no less—on the naval maneuvers being employed in the Persian Gulf. The following day the paper had run a three-column, front-page color picture of the senator saying good-bye to a bunch of sailors who were shipping out to the Middle East from the naval base in Jacksonville. Parabrise therefore had good reason to believe that Wanda's call was yet another opportunity for his hometown newspaper to provide him with some excellent publicity, as it had throughout Operation Desert Storm and its precursor, Operation Desert Shield, so he told his secretary he would talk to her.

"What can I do for you, Ms. Donnerstag?" he asked.

"You can meet me tomorrow night at eight in the lounge of the Woodbridge Holiday Inn off I-95," she said. "I want to talk to you."

"Is this a story you're doing?" Parabrise asked. " 'Cause if you want an interview, we could do it either here in my office or at my house."

"It's an interview," Wanda said. "It would be so much easier for my schedule if you met me at the hotel."

Her voice was soft and provocative, slightly reminiscent, actually, of the tone used at times by Nikki Waters, though Parabrise did not at first make that connection. He was, however, just a little aroused by Ms. Donnerstag's voice, and being far too sure of his appeal to women, was intrigued rather than suspicious. Nevertheless, as a matter of habit he decided to make sure this woman was who she said she was. He put Wanda on hold and had his secretary call the *Journal-Express* to make sure a Wanda Donnerstag was in fact an editor at the paper. Less than two minutes later, Parabrise's secretary assured him that Ms. Donnerstag was indeed an editor at the paper, *the* editor, actually, of the life-style section.

"This is rather unusual, Ms. Donnerstag," Parabrise said. "Could you give me some idea of what this interview is about?"

"I would really rather talk to you in person," Wanda said. "I'm flying into Washington tomorrow afternoon for a meeting and have to leave the following morning. If you can't make it tomorrow night, then I'll catch up with you some other time."

"No, I think I can make it," Parabrise said. "I haven't got anything pressing tomorrow night. How much time will you need?"

"An hour should be plenty," Wanda said.

"Okay. I'll see you at eight. What do you look like, so I'll know who you are?"

"I have dark hair," Wanda said. "I'll be wearing a tan suit and a white silk blouse. Anyway, I'll know who you are. I have the picture of you we ran on the front page right here on my desk."

"I know about you and Nikki Waters," Wanda said. She was sitting across from Parabrise in a booth in a dimly lit corner of the lounge. The jacket of her suit was open and the top two buttons of her blouse were undone. Parabrise could see that she wasn't wearing a bra. He took a sip of his drink and waited for her to continue, waiting for what was coming next, trying not to show any reaction to what he had just heard.

"Nikki and I were very close. As close as two people could possibly be," Wanda said. "She told me about you and her. I know what you're probably thinking, but don't worry, this is not about blackmail. Not at all. It's just that when she told me about you ... about how you made her feel ... I thought it would be exciting to find out in person ... find out if you could make me feel the same way. I know it would be exciting for me if I could make you feel the way she did ... if I could turn you on like that. Would you like that?"

As Wanda spoke, Parabrise watched her scarlet-tipped fingers move to her breasts and begin fondling the nipples. At the same time, he was aware of the pressure of her leg against his own. He took another sip of his drink and looked into Wanda's eyes, where he saw pure madness intermingled with lust. Good sense told him to get up and walk out of the lounge, but he could feel this woman's body straining toward him, could feel the heat coming off her in perfume-laden waves, and he was inflamed beyond reason. It had been a while since he had come across someone as kinky as Ms. Wanda Donnerstag, and he was up for something out of the ordinary.

"Do you have a room here?" he asked.

"Let me show it to you," Wanda Donnerstag said.

She came at him in the darkness of her room as soon as the door was closed, unzipping his pants and taking him into her mouth. "Did she do this to you?" she asked. "Did she do this, and this?"

When they were both naked on the bed and she was writhing under him, she began to talk again. "Did you call her names?" she said. "You did. I know you did. You called her a whore and a bitch. Talk to me like you talked to her. Call me names. Call me Nikki," she said when he was about to come.

In the two months before Katherine Troy's wedding, Roland and Clara worked ceaselessly on the Nikki Waters case, retracing every conceivable lead, reexamining every shred of evidence, combing Billy's office, his barn, and the ground around the Deet's Creek cabin.

Troy had cleared a space along one wall in the large downstairs room where he kept the miniature replicas of crime scenes that he built. Next to the wall were newly constructed models of Billy's office, the stables, and the area around the cabin. The wall itself was covered with thirty-five-millimeter photographs Troy took of all three locations. Troy had discovered the passageway above the stables and had sensed there was a strong possibility it had been used by Nikki's killer; there were pictures and a model of that passage as well, but neither Troy nor the crime-lab technicians he persuaded John Smith to send to the track were able to find anything conclusive.

"What I can tell you is that sometime during the past two years human beings have been up there," Smitty said, "but there ain't a fingerprint, a footprint, a pubic hair, a trace of manly or womanly excretion, or anything else stuck to those boards that matches what we found in the office. You can spend the rest of your life up there, Tooth, you ain't gonna do no better than us."

Together, Clara and Troy flew to Mississippi to talk to Nikki's family and friends. They flew to New York City and tracked down the models Nikki worked with, the photographers who took her picture, and the men she dated, searching for someone with a motive for killing her and the ability to carry out the act. They talked to Howard and Bonnie Hinshaw. They talked to the manufacturer whose office Nikki trashed and to the former manager of the Orlando radio station where Nikki worked—the religious fanatic who had lusted for her and hated himself for it. Not one of them was anywhere near Orlando on the night Nikki Waters died. In the end, the only thing Troy and Clara achieved was a new level of frustration, blunted only by their determination that Katherine's wedding be a joyful occasion.

In central Florida, just before the land is wrapped for six months in a blanket of intense, unrelenting, moist heat, there are certain days in spring when there is a pureness and clarity to the warm air that brings even distant objects into sharp focus and causes normal sounds to travel great distances with distinct, cohesive resonance. On days like this, the tail feathers of a hawk circling above the trees, for instance, are plainly visible to anyone with decent vision, and the laughter of a child on a playground a half-mile away seems as though it were coming from across the street.

Sheridan Halpatter predicted a day like this for Katherine's wedding, and he was right. The afternoon temperature was around eighty degrees, the sky was cloudless, and there was no wind to carry away the music played by several local jazz musicians, who were Roland Troy's friends. Instead the music wafted over the sloping ground between the house and pond and hung there, swirling among the trees as though it were being played in a concert hall with perfect acoustics and not outdoors.

After the ceremony, at which Halpatter recited an ancient Indian blessing for newlyweds, dinner was served while the musicians continued to play on Troy's front porch and people danced on the lawn. Clara danced one dance with Teddy Chambers during which she said she didn't blame him in any way for what had happened, and Katherine joked about her mother, who had ignored the invitation Troy had sent. "The only thing she'd celebrate would be Ragnorok, the period in Norse legend that signifies the coming of the end of the world," she said.

Shortly before midnight, when nearly everyone had left, a man in a chauffeur's uniform delivered a package to Troy's house addressed to "Mr. and Mrs. Turner Abbey." Inside, protected by shredded Styrofoam and wrapped in tissue paper, was an Oriental jade statue of a man with long hair hanging over his shoulders, a long, pointed beard, and an equally long mustache. The man was wearing a flowing robe and was seated on an ornate throne made of ebony. The entire carving was only twelve inches high and had a card tied to it with gold string. On the card was an inscription written in precise, flowing script.

"This is a representation of Kuan Ti," the card read. "In ancient China he was the god of war, the patron of literature, and the upholder of justice. Kuan Ti was regarded not as a god who waged war, but rather as one who prevented strife and protected those under his care from evil. May Kuan Ti's influence always prevail in your home."

The card was signed by Chotoku Nakama. Weeks later, when Katherine had the carving appraised at Sotheby's in New York, she was told there were only two others known to exist that were exactly like hers. One was in a British museum, and the second was owned by a reclusive former rock star who lived in the woods of northern California. The appraiser valued the carving owned by Katherine and Turner Abbey at somewhere between two hundred and fifty and three hundred thousand dollars, though he admitted his appraisal was conservative and that the right buyer might pay considerably more.

"You never told her about Nakama," Clara said.

"Never," Troy said. "Until today."

It was three in the morning, but neither Troy nor Clara were able to sleep so they brought the portable cassette player outside and were sitting next to each other in the old chairs mounted on blocks on the porch, listening to a tape Troy had made from an old Latin jazz album cut by Cal Tjader and Charlie Palmieri. Fog had rolled in on a light northeasterly breeze and tiny droplets of moisture blew against their faces. They were drinking mugs of hot apple cider and eating leftover wedding cake and Troy was smoking his fourth cigar of the day.

"What did she say?" Clara asked.

"She said, 'He's a criminal but he saved your life so I can't send the statue back.' I told her about the orphanage Nakama built in Bangkok and the hospital in Rangoon, both named after his wife. She asked me what Nakama would say if she sold the statue and split the money between them. I told her I didn't know. I told her he was totally unpredictable—he might think it was wonderful or he might be pissed off. She said maybe she'd wait until he died so he wouldn't be insulted."

"And you said . . ."

"I said, 'Go enjoy your honeymoon. I'll put it in a safe place and you can think about it later.' I probably should've kept my mouth shut."

"I don't think so. She seemed real happy when she left. She's young and in love, Roland. And she's a lighthearted soul. An optimist. Look at the way she dealt with the fact that her mother wasn't here. Things like where that statue came from don't weigh on her like they do on you. She'll sell it or keep it. One way or the other, she won't feel guilty. You shouldn't either."

"Clara, when I was down in Texas three months ago, I killed two men," Troy said. "It was them or me, and they probably deserved it anyway, but I took their lives. You'll never read about it anywhere. It ain't in any police file, but that don't mean they ain't gone. I made Villegas, the drug dealer, sit on one of their bodies so I could get information out of him. He deserved to die even more than the other two, and he did, right in my kitchen. You deal with people like that, you involve yourself in that world, you have to expect violence. I learned that a long time ago. I learned I was good at dealing with it. I learned I *liked* dealing with it. I mean nobody forced me to become a cop after I got back from Southeast Asia. I could've become a lawyer or a teacher or gone into business or a thousand other things. But I didn't. It was like I had this sleeping beast inside me that woke up one day when I was over there and part of me hated the creeping and crawling through the jungle, the constant hiding, the tracking and sneaking and the death that was always in the shadows, around the next bend, behind the trees, in every village. Part of me hated it and was scared of it, but the beast liked it. The beast craved it. The beast made me good at it.

"When I came home, it was the beast that made me the best homicide detective in this state. That ain't late-night braggin' bullshit, Clara. I was the best. I hauled 'em in like they were catfish. I did jobs on the side for government agencies nobody knows exist. I was asked to do 'em because I did 'em better than anyone else, and that's the pure and simple truth. Then one day I'd had enough. I pulled a dumb stunt with a gun in a courtroom and I had to quit, but it was coming anyway. I put the beast back to sleep and went to building models. I put him to sleep, but he was still there, waiting to wake up again, waiting for another chance.

"When I went to Texas the beast was ready, and he was happy and excited when I made Raimundo Villegas sit on the dead body of his friend. It was a good move. The beast *knows* the moves. Villegas was scared shitless and he talked. When it was over, I didn't feel guilty, I felt sad. I was depressed. I felt even worse after I went to visit Nakama. All the way down there I was thinking I had Billy's deal almost wrapped up, and once it was over I could put the beast to rest for good because I wasn't alone. I had you. Together we could live the peaceful life. But Billy's deal isn't over. Poor fuckin' Billy.

"So now I feel sad again. Not guilty. Sad. I didn't want my daughter's wedding sullied. I should've kept my mouth

shut about Nakama. I shouldn't have told her about him today."

That summer, in the evening, Roland Troy took to driving to the track, where he would sit in a lawn chair outside
Billy Roseman's office. The track was empty; all the horses
and the owners and the trainers were off racing up in the
Northeast or the Midwest. Billy's horses were gone too,
sold to John Chadwick for less than half their worth.

Once in a while, Troy would see a jogger circling on the
red clay oval and occasionally a patrol car would drive up
and down in front of the rows of barns, checking for tran-
sients, checking for kids with booze or drugs, but otherwise
he was alone. Behind him, the long row of stalls were
empty, their concrete floors cleaned of hay, and Billy's office was locked. Troy had a key but he didn't go inside. He
didn't feel the need anymore. He sat instead under the
faded, tattered awning that flapped in the breeze, the awning with the logo of the crossed six-shooters, the words
QUICKDRAW STABLE, and the outline of a race horse—an
outline taken from a photograph of Steakhouse Papa as he
was crossing the finish line ahead of the pack. Troy sat and
smoked a cigar and let his thoughts wander, hoping something would occur to him that had slipped by, some clue he
had missed, some avenue of discovery that would manifest
itself there in that place.

Occasionally, just after sunrise, he paddled his canoe
down the Coacoochee and up Deet's Creek, stopping at the
cabin where the bikers saw Nikki Waters's Porsche. Tom
Waxe, who still searched the ground around the cabin regularly, swore he felt the presence of Nikki's killer there,
but, sitting in his canoe next to the old wooden dock, Troy
sensed nothing. During the day, he went back to building
crime-scene models in his shop while Clara worked as a
paralegal in Stanton Feinberg's law office. She took the job
not because she needed the money but to keep from going
crazy.

It was at the track one evening in July that Cool Babba
Wisdom found Roland Troy. Cool Babba pulled his black
Camaro IROC up alongside the row of stalls, unfolded his
enormous frame from the car, leaned across the roof, and

smiled. Troy puffed on his cigar and watched him from the lawn chair.

"Mr. Troy," Cool Babba said. "How was it I knew you might be here?"

"That's an interesting question, the way you pose it," Troy said.

"How about I join you over dere?" Cool Babba said.

"C'mon over," said Troy. "Have a seat. Have a cigar." Fact was, he welcomed the company and was suddenly filled with goodwill.

"Now you speakin'," Cool Babba said. He ambled over, flopped down in the empty lawn chair, and stretched out his legs. They extended all the way across the concrete apron that ran in front of the barn so that his heels rested in the dirt, a good ten inches past Troy's own.

"Those are some long legs," said Troy, proffering a cigar.

"And they all mine," Cool Babba said, lighting up with considerable gusto. "Fine smoke, dis. Mighty pleasant indeed."

"What brings you around?" Troy asked. "You ever get another job?"

"Oh, got de job, got de job. Been managing a reggae club down Disney way, but somet'ing better popped up. Another radio gig in Atlanta. Leavin' for dat very place next week. Just so you t'ink I don't forget you, I don't forget," Cool Babba said. "I take my time be de only t'ing. I don't have much but it be as good as yours now dat Mr. Peanut Butter have his say."

"What the hell are you talkin' about?" said Troy.

"Mr. Peanut Butter say you a man of your word. You did exactly what you say you do for him. He say you be de one to trust."

"Mr. Peanut Butter took care of his end of the deal," Troy said. "He took care of my friend for as long as he had to. He ain't so bad, Mr. Peanut Butter. For a fuckin' dope dealer."

"Now den, no cause to rile yourself up," said Cool Babba. "T'ing is, I need some confidence from you. Some sense of security, you see where I'm heading."

"I ain't gonna turn you in, if that's what you're afraid of," Troy said. "What do you have for me?"

"I got de tape from de Raven's machine," Cool Babba said.

"What machine?"

"De one dat was in her house. De one dat record de phone calls dat came 'trough." Cool Babba took a pull on his cigar and studied the ash with lidded eyes. Troy waited.

"See, Mr. Troy, it be like dis," Cool Babba finally said. "Me be de one give de Raven de ganja on dat fateful night. Me be de one lissen to de Bearcat while my show roll on so dat me happen to hear de dreadful news broadcast by de police. Dey say her name on de scanner, you understand? Dey say her name and quick as can be I hurry over dere in case some evidence be about to cause de implications of I. Raven's place show no sign of Cool Babba. No significance dere of I."

"So you broke into Nikki Waters's house the night she was killed, *before* the cops got there . . ." Troy said.

"An' took de tape, which was all dere be. But de tape prove useless too, Mr. Troy. Me lissen an' all dat is is some Raven's friend, some lady who suggests dey meet to have demselves a drink. No killer dere, I'm afraid. No message of a threat. Still, it be somet'ing. It now be yours."

Cool Babba reached into his pants pocket and produced a cassette tape, which he gave to Troy. "De ganja be a factor in her death, I know. But Mr. Peanut Butter . . . he say what he say." Cool Babba drew his extraordinary legs in, rested his arms across his thighs, and turned his head to look at Troy. He smiled, showing his two gold teeth.

"Your secret's safe with me, pard," Troy said. "Stoned or straight, she was gonna be dead anyhow. You go have yourself a life in Atlanta and don't sweat it."

"She was somet'ing else, dat Raven," Cool Babba said. "She had her problems, but den who be dat don't. I'm sorry at what happen to your boy. She talked about him time to time. No chance he did it, not dat one." He rose and stretched his arms up over his head so high his hands touched the framework of the awning.

"How the hell tall are you anyway?" Troy asked.

"I?" Cool Babba said. "Maybe six-nine, six-ten. All depend on de weather. Got a sixteen shoe. Cool Babba step a toe, you know it. Oh, one t'ing more. Could be another make de Raven's house before my time. Could be."

"How's that?" asked Troy. He was beginning to feel locked in, like someone who suddenly was able to understand a foreign language. "Was her house turned upside down or something?"

"Not upheaved or not'ing. Not dat way," Cool Babba said. "But de cat was in an' dat be Raven's task. Maybe not dis night. It be hard to tell, Mr. Troy. No way to hang t'ings upon dat one, but it was a wonder for I so now it be for you."

"Thanks," said Troy. "Happy trails."

"Same for you, Mr. Troy. You don' worry. T'ings be set right in de soon time, dat for sure."

Cool Babba bobbed and weaved over to his car and folded himself back inside. He cranked the IROC over, stuck an arm out the window in a power salute, and hung a one-eighty, spewing dirt in a rooster tail behind him. When he was gone, Troy stubbed out his cigar, climbed into his El Camino, and put the tape into the deck. Before he reached the gate at the entrance to the track he had listened to it three times.

"Listen to it again, Smitty," Roland Troy said.

"I been listening to it, Tooth," Smith said. "I been listening over and over. It's a woman asking Nikki Waters to meet her for a drink so they can talk. What the fuck else do you want to make out of it?"

"It's a desperate woman," Troy said.

"Yeah, right," Smitty said. "So she sounds strung out. Maybe her husband quit talking to her. Maybe her boyfriend dumped her for another girl. Maybe she lost her job. Maybe she found a lump in her breast. She wants to talk. She don't say jack shit in the way of a threat."

"Listen to her, Smitty," Troy said. "She doesn't say, 'I need to talk to you.' She says, 'You have to see me.' There's a difference. 'You have to see me' implies Nikki was ducking her. It implies she shut her off. There's more goin' on here than a friendly drink with a sympathetic ear. Take my word for it."

"Like I took your word for that roach-infested attic or

whatever you want to call it up over those horse stables? This is where the killer hid, you said. 'Smitty, I can feel it in my bones. Take my word for it.' So I dusted that place better'n my old grandma used to dust her piano. I got lab dudes still on my ass to this day talkin' about how hot it was up there and all the splinters they received."

"Fuck the lab dudes," Troy said. "That's their goddamn job. I crawled through shit those downtowners never imagine in their wildest dreams. The lab dudes. Nobody ever took a shot at a lab dude, to my knowledge. You tellin' me they won't do a voice analysis?"

"My man, you are grasping at straws. I ain't sayin' I blame you, but that is what you're doin'. I could have 'em analyze that tape 'til next Christmas, it ain't gonna prove nothin'. I can't send out an APB for a voice. I can't tell my guys to go searchin' for one either. Not unless there's a body attached to it. Tooth, Tooth. You know that, man. C'mon, man."

"What about her address book? Your guys are all busy, let me have it and I'll call every woman in it. I get a match, I'll let you know, we can have a chat with her."

"There *was* no address book," Smitty said. "No address book, no diary, no appointment book. Not in her house or her car or at the radio station. That Raven either flew non-scheduled all the time or else she never did nothin' needed writing down. She was never late for work, I can tell you that."

"Well, we both know there were things she did, now, don't we?" said Troy. Months before, he had told Smitty everything he found out about Nikki Waters, only omitting his sources of information.

"We found scraps of paper," Smitty said. "Business cards. Matchbooks with phone numbers. Shit like that. People live that way."

"Not people like Nikki Waters," Troy said. He scratched at his beard, thinking about what Cool Babba Wisdom had said—that someone may have beaten him to Nikki Waters's house the night she was killed.

"You want a wing?" Smitty asked, holding out the Styrofoam container filled with Buffalo-style chicken wings. "These are the best Buffalo wings in town. Brother down on the Trail makes 'em. Dude used to *play* for Buffalo, back in O.J.'s time. Cleveland Wingfield. You remember him?"

"Uh uh," said Troy.

"That figures," Smitty said. "He was an offensive lineman. 'Wingy's' is what he calls his place. Here, try one."

Troy shook his head. "It's nine o'clock in the morning, Smitty. How the hell can you do it? Eat them greasy things this early in the day. You ought to lose some weight anyway. You're starting to look like every other desk cop I know."

"Lose weight my ass. I ain't overweight. By much. Besides, it's chicken. Low cholesterol, low fat, all that good shit."

"You're right about the last part," Troy said. "Can I have my tape back?"

"Now see, you're goin' away pissed off," Smitty said. "What you want me to do? Tell me what you want me to do."

"I don't know," Troy said. "You're right about the voice. There's nothing to *be* done. I'm sorry, man."

He stood up. Smitty rose from his chair, gave Troy the tape, and they shook hands. Smitty patted Troy on the shoulder.

"I thought the same thing you did, Tooth," he said. "Where's her records? But believe me, if there was anything in her house or her car or that station, we'd 've found it and you'd know about it."

"I believe you," Troy said.

"C'mon then. Try one of these wings."

"Just because I believe you, Smitty, don't mean I'm gonna poison myself," Troy said.

"Suit yourself," Smitty said. "Be one more for me. But I gotta say, man, all due respect to this situation here, you ain't the fun fella you once was. Time come, you gotta cut it loose. Even you, Mr. Tooth."

"Took me two years, maybe more, I forget, it's been so long, 'fore I found that tooth, Smitty. Ain't no statute of limitations on murder. Ain't no statute of limitations on me neither."

It sounded good, Troy thought, putting it like that, but as

he stuck the tape into the console of his El Camino, in with
the maps and a small notebook he kept in the car, he had
the cold premonition that the words were hollow, a tough-
guy response spoken on the wooden sidewalk in front of
the façade of a Hollywood movie-set saloon. He sat in the
El Camino with the keys in his hand. The growing heat of
the July morning came through the open windows, but the
coldness he felt persisted. He watched the clerks and secretaries and lawyers hurry up and down the steps of the criminal court building across the street. He watched the
scraggly men and women with their scraggly husbands and
wives and boy friends and girl friends, moving slowly, dog-
gedly, up the same steps on their way to trial. He watched
the pretty blond hot-dog lady in her tight shorts and halter
top unfurl the umbrella above her shiny stainless steel cart.
He'd heard she was taking in close to a thousand a week,
and by the looks of her he didn't doubt it. He watched an
old woman with a large black plastic trash bag slung over
her shoulder come up the street, stopping to check every
refuse basket for aluminum cans. He watched a tall young
black woman walk past, doing some sort of dance to music
in her head as she disappeared from sight. He sat and he
watched, flipping the keys from one hand to the other, wondering if he knew the black woman's song, wondering
where to go.

XXV

◆

The new editor-in-chief of the *Journal-Express*, the man from Buffalo who was exchanged for Byron O'Reilly, was named Jason Masterson. He was a man so bland, so devoid of charisma, so neutral in appearance, that the writers who hung out at Joyce's Tavern decided one night his name should have been Mr. Gray. From then on, that's what they called him. The appellation stuck and soon spread throughout the paper. Whether Masterson was aware of it or not was impossible to determine.

With Jason Masterson in command, the *Journal-Express* began slowly to deteriorate into a paper with about as much character as a grilled-cheese sandwich, a paper that was little more than a localized version of *USA Today*, although the change was very gradual and during Masterson's first few months was not really evident at all. What was evident, however, to someone with the manipulative instincts of Wanda Donnerstag was that as long as her department kept churning out product on time and with at least a semblance of creativity, Jason Masterson was not about to intrude into her territory nor diminish her power. As long as the wheels of the life-style section turned without squeaking, Wanda Donnerstag was free to terrorize those hapless souls under her direct command as she never had before. Since the *Journal-Express* was a non-union paper, a disgruntled writer or editor's only recourse was to find a job somewhere else.

Through the window of her office Wanda watched the writers and editors in her domain bend to their work. Occasionally one would look up and glance over in her direction, checking to see whether she was watching. What a bunch of cowards they were. Not one of them dared challenge her, but she knew the way they'd gather around their customary table at night in a corner of Joyce's Tavern to curse her out. They would tell their pathetic little stories about how she had mistreated them, trade meaningless gossip about what they had heard about her from friends at the other papers where she had formerly worked, and invent clever new epithets for her. It was exquisite, knowing that only the night before she had screamed and wriggled beneath Drew Parabrise, Senator Parabrise, the man already being mentioned in op-ed pieces as a possible contender for his party's presidential nomination.

It was delicious knowing that *she*, the ice-woman, the snow-cunt, the bloodless Bavarian bitch (she had her sources in the department and knew all the names they called her) was the handsome senator's available piece of ass. True, she had only been with him three times, but she was in no hurry. She was too smart to rush things. The important point was that she had access to him, almost the way Nikki Waters once did.

She looked at them out there beyond the window, busying themselves like a bunch of dogged ants. What would they think if they knew who she really was, these industrious, erudite journalists? What would her former classmates at Wellesley think? The ones who nicknamed her "Ms. Prune." Or her father. Especially her father, that cold-hearted bastard of a Lutheran minister who reduced her mother to catatonia by refusing to speak to her for almost a year, just for having an innocent drink with another man. What would he think of the language she used with her senator? Too bad he was dead, or she'd send him a tape. Too bad she couldn't tie her father to a chair and make him watch the things she'd done with her senator, make him watch while Parabrise jerked off into her mouth, or make her father watch her in bed with the women she picked up at the mall. That would be the best. That and making him watch how Nikki, her true love, her true dead love, helped her come. Her hand, hidden from view by her desk, reached under her long cotton skirt and touched the place above the elastic band of her panties where the bird decorated her skin. What would all of them think of that, if they knew? What would they think if they could see the outstretched wings, the grasping talons, the sharp, insistent beak of her raven?

At first, the fact that Billy Roseman had no VCR in prison and hence could not watch the videotape of Steakhouse Papa's great race the way he had over and over again at home was quite distressing to him. He found that he was agitated all the time, which only added to his anger at having pleaded guilty to Nikki Waters's murder. Then he lit upon the idea of trying to remember every single detail surrounding his Breeders' Crown victory, the same way that prisoners of war he'd read about recreated their childhoods, dredging up the most minuscule events and obscure conversations with friends and family members in order to survive their captivity. To help him do this, Billy began a study of the history of civilization, figuring that if he read about antiquity during the day it would be easier to conjure up his own past at night.

He began with a book by one J. Mellaart entitled *Early Civilizations in the Near East*. When he finished that he read Gardiner's *Egypt of the Pharaohs*, followed by Arthur Waley's *Three Ways of Thought in Ancient China*. By the time he had worked his way through those three volumes, Billy could actually smell the cold night air that swirled around him as he drove his Corvette convertible to the track in upstate New York where he and Steakhouse Papa became champions of the world. Billy could have stayed in town in a fancy hotel with all the other people associated with the big race, but instead he rented a tiny cabin at a motor court way out in the country. He had wanted to be alone, with no distractions, away from all the hoopla surrounding the event. Although the race had been run in late October, and it was cold, he had put the top down for the twenty-mile ride to the track. There was a full moon, he remembered, and the woods shimmered with electric blue light. He could close his eyes and see the headlights of his car slicing through the darkness on the winding country road, and feel the throb of the powerful V-8 engine in his right leg. "Tonight I find out whether I'm worth anything or not," he remembered telling himself.

Soon, as he lay there on his back, he could taste the

sweat that had rolled down his face while he waited for the race to begin, and hear individual voices calling to him from the grandstand, urging him on, lending him support, cheering for his horse. He could feel the sting of dirt against his face thrown into the air by the hooves of other horses and the overwhelming sense of triumph when Steakhouse Papa moved into the lead.

This nightly exercise in concentration, now the focus of his life, actually produced beneficial side effects for Billy, since he discovered his memory was more precise if he ate regularly and exercised. Furthermore, his daily regimen of intense study became a productive outlet for his rage. He made application for college-credit courses as Roland Troy had advised, intending not to rest until he earned a Ph.D. He figured he had plenty of time. Billy had no illusions about an early release; he was convinced he would serve every day of the sentence he had been given.

XXVI

♦

One Sunday in the fall, when the intense heat began to wane, Roland Troy built a fence to keep the animals out of Clara's garden.

"You know, I was watching you while you were digging the holes for the fence posts," Clara said to him that night. "I saw your tattoo in the bright sun and I noticed that it's faded quite a bit, Roland. You can hardly tell that it's a tiger now at all. You should go back to that guy in Daytona who did it and have it fixed or whatever they call it. Touched up? Redone?"

Troy didn't answer, but that night he privately studied the tattoo in the mirror. Under the bright bathroom lights he could see she was right. The clarity of the lines that originally gave the tiger such a ferocious and dynamic aspect was gone; the animal looked now more like somebody's dancing pet. In addition to that, the Chinese characters were faded. Troy thought about the last time he had shown the tattoo to anyone. It was in Costa Rica, on Monkey Creek, when he had been confronted by Nakama's men. Faded though the tattoo was, Nakama's soldier—the one with no tongue—had had no trouble recognizing it. The silent Oriental had tried to remain impassive, but he had been impressed. Troy could still picture the man standing in the powerful jet boat. He had tensed slightly when he saw the prancing tiger on Troy's arm.

Remembering the incident on the jungle river reminded Troy of Nakama. What if the crafty old pirate had lied to him? What if all the highfalutin' talk and political rhetoric had been nothing but a bunch of bullshit—a smoke screen—and Nakama *was* the one responsible for the murder of Nikki Waters? All that stuff about not making a mess of it—who knew if that was true? The best hit men in the world occasionally fucked things up. Look what happened to that guy who tried to take out Charles de Gaulle.

Troy sat down on the closed toilet seat and put his head in his hands. It was useless, he thought, rehashing that scenario. Pointless. He had gone over it so many times it literally made him sick to his stomach. It was useless because there was absolutely nowhere he could take it. This murder hadn't been committed by some piney-woods redneck who left a telltale tooth behind in his hit-and-run car. In nearly ten months he hadn't been able to uncover one single shred of evidence pointing to anyone other than Billy Roseman, and the trail was now as cold as the stone on Nikki Waters's grave. Troy stood up, put his shirt back on, turned out the light, and left the bathroom. He had totally forgotten about the tattoo.

Actually, Troy and Clara didn't talk much about the murder anymore. There really wasn't a whole lot left for them to say, and though neither mentioned it to the other they were beginning to resign themselves to watching Billy serve out his sentence. Clara, the mother, the Jewish mother no less, was handling it better than Roland Troy.

"We go on with our lives," she told him one night when he asked her what they should do. "Billy isn't dead. There's always hope. We stop feeling guilty and go on with our lives. Maybe we should take a trip."

"Soon," Troy said. "Not just yet. Maybe around Christmas. We'll go up to Massachusetts to see Katherine. How's that sound?"

"I was thinking more like Greece," Clara said. "Israel and Greece. That's what I was thinking. We can go to Woods Hole in the spring."

"Okay," Troy said. "That's what we'll do. Israel and Greece. Right after Christmas. After all the crowds. Woods Hole in the spring."

"I'm serious, Roland," Clara said.

"Oh, I know," he said. "So am I."

"I hope so," she said.

A week after Troy built the fence, Clara mentioned his tattoo again. "It used to just jump out at you," she said. "It looks all blurry now."

"Sometimes that's how I feel," Troy said. "Blurry."

"Oh, Roland, don't be so damn morose," Clara said. "What was the guy's name who did it? The guy in Daytona?"

"LaFountain," Troy said. "Maurice, I think his first name is. Or Morris. Something like that. Nobody ever calls him by anything but his last name. I haven't seen him for ten years, since the last time I had him touch it up."

"Well, I think you should call him and go on up there."

"I never knew you liked tattoos that much," Troy said.

"Some I do, some are simply awful," Clara said. "Yours I happen to like a great deal. The prancing tiger. Shima told me all about what it stood for before he left. Honor, courage, loyalty. That's who you are, Roland. But I'm not trying to talk you into anything. Whether you fix it or leave it like it is, I'll love you just the same."

"Roland Troy. Jesus Christ, man, I was just thinkin' about you the other day," LaFountain said. "Hell, c'mon up, c'mon up. Let's fix that bad-boy 'fore it turns into a blob of blue mud. You remember how to get to my house?"

"Yeah," Troy said. "When you want to do it?"

"Shit, let's do it now," LaFountain said. "Today. This afternoon. How's that sound?"

"Sounds good to me," Troy said.

After lunch that day, he drove north on I-4 until it branched off to connect up with I-95, then took 92 past the speedway and on across the Intracoastal Waterway, heading east toward the ocean. When he reached A1A, he turned south, away from the convention center and the towering Hilton and Marriott hotels. Driving slowly, he continued past blocks of fast-food restaurants, souvenir stands, surf shops, and gaudy motels, searching for the old, run-down part of town where LaFountain told him he still lived.

Troy drove until the honky-tonk atmosphere gave way, on the ocean side of the highway, to high-rise condos with lighted tennis courts and expensive, single-family, ocean-front homes. There, he made a right turn away from the ocean into a neighborhood of narrow streets filled with rusty old cars and lined with weather-worn cinderblock houses. In spite of all the new construction along the shore-

line, these streets and houses remained unchanged from the
day thirty years before when Ansai Shima brought Troy
here—when Shima made him a Prancing Tiger.

Troy smiled to himself. When the next big Atlantic
hurricane hit (and there was no doubt that sooner or late
it would), the fancy condos standing cheek-to-jowl along
the ocean would bear its brunt, in essence providing
LaFountain and his neighbors with a seawall to absorb at
least part of its fury.

LaFountain was waiting for him outside in his yard, leaning against the 1947 Hudson pickup truck he drove. He
wore a pair of faded old jeans, but in spite of a cool offshore breeze was shirtless, displaying his panoply of inter-
woven, inked designs. Troy climbed out of his El Camino
and studied the artwork covering LaFountain's tanned arms
and torso, which, despite his age, were relatively wrinkle-
free.

"My favorite's still the spider," Troy said.

"Everyone says that," LaFountain said. "I think it's because it's on my head. Freaks 'em out. Old as I am, chicks
still want to run their tongues over it."

"How old are you anyway?" Troy asked.

"Sixty-two this month," LaFountain said. "But my
hand's still steady as a rock. Let's go inside."

LaFountain's house, filled with books, records, stereo
equipment, and a number of electric and acoustic guitars,
was as unchanged as the streets outside. LaFountain motioned Troy to an easy chair in his cluttered living room,
brought them each a beer from the kitchen, pulled on an
Orlando Magic T-shirt, and sat across from Troy on the
back seat of an old Packard that served as a couch. "I was
actually gonna give you a call," he said. "Got a story I
thought you might like to hear."

"Lay it on me," said Troy. He was in no hurry and in
fact welcomed the opportunity to unwind before LaFountain went to work on his arm.

"Had this woman in here, a month, maybe six weeks
ago," LaFountain told him. "Sexy-looking, in a strange
kind of way. Wearing this real slinky dress and high-heel
shoes.

"Right off the bat she says to me, 'I've come all this way

because I was told you do the most exquisite miniatures, absolutely the best of anyone in central Florida.' Those were her exact words—'Exquisite miniatures.' Who the fuck talks like that to a tattoo artist? Exquisite miniatures. Maybe I should hang out a sign with that on it. LAFOUNTAIN'S EXQUISITE MINIATURES. Go over great with the bikers, don't you think?

"Anyway, I say, 'What would you like?' and she says, in this very sophisticated way, 'I'd like a horse.' The way somebody would say, 'I'd like a Monet.' 'Can you do that for me?' she says. I tell her no problem. I say, 'I think I've done three, four hundred horses since I started. You shouldn't have a whole lot to worry about.' She tells me fine, but this is a very special horse, a particular horse, that she wants, and proceeds to take out a newspaper clipping with a picture of a horse in it. I take a look at the picture and right away I know the horse she's talkin' about. I know him good. He's Steakhouse Papa. I made some serious change with that sucker. You want another beer?"

"Uh uh," Troy said. "I'm good." He felt as though he had just boarded a train that was starting to pick up speed—that he was watching the landscape going by faster and faster through a window.

"Me too," said LaFountain. "One beer's my limit when I'm workin'. Don't want me puttin' a buffalo or a Confederate flag where you got that tiger now, do we?" LaFountain laughed and then began to cough. He didn't sound as healthy as he looked.

"Occupational hazard," he said. "Something in the ink, my doctor tells me. Thirty-six years breathing it in has taken its toll on my lungs. And here I never smoked, except for an occasional taste of the herb. What can you do, right? Anyhow, now I have your attention, don't I? There's more. I know you know all about that horse. Let me tell you how come I do too.

"Back about two or three years ago, in the summer, things were really slow. One day I'm sittin' around drinkin' beer, riffin' my old lady, and who comes knockin' on my door but my nephew from upstate New York and three of his friends, all wantin' a horse on their arm. They were all in the same college fraternity and they wanted to get themselves tattoos, so naturally my nephew told 'em I was the man to see. They piled into a car and drove nonstop from New York to my front door.

"A horse with wings was what they wanted. One that could fly, they told me. Like Steakhouse Papa. I say, 'Like who?' They say, 'Shit, don't you know about Steakhouse Papa, the horse that's tearin' it up at all these tracks in the Northeast? That horse trained right down the road from here in Orlando, at the Ben White Raceway.'

"I said, 'Boys, not only don't I know about him, I didn't even know there *was* a place called the Ben White Raceway. Only raceway I know about is the one across the bridge for auto*mo*biles.'

"Now up where my nephew was going to school the economy was in the pits. Everyone's depressed. They're lookin' for somethin' to cheer for. Along comes Steakhouse Papa, the underdog, the Little Engine That Could, and he's stabled at the Hudson Valley Raceway, right outside of town. He's beating everything in sight—the horse has become a hometown hero.

"My nephew's fraternity kind of adopted Steakhouse Papa. Went to all his races. Shit, it's summer vacation. They got time. And they're makin' money bettin' on him. So I do their flying horses and all the while they're talkin' and talkin' this horse to me, like it was Babe Ruth or Red Grange they were watching until finally I say I'm convinced. I want to see him race.

"My wife had been wanting to take a master class with Domingo Santiago, this very famous guitar instructor in Manhattan, so I said to her, 'Tell you what. We'll fly up there, you take the class, I'll go see this horse race.' She was all for that. I saw him twice at the Meadowlands. Won both times by . . . I don't know, ten, fifteen lengths, maybe more. What an experience. Did you ever see Steakhouse Papa run?"

"Once," Troy said. "At Yonkers."

"Well, man, in that case you know what I'm talking about. I'd never seen a harness horse pull like that before. Billy Roseman wasn't driving him, brother, he was hanging on. It was like he'd strapped his sulky to a Lamborghini and the rest of the guys were tied to Volkswagens.

"So now I'm a believer. The big race comes around—the Breeders' Crown—and I got this feeling Steakhouse Papa's gonna whip that favorite horse, Blue Monday, so I'm bettin' the farm. I put ten big ones down on Steakhouse Papa to win."

"You bet ten thousand bucks on that race?" Troy asked. "Are you telling me the truth?"

"As God is my witness, Roland. Steakhouse Papa went off at four to one. That horse made me forty thousand dollars, minus what I had to pay the fuckin' government. That's why I felt so bad when I read what happened to him, and how your man got nailed for that murder. The Daytona paper did a long piece on it—how the horse died and the guy's life went to shit and then he raped and killed that woman. Somehow I felt personally involved because I followed the horse and bet on him and made all that money. They even mentioned you in the story. Did you ever see it? Here, I dug it out when you called."

LaFountain went over to an old roll-up desk in the corner of the room and returned with a folded newspaper. "Right here," he said, spreading the paper in front of Roland Troy and reading while he ran his index finger across the line of print. " '. . . Even with the help of Roland Troy, former homicide detective and super-sleuth investigator for the State Attorney's office, the efforts of Roseman's defense team proved fruitless. Facing overwhelming evidence against his client, defense attorney Stanton Feinberg entered a plea of guilty in Roseman's behalf . . .' "

"I never saw this one," Troy said. "I didn't know I'd been mentioned at all. I'm very close to Billy Roseman's mother. That's how come I became involved in the case."

"I figured it was personal, you being retired and all," LaFountain said. "Anyway, I don't say a word to this woman about me and Steakhouse Papa, but naturally I'm curious as hell, so I ask her why she wants that particular horse. She gives me this look, straight on, like she's staring at something inside my head. 'That particular horse is very special to me,' she says in that English-teacher voice.

"I don't push it. Thirty-six years in this business and I've heard it all and seen it all. I never push it. I do what the customers want and send 'em on down the road. I ask her where she wants it and without a bit of hesitation she pulls up her dress and says, 'I want the horse right here, next to the raven. They belong together.' "

"She had a raven . . ." Troy said.

"Tattooed on her belly," said LaFountain. "Not bad work either. I did the horse and she split. She never flinched while I was working. It was like she was in a trance. After she left I got out this clipping and reread it. They mention that the woman who got killed was known on the radio as 'the Raven.' I'd forgotten about that. I thought about calling you, but then I figured she was just some fruitcake with a fixation. I see plenty of those, believe me."

"You see what she was driving?" Troy asked.

"Oh yeah, that's another thing," LaFountain said. "I'm glad you asked. She drove a Saab. A black one. Two-door, non-turbo. Two, three years old at the most. Orange County tags. I'm a car fanatic, man. I always look. It's part of this personal long-term study I've been making since . . . hell, since I got out of the navy and started working. I've always been fascinated by what kind of cars different kinds of people drive.

"Check it out. You could walk me through a Winn Dixie and I could tell you, with ninety percent accuracy, which people in the store went with which vehicle in the parking lot. I could. I've done it. Like you and your El Camino. That fits perfectly, man. Part hot rod, part truck. An El Camino is you. Cowboy with long hair and a beard. Corvettes are middle-aged guys with young girl friends. Jeep Cherokees are country squires. Closest they get to dirt is walking across the front lawn. Retirees from Michigan are Crown Vicky Fords or Mercury Grand Marquises. Volvos are parents. Swamp rats drive rust-bucket Monte Carlos or those old Buick LeSabres that drag on the ground. They must look for ones without any springs. Chicks I do—the ones who aren't attached to bikers—generally dig Camaros, Firebirds, Mustang GT convertibles, maybe a 300ZX if they have some money. It goes on and on. I ain't always right, but just about, and I can tell you this, in all the years I've done tattoos, that woman is the only person I ever did who drove a Saab."

LaFountain refolded the newspaper clipping and returned

it to its folder in his desk. "Some story, huh?" he said, sitting back down on the Packard-seat couch. "It's a crazy world out there, my friend. The Saab sister. Talked like an English professor. Pulled up that tight silk dress and she wasn't wearing any panties. A crazy world. Broad like that showin' up here, gettin' me to do a tattoo of that horse. Can you dig that? Speaking of which, let me get to work on *you*. That damn tiger looks like it's been run over by a bus."

"Come outside with me a second," Troy said. "I got something I want you to listen to."

LaFountain walked with Troy over to the El Camino parked in front of the house. The breeze off the ocean had picked up and was blowing eddies of sand up the street. The sand swirled around the feet of several gulls that were pecking at a gummy substance on the concrete. "Hop in," Troy said. "I'm gonna play something on the tape deck I want you to hear."

As LaFountain got into the car, Troy turned his face into the wind and took several breaths of the clean, salty air. He felt as though he were running downhill, down a long, easy grade that allowed him to gather energy rather than exhaust himself. 'Slow down,' he told himself. 'Slow down. If it's gonna happen then it's gonna happen.' He climbed into the El Camino's driver's seat, reached into the console, removed the tape Cool Babba Wisdom had given him, and put it into the tape player. "Recognize the voice?" he asked.

LaFountain turned not just his head but his entire body to face Roland Troy. His face bore the look of someone who had been awakened from a deep sleep with a bucket of ice water. The tape ended and Troy could hear LaFountain's breath rasping deep in his chest.

"Want to hear it again?" he asked.

"I don't need to," LaFountain said. "That's her."

"As I live and breathe, it's Roland Troy," Joanie Flowers said. "God, we ain't seen you down here in forever, it feels like. How you been, sugar?"

"I'm doin' all right," Troy said. "How 'bout you?"

"I'm makin' it," Joanie said. "Same as everybody. I

dance half as long and fall asleep watching the TV. Does that mean the end is near?"

"In your case, not a chance," Troy said. "Skinny women live forever. They enjoy sex at eighty. That's what my grandma said."

"You're so full of shit, Roland Troy. Same as you used to be. That's okay. I still love you. What's up?"

"I'm lookin' for somebody," Troy said.

"Ain't we all," Joanie said. "Mine's six-two, one-eighty, tight butt, about twenty-four years old. No short hair. I hate men with short hair. I want him for about a month. Then he can disappear. I'll die happy."

"Mine's driving a Saab. Black two-door. Orange County tags. Can't be a whole lot of those registered to women, you think?"

"A black Saab. What is she, a Swedish funeral director? You gettin' kinky in your old age?"

"Can you run it back five years?" Troy asked.

"For you? Yeah, why not?" Joanie said. "It'll take me some time though. You want me to call you?"

"That'd be fine, Joanie," Troy said. "I do appreciate it. No foolin' around. I truly do. This is a big one."

"I figured," Joanie said. "Good luck."

"You too," Troy said.

"Oh, it's long past luck for me, sugar," Joanie said. "It's pure skill gets me over, don't you forget it."

"Who would you come to?" Teddy Chambers said. "Who'd pull all these strings for you if I wasn't here anymore? If I'd taken that teaching job up there in Tennessee?"

"Those are irrelevant questions, Teddy," Roland Troy said. "On account of you didn't take the job. You're still here."

"Well, then," Teddy Chambers said, "let me ask you one that *is* relevant. Let me ask how the fuck you know for sure you're gonna find this evidence in this house with this search warrant you want me to get for you? How about I ask you that instead?"

"I don't think you want to know the answer," Troy said.

The two of them were in the gym Teddy Chambers had built onto the side of his garage. The twenty-by-thirty-foot

room was filled with Nautilus equipment Teddy had purchased at an auction of property formerly belonging to a
Colombian drug smuggler. Everyone at the auction but
Teddy had been interested in the speedboat, the Porsche
Carrera, the ZR-1 Corvette, and the four Rolex watches. He
had been the only bidder for the exercise machines, which
he bought for 10 percent of what they were worth. Teddy's
wife had done even better. She purchased an original James
Rosenquist that wasn't listed on the inventory for sixty-five
hundred dollars.

Chambers finished a set of flys on the double chest machine and turned to Troy, who was pedaling lazily on the
stationary bike. Perspiration poured off Chambers's face
and his shorts and T-shirt were wringing wet. Troy, in his
street clothes, hadn't broken a sweat.

"I want to know, Roland," Chambers said. "Off the record. Here in the seclusion of my home."

"You already know," Troy said.

"I need to hear you tell me," Chambers said. "Gettin' you
deputized is one thing. Gettin' my buddy the judge—my re-
pressive, punctilious buddy who'd love to nail my ass to the
wall—to issue a search warrant is something else again."

"Punctilious," Troy said. "And repugnant, as I recall."

"He recalls you very well, the judge," Chambers said.
"He'd like your ass on the same wall."

Troy grinned at him. "Ah, Teddy, me boy," he said. "After all these years we've been knowin' one another you're
still such a cautious fella. Such a circumspect soul. Fair
enough. It's a righteous warrant, 'cause what I'm gonna
find has been previously determined. I've already been in
the house."

"That's what I thought."

"I know that's what you thought," Troy said. "I'll even
tell you what I found, off the record, like you said. She's
got Nikki Waters's address book. She's got Nikki Waters's
diary. She's got some of Nikki Waters's clothes. I checked
the laundry marks. And, in her own little journal, she's
even got a couple of pages about what she did with Nikki
Waters's nipple, how she preserved it with liquid plastic.
Six coats, as I remember. She made a ring out of it. There's

even a diagram. She could teach your buddy the judge a thing or two about punctilious. I didn't have time to look for the ring, but it's there and I'll find it. She uses it to get herself off. You don't have to worry about the search warrant, Teddy. This one's tighter than a hooker's skirt."

"Not quite," Chambers said. "What about probable cause? How'd you know what you found was gonna be there, the judge is gonna ask. To say nothing of what any defense lawyer worth a pound of piss is gonna say."

Troy stopped pedaling and scratched his beard. "I forgot to tell you," he said. "There's enough toot in that place to prosecute for distribution. And I know the man who knows where every last spoonful in this town came from. He already told me where she got hers. This is goin' down as a drug bust. What else I find along the way . . ." Troy shrugged. "Lucky me," he said.

"Obviously, I don't want you going in alone," said Chambers. "Your position in all of this . . . shit, you ain't even a real cop anymore. It wouldn't fly."

"Smitty's goin' with me," Troy said. "The politically correct, well-credentialed Captain Smith, out to demonstrate that even those in command are not above the nitty-gritty when it comes to fighting crime. It's his show. A morale-booster for his overworked, underpaid men. He gets the credit. *You* get the credit. Your buddy the judge gets the credit. Everybody's happy."

"I hope so," Teddy Chambers said.

Afterwards, those in attendance said the speech Senator Drew Parabrise gave that Saturday evening at the Lake Buena Vista Resort Hotel next to Disney World was the best of his career. "Inspired," the *Journal-Express* editorial called it the next day. "It was a gutsy speech, a welcome departure from the fence-straddling Pablum that's been coming out of Washington lately. Senator Parabrise showed the world that he knows how to take a stand."

The stand Drew Parabrise took, in front of an enthusiastic crowd who paid five hundred dollars a plate to hear him, concerned the issue of the nation's economic recovery. He began by painting a glowing portrait of America as an industrial giant. In flowery, poetic language, he spoke of wagons rolling west, of railroad track being laid, of huge factories rising along the banks of great rivers, of cattle grazing on the open plains. "Where would this country be," he asked, "if the men who built the steel mills had been prevented from venting the smoke from their smelters into the air? Where would this country be if the government had prevented coal mines from being tunneled into the earth and oil wells from being drilled? Where would this country be if loggers had been prevented from cutting any trees?

"What has happened to America," Senator Parabrise said, "is that fear has replaced vision, timidity has replaced courage, lack of a bold plan for growth has crippled our economy."

It was a risky but calculated move on the part of Drew Parabrise. On the surface he seemed to be supporting the president's position, but the underlying message of the speech was clear: A weak, ill-defined presidential plan to cure the nation's economic woes called for someone to prop it up, someone with the temerity to say the things the president did not have the balls to say. When Parabrise made his own run for the presidency, no one would be able to accuse him of being some rubber stamp left over from a previous, ineffectual administration.

Drew Parabrise lingered at the hotel for more than an hour after his speech was over, basking in the warm atmosphere of support provided by those who had heard him. He had delivered the speech against the advice of his top aide, who told Parabrise it was foolish and premature for him to present even a veiled attack of the president. Now, judging by the reception he had just been given by a roomful of the most influential and wealthy people in the state, the wisdom of his decision was confirmed. He was, after all, his own best advisor.

Finally, after the last well-wisher had shaken his hand, Parabrise slipped out of the hotel, climbed into the Chrysler New Yorker that had been rented for him, and drove northeast on the interstate toward Orlando. He got off at the Princeton Street exit and began working his way along the tree-lined cobblestone streets of College Park.

He drove very slowly, since he was not positive he wanted to keep the rendezvous he had arranged at the home

of Wanda Donnerstag. Part of him said to turn back, that a
couple of hours with Wanda was too risky. Each time
Parabrise had been with her, part of him had said stay away
from this woman, cut her off. But another part of Drew
Parabrise compelled him to continue down the narrow,
darkened streets. That part of him was enticed by the
games Wanda played and her obsession with gratifying his
wildest fantasies. He was thrilled by the thought of her
haughty demeanor crumbling, her educated, finishing-
school diction dissolving into the language of the gutter as
she submitted to whatever he desired. That part of Drew
Parabrise pulled him toward Wanda's house with the force
of a whirlwind. In its face, on this night, his rational side
didn't stand a chance.

At nine-thirty that same Saturday night, Wanda Donnerstag pulled her black 1989 Saab 9000 into the one-car garage attached by a breezeway to the small house she owned
in College Park. She let herself into the house through the
kitchen door, locked the door behind her, and placed her
pocketbook on the round oak table that sat in a corner of
the room beneath a reproduction of a Tiffany lamp. She
gave her cat a can of food and some fresh water, made herself a cup of Celestial Seasonings Sleepy Time tea, and
took the cup into the living room. She turned on a tape of
pianist Glenn Gould playing Bach's "Two- and Three-Part
Inventions" and sat down on her beige leather couch to sip
tea and listen.
Halfway through the cup of tea, Wanda lit a joint and became lost inside the music. She closed her eyes and imagined herself at the back of an empty concert hall. On the
stage, Glenn Gould was playing on a marvelous pre–World
War Two Steinway, a piano with almost the baroque resonance of a harpsichord. It was the perfect instrument for the
inventions. In her mind she could see the individual notes
rise from this piano, drift across the stage, and assume seats
in the empty rows before her. Several of the notes turned
around to look at her. She nodded to them and they nodded
back. The notes didn't cough or make any rustling sounds.
They were much better concert companions than people.
The tape ended and Wanda returned to her living room.

She looked at her watch and saw that it was almost ten-thirty. The half-finished cup of tea and the rest of the joint lay on the glass coffee table in front of her. Her cat was curled up by her feet. She looked at her watch again. Very soon, her senator would be with her. What surprise had she planned for her senator tonight? She went into the bedroom with the partially smoked joint and put it on top of her dresser, on the music box filled with coke. She would decide later which one they'd have, or they could have both. Both would be nice. She had learned about that one night in the dressing room of Victoria's Secret, after the store was closed.

Wanda looked at her watch. The trip from the living room had taken less than a minute but had felt more like a week. "No more watch," she thought. "We definitely do not need any more watch." She removed the watch from her wrist and placed it on her night table. That made her feel much better and she began to hum a portion of the Glenn Gould tape as she took off her clothes, put on a new black camisole, and went over to her dressing table to see how she looked. For several minutes she busied herself with her makeup, taking great pains to achieve the high-fashion model look—the Nikki Waters look—she knew turned Drew Parabrise on. It was then she remembered the surprise she had for him. She would wear her special ring for him tonight.

She took a piece of notepaper from her night table, wrote something on it, brought the note and the unfinished joint back into the living room, and placed them together on the coffee table, where Parabrise was sure to see them. Then she quickly returned to her bed. She wasn't sure how long it would be before he appeared in the doorway of her bedroom, but that didn't really matter. Now that she knew what it was she'd planned she could lose herself again, the way she had with the music. She could relax and just let things happen, taking as little or as much time as was necessary.

Drew Parabrise found the key to Wanda's front door under the sisal mat, where she told him it would be. He let himself into her house, locked the door behind him, and stood quietly in the dimly lit living room. The single-story

house was not large. In addition to the small living room
with an even smaller dining area at one end, there was a
kitchen, two bedrooms, and two bathrooms, one off
Wanda's bedroom, the other off the hall. As Parabrise stood
silently in the living room, listening intently, he could hear
Wanda Donnerstag in the throes of self-arousal in her bedroom down the short hallway to his left. He continued listening, savoring the sounds. If his performance at the Lake
Buena Vista Resort Hotel had been the evening's main
course, this was now dessert.

Parabrise removed his jacket and tie and tossed them on
the leather couch. He saw the note and the half-smoked
joint on the table and smiled. Dessert was going to be even
tastier than he had hoped. He lit the joint, inhaled deeply,
and held his breath. He repeated this twice more, then set
the roach in an ashtray and again stood still and listened.
The low moaning sounds coming from the master bedroom
remained unchanged, only now he could hear with perfect
clarity their rise and fall. If Wanda knew he was in the
house she gave no indication, an embellishment that added
considerably to his excitement. The fantasy of creeping unseen and unheard into a woman's bedroom while she mas-
turbated was certainly a good start. He removed his shoes,
walked softly from the living room down the dark hallway,
paused once more, and noiselessly entered Wanda Donnerstag's bedroom.

The only light came from the bathroom, through its door
that was partially opened in a way that lit a strip of carpet
and a narrow section of the bed along which Wanda lay.
The shaft of light fell along Wanda's face and body, as
though she were the focal point of an erotic painting. The
light illuminated her wild eyes, her wet, panting mouth, her
breasts that hung free of the black lace camisole, and her
belly, decorated with the raven and the horse. It was there
that Drew Parabrise fixed his gaze, on the pair of perfectly
portrayed tattoos and on Wanda's hand, moving slowly,
rhythmically, below them. A gold ring was attached to the
middle finger of that hand, a gold ring with its setting
turned inward so that Wanda could rub whatever the setting
was against herself.

Parabrise was transfixed. He wanted to say something, to

break the silence that had suddenly become oppressive, but he was rendered mute. It was not time yet. Something further had to happen before he spoke. He watched the ring and listened to the sound of Wanda's breath. He wanted to undress and lie down on the bed beside her, but he forced himself to wait. Not yet. Then it seemed that he was standing in a tunnel with Wanda's bed at the far end and that the bed was rocking back and forth, making him slightly dizzy. He saw the gold band on Wanda's finger sparkle in the shaft of light, then disappear between her legs. Her cries grew louder and she began to toss her head from side to side.

"Now," the woman said. "Now. Hurry."

Drew Parabrise stepped further into the bedroom and spoke to Wanda, but his words were lost in the loud crash that came from the living room as the front door banged open against the wall. There were sounds of running feet in the hallway. Parabrise froze. He looked wildly around. His mouth went dry and his throat constricted. He saw Wanda Donnerstag sit up. She had an object in her hand but the hand was in the darkness, behind the shaft of light, and he couldn't see what it was.

"You bastards," she said as two bulky forms rushed into the room.

For three days Roland Troy tracked Wanda Donnerstag. He learned what time she came to work and when she left. He watched the way she moved, calculating her strength, gauging her speed and her reflexes. Although he had found no weapon when he searched her house, he assumed she was armed. Even if she weren't, Troy knew of skinny women who'd knocked two-hundred-pound men across a room, and of children who had wrested weapons from unwary adults. From the day Troy left Nakama's fortress in the Burmese mountains, he had never walked through the door of an occupied house unprepared.

"She's got company," he said to Smitty when he saw the rented Chrysler. "Wait here." They were crouched behind a tree in Wanda's front yard. Staying low, Troy crept along the driveway, wriggled between two bushes, and peeked through the kitchen window. The kitchen, he saw, was empty. He checked one of the living-room windows and saw no one there either. The excitement, the expectation of capturing Nikki Waters's murderer, had kept Troy from sleeping more than three hours a night for nearly a week and he felt slightly shaky but he calmed himself. Total focus was essential. *She's killed once,* he thought. *The first one's the tough one. It won't be as hard for her to kill again.*

"They're in the bedroom," he said to Smitty. "Her and her friend. There's no need to split up. They can't get to the kitchen door without coming through the living room. We can both go in through the front."

"Let's get it done, Tooth," Smitty said.

Then Roland Troy moved, staying low across the lawn and up the porch steps, never slowing as he hit the front door with his shoulder, feeling none of the resistance as the latch gave way, feeling none of the pain in his crippled hip, feeling nothing, only seeing, only hearing. Across the living room and down the hall he raced, thinking *Don't flush it, don't flush that fucking ring down the toilet before I get to it, you murdering bitch. Don't throw my evidence away.* Sideways now he moved in a shuffle like a dance step that had him in the bedroom with Smitty right behind him and the woman on the bed and the shadow of a man before his eyes.

In a shaft of light Troy saw the ring. On the woman's middle finger he saw it, made out of gold and Nikki Waters's severed tit, and then, as Smitty passed him and approached the man, he saw the automatic, rising from the pillow, entering the shaft of light, clutched like a scepter in the woman's other hand.

"Smitty, look out," Troy hollered. "Get down. She's got a gun." He hurled himself across the bed, across her body, reaching while he was in the air for the hand that held the weapon and the other with the ring, but he was not in time. Before his hands could clamp her wrists and pin her arms, Wanda Donnerstag got off three quick shots with her .22-caliber, short-barreled Steel City Double-Deuce, and the acrid smell of gunsmoke filled the room.

"Are you hit, Smitty?" Troy shouted. "Are you okay?"

"I'm fine," Smitty said from somewhere on the floor. "But this other guy ain't doin' too good at all."

"Don't move," Troy said to Wanda. The smell of her sweat and her perfume enveloped him, mixing with the gunsmoke, and her hoarse breathing rasped in his ear. "Don't you fuckin' move," he said, "or I'll break your arms."

His warning was unnecessary; she lay motionless beneath him like a spent lover. He could feel her heart beating against him. She said nothing. Then Troy saw the ring, the ring that would convict her, still caught in the shaft of light, on the hand now tightly in his grasp. Its shape was like the diagram he had studied in the journal: four spidery gold fingers curled around a setting that was coated with a transparent polyurethane shield. The setting looked like a small flesh-colored cone, darker near its tip. It was the size and shape of a woman's nipple and a tiny portion of her breast, but as Troy stared at it, ten inches from his face, a knot grew in his stomach and sour bile rose into his throat. Whatever lay beneath the transparent coating was artificial, with none of the striations of a woman's skin. It was a piece of rubber, or plastic, or silicone, or painted wood made to look like human flesh, maybe even made to feel like human flesh, but clearly something else. The setting of Wanda Donnerstag's ring had not come from a human being. The entries in her journal—the diagram and the detailed descriptions—were a fantasy, a delusion, a figment of Wanda's imagination.

"You didn't do it," Troy said to this woman with the garishly painted face, and the raven and horse tattoos, and the ring that was a replica of Nikki Waters's breast. "You aren't the one who shot Nikki Waters."

"No," said Wanda. Her mouth was inches from his ear. "Not me. Never me."

"Who killed her then, goddammit?" Troy screamed. "Who the fuck killed her if it wasn't you?"

"You killed her," Wanda hissed. "You, and my senator, and that black motherfucker over there. And the one with the horse. That's who killed her. You all did."

* * *

"Nice piece they wrote about that fine speech our late senator made, don't you think?" Teddy Chambers said. He was leaning on the roof of his new Dodge Dakota that he'd pulled to within two feet of Roland Troy's porch. "Those reactionary assholes made Parabrise sound like he was William Jennings Bryan. If they put the paper to bed a couple hours later, they could 'a run it right alongside his obituary."

Troy relit his dead cigar and regarded his friend in silence.

"I had a talk with Wanda," Chambers said after a minute. "She made the ring herself. She showed us her gold-soldering equipment. She even told us where she got the nipple. Place in Winter Park that sells artificial breasts to mastectomy patients. She had to buy a whole one. She was wondering whether she cut off the same amount as Nikki Waters's killer. She'll never stand trial. They'll put her in the nuthouse and throw away the key."

"Don't you wish you'd gone to Tennessee?" Troy asked.

"A few more days like this and I still might," Chambers said.

"I'm glad you stayed," Troy said.

"Wanda broke into Nikki's place two days before the murder," Chambers said. "She must be pretty slick, or Nikki had her mind on other matters and never missed her things. She never reported anything stolen. How much of that diary did you read anyway?"

"Enough," said Troy. "Miss Nikki didn't spare the details. She pretty well told it like it was. Especially the stuff about her and Parabrise. Maybe she planned to write a book."

"The strangest part to me is that she was falling in love with Billy," Chambers said. "If somebody hadn't killed her, I think the two of them would've wound up together, in spite of what she did to his horse."

"Uh uh," said Troy. "Never would've happened. Nikki Waters was a doomed woman. Sooner or later she would've disappeared. Vanished from the face of the earth. Poof. Sayonara."

"You're sure of that, huh?"

Troy sighed. "I don't know what I'm sure of anymore,

Teddy," he said. "What can I tell you? I have reason to believe that's the case."

"I'm sorry, Roland," Chambers said. "I thought you had the goddamn thing solved. I thought it was finally over."

"So did I," Troy said. "But it ain't."

"I'm sorry for Clara, mostly," Chambers said. "God, what a fucking roller-coaster ride. What a nightmare. I never could have brought myself to ask for the death penalty, you know. I never would have been able to look you or Clara in the face again. If it had gone to trial I would have resigned."

"Clara's handling it," Troy said. "She's tougher 'n you and me both. You remember that Cadillac she used to drive around town in when we were kids? The gold Eldorado convertible? She kept it all these years, stuck away in the corner of a barn at Jimmy Swinton's airport. Shop up in Sanford's gonna do a little work on it, get it running like new. She's talked me into taking a trip to Texas in it with her just as soon as they're finished. It'll be our honeymoon. Speakin' of which, my wife's inside, fixing us some dinner right now. She'll be real insulted if you don't stay."

"Your wife?" Teddy Chambers said. "Your wife?" He brought his fist down on the Dakota's roof, leaving a pronounced dent. "You and Clara got married? You went and got married? Son of a bitch! Why didn't you tell me?"

"Take it easy, pardner," Troy said. "You're gonna ruin your brand-new truck. It only happened last night. Come on in the house. You can be the second person to kiss the bride."

Teddy Chambers climbed the steps to the porch, where he paused and sat on the railing facing Roland Troy. "There's something I want to ask you, Roland," he said. "It's been on my mind since Smitty called me Saturday night and it won't go away." Chambers shifted his weight and cleared his throat. "Shit," he said. "Forget it."

"Hell, it can't be that bad, Teddy," Troy said. "Ask away."

Chambers cleared his throat again and flicked a piece of dirt off his perfectly polished boot with his index finger. "What I was wondering," he said, "was how you felt when you realized it was Parabrise lying on her bedroom floor?"

Troy took his hat off, repositioned it on his head, and studied Chambers's face for a moment while he searched for the right words. He puffed once on his cigar, tilted his head back, blew a stream of smoke straight up, and watched it spread out against the weathered boards of the porch roof.

"How did I feel?" he finally said. "How did I feel? I've been asking myself the same thing. I felt like a house that was lived in for a hundred years and suddenly was vacant. That's how I felt." He smiled at Chambers and shrugged.

"I hope you didn't mind my asking," Chambers said.

"Nah," said Troy. "C'mon. Let's go inside."

XXVII

♦

In November, a week before Thanksgiving, Tom Waxe died. He was out on the Coacoochee with Sheridan Halpatter, searching for an alligator that Halpatter had spied the day before. They were in Halpatter's flat-bottomed boat. Halpatter said something to Tom Waxe and Tom Waxe began to answer when he tumbled forward from his seat. Halpatter cut the motor and knelt immediately beside his friend, but his quick attention didn't matter. Tom Waxe was already gone.

He was buried on the slope by the river near the pine grove where his ancestors and those of Sheridan Halpatter lay, near the place where Wiley Troy had seen the wildcat and where he and his wife and son were buried and where someday they would bury Roland Troy.

"We live out here in the swamp," Sheridan Halpatter said to the small group of people assembled by the river. "Those of us who are left. We live in the swamp and in the forest, on land where layers and layers of bones lie buried. We understand what this land meant to the people who lie here, to people like Tom Waxe. The new ones who live here now do not. They insult the land with their acres upon acres of concrete. Before long they will pave so much the land will be out of water despite how much it rains. By then the rest of us will lie with Tom Waxe, our friend, so it will not matter to us, but it is a sad thing just the same.

"I mention this now because the land was a subject close to Tom Waxe's heart. He was a fine man who brought others together when they had differences. He was an excellent friend. In his memory, let those of us who are left preserve this place that we love for as long as possible. It isn't much, considering what's been lost, but it's all we've got. That and each other.

"One thing more. Tom's house will now belong to Roland's daughter, Katherine, and her husband. I have taken the liberty of removing the TIMPANA sign from the front porch and am going to place it here, on a post, near Tom Waxe's grave. I don't know about the rest of you, but it's still a mystery to me how the hell Tom Waxe got that house stuck way up in the air."

"Tom Waxe sensed something ominous near the Deet's Creek cabin," Sheridan Halpatter said. "He told me that time after time. Matter of fact, he mentioned it yesterday, not long before he died."

Halpatter was leaning on his post-hole digger. One of his enormous feet rested like a dozing otter on top of the digger's blades. Beads of sweat glistened on his broad forehead, which he wiped with a flick of his index finger. After the other mourners left, he and Roland Troy had remained at the grave site to erect the TIMPANA sign. Halpatter had just dug a hole for the cypress post on which the sign would be nailed.

Roland Troy poured the bucketful of concrete he had mixed into the hole, centered the post in the concrete, and motioned with his head for Halpatter to fill the rest of the hole with dirt.

Halpatter quickly scooped dirt around the post with his hands and expertly tamped it down with his bare feet. "Tom went there twenty, thirty times, he was so convinced," he said. "He didn't think you took him seriously."

"I looked the place over, same as him," Troy said.

"He thought you may have been humoring him," Halpatter said.

"He knew me better'n that. So do you."

"All I know is Tom Waxe was nearly blind. He crawled around like an old beagle, but what could he see? He may have missed something."

"I was out there more'n once, Sheridan. I couldn't find a thing."

"Maybe you were blind too. Maybe you looked in the wrong place."

"You want to go back there? Is that what this is all about? Why don't you just say, 'Hey, Roland, let's go on back there a time or two and see what we can turn up?' Why not do it that way?"

"I'm feeling oblique," Halpatter said. "It's the Indian way at times like this."

They took Troy's canoe, setting out at dawn, saying little until they tied up at the old wooden dock. When they had made the canoe fast and walked from the dock, Troy stooped, picked up a small stone, and tossed it into the water. "That's how we'll search," he said to Halpatter. "Like widening ripples. We'll cover this whole neck, from the creek to the highway. We'll do it right."

He stooped again, picked up a stick, and walked about ten yards from the dock. "This where you reckon she spun that Porsche around?" he asked.

"Yep," Halpatter said. "That's the spot."

Troy stuck the stick into the ground, straightened, and faced Halpatter. "I'm gonna give it a week, Sheridan," he said.

"A whole week?" Halpatter said. "You aren't fooling around. Tom Waxe would feel very good about this."

"Couple people out sick in Stanton's office, so Clara's working full-time," Troy said. "I got nothing better to do. Anyway, I been thinkin'. Maybe I *was* blind."

"Well, it won't take you a week," Halpatter said.

"Is that you talkin' or Tom Waxe?" Troy asked.

"Oh, no one but me, Roland, that's for sure," Halpatter said. "But then again, who knows? That old Indian had a long reach for a little guy."

On the fourth day Halpatter went off to hunt for a rogue alligator that had come ashore at the edge of the swamp and killed a goat, so Troy searched alone. It was just as well. Halpatter, for all his initial enthusiasm, had grown weary of tediously picking through dead leaves and undergrowth, and at the end of the third day asked Troy whether he thought he was overdoing it just to prove a point.

Shortly before noon, not long after Troy had begun to consider whether he would eat his lunch of homemade bread, three-bean salad, fruit, and iced tea on the dock or in his canoe, down along the creek, he saw a glimmering about six feet off the ground, on the trunk of a camphor tree. He was behind the cabin, on the side not visible from the clearing, working his way slowly into the woods, away from the dock and the open ground, away from where someone would have had to stand in order to see Nikki Waters in her Porsche. For this reason neither he nor Tom Waxe nor Halpatter had ever searched there before. Troy was on his hands and knees, sifting through the grass and dirt, when he looked up and saw something on the tree trunk reflecting sunlight.

In three days he and Halpatter had found a six-pack of empty Coors beer cans, several cigarette butts, and a torn pair of panty hose, all at the edge of the clearing within six feet of some charred logs. Troy determined instantly that the remains of the campfire, as well as the rest of the stuff, had been there no more than two weeks. With similar expectations for the shiny object stuck or hung upon the tree, he rose slowly and walked perhaps ten feet to get a better look. When he reached the tree he stopped. Level with his forehead, embedded in the wood, was a silver coin that looked to be about the size of a half-dollar. Only a third of the coin protruded, but Troy could clearly see that its edge had been honed to the sharpness of a razor. He took a deep breath, and, not quite believing what he saw, reached his hand out toward the coin like someone groping for a light switch in the dark.

"I'll be goddamned," he said out loud. "He was right. That old son of a bitch Tom Waxe was right."

Troy got out his folding Buck knife and began digging, taking care, in spite of his excitement, not to scratch the coin. It took him nearly ten minutes, and when he finished he sat down and let out a long, low whistle. The coin, lying in his open handkerchief on the ground between his legs, was a ten-colones piece minted in 1955, in the republic of Costa Rica.

"I'm going with you," Clara said.

"Look, Clara . . ." Troy began, but she didn't let him finish.

"There's no look Clara to it," she said. "I'm your wife. I'm going with you. End of discussion."

They flew from Miami to San Jose, spent the night at the Bougainvillea, then met Lester in the hotel's restaurant, the same as Troy had done ten months before.

"I flew by the place yesterday when I heard you were coming," Lester said. "No sign of life, far as I could tell. Nobody's seen any of his men for quite a while. Word is, the man done left town. Could be you're on a wild-goose chase."

"I don't think so," Troy said.

"Hey, you're the Shadow. I ain't about to argue," Lester said. He turned from Troy and looked directly at Clara. "But you might consider a weapon this time," he said.

"What do you have?" Troy asked.

It came to him, as they paddled the cayuca up Monkey Creek, that they had done this on the Coacoochee when they first met—on their first date, in fact—she in the bow, he in the stern, her lean, supple back bending with each stroke, the ends of her long dark hair touching the water. Her hair was shorter now, but she paddled with the same determination, the same style. He reached forward to touch her, squeezing her shoulder gently. She turned her head and smiled, unafraid. She was right; he could take her anywhere. At the last minute he had declined the automatic rifles Lester brought in his Cessna, opting for a single four-inch-barreled .357 he stuck in the pocket of his vest.

"I ain't goin' to war," he said. "But then, you can't tell that to a shark."

"What is it we're looking for, if Nakama isn't here?" she asked him after they left Lester at the German's lodge and set out for Monte Mono, the mountain of the howler monkeys.

"The man who killed Nikki Waters," Troy replied. "The Oriental guy with no tongue. Last trip that dude ever took was up this river. That you can take to the bank."

They found him, as Troy suspected they might, inside the house, in the former communications room that was now stripped bare of TV sets and computers and any other links to the outside world. He was seated in the only piece of furniture in the place—a high-backed swivel chair—or his skeleton was, positioned so that it faced them when they walked into the room.

They had moored the cayuca at the wooden bridge and walked up the jungle path to the helicopter pad. There was no Jetranger parked there now, no cowboys strapped with Uzis, no satellite dish there either, and the house was as still as a tomb. It was boarded up, save for the sliding glass door that opened onto the deck overlooking the ocean. Troy had been about to smash the glass with a log when he thought to try the door and found it unlocked.

"Oh, God," Clara said. "Oh, dear God."

She began to cry uncontrollably, pointing as she did in the direction of the tongueless Oriental in the chair.

Troy thought at first she might be sick, or that the sight of the fleshless bones, arranged in a bizarre imitation of a man awaiting a guest, might cause her to pass out. He put his arm around her for support, but she had not cried out in terror. It was not the skeleton with the gold chain still around its neck and the sharpened gold coin pushed into its eye socket that she was pointing at. Nor were the remains of the murderer the cause of her tears. It was instead the small sealed jar, set on the floor between the bones of the Oriental's feet. The jar was filled with a clear liquid, no doubt formaldehyde, in which floated what Troy knew in an instant was the severed tip of Nikki Waters's breast.

Epilogue

◆

"He was going to kill her with the coin when she got out of her Porsche," Jack Ubinas said. "Hit her in the jugular like the old *boo tow doy*—the tong assassins—but she spooked and took off instead. He was furious. His plan was blown, his ninja ritual, so he turned around and in a moment of anger flipped the coin into the woods, where it stuck in the tree. Am I right?"

"As always," Troy said. He was sitting on his porch, watching a pair of pelicans fish his pond, smoking a cigar, talking to Ubinas on the portable phone.

"Hey, don't be smug," Ubinas said. "How long you figure he'd been there? In the desk chair?"

"Judging by the layer of dust, he'd been there for a while," Troy said, "but it's hard to say. They probably shot him in the jungle and hung him in a tree so the wild dogs wouldn't scatter the bones. That climate . . . the maggots and birds'd pick a corpse clean in two weeks. My guess, though, is that the guy was dead the day after I left, way back last winter."

"Nakama wanted you to get a look at him first," Ubinas said. "While he was still alive. See what course you took. See whether Mr. Tooth could figure it out."

"It seems that was the plan," Troy said. "Nakama knew nobody'd go in there but me. Not for a long time, anyway. He wasn't coming back. The house reminded him too much of his wife. And everybody who lives down there steers clear of the place. Even the *bandidos* are scared shitless of him. That skeleton could've sat there for ten years unless a hurricane blew the sliding glass door in."

"So," Ubinas said. "You want me to find out where old Bassai is?"

373

G

Philip Singerman

"No offense, Jack," Troy said, "but I don't give a shit about Nakama. Not anymore."

"You think the game is over?" Ubinas asked.

"It is for me," Troy said. "The DNA test on the nipple was conclusive. Billy gets out in a month, six weeks at the most. Meantime, Clara and I are taking a ride to Texas in her old Eldorado. Put the top down if it ain't snowin'. Play George Jones and the Fabulous Thunderbirds on the tape deck. Visit her old high school."

"What if Nakama still wants to play?"

"He left a card," Troy said. "Underneath the jar."

"A card?"

"A Hallmark card, wishing the recipient a long and happy marriage," Troy said. "Then again, he didn't sign it."